The Journalism Behind Journalism

Today's journalists need to know both the skills of how to write, interview, and research, as well as skills that are often thought of as more intangible. This book provides a practical, how-to approach for developing, honing, and practicing the intangible skills critical to strong journalism.

Individual chapters introduce journalism's intangible concepts such as curiosity, empathy, implicit bias, community engagement, and tenacity, relating them to solid journalistic practice through real-world examples. Case studies and interviews with industry professionals help to further establish connections between concept and practice, and mid-chapter and end-of-chapter exercises give the reader a concrete pathway toward developing these skills. The book offers an important perspective for the modern media landscape, where any journalist seeking to make an impact must know how to contextualize events, hold power to account, and inform their community to contribute to a healthy democracy.

This is an invaluable text for courses in journalism skills at both the undergraduate and graduate level and for anyone training the next generation of journalists.

Gina Baleria is assistant professor of digital media, media writing, and journalism at Sonoma State University, California, USA, and a former broadcast and digital journalist. She produces and hosts the podcast *News in Context* (@NewsInContextSF). Her research interests include digital media literacy, engagement across difference, and the practice of journalism.

The Journalism Behind Journalism

Going Beyond the Basics to Train Effective Journalists in a Shifting Landscape

Gina Baleria

LONDON AND NEW YORK

First published 2022
by Routledge
2 Park Square, Milton Park, Abingdon, Oxon OX14 4RN

and by Routledge
605 Third Avenue, New York, NY 10158

Routledge is an imprint of the Taylor & Francis Group, an informa business

© 2022 Gina Baleria

The right of Gina Baleria to be identified as author of this work has been asserted by her in accordance with sections 77 and 78 of the Copyright, Designs and Patents Act 1988.

All rights reserved. No part of this book may be reprinted or reproduced or utilised in any form or by any electronic, mechanical, or other means, now known or hereafter invented, including photocopying and recording, or in any information storage or retrieval system, without permission in writing from the publishers.

Trademark notice: Product or corporate names may be trademarks or registered trademarks, and are used only for identification and explanation without intent to infringe.

British Library Cataloguing-in-Publication Data
A catalogue record for this book is available from the British Library

Library of Congress Cataloging-in-Publication Data
A catalog record has been requested for this book

ISBN: 9780367558239 (hbk)
ISBN: 9780367558222 (pbk)
ISBN: 9781003095309 (ebk)

Typeset in Bembo
by Deanta Global Publishing Services, Chennai, India

For my sweet, stoic, and funny husband and teammate: Romus.
Thank you for always encouraging me to fly
while helping me keep my feet on the ground.

For my nieces and nephews.
I hope you are always curious, empathetic, and tenacious
and that you see and embrace the humanity of everyone you meet.

Contents

A note on perspective ix
Acknowledgments x

1 The who, what, when, where, & why of intangibles 1

PART 1
Internal intangibles 21

2 Cultivating curiosity: The foundation of exceptional journalism 23

3 Empathy, solidarity, & compassion: Covering subjects fairly & countering echo chambers 45

4 Good stewards: Facing our implicit & unconscious biases 70

5 The intrepid journalist: Tapping into tenacity, doggedness, & resourcefulness 96

PART 2
Looking outward 121

6 Community engagement: Identify, connect, & engage (but don't pander!) 123

7 Inclusive writing & storytelling: Speaking the language of your communities 149

8 Speaking truth to power: Embracing the journalist's accountability role 179

PART 3
Contextualizing your practice 205

9 The importance of stepping away: Managing safety, trauma, & self-care in journalism 207

10 Navigating & understanding the journalism industry & operationalizing your passion 235

Glossary 260

Index 263

A note on perspective

This book was written with passion and a sincere love for the profession of journalism, a career in which I immersed myself for many happy and fulfilling years. Inherent in that love is a desire to see my profession be the best it can be, recognize my part in working sometimes uncritically within the system, and contribute to making it better. It was in this spirit that I approached this text.

In addition, I – as a cisgendered, able-bodied, middle-class woman of Italian descent who is considered white in the US societal context – am only capable of writing from the perspective that I hold.

Every effort was made to incorporate voices from as many diverse perspectives as possible. I am grateful to those who reviewed chapters and contributed to expanding my perspectives, calling out my biases, and contributing their perspectives: Edith Asibey, Anne Belden, Ed Beebout, Fawn Canady, Chandra Clark, Carolyn Copeland, Marty Gonzalez, Patrick Johnson, Lila LaHood, Misha LeClair, Lisel Alice Murdock-Perriera, Kevin Nguyen, Dave Padilla, Samantha Stanley, Theresa Burruel Stone, Walter Thompson, and Kyla Walters.

I am also grateful to those who consented to be interviewed, including David E. Kaplan, Glenn Kessler, George Kiriyama, Misha LeClair, Elana Newman, Keith Woods, Anita Varma, and Karen Yin.

Inevitably, any effort will fall short, and I am sure that is also the case here. I ask that the reader read from a place of empathy and compassion, and with a spirit of contributing to holding to a higher standard this profession that sustains healthy, functioning societies.

Acknowledgments

First and foremost, thank you to my husband Romus for supporting me in this idea, dealing with my writing process, rigorously debating ideas with me, helping me procrastinate AND get back on track, and always believing in and celebrating me. You're simply the best teammate, partner, and friend, and I'm lucky to have you.

A huge thank you to Samantha Stanley who, for some reason, agreed to read and provide invaluable feedback on every chapter in this book. I am ever grateful to you. The book is significantly better because of your generosity of time, perspective, and expertise.

Thank you also to others who reviewed chapters: Edith Asibey, Anne Belden, Ed Beebout, Fawn Canady, Chandra Clark, Carolyn Copeland, Marty Gonzalez, Patrick Johnson, Lila LaHood, Misha LeClair, Lisel Alice Murdock-Perriera, Kevin Nguyen, Dave Padilla, Theresa Burruel Stone, Walter Thompson, and Kyla Walters. Your feedback and guidance strengthened the book, and I am grateful to you.

Thank you to my writing group, "The Best Faculty Cohort Ever," for your support and for the space we created together to help me craft this book.

Thank you also to my dear friend Joyce "Joycie" Cheng for your friendship, support, our twice-weekly work sessions, AND for creating an amazing graphic for this book! An additional thank you to my dear friend Navid Dayzad for walking me through the legal side, listening, letting me bounce ideas off you, and your unwavering support and belief in me.

Thank you to Margaret Farrelly (formerly at Routledge) for starting this journey with me by believing in the idea. Thank you to Priscille Biehlmann for shepherding this idea, to Rachel Cook for guiding me through the editing process, to Geraldine Martin for seeing this book to fruition, and everyone else at Routledge who contributed to the process.

Thank you to my nieces and nephews, as well as my students past and present, my constant reminders as to why I wrote this book and made the effort to offer something that might be helpful and useful to the training and practice of journalism.

Thank you to my parents and in-laws for their unwavering support. An additional thank you to my parents for always challenging my perspectives, so that I learned how to both defend my position and understand someone else's.

1 The who, what, when, where, & why of intangibles

> The people must know before they can act,
> and there is no educator to compare with the press.
> – Ida B. Wells (1862–1930), Pulitzer Prize-winning journalist and activist[1]

WHY must we develop intangible skills?

Journalism has been called "the noble profession;" a "watchdog" and check on power; a conduit for information gathered and presented "without fear or favor."[2] In the US, it has been called "the **fourth estate**." Journalism is not only mentioned in the US Constitution, it is protected in the very First Amendment. Countless people have pointed to journalism as a guardian for democracy and a healthy, functioning society, including Thomas Jefferson, who said, "Our liberty depends on the freedom of the press, and that cannot be limited without being lost."[3]

French philosopher, author, and journalist Albert Camus said, "A free press can be good or bad, but, most certainly, without freedom, a press will never be anything but bad."[4]

And, the late, legendary CBS anchor Walter Cronkite said, "Journalism is what we need to make democracy work."[5]

In the age of social media and deepening political divisions, journalism has come under sharp attack. In some quarters, there has been a sustained effort to undermine the public's trust in the profession, including in the Philippines, Russia, China, Eritrea, Japan, Egypt, Saudi Arabia, Nigeria, and the US.

In 2017, US Navy Admiral William H. McRaven, ninth commander of the US Special Operations Command, touted journalism's role in a healthy society and the dangers of eroding journalism's position. "We must challenge this statement and this sentiment that the news media is the enemy of the American people," McRaven said. "This sentiment may be the greatest threat to democracy in my lifetime."[6]

At the same time, corporate-owned outlets have gone through layoffs and other resource cuts over the past several years, in particular in 2020 during the COVID-19 crisis,[7,8] making it even more difficult to cover the stories that need to be told. Corporate-owned media has also played a role in creating content that has contributed to political polarization and an erosion of trust in media outlets.[9]

Given journalism's aspirational position as a provider of public information, a defender of democracy and healthy societies, and a way to afflict the comfortable and comfort the afflicted, it is incumbent upon anyone considering entering the field to learn what it takes to pursue this role.

WHAT is the journalist's mission?

The mission of those doing journalism is to inform the public so citizens have the information they need to make decisions about their communities, as well as their own health and safety. The American Press Association (APA) describes the central purpose of journalism as "to provide citizens with accurate and reliable information they need to function in a free society."[10] The International Consortium of Investigative Journalists (ICIJ) says journalism has the "power" and responsibility to "empower our readers to engage with their local communities about issues of global importance, such as broken systems and abuses of power."[11]

The United Nations also names freedom of the press as critical to healthy nations, writing in 1948, "Everyone has the right to freedom of opinion and expression; this right includes freedom to hold opinions without interference and to seek, receive, and impart information and ideas through any media and regardless of frontiers."[12]

Around the world, many have given their lives in service of this mission, and many more have been detained, harassed, threatened, and attacked. In 2020 alone, 50 journalists were confirmed killed for doing their job, with 68% of those deaths occurring in countries that were "at peace."[13] In the past ten years, nearly 600 journalists lost their lives because of the work they were doing,[13] including *El Mundo* reporter Julio Valdivia Rodriguez in Mexico and Rakesh "Nirbhik" Singh with the publication *Rashtriya Swaroop* in northern India. In 2020, multiple journalists in the US and around the world were targeted and attacked while covering Black Lives Matter protests.

Reporters Without Borders (RSF) Secretary-General Christophe Deloire said in the report,

> Some may think that journalists are just the victims of the risks of their profession, but journalists are increasingly targeted when they investigate or cover sensitive subjects. What is being attacked is the right to be informed, which is everyone's right.[13]

Yet, even in the face of threats, violence, and efforts to censor and suppress, journalists around the world continue to doggedly pursue the truth and reveal important information to the public. Journalists all over the world put themselves on the front lines of seeking truth and holding power to account every day, and those who practice journalism continue to hone their skills, develop tools, and build the foundations they need to fulfill this critical mission.

Strong journalism is even more important in our current socio-political landscape. In recent years, the World Press Freedom Index has seen a decline in freedom of the press around the world, alarmingly including the US and other Western nations. Between 2013 and 2019, the RSF's US press freedom ranking (out of 180) fell from 32 to 48, and then to 44 in 2021.[14]

We saw examples of this in how the Trump administration engaged with the news media during its tenure. In addition to holding few news conferences, the administration attempted to block journalists working at reputable news outlets from covering certain events simply because the then-president was not happy with an outlet's coverage, even if that coverage was verified and factual. His administration excluded from events reporters from such outlets as NPR, CNN, *The New York Times*, *The Washington Post*, Univision, the *LA Times*, BuzzFeed, *Politico*, the BBC, *The Guardian*, and even *The Des Moines Register*.[15,16,17,18] The former president also regularly attacked journalists during his speeches, calling them "the enemy of the people," "**fake news**," and "crazed and dishonest."[19,20]

When several reporters were banned from the White House press secretary's daily briefing in 2017, *The New York Times* described it as "a highly unusual breach of relations between the White House and its press corps."[21] In a separate statement, *New York Times* Executive Editor Dean Baquet wrote, "Nothing like this has ever happened at the White House in our long history of covering multiple administrations of different parties …. Free media access to a transparent government is obviously of crucial national interest."[8]

Ben Smith, editor-in-chief of BuzzFeed, also protested, saying, "While we strongly object to the White House's apparent attempt to punish news outlets whose coverage it does not like, we won't let these latest antics distract us from the work of continuing to cover this administration fairly and aggressively."[8]

Protests also came from the White House Correspondents' Association and the Committee to Protect Journalists. Even outlets that were not excluded spoke up on behalf of the outlets that were, based on their conception of journalism's role in a healthy society, including *The Wall Street Journal*. The Associated Press and *Time* magazine boycotted the briefings, and Fox News anchor Bret Baier tweeted, "a White House gaggle should be open to all credentialed orgs."[8]

Leaders in other nations have attempted similar tactics in an effort to silence or discredit the news media, including the Philippines, Russia, Nigeria, and Saudi Arabia. In this climate, journalism is more important than ever, and doing journalism well is imperative.

WHO is affected by a lack of strong journalism?

Our communities and society face several persistent and growing problems, including a lack of trust in our information sources;[22] an inability to distinguish between news, tabloid, opinion, and propaganda;[23] and a desire to see only information we like or agree with.[24,25] If on any given day or at any given hour we compared the home pages or top stories of Fox News and MSNBC or of OANN and CNN, or even of the BBC, ABC Australia, and NPR, our understanding of major news stories would be largely different, including the impeachment of Donald Trump, the 2020 US presidential election; the insurrection at the US Capitol, the protests in Hong Kong; COVID-19; the Black Lives Matter protests, mass shootings, Anti-Asian violence, and other news stories.

For example, those landing on MSNBC.com on the day either Senate impeachment trial ended – in February 2020 or 2021 – would come away with the understanding that there had been a serious miscarriage of justice that may strike at the very heart of our democracy. While those ending up on FoxNews.com at the same moment would come away with the understanding that the nation had been saved from a partisan effort to subvert the electoral system. Those who went to CNN's homepage in the wake of the 2020 US presidential election would have understood that, though votes were still being counted, Joe Biden had won the election. However, those going to OANN.com would have thought that the election was somehow stolen from Donald Trump. No matter which of these frames resonates with you (if any), the point is that it can be difficult for someone with one **constructed reality** – a perception of the world constructed by the media they consume and the filter bubbles they inhabit – to relate to, talk with, or come to an understanding of a person with another constructed reality.

These differing constructed realities, **filter bubbles**, and **echo chambers** are exacerbated by fake or misleading news from questionable sources and on-air pundits looking to capitalize on the confusion. They are also fueled by the demands of a 24-hour news cycle, which needs to find ways to hold **audience** attention, as well as the fact that those seeking to inform or misinform have become more and more sophisticated in their strategies to design rhetoric, messaging, and narratives that foment emotion.

When each audience member makes different assumptions and comes to different conclusions about the cause or solution to an issue or problem based on the information sources on which they rely, it makes it hard for us as citizens to come together and solve the problems plaguing our communities and society. In this climate, journalists must figure out how to do the job of informing citizens who may hold vastly different views based on divergent constructed realities, as well as those who may be suspicious of information that does not match their reality, even if that information is sound.

WHERE are these issues playing out?

In addition to living in differing constructed media realities, many people have difficulty navigating the massive amounts of information that bombard them on their digital devices. Content creators and information providers are not all journalists, and they may not be doing their best to fact check, inform, and educate. Rather, some may simply share information without assessing it or share an opinion without fully investigating the issue or topic, while others seek to misinform, mislead, obfuscate, or spin. This has led to a deep distrust among audiences seeking information, and confusion about which sources to trust.

The proliferation of voices in digital spaces, while liberating for those who had not before had a seat at the table, can be confusing for those trying to navigate the massive number of blogs, headlines, videos, podcasts, and social media posts in their feeds, all seeking a piece of each user's attention and time. To make sense of this onslaught, research shows that people are far more likely to consume content that is simple, but this may mean false information because such content is often presented as black-and-white, which is easier to understand and process.[26] Actual news stories are often more complex, meaning they may take more time to process or consume in their entirety. A 2018 Massachusetts Institute of Technology (MIT) study published in the journal *Science* found that lies spread faster than truth on Twitter, proving Jonathan Swift's adage that "Falsehood flies, and truth comes limping after it."[27]

Many people seeking reliable information get frustrated and simply tune out, meaning they may not get information from any reliable news sources and instead rely on information shared by their friends and family. This information may or may not be sound. These trends are concerning because they mean more power is given to those who seek to misinform or spin, while those seeking to report the truth fight to be heard.

EXERCISE BREAK

See how well you do at differentiating fact-based information from misinformation.

Take the News Literacy Project's News Lit Quiz: "Should You Share It?"

https://newslit.org/tips-tools/quiz-should-you-share-it/

In addition, many local newspapers across the US have been hobbled or shuttered by a lack of or a siphoning off of resources. Even once-powerful newspaper chains are suffering, such as McClatchy, which filed for bankruptcy in 2020 and was subsequently bought by a hedge fund, and Tribune Publishing, which finally succumbed to its hedge fund majority shareholder when a proposed sale was announced in February 2021. After the Gannett–GateHouse merger in 2019, layoffs followed at several local newspapers.[28] In addition, outlets owned by hedge funds, such as Alden Global Capital (Tribune buyer), have seen legacy properties sold, resources siphoned off, and staffs cut as Alden seeks to reward shareholders rather than reinvest in local journalism.[29,30] This downsizing can create barriers to doing journalism well and allow mis- and dis-information purveyors to fill the gap and flood social media feeds and local news markets with sensational stories or fake, misleading, or **biased** information.[31] In this cycle, audiences find it even more difficult to trust what is true and what is "fake news." Researchers find that this trend is taking a significant toll on our ability to communicate with each other, trust our information sources, and ultimately sustain democracy or a healthy, functioning society.[32,33]

WHEN do we employ intangible skills?

To counter the trends and cycles that dominate our digital news and information landscape, it is critical to have strong, well-trained, steadfast journalists that hold power accountable and shine a light on corruption.[34,35] Those practicing the most comprehensive and impactful journalism have skills that set them apart, including an insatiable **curiosity**, a deep **empathy** for those they cover, an understanding of their own **implicit biases**, an internalized and clear ethical compass, and a **tenacity** to pursue a story to the fullest.[36,37] But newsroom leaders and journalism professors across the country have noted a deterioration of the foundational, intangible skills that define successful and intrepid journalists, as the industry grapples with efforts to undermine journalism.[22]

In addition to mis- and dis-information competing with journalistic content, news publishers trying to increase revenue are adding competing content, such as **native advertising** – content designed to look like editorial content, but actually a sponsored ad. "Native ads are intended to resemble the look of news stories, complete with eye-catching visuals and data displays. But, as with all advertisements, their purpose is to promote, not inform."[38] Research shows that audiences had trouble distinguishing native advertising from journalistic content,[38,39] and that when they did recognize content as native advertising, their opinion of the outlet utilizing this revenue strategy was diminished.[39,40] This presents another challenge to journalists seeking to cultivate and maintain audience trust. By developing and employing the skills discussed in this book and pairing them with strong newsgathering, interviewing, writing, and reporting skills, as well as transparency, you can help build and keep that trust with your audience.

This book focuses on how to cultivate these critical intangible journalistic skills that are foundational to coverage that truly informs. Explicitly teaching and learning these intangibles ensures the continuation of strong journalism, and therefore strong, healthy societies. In the chapters that follow, I seek to provide a practical, concrete, how-to approach for developing and honing these foundational intangible skills.

WHAT are intangible journalism skills?

If you have taken a beginning journalism course, then you were likely trained in the elements of newsgathering, researching, interviewing, verifying information, and writing. These basic skills are all critically important to the practice of journalism. However, doing effective journalism also requires a mastery of many other skills that may seem intangible or innate. "A great journalist will see, hear, smell, touch and feel the story," said George Kiriyama, managing editor of KTNV-TV (ABC) in Las Vegas, a Scripps station.[41]

To see, hear, smell, touch, and feel a story, a journalist needs to be curious about it. **Curiosity** drives the entire process of journalism. It leads us to want to know more, to want to know *why* something happened – or didn't happen; to want to know *how* something ended up the way it did – or didn't. This wanting to know *why* or *how* – or even what, when, where, who, in what order, etc. – leads the intrepid journalist to ask questions and then seek out the answers. This process of seeking may lead to more questions, additional avenues, and connecting the dots. This process is foundational to good journalism. *Chapter 2* will explore curiosity in depth, including the role it plays in the practice of journalism, and how a lack of curiosity affects the work of doing journalism. Most importantly, this chapter will discuss how to cultivate curiosity and build it into student journalistic learning and practice.

Curiosity involves looking up, looking around, and paying attention to the world that surrounds you, which can cause you to *wonder* what is happening in front of you, why something is set up a certain way, and how something works. For example, after Hurricane Andrew in 1992, a *Miami Herald* reporter *wondered* why so many houses lost their roofs. This curiosity led to a story uncovering sub-standard construction practices, which garnered the paper a Pulitzer Prize.

Using all of our senses when covering a story means we must engage our **empathy**. *Chapter 3* explores why it is so important to cultivate and practice empathy in all aspects of journalism, from research and story development to covering subjects and cultivating sources; from connecting with audiences to writing and presenting narratives. Empathy can help us forge meaningful connections and build trust, which for a journalist contributes to building credibility.

Research on empathy shows that it can help people feel as if they belong, cultivate trust, and lead to humanization, rather than stereotyping and *othering*. But, when applied in an echo chamber, empathy can also lead to hyper-defense of **in-groups** and dehumanization of **out-groups**.[42,43] For example, studies show that missing white children tend to receive more news coverage than missing children of color.[44] Part of the reason for this phenomenon is that law enforcement officials, journalists, and mainstream community members, who are generally largely white in US communities, have greater familiarity with those who resemble them. This empathy may not extend to those outside of the mainstream community, where stereotypes may lead to misperceptions.

Given that the central purpose of journalism is to inform the public so the public can participate in how its community functions, audience members must feel some sense of belonging to that community. How a journalist covers a given community or sub-community will play a role in whether that group of people feels a sense of belonging or alienation; a feeling of being understood or stereotyped. Journalists who cultivate empathy are more likely to see the humanity in everyone they cover, leading to more well-rounded and complete coverage, including fairer and more equitable treatment of missing persons cases.

Of course, a major barrier to curiosity, empathy, and trust is **implicit bias**. The perception of journalism cultivated in the US is that those working in news are supposed to be "objective." In truth, neither journalists nor any human being who ever walked the Earth has ever been objective. The idea of journalistic **objectivity** was cultivated in the early 20th century when journalists began to apply the objective scientific method to newsgathering and story coverage.[45] But the concept of objectivity soon migrated to the journalists themselves, and the idea of the objective journalist has stuck.

We all have our own set of **biases**, and the proliferation of clickbait and influencer content does not make it any easier to navigate biased content. The key is to learn what your biases are, double check every story you write to see how those individual biases may affect how you're covering a story, and adjust to ensure that you are working to overcome your biases to cover a story fully and fairly. *Chapter 4* will provide pathways for doing just that, teaching you to discover and face your own biases. Once you become aware of your implicit biases, you may then begin to notice how they might influence the way you approach and cover a story, including which angle appeals to you, which sources you choose – and don't choose, your word choice, which stories you find newsworthy and not newsworthy, and which story ideas you notice – and miss.

In addition to recognizing and countering your own biases, it is important in journalism to pursue and stick with a story to its bitter end, whatever that might be. A primary defining element of a strong journalist is **tenacity**, doggedness, persistence – a willingness and ability to keep pursuing a story, no matter whether there are setbacks, challenges, twists, or turns. *Chapter 5* will explore some of the strongest examples of tenacity in journalism, including *New Yorker* reporter Ronan Farrow and *New York Times* reporters Megan Twohey and Jodi Kantor, who displayed tenacity and persistence in their coverage of sexual assault allegations against media mogul Harvey Weinstein. In his book *Catch and Kill*, Farrow described extreme measures he said Weinstein took during the newsgathering phase to silence Farrow and deter him from the story, including having proxies make threats, hiring private eyes to trail Farrow and unsettle his loved ones, and cyber-hacking. Twohey and Kantor worked to build trust among women who had been harassed and assaulted but were afraid to speak out. Farrow, Twohey, and Kantor were not deterred, and their work led to Weinstein's arrest and ultimate conviction.

Along with tenacity comes resourcefulness, a key skill to surmount many of the challenges you may face in your newsgathering. *Chapter 5* will also explore strategies to increase resourcefulness, as well as when to go with the information your resourcefulness has yielded and when to set that information aside. For example, you may secure the name of a sexual assault victim, but it is generally accepted that you would not publish that name because of privacy concerns.

It would be irresponsible to fail to acknowledge the sincere challenges and even dangers inherent in doggedly pursuing a story. For example, Rappler journalist Maria Ressa has faced harassment and legal challenges for reporting critically on Philippines President Rodrigo Duterte. *Washington Post* reporter Jamal Khashoggi lost his life in October 2018 because of his coverage of Saudi Arabian leadership. In addition, CBS News and 60 Minutes correspondent Lara Logan was sexually assaulted while covering the 2011 Arab Spring protests in Cairo, Egypt. When Logan shared her story with 60 Minutes colleague Scott Pelley later that year, she said even though the experience was horrific, she heard from many other female journalists that they were thankful she shared her story.

> I think there are a lot of women who experience these kinds of things as journalists and they don't want it to stop their job because they do it for the same reasons as me – they are committed to what they do. They are not adrenaline junkies, you know, they're not glory hounds, they do it because they believe in being journalists.[46]

Indeed, journalists face many challenges when doing their jobs, and while it is not always life or death, these challenges can involve a lack of resources, an inability to gain access to an important source, online harassment from those who wish to silence you, and other barriers to fulfilling your journalistic role, which is to inform your community. In *Chapter 5*, we will discuss how to cultivate tenacity in the face of challenges.

One way to smooth the way toward rich, holistic, nuanced, and impactful coverage – as well as shatter biases and see humanity – is to connect and engage with those you cover. *Chapter 6* will focus on the importance of **community engagement** – in both in-person and digital communities. *Chapter 6* will explore how to identify, cultivate, and engage with audiences who may not be in the mainstream of a community. People in these communities often say they are overlooked by the news outlets that cover their area, and when not overlooked they are stereotyped. When people in traditionally under-served and marginalized communities do make the news, it is often for something negative. And, when comparing two stories about a similar incident, people in marginalized communities often say they are not covered or treated fairly. For example, when a mob of Trump supporters stormed the US Capitol on January 6, 2021, in an insurrection to stop the lawful counting of electoral college votes, footage showed some Capitol Police officers making way for them, even going so far as to open gates and pose for selfies with members of the mob. Many observers were quick to point out how different this largely white group of people was treated compared with how Black Lives Matter protesters were treated throughout 2020, when they were often greeted with rubber bullets, tear gas, and rough treatment.

Connecting with those in your community will help you cultivate sources, leads, and story ideas, as well as combat any implicit biases you may have as you get to know members of the community who may have different experiences and perspectives, and whom you may have unwittingly stereotyped. Or if you are a member of an under-served community, then you can fight to ensure your community and others are represented truthfully in coverage. In addition, connecting with digital community spaces relevant to your audience can help you build journalistic trust and credibility. It's your job to be aware of all members of a given community and to ensure fair and unbiased coverage. *Chapter 6* will explore how to truly see and hear the people in front of you, and how to sincerely engage in their stories. Strategies learned in this chapter can also help when dealing with antagonistic community members, harassment, and other challenges that come with interfacing with the community.

In *Chapter 7*, we'll focus on how to adapt your journalistic **writing** style to ensure you are speaking **inclusively** to audiences and avoiding language and framing that may center one community – namely the white, male, cis-gendered, middle-to-upper class, able-bodied audience in the US or dominant audience in other countries – over other audiences in your market. This includes content pushed out via social media, digital articles, video, and audio, so that your community can more fully connect with your content. The chapter will explore the importance of taking into account how people might hear, see, or understand what you are saying, writing, or presenting. Those from different backgrounds or with different personalities or experiences may interpret things very differently, making it critical that you use language precisely and with an understanding of its multiple meanings, as well as consider the ethics around sharing upsetting visuals and audio.

Two non-news social media examples include "the dress" in 2015 – whether you saw it as blue or white; or whether on a social media audio post from 2018 you heard the word "Laurel" or "Yanny." These simple examples illustrate that we do not all consume or interpret content in the same way. In a news context, it can come down to how we describe a source, suspect, incident, or event. For example, the words "demonstration," "protest," "unrest," and "riot" can be used for the same event but convey very different meanings and resonate with or alienate different audiences.

Of course, the desire to connect can also go very wrong, turning instead into pandering, clickbait, hyperbole, or putting the desires of the audience above the journalistic importance of a given story. We will explore tools and strategies to help you avoid these lazy and damaging tactics for forcing engagement, and instead find balance in your writing. Mastering these skills can help you stay on the journalistic side of promotion and content creation.

For example, images used in stories involving the same crime may visualize a white perpetrator as a family man who has fallen on hard times, while a perpetrator of color may be depicted without these humanizing aspects, even if they are also true. A Media Matters study of New York City Police Department statistics found that while less than half (48%) of suspects arrested for assault were people of color, news coverage included people of color 73% of the time.[47] The same study found similar results in other major cities. Because of this, several news outlets have decided not to use mugshots when covering crime stories.[48] When writing about this trend in February 2020, the Poynter Institute, in partnership with The Marshall Project, explained that newsrooms like the *Houston Chronicle* made this decision, because "people who are arrested but not yet convicted are still innocent under the law."[47] Mugshots can reinforce negative stereotypes and undermine the presumption of innocence, wrote Keri Blakinger for Poynter. "It reaffirms existing biases and creates biases where none exist," said Johnny Perez, formerly incarcerated and now director of US prison programs for the National Religious Campaign Against Torture.[47]

One of the most important roles journalism plays in society is as a **watchdog** of and **accountability** check on local, regional, and national governments, corporations, organizations, and other entities that may affect citizens and their communities. *Chapter 8* will explore how journalists can adhere to this journalistic tenet of serving as a watchdog and steward of information, as well as how to cultivate a thick hide as they practice journalism throughout their careers. Specifically, *Chapter 8* will explore how to effectively and professionally interview politicians who want to answer only with talking points, how to remain professional and calm when being challenged by an interviewee or crowd or when an interviewee or crowd turns hostile, and how to seek out and find information that a given source may be unwilling to provide.

NPR's Mary Louise Kelly personified these tenets when she interviewed then-Secretary of State Mike Pompeo in January 2020. During the interview, Kelly calmly and persistently asked questions of journalistic importance, including about Pompeo's Ukraine policy and his lack of defense of State Department officials who testified in the impeachment hearings. After the interview, Kelly reported that Pompeo yelled at her for several minutes. While reporting (and during the interview itself), Kelly remained calm and reported matter-of-factly, without losing her cool or resorting to disparaging Pompeo. She focused only on the facts of the events as they unfolded.[49] We also saw an example of journalistic professionalism and calm in March 2019, when CBS This Morning co-host Gayle King interviewed R. Kelly.[50] In that interview, Kelly yelled at King on camera, and she remained calm and professional the entire time, pursuing questions meant to inform the public. In each of these cases, remaining calm and continuing to pursue lines of questioning important to the public at large established credibility, tenacity, trustworthiness, and journalistic presence. While most interviews will not be openly hostile, it is always important for reporters to pursue lines of questioning that are meant to inform, even in the face of sources who may be unwilling to answer.

Chapter 8 will also discuss the importance of using your good judgment to ensure a story is truly informative and helpful for a community, and to ensure that your journalistic credibility remains intact. This can include keeping a healthy skepticism, as well as understanding the difference between skepticism and cynicism. It also includes resisting the urge to pursue a he-said-she-said or two-sides approach to story coverage. This can mean avoiding the easy temptation to place disparate sources at the same level of credibility – for example, a scientist who provides well-researched and validated data on climate change and a person on the street who says they do not believe in climate change; these two sources do not have equal credibility and should not be treated as such in any story.

Honing this set of skills and strategies can be intense and overwhelming, and doing the job of journalism can be challenging and exhausting, while at the same time exhilarating, meaningful, and validating. Journalists serve as **professional witnesses** and often cover stories involving death, **trauma**, violent and exploitative behavior, or other difficult topics, such as mass shootings, natural disasters, fires, and the deaths of children. Covering these types of stories can take an emotional and physical toll. In addition, journalists, in particular female journalists, often deal with online harassment and even threats.

Journalists often minimize the importance of **self-care** in processing any trauma they witness, which can lead to unhealthy coping strategies rather than healthy coping skills.

"You shut it off. You just don't feel it," said former TV and digital producer Misha LeClair. "You would be a mess all the time if you felt all the feelings about all of the stuff that happens ... but it comes out somewhere. It just comes out in unhealthy ways," such as excessive drinking or eating, drug use, or withdrawal from friends and loved ones.

To ensure that you are able to continue doing the important work that is journalism, you need to take care of yourself. *Chapter 9* will explore the importance of processing and dealing with the **trauma** we witness, sometimes on a daily basis. **Self-care** is key to your longevity as a journalist, allowing you to recharge, so you can be ready to face the stories you cover and authentically, honestly, and ethically engage with sources and audiences.

Once we've explored how to develop these intangible journalistic skills, in *Chapter 10* we will explore how to **operationalize** them – how to do journalism in a landscape that is evolving, shifting, and changing at a faster pace than ever before. We're in the midst of a contraction of the corporate journalism model, which has dominated the US journalism industry throughout much of its history.

Though it has been well reported that advertising and subscription revenues have fallen over the past two decades and that many people enjoy reading news articles for free, another central factor in the corporate journalism arena involves the fact that hedge funds have been purchasing local news outlets to take advantage of the real estate and resources held by legacy newspapers and broadcast media companies. Instead of investing and re-investing profits into the news outlets so they can continue to engage in strong journalism and inform their communities, hedge funds have siphoned resources out of the community and into the pockets of shareholders, leaving news outlets gutted and many communities without a watchdog. This hobbles news outlets as they strive to inform the public, speak truth to power, and hold power accountable.

Shrinking resources have led to decreased local news coverage and increased corruption.[51,52,53,54]

Young journalists are entering the field in this challenging time, but that does not mean all is lost. Many corporate outlets are still engaging in valiant coverage, including *The New York Times*, *The Washington Post*, *The New Yorker*, and others. And other journalism models are emerging to help ensure strong local coverage. For example, in Half Moon Bay, CA, a group of local investors decided to purchase the local newspaper, the *Half Moon Bay Review*, with a commitment to support strong journalism rather than siphon off profits. The same thing happened in Santa Rosa, CA, when local investors decided to purchase *The Press Democrat* to protect it from outside corporate takeover. While this is noble, it relies on the kindness and integrity of individuals. Systemically, solutions are still needed.

We are seeing exciting journalism happening in the nonprofit, public, and community sectors. Reveal and ProPublica regularly cover important and impactful investigative stories. The Marshall Project, helmed by former *New York Times* Executive Editor Bill Keller, covers the criminal justice beat. The 19th centers the stories of women in news coverage, and Prism focuses on stories that are under-represented in mainstream news coverage. As the nonprofit news sector grows and evolves, nonprofit outlets will need well-trained journalists ready to do the job of informing their audiences and serving as watchdogs for healthy societies.

You may also choose to do solo journalism. In *Chapter 10*, we'll discuss the opportunities and challenges of each possibility, and offer concrete strategies and tips for how to cover and publish stories, get compensated for labor, and build credibility in a crowded landscape.

HOW do we move forward?

Staying on the journalistic side of any aspect of news coverage requires a strong and developed ethical compass. As a student of journalism, you are beginning to develop your own ethical foundations. Each chapter in this book is framed by the ethical standards that guide journalists, including the Society of Professional Journalists' (SPJ) code of ethics, which includes the tenets:

- Seek Truth and Report It
- Minimize Harm
- Act Independently
- Be Accountable and Transparent

It is important for every journalist to cultivate strong ethical standards to ensure that their audience sees them as credible and trustworthy. This includes acting ethically toward the people you cover, interview, use as sources, and engage with during your newsgathering; as well as toward the information you engage with, including documents or datasets entrusted to you, and information that may be compromising to an individual or organization. You will learn how to weigh various considerations when making journalistic choices about how to treat people and information in news coverage.

Of course, digital access opens the door to opportunities and pitfalls, so we will also explore how to apply ethical standards to help guide decision-making in this context. This may include whether to use information, how to share it, how to frame it, how to contextualize it, and how to break it down so that your audience understands all aspects of it. The more ethically you handle complex topics, sensitive information, and information onslaughts, the more you can increase understanding and cultivate relatability and trust. Hopefully, this book will give you an opportunity to begin or continue to define your own ethical guideposts and standards.

The intangibles discussed in this book are foundational to strong journalism. The time has come to deliberately and consciously develop these skills, so we can ensure that we in the field of journalism continue to hold power to account, serve as watchdogs, tell stories that need to be told, and better inform the public.

Mastering intangibles, such as curiosity, empathy, tenacity, and recognizing implicit biases, will help you stay nimble in our shifting and evolving journalistic, digital, and societal landscapes. Then, you can use your skills to contribute to informing your public and holding power to account. You are the next generation of journalists preparing to do the important work of ensuring that journalism remains viable and thrives.

Key takeaways

- Journalism is considered a watchdog of a healthy society and a profession with a responsibility to hold power to account, meaning those who do this work must do their best to practice strong, informative, explanatory, contextual journalism.
- Developing intangible skills, such as curiosity, empathy, tenacity, and awareness of implicit bias, can position you as a strong journalist.
- Journalists must also take care of themselves so they can face challenging stories, potential online harassment, and difficult newsgathering scenarios.

Discussion questions

1. Why are you studying journalism? Imagine yourself working as a journalist. Describe your primary ethical tenet(s) and explain why these are the tenets that will guide you.
    a. For example, how will you handle sensitive information, engage with sources, etc.?
    b. What do you consider as your responsibility (to society) as a journalist?

2. Which of the intangible skills discussed in this chapter resonates the most with you? Why? How do you think it will inform your journalism practice?
3. Which of the intangible skills mentioned in this chapter do you feel might be your greatest challenge? Why?
4. Consider how you might respond if an audience member seeking coverage to represent a different constructed reality criticizes your news coverage. Write about a possible approach you might take to address this situation.

Exercises

1. Choose a working journalist who you think embodies one or more of the practices of intangible journalistic skills outlined in this chapter in service of informing the public. Answer the following questions:
   a. Why did you choose this journalist?
   b. How do you think this journalist embodies intangible skills?
   c. Discuss an example of this journalist's work that inspired or impacted you.
      i. Why this example?
      ii. What can you take from it?
   d. What can you learn from this journalist?
2. Choose a news story from a reputable outlet from the past two weeks. Analyze and annotate the story by answering the following questions:
   (For guidance on reputable outlets, refer to this bias chart and choose an outlet in the Green Box https://www.adfontesmedia.com/interactive-media-bias-chart/)
   a. List the headline, byline, date, and URL.
   b. What is the main point of this story?
   c. How well did the writer support their main point?
   d. Whom do you think this story is for? Who is the intended audience for this story?
      i. NOTE: It is not everyone – be specific.
   e. Did you detect any bias in the story as it was presented?
      i. If so, describe what elements of the story led you to this conclusion.
   f. List the sources used in the story.
      i. What information did each source provide that helped you better understand the story?
      ii. If you think the source did not advance understanding, explain why.
   g. Identify the diversity in the sources, if any, or lack thereof.
      i. Diversity can include race, ethnicity, gender, gender identity, sexual orientation, geographical/regional, political leaning, etc.

h. Identify whether any perspectives are missing from the story. If so, explain.
i. Which sources might you have included to ensure other perspectives are represented?
3. Reflect on your own news media consumption.
   a. Which outlets do you primarily visit to get your news? Why?
   b. Which outlets do you avoid? Why?
   c. Which types of outlets are missing in your news consumption habits? How do you plan to incorporate them into your regular news consumption?
4. Choose a news story you are critical of or believe contains "bad journalism" or shoddy work.
   a. What are your issues with the story?
   b. What intangible skill/s do you think is/are lacking?
   c. What steps could the writer have taken to guard against this?

Notes

1. Wells-Barnett, Ida B. "Self-Help." In *Southern Horrors: Lynch Law in All Its Phases*, 1892.
2. Ochs, Adolph S. "Without Fear or Favor." *The New York Times*, August 18, 1996. Accessed February 11, 2021. https://www.nytimes.com/1996/08/19/opinion/without-fear-or-favor.html.
3. Jefferson, Thomas. "Founders Online: From Thomas Jefferson to James Currie, 28 January 1786." National Archives and Records Administration. Accessed February 7, 2020. https://founders.archives.gov/documents/Jefferson/01-09-02-0209.
4. Camus, Albert, and Justin OBrien. *Resistance, Rebellion and Death*. London: H. Hamilton, 1964.
5. Nichols, John. "Walter Cronkite: Definitional Journalist Saw Big Media's Flaws." *The Nation*, June 29, 2015. https://www.thenation.com/article/archive/walter-cronkite-definitional-journalist-saw-big-medias-flaws/.
6. Phillips, Kristine. "'Greatest Threat to Democracy': Commander of Bin Laden Raid Slams Trump's Anti-Media Sentiment." *The Washington Post*. WP Company, February 24, 2017. https://www.washingtonpost.com/news/checkpoint/wp/2017/02/23/greatest-threat-to-democracy-commander-of-bin-laden-raid-slams-trumps-anti-media-sentiment/.
7. "Final Job Cuts Report for 2020; Over 2.3 Million, Nearly Half Due to COVID." Challenger, Gray & Christmas, Inc., January 08, 2021. Accessed February 11, 2021. https://www.challengergray.com/blog/job-cuts-dec-2020-over-2-3-million-nearly-half-due-to-covid/.
8. Fischer, Sara. "More than Half of Media Jobs Lost This Year Are in News." *Axios*, December 08, 2020. Accessed February 11, 2021. https://www.axios.com/media-unemployment-job-loss-44acca2d-a339-463f-924d-c7963f5d5601.html.
9. "American Views 2020: Trust, Media and Democracy." Knight Foundation, August 4, 2020. Accessed February 11, 2021. https://knightfoundation.org/reports/american-views-2020-trust-media-and-democracy/.
10. "Principles of Journalism." American Press Association 2007. Accessed February 7, 2020. https://americanpressassociation.com/principles-of-journalism/.
11. "What Is ICIJ?" International Consortium of Investigative Journalists (ICIJ), November 25, 2020. Accessed February 11, 2021. https://www.icij.org/about/.
12. "Claiming Human Rights." The Universal Declaration of Human Rights, Article 19, December 10, 1948. Accessed February 11, 2021. http://www.claiminghumanrights.org/udhr_article_19.html.

13 "RSF's 2020 Round-Up: 50 Journalists Killed, Two-Thirds in Countries "at Peace": Reporters without Borders." Reporters Without Borders (RSF), December 29, 2020. Accessed February 11, 2021. https://rsf.org/en/news/rsfs-2020-round-50-journalists-killed-two-thirds-countries-peace.
14 "2021 World Press Freedom Index: Reporters Without Borders." Reporters Without Borders (RSF). Accessed February 11, 2021. https://rsf.org/en/ranking.
15 Kludt, Tom, and Brian Stelter. "'The Blacklist': Here Are the Media Outlets Banned by Donald Trump." CNNMoney. Cable News Network, June 14, 2016. https://money.cnn.com/2016/06/14/media/donald-trump-media-blacklist/index.html.
16 Carissimo, Justin. "White House Blocks News Outlets from Media Briefing." The Independent. Independent Digital News and Media, February 25, 2017. https://www.independent.co.uk/news/world/americas/white-house-blocks-news-outlets-from-media-briefing-a7598641.html.
17 Siddiqui, Sabrina. "Trump Press Ban: BBC, CNN and Guardian Denied Access to Briefing." The Guardian. Guardian News and Media, February 25, 2017. https://www.theguardian.com/us-news/2017/feb/24/media-blocked-white-house-briefing-sean-spicer.
18 Farhi, Paul. "CNN, New York Times, Other Media Barred from White House Briefing." The Washington Post. WP Company, February 25, 2017. https://www.washingtonpost.com/lifestyle/style/cnn-new-york-times-other-media-barred-from-white-house-briefing/2017/02/24/4c22f542-fad5-11e6-be05-1a3817ac21a5_story.html.
19 Sugars, Stephanie. "From Fake News to Enemy of the People: An Anatomy of Trump's Tweets." Committee to Protect Journalists, January 30, 2019. Accessed February 11, 2021. https://cpj.org/2019/01/trump-twitter-press-fake-news-enemy-people/.
20 Samuels, Brett. "Trump Ramps Up Rhetoric on Media, Calls Press 'the Enemy of the People'." TheHill, April 05, 2019. Accessed February 11, 2021. https://thehill.com/homenews/administration/437610-trump-calls-press-the-enemy-of-the-people.
21 Davis, Julie Hirschfeld, and Michael M. Grynbaum. "Trump Intensifies His Attacks on Journalists and Condemns F.B.I. 'Leakers'." The New York Times, February 24, 2017. https://www.nytimes.com/2017/02/24/us/politics/white-house-sean-spicer-briefing.html.
22 Newman, Nic, and Richard Fletcher. "Bias, Bullshit and Lies: Audience Perspectives on Low Trust in the Media." SSRN Electronic Journal, 2017.
23 Mcgrew, Sarah, Joel Breakstone, Teresa Ortega, Mark Smith, and Sam Wineburg. "Can Students Evaluate Online Sources? Learning from Assessments of Civic Online Reasoning." Theory & Research in Social Education 46, no. 2 (August 2018): 165–93. doi: 10.1080/00933104.2017.1416320.
24 "Political Polarization in the American Public." Pew Research Center for the People and the Press. Pew Charitable Trusts, December 31, 2019. https://www.people-press.org/2014/06/12/political-polarization-in-the-american-public/.
25 Thompson, Alex. "Journalists and Trump Voters Live in Separate Online Bubbles, MIT Analysis Shows." Vice, December 8, 2016. https://www.vice.com/en_us/article/d3xamx/journalists-and-trump-voters-live-in-separate-online-bubbles-mit-analysis-shows.
26 Vosoughi, Soroush, Deb Roy, and Sinan Aral. "The Spread of True and False News Online." Science 359, no. 6380 (August 2018): 1146–51.
27 Arbuthnot, John, and Jonathan Swift. The Art of Political Lying. New York: K. Tompkins, 1874. doi: 10.1126/science.aap9559.
28 Allen, Barbara. "Gannett Layoffs Underway at Combined New Company." Poynter. Poynter Institute, February 28, 2020. https://www.poynter.org/business-work/2020/gannett-layoffs-underway-at-combined-new-company/.
29 Pompeo, Joe. "The Hedge Fund Vampire that Bleeds Newspapers Dry Now Has the Chicago Tribune by the Throat." Vanity Fair, February 5, 2020. Accessed February 11, 2021. https://www.vanityfair.com/news/2020/02/hedge-fund-vampire-alden-global-capital-that-bleeds-newspapers-dry-has-chicago-tribune-by-the-throat.
30 Benton, Joshua. "Hundreds of Tribune Employees Are Protesting Alden Global Capital's Sudden Interest in Their Newspapers." NiemanLab, December 11, 2019. Accessed

18 Who, what, when, where, & why of intangibles

February 11, 2021. https://www.niemanlab.org/2019/12/hundreds-of-tribune-employees-are-protesting-alden-global-capitals-sudden-interest-in-their-newspapers/.
31. Alba, Davey, and Jack Nicas. "As Local News Dies, a Pay-for-Play Network Rises in Its Place." *The New York Times*, October 18, 2020. Accessed February 11, 2021. https://www.nytimes.com/2020/10/18/technology/timpone-local-news-metric-media.html.
32. Darr, Joshua P., Matthew P. Hitt, and Johanna L. Dunaway. "Newspaper Closures Polarize Voting Behavior." *Journal of Communication* 68, no. 6 (May 2018): 1007–28. doi: 10.1093/joc/jqy051.
33. Rubado, Meghan E., and Jay T. Jennings. "Political Consequences of the Endangered Local Watchdog: Newspaper Decline and Mayoral Elections in the United States." *Urban Affairs Review* 56, no. 5 (2020): 1327–56.
34. Gao, Pengjie, Chang Lee, and Dermot Murphy. "Financing Dies in Darkness? The Impact of Newspaper Closures on Public Finance." *Journal of Financial Economics* 135, no. 2 (2020): 445–67. doi: 10.1016/j.jfineco.2019.06.003
35. "IS A CITY MANAGER WORTH $800,000?" *Los Angeles Times*, July 15, 2010. https://www.latimes.com/archives/la-xpm-2010-jul-15-la-me-bell-salary-20100715-story.html.
36. Gillmor, Dan. "Towards a New Model for Journalism Education." *Journalism Practice* 10, no. 7 (2016): 815–19. doi: 10.1080/17512786.2016.1164998.
37. Zelizer, Barbie. "Why Journalism Is about More than Digital Technology." *Digital Journalism* 7, no. 3 (2019): 343–50. doi: 10.1080/21670811.2019.1571932.
38. McGrew, Sarah, Teresa Ortega, Joel Breakstone, and Sam Wineburg. "The Challenge that's Bigger than Fake News: Civic Reasoning in a Social Media Environment." *American Educator* 41, no. 3 (2017): 4.
39. Amazeen, Michelle A., and Bartosz W. Wojdynski. "The Effects of Disclosure Format on Native Advertising Recognition and Audience Perceptions of Legacy and Online News Publishers." *Journalism* 21, no. 12 (December 2020): 1965–84. doi: 10.1177/1464884918754829.
40. Iversen, Magnus Hoem, and Erik Knudsen. "When Politicians Go Native: The Consequences of Political Native Advertising for Citizens' Trust in News." *Journalism* 20, no. 7 (July 2019): 961–78. doi: 10.1177/1464884916688289.
41. George Kiriyama (Managing Editor at KTNV), in conversation with Gina Baleria, February 2020.
42. Ellingworth, James. "Attacks on Black Fans Show Tide of Fan Racism in Ukraine." *AP NEWS*. Associated Press, November 3, 2015. https://apnews.com/article/a760a7770b6a4631bae5ed123af569c0.
43. Johnson, James D., Nelgy Olivo, Nathan Gibson, William Reed, and Leslie Ashburn-Nardo. "Priming Media Stereotypes Reduces Support for Social Welfare Policies: The Mediating Role of Empathy." *Personality and Social Psychology Bulletin* 35, no. 4 (2009): 463–76. doi: 10.1177/0146167208329856.
44. Sommers, Zach. "Missing White Woman Syndrome: An Empirical Analysis of Race and Gender Disparities in Online News Coverage of Missing Persons." *Law & Criminology* 106, no. 2 (2016): 275–314. doi: 10.1177/1931243115572822.
45. Mindich, David T. Z. *Just the Facts: How "Objectivity" Came to Define American Journalism*. New York: New York University Press, 2006.
46. Pelley, Scott. "Lara Logan Breaks Silence on Cairo Assault." *CBS News*. CBS Interactive, May 1, 2011. https://www.cbsnews.com/news/lara-logan-breaks-silence-on-cairo-assault/.
47. Colleluori, Salvatore, and Daniel Angster. "REPORT: New York City Television Stations Continue Disproportionate Coverage of Black Crime." Media Matters for America, February 18, 2015. https://www.mediamatters.org/legacy/report-new-york-city-television-stations-continue-disproportionate-coverage-black-crime.

48 Blakinger, Keri. "Newsrooms Are Rethinking Their Use of Mugshots in Crime Reporting." Poynter Institute, February 11, 2020. https://www.poynter.org/ethics-trust/2020/newsrooms-are-rethinking-their-use-of-mugshots-in-crime-reporting/.
49 Kelly, Mary Louise. "Transcript: NPR's Full Interview with Secretary of State Mike Pompeo." NPR. National Public Radio, January 24, 2020. https://www.npr.org/2020/01/24/798579754/transcript-nprs-full-interview-with-secretary-of-state-mike-pompeo.
50 King, Gayle. "The Gayle King Interview with R. Kelly." *CBS News*. CBS Interactive, March 9, 2019, https://www.cbsnews.com/news/r-kelly-interview-full-coverage-of-the-gayle-king-interview-with-r-kelly-on-cbs-2019-03-08/.
51 Elgot, Jessica. "Decline of Local Journalism Threatens Democracy, Says May." *The Guardian*. Guardian News and Media, February 6, 2018. https://www.theguardian.com/media/2018/feb/06/decline-of-local-journalism-threatens-democracy-says-may.
52 Gendreau, Henri. "Don't Stop the Presses! When Local News Struggles, Democracy Withers." *Wired*. Conde Nast, January 29, 2018. https://www.wired.com/story/dont-stop-the-presses-why-big-tech-should-subsidize-real-journalism/.
53 Hamilton, Lee. "Why Good Journalism Matters." Global Investigative Journalism Network, November 20, 2019. https://gijn.org/2015/05/22/why-good-journalism-matters/.
54 Wihbey, John. "Six Powerful Examples of Journalism's Importance: Recent Civic Impacts of the Press." *Journalist's Resource*. Harvard Kennedy School's Shorenstein Center and the Carnegie-Knight Initiative, May 13, 2014. https://journalistsresource.org/tip-sheets/reporting/six-shining-examples-power-journalism-recent-civic-impacts-of-the-press/.

Part 1
Internal intangibles

2 Cultivating curiosity
The foundation of exceptional journalism

> If you're curious, you'll probably be a good journalist because we follow our curiosity like cats.
>
> – Diane Sawyer[1]

One day, when KGO-TV reporter Wayne Freedman was walking toward work in San Francisco, he noticed something that got him wondering. Two women were at work. One was a vendor along the sidewalk and the other was an office worker. But what Freedman noticed was that the two women worked just a few feet from each other all day, separated only by the large pane of glass of the building where the office worker worked.

Freedman decided it would be interesting to interview the women to see whether they knew each other, had ever talked, or realized how physically close they actually were – even though it would take them a while to actually walk to each other's spaces.

His curiosity and wonder led to an intriguing human-interest story that caused viewers to wonder about the barriers we abide by and what that means for how we perceive proximity and human connection.

WHY is curiosity important?

Without curiosity, there would be no journalism.

To some, this statement may seem hyperbolic, and we strive to avoid hyperbole in journalism. But the fact is that curiosity drives the entire process of journalism. It leads us to want to know more, to want to know *why* something happened – or didn't happen; to want to know *how* something ended up the way it did – or didn't. "It is the foundation of asking questions and wanting to get to the bottom of any story," said Vanessa Nevarez, news assignment editor at KGTV in San Diego. "The only way to be able to tell a story fully is to be curious to learn about it."[2]

WCBS reporter Janice Wright agreed. "Curiosity is what motivates a journalist to keep looking for the facts, the fun, the twists and turns and surprises in a story."[3]

This wanting to know more – *why* or *how* or even what, when, where, who, in what order, etc. – leads the intrepid journalist to ask questions and then to seek out answers to those questions. This process of seeking may lead to more questions, additional avenues, connecting dots, filling in gaps, and putting pieces together. The general public may not be in a position to connect those dots on their own, and so your newsgathering can inform them, allow them to better understand and engage with their community, and perhaps inspire their curiosity to know more.

Without this process, no stories would be written, no investigative avenues explored, no processes or situations explained – i.e. no journalism.

Given the central role of curiosity in journalism, it is important that this skill is cultivated among today's journalism students. News directors, managing editors, and college professors have expressed concern about the decreasing level of curiosity they see among some students and new journalists, which could be for many reasons, including more time spent in digital spaces that provide pathways to new content; and because the educational focus in the US has been on standardized teaching approaches – in which students are drilled to know specific information – with less attention paid to allowing students to explore and discover – i.e. cultivate their curiosity.

Curiosity is not just about getting the story. Kathryn Schulz, author of *Being Wrong*, found that curiosity, along with empathy and humility, make it less likely that journalists will get the story wrong.[4] This means that curiosity plays a role in accuracy, a foundational tenet of strong journalism.

In this chapter we define the term "curiosity" as it relates to journalists and journalism; discuss the role curiosity plays in journalism practice; and explore how a lack of curiosity can negatively impact journalism and ultimately a healthy, functioning society. We'll also look at how exactly you can cultivate your own curiosity and use it to inform your journalism practice.

WHY might some students appear less curious?

The feeling that students seem less curious today than in years past may be tied to external factors. Santa Rosa Junior College journalism instructor Anne Belden said she thinks the current media landscape may play a role.

> I think they're bombarded by so much media and social media – they've got their Spotify, they're Netflixing and binging, and they've got TikTok and Instagram and video games, and they're just scrolling through so much media that it's hard to pick out what's important. It's hard for them to stop, sit back and say, "well, why is this happening?" There's no room.[5]

Rick Brunson, associate instructor at the University of Central Florida, agreed. "For all the technology at their fingertips that literally makes the world available to them, far too many are living in digital bubbles," Brunson said. "Moving them out of their own comfort zones is our greatest challenge – and our greatest joy when it happens."[6]

Julian Rodriquez, lecturer at the University of Texas at Arlington, said technology use – or dis-use – can indicate level of curiosity. "Students who show a higher level of curiosity are usually the ones who are not distracted in class (e.g. distracted with smartphones)," he said. "They are simply more engaged with the lecture and have more interesting and complex questions and comments."[7]

Laura Smith, who teaches journalism at the University of South Carolina, said she thinks our education system plays a role in how students approach their work. "I believe it's an artifact of the public school/excessive teaching to the test," she said. This has led students to focus on "getting it right" rather than exploring avenues of inquiry.[8]

In addition to the influence of technology, mass media access, and the P-12 school system, today's young people are increasingly anxious about issues such as climate change,[9] the global COVID-19 pandemic, social justice and institutional racism, feeling safe in their communities, and other issues that constitute potential existential threats. That anxiety could also be overriding curiosity, as students seek comfort rather than novelty.

Students in Belden's community college classroom have experienced the impacts of climate change first-hand multiple times over the past few years, including massive fires and significant floods. Belden said these experiences have been overwhelming for many, and some of her students want to give up. "They say, 'Why should I bother, if the world is not going to be there for me?' So, I try to impress upon them the fact that journalism is one way to combat it. Journalism is something they can do to shine a light on issues that need attention and are important to them," Belden said. "I try to show them how important journalism is and how good journalism can effect change. If they want to change the world, journalism is one way to do it."[5]

Belden continually evolves her curricula to meet students where they are and address the shifting needs of the student journalists who end up in her classes each semester.

WHAT is curiosity?

Curiosity is the desire to know; an eager wish to know or learn something;[10] an inquisitive interest in others' concerns that leads to inquiry.[11] In short, curiosity is the foundational structure of doing journalism.

Robert Niles of the Orange County Register wrote, "The most important characteristic shared by good journalists is curiosity. Good journalists love to read and want to find out as much as they can about the world around them."[12]

Terry Conway worked for two legendary radio stations, as a writer and editor at KCBS All News 740 AM and assistant news director at KGO 810 AM. She said curiosity guided all aspects of her news life.

"I think you have to be naturally curious to determine what questions you should be asking in your interviews and what questions need answering in your writing," Conway said. "It played a role every time I conducted an interview – in other words, every day!"[13]

Legendary reporter and DJ Peter Finch said, "there are literally hundreds of thousands of examples" of when curiosity played a role in his newsgathering process. For example, when he convinced his radio station to send him to Nicaragua in the 1980s,

> as the Contras and Sandinistas were going at it, so I could see for myself what a 'war-torn' country looked like. The owner of the station let me go, but I had to sign a release saying I wouldn't sue him if I were hurt or killed.[14]

Finch's curiosity drove his desire to know first-hand what was going on in this pivotal, international story, and the threat of harm was not going to deter him from trying to get the story. This is not to say that you want to put yourself in harm's way. It's important to weigh the risks and benefits of any story and do your best to stay safe. But the curiosity to understand drove Finch's desire to cover the story.

WCBS's Wright also recalled several examples of how curiosity drove her journalism.

"When Asiana Airlines flight 214 crashed at SFO (in 2013), I was curious to know if runway construction might have played a part," she said. "It was an issue no one was talking about, until I asked 'Hero on the Hudson' Captain Sully Sullenberger his opinion. He thought the construction could have contributed. That angle became the lead of the story."[3]

In addition, "when I went into San Quentin State Prison to watch prisoners perform Shakespeare, I was curious to know what their crimes were. I thought it was an essential part of the story," said Wright. "I couldn't just do a feel-good story about them. One prisoner, who was the star of the show, started to cry as he told me he had brutally murdered three people."[3]

In the first example, Wright's curiosity led her to find a fresh and important angle about a significant plane crash, an angle that informed her audience, shed light on a systemic issue, and held the correct officials accountable. In her second example, curiosity helped Wright tell a more holistic story, adding humanity, complexity, and realism, and allowing audiences to hear a prisoner's remorse.

All these examples involve an important element of curiosity – wonder. When we have wonder about the world around us – how things work, why they're structured a certain way, what occurred, and who was involved – it can cause us to want to learn more. Children tend to have an attitude of wonder about the world around them, leading them to ask questions (so many questions) about why things are the way they are, how something works, what something is, who did something, when something might happen, or where things may be going. Adults tend to lose this sense of wonder, perhaps because we become afraid to admit that we don't know something, less interested in the world around us, or distracted by our immediate responsibilities. But wonder can drive our curiosity and thus our newsgathering.

One way to jumpstart a sense of wonder is to slow down – or stop – and take a breath. Disconnect from what is familiar to you and seek out experiences that are new for you. Another is to deliberately walk into a situation adopting the mindset of a child or someone unfamiliar with the situation or circumstance (even if you think you know) and who wants to learn all about it. This can give you permission to go ahead and ask those questions you might normally censor. But, with a seemingly endless list of to-dos and responsibilities, and with smartphones at our fingertips ready to entice us into hours of mindless scrolling, it can be difficult to make these things happen. Nevertheless, choose some topic, issue, or situation and give it a try.

EXERCISE BREAK

1. Think of a topic, issue, or situation you are interested in or have wondered about.
2. Open a Google doc, Word doc, or Pages doc, or grab a piece of paper and pen.
3. Write the topic you chose at the top of the page and then set a timer for three minutes.
4. As soon as you hit start, write or type everything you wonder, everything you don't know, and everything you think you already know about the topic.
5. Once three minutes have elapsed, look at what you wrote and come up with a story idea you might start to pursue based on your musings.

To jumpstart wonder, look up and look around. Then, ask questions and *wonder* about what you see. When Wright was covering the Asiana Airlines crash, she found a new angle by looking up from her notes and looking around. While looking around, she started to take in the runway. That, coupled with her knowledge of recent construction, jumpstarted her curiosity and caused her to ask the question, "I *wonder* if that recent construction played a role in this crash?" The first step on Finch's journey of covering the war in Nicaragua was him saying to himself, "*I wonder* what it's like for people who live in a war-torn country?"

To cultivate wonder and curiosity, start making it a habit to look around. If you're at home, take in your space. Ask questions about what you see, hear, smell, and sense. Take a closer look at items you glance over every day. Stop and consider them for longer than a moment. If you are in the library, a classroom, or a café, take note of what you see, hear, smell, taste, and sense.

If you're walking or driving or riding public transit to school or work or anywhere else, look up. Look around. Notice what's happening. Pick out an element you do not usually pay attention to. Ask the five Ws about something you observe, and endeavor to answer them. Ask yourself, "*I* wonder...." Let these ruminations lead you to a possible story idea. Then, begin researching that idea and developing it into a news pitch.

For example, as I write this, I am sitting in a café. If I look up, I see three employees behind the counter, working and chatting with each other. There are only three other people in the café with me. Two are talking to each other, and one is working on his laptop. A handful of others have come to order something to go. As I smell the coffee brewing, hear the conversations, and taste my now cold drink, I wonder whether there's a way to keep my drink warm, why three people are working on such a slow day, whether this particular coffee shop is getting enough business to stay solvent. How about the shopping center? I might then get up and ask one of the employees how business is going, whether they've seen any changes in recent months. If the answers support my ruminations, then I might pursue the story further by talking to city representatives about the current economy. The act of looking up from my laptop to take note of what was around me led me to develop some possible story ideas.

On the opposite end of the spectrum, killers of curiosity are:

- Making assumptions
- Drawing conclusions before collecting all the facts
- Allowing our biases to lead
- Failing to give time to the newsgathering and assessment process

You may go into your newsgathering with preconceived ideas about how the story will go, but be careful about letting your ideas frame the outcome of your story. If your newsgathering leads to contradictions to the preconceived notions you started with, then let go of your preconceived notions. Let your curiosity about these new ideas lead you down new roads, so you can really learn what is going on with your story.

For example, I might be sent to cover a city council meeting. If I've covered these meetings before (and if I've been working as a journalist, then chances are I have), then I likely have a preconceived idea of how the meeting is going to go. I'll get there a bit early (or maybe a bit late), and then when the meeting is called to order, the city council members will go through the agenda using governmental protocol. A handful of regular attendees will participate in the public comment, likely about something that should probably be addressed but is likely not newsworthy – but maybe it is; my preconceived ideas about public comment could cause me to miss something. Then, when the city council takes its vote on the newsworthy agenda item, I'll make some notes, snap a few photos, perhaps get video of the vote. Once the meeting is over, I'll interview one or two city council members and any attendees who had an interest in the particular item I am writing about. Or, I might leave early, after the vote perhaps. However, the meeting may not go the way I expect. Some city council members may change their vote; many members of the public may show up to advocate a position; protesters may storm the chambers and disrupt the meeting; the power could go out; etc. One of the regular public commenters may make a point I had not considered before, opening an avenue of curiosity for me to explore. I never truly know how things will unfold, and so I need to be ready to cover the story as it presents itself, not just as I expect it to go. I need to walk into the city council chambers or enter the Zoom room with some sense of curiosity and wonder. How might this meeting go? How might it be different from previous meetings? This will prime me to be able to catch the elements that may lead to important news stories.

HOW does curiosity influence journalism & HOW do you get curious?

Curiosity influences journalism in so many ways, including:

- Coming up with story ideas
- Observing the world around us
- Prompting us to ask questions about what we see, hear, feel, touch, taste, and smell
- Noticing when something does not match an expectation or statement
- Following up on an answer that does not seem complete or authentic
- Finding connections that aren't always obvious

To explore how curiosity affects journalism and how you can get curious, let's start at the very beginning of the journalistic process – coming up with story ideas. Journalists consider countless ideas every day. Some ultimately turn into stories, and some don't. But the point is that journalists are constantly generating idea upon idea – through observation, reading, listening, watching, noticing – and then exploring those ideas to see where they lead. Once you start doing this, I promise it will get easier, until you reach the point where you can't stop being curious and coming up with ideas.

Story ideas cannot be generated if there is no curiosity. By being curious about the world around you, you can quickly come up with a list of story ideas. Similar to the café example above, at the time of this writing, in my neighborhood, right outside my window, construction crews and equipment are digging into the street. I could simply glance out the window and wish the construction noise would stop. I could also ignore what is going on outside my window and continue writing this chapter or scrolling on social media. Or, I could get curious about what's happening right outside my window.

Getting curious may take many forms. It may lead me to do some online research about my city's construction plans. It may lead me to make a few phone calls or send a few emails to city representatives asking about the construction. If I don't know anyone at the city, then I may do some research to figure out exactly whom to contact. I may run across a city council agenda or minutes discussing city street construction. This discovery may lead down several paths, depending on what was said on the agenda or in the minutes. I may discover that the city plans to revisit the issue of street work at an upcoming meeting. I may also ponder the environmental impact of the machines working so many hours, the pollutants kicked up by digging through concrete, etc. This will lead me down other paths toward a potential story.

I may also discover that the issue has been written about – which does not mean I should then drop it. Every story has many angles, updates, and perspectives – so continue to be curious, even if a story has already been covered. In the published articles I find, I may discover that the city has allocated special funds to the process of updating sewer lines, and that may lead me to explore where these funds are being spent. If I discover that only certain neighborhoods are receiving the funding, then that may lead me to ask why other neighborhoods did not. There may be a story there – and there may not be a story there – but the important thing is to be curious enough to ask the question and then seek out the answer.

My seeking may lead me to discover that only neighborhoods that are wealthier or gentrifying are seeing construction to update sewer lines, while neighborhoods without as many resources or with a lower socio-economic demographic may not be on the list or may be slated for future funding. Hopefully, this information leads you to ask WHY and HOW – WHY are only certain neighborhoods on the list and not others? HOW was the decision made? Though you may make some assumptions at this point, such as that the city is ignoring residents in lower socio-economic groups or residents of color, be careful. Your assumptions may prove correct. Or, you may discover upon further inquiry that the neighborhoods not currently on the list had their sewer lines updated in a previous round of funding just a few years prior, thanks to demonstrations by residents and a lawsuit that prompted the city to prioritize under-served neighborhoods. The point is to be curious, and allow your curiosity to lead you to ask questions, seek answers, and explore all avenues of inquiry.

My curiosity may also lead me to step outside my door and observe what is going on along my street. If I see "no parking" signs in my crowded neighborhood, then I may consider pursuing a story about how ongoing construction impacts neighborhood parking, and how residents may respond. This might lead me to grab my video or audio recorder – or smartphone – and begin walking around and talking to people I see on the street. I may ask them whether they are affected, how they feel about it, whether the city communicated with them about the street closures and parking restrictions, and how they would like the city to handle construction restrictions.

While I'm out and about, I may capture some video of the construction going on, how traffic is moving through the area, if at all, and other aspects of the scene that I find relevant. I may also capture audio of the construction, cars going by, and workers communicating.

I may approach one (or more) of the construction workers to ask what they are doing and why, as well as how long they expect construction to last, whether they've hit any snags, etc. If I'm able to record these interviews – either audio or video – then I will do that. However, given that government employees or contractors may not be authorized to officially talk to the news media, and given that they may show hesitation before talking to me, I will keep the conversation casual and let them know it's **off the record**, and that I appreciate them giving me some basic information. By the way, in addition to curiosity, a journalist should always engage with integrity. If you agree that something is off the record, then you need to honor that promise and keep it off the record, which means shared in confidence and not to be used for publication.

My conversations with construction workers may reveal that union employees are frustrated by the fact that the city hired a non-union firm to work on some aspects of the project. This piece of information can absolutely be explored and will potentially make an interesting and informative story. I'll need to think about what sources I may pursue to discover more – such as a union rep, a city administrator, and a representative from the non-union firm.

This entire time, I am jotting down notes that may occur to me about newsworthy items, areas for further inquiry, questions that have come up that I am unable to answer on the scene, thoughts that have occurred to me in general, and anything else that may be worth exploring later.

Once I've explored as many aspects of the scene as I can, I'll take one last look around, give the scene one more listen, and contemplate what I've already collected one more time. If anything in that assessment piques my curiosity, then I'll explore it further, either on the scene or back at my computer.

So, hearing construction outside my window, when considered with journalistic curiosity, led me to discover not just one but several possible story ideas and avenues for further inquiry. These ideas include:

- How city funds are allocated and whether certain neighborhoods get favorable treatment.
- How parking restrictions and street closures affect neighborhood residents and businesses.
- How the city is working with unions.
- Whether this type of construction causes environmental pollution, and if so, what exactly are the impacts?

And, you may have come up with other ideas, as well. If so, great! You're getting curious.

WHO is affected by a lack of curiosity?

In truth, all of us are affected by a lack of curiosity or a silencing of curious voices in journalism. Without curiosity, we have no meaningful news stories. Given that news stories inform the public and allow people to understand and engage with their community, a lack of curiosity means that neither we journalists nor the publics we serve will learn about the things we all need to know to hold our officials accountable, understand decision-making processes, learn about how tax dollars are being spent, and add our voices to the process. We see the effects of too little curiosity in some of the major stories of 2020 and 2021. A lack of curiosity about the perspectives of Asian Americans, African Americans, immigrants, and other people of color in the US has led to a failure to adequately reflect these perspectives and voices in much mainstream news coverage. As a consequence, these groups have been more affected by violence, stereotyping, COVID-19, and targeting.

Another way journalism largely failed the public was leading up to the 2016 presidential election, when a lack of curiosity (among other things) led to lackluster reporting from many news outlets and ultimately a failure to accurately report the nuances of a major story. The *National Review* called out what it saw as "incurious reporters" for the fact that so many major national news outlets got the 2016 election so wrong, with Senior Political Correspondent Jim Geraghty arguing that the real problem is journalists at major national outlets who

George Kiriyama: Journalism, storytelling, & curiosity

George Kiriyama's first career goal was to become president of the US, but once he learned presidents could be assassinated, he switched gears and by 12 had settled on journalism.

In high school, he told his math teacher, "You're a fantastic teacher, but I have to let you know that what you're teaching me has no relevance for my career." When his teacher responded, "you never know when you may need trig. What if you're covering a serial killer who uses math to kill his victims," Kiriyama said, "if indeed there is someone out there doing that, I want that story, and I may have to call you to crack the case."[15]

Kiriyama, now managing editor at the Scripps Station, KTNV in Las Vegas, carried that drive and passion into his career, first as an assignment editor in Los Angeles; then reporting in a small town in south-west Texas; Michigan; Kansas City, Missouri; the San Francisco Bay Area; and later to management roles in Central California and Las Vegas.

While in Texas, Kiriyama said he realized he was living his dream. "Covering different types of communities, from the church community to have little curiosity about communities outside their own cultural filter bubbles – the very communities who voted to put Donald Trump over the top in the electoral college count. This led these news outlets to miss or ignore stories until they themselves were affected. Geraghty also detailed another example:

> In 2013, writing for *Slate*, Matthew Yglesias noted with great incredulity the considerable bureaucratic and paperwork hurdles he faced to get a license to rent out his old condominium in Washington, DC: "I've been to three offices, filed five forms, spent $200, lost a day of work – and I'm not even close to getting the simple license I need," he wrote. "Cities make it ridiculously hard to start a small business. They need to stop."

"No kidding!" plenty of conservatives scoffed, noting this was the sort of argument Yglesias rejected before his experience with the local bureaucracy. We shouldn't knock someone for adjusting his perspective based upon firsthand experience. But a good journalist will attempt to get a detailed feel for an issue or the people involved *before* making a blanket judgment.[16]

Often, lack of time and resources become barriers to truly allowing curiosity to flourish, and this is a real challenge in the news industry. Though you cannot do much about the forces at work in layoffs, newspaper closures, and other factors

communities of color – it was exactly what I envisioned myself doing, and I was actually doing it."[24]

His satisfaction persisted, even though, "I wasn't making much money. Those who think it's glamorous, they get a reality check in their first job."[24]

Kiriyama also began honing his journalistic approach, leading with curiosity to connect with people in the area. "It wasn't just the movers and shakers, the politicians and mayors of those communities, it was more connecting with people in the neighborhoods. I liked hearing their stories."[24]

Journalists are storytellers at their core, said Kiriyama. "You want to know what people are doing, how people think. It's more observing and monitoring, but at the same time asking questions about why."[24]

While at KNTV in San Jose, CA, in 2007, Kiriyama hoped to pique the curiosity of his audiences by turning the lens on his own story.

It was the 65th anniversary of the incarceration of Japanese Americans in concentration camps in the US. Kiriyama pitched sharing his family's experience in the camps. He asked for five minutes, but his executive producer offered an hour and encouraged him to include his colleagues of Japanese descent, as well as prominent Japanese Americans.

"It was a phenomenal thing for me," Kiriyama said of the Emmy-nominated piece. "I'm glad the station did it. The station really thought that my story, Mike and Rob Mayeda's story were important. When a station does something like that, you feel valued and respected, and that's what all stations should strive for."[24]

impacting journalism, you can be curious about these factors and trends. You can explore them and report on them yourself. The fact that so few members of the public realize that their newspaper faces financial and resource challenges[17] is in part due to the fact that not enough reporting has been done; not enough journalists have been curious enough about the issue to take it on (though several have). You, with your developing journalistic curiosity, can change that.

Student journalists in many communities have been filling voids left by the loss of local news outlets. "Sometimes they are the only reporters in the room at important public meetings," wrote the Student Press Law Center when it named 2019 the year of the student journalist.[18]

When Belden's students covered the 2017 Northern California fires, they had advantages over the national news media. "These SRJC students had a knowledge of the area that the national press that was just descending did not," Belden said. "They had contacts. They knew whose houses had burned down. They had neighbors and friends all over the county, so they really had an upper hand over the national media." This realization gave students the confidence to be more curious and seek out more angles, which led to incredible coverage, praise from community members, and ultimately accolades and awards. "They learned – as I did – that they could compete in covering breaking news and be a resource to their community, and they had the edge, because they knew the community," Belden said.[5]

Kiriyama pointed out that newsroom diversity mattered. "The argument could be made that if I wasn't there, Rob wasn't there and Mike wasn't there, that documentary probably wouldn't have happened."[24]

To that end, Kiriyama volunteers his time to support and mentor Asian American journalists, and he served as national vice president for broadcast for the Asian American Journalists Association from 2009–2012.

"I am actively involved in making sure that Asian-American journalists are represented in newsrooms across the country," he said.

When I walk into a newsroom, obviously I see who's there, and then I look at the community to see what the community looks like. Anyone who supports diversity and inclusion believes that every newsroom must reflect the community. You can't have a newsroom that is out of touch or not connected, or you just won't survive.[24]

As for reporting in a politically fraught social context, Kiryama said newsrooms "have to do a better job at making sure they explain to the viewer where they got their information, who they talked to, and that anything that comes from outside is clearly verified."[24]

Overall, Kiriyama still sees his chosen profession as a calling.

"I think being a journalist is a very powerful position. It's a responsibility you should not take lightly. Your words are power," Kiriyama said. "Your responsibility is to educate and inform and empower people to be better."[24]

A lack of curiosity can also have a more insidious outcome – further stereotyping, *othering*, and marginalizing under-served communities. Journalists at mainstream news outlets, who are often white, enter under-served communities or communities of color only when something bad happens, such as the death of a high school student or a shooting. Very little time may be invested in getting to know the community, and coverage may rely instead on preconceived ideas and assumptions. Curiosity can help address this persistent issue by encouraging journalists to want to know more about people and communities with whom and with which they are not familiar.

WHEN can we practice curiosity?

The answer to when you should engage your curiosity is any time and all the time. You never know when a story idea may present itself. By always being curious, by always paying attention and keeping your journalistic senses honed, you can catch those opportunities and ensure they do not slide by.

Dory Culver worked for many venerable print and broadcast news outlets before retiring, including the *St. Louis Post-Dispatch*, the *Arizona Daily Star*, KTAR, and finally as assistant news director and managing editor at KCBS All News 740 in San Francisco.

Culver said curiosity is "the spark that creates interest."[19]

"As a reporter or as an editor I always challenged myself or my reporters to be curious before they covered a story," she said.

> Curiosity means listening and asking questions that elucidate, clarify, challenge, and provoke. Whether you are a print or broadcast reporter it is your responsibility to understand your story well enough so you can tell it to others. Asking questions is the only way to do that. Maintaining your own sense of curiosity is the only way to help others understand it.[18]

Beyond just curiosity for stories, journalists should practice curiosity about every aspect of their profession – including new tools and apps; new ideas for how to practice journalism; and emerging technologies, such as augmented reality (AR), virtual reality (VR), artificial intelligence (AI), and 360 video. At so many turns in the history of journalism, reporters have lacked curiosity about and shunned new technologies and ideas that showed potential to advance the profession, thus hindering the important work of doing journalism.

Most recently, many broadcast and print journalists belittled digital as it emerged, clinging to the paradigms with which they were familiar, rather than exploring the possibilities and opportunities to do impactful journalism utilizing digital technologies. This likely held the profession back as other voices initially filled the void.

But this attitude was not born in the past few decades. In the late 1880s, when the typewriter was introduced to newsrooms, many journalists dismissed it as a fad and gimmick, clinging instead to their familiar practice of handwriting articles. In actuality, the resistance was largely driven by fear and inertia. Some were worried about learning how to type, while others thought typewriters would compromise writing.[20] How ironic then that typewriters became an iconic image of journalism and that many journalists of the 1980s and 1990s clung to their typewriters as word processors and then computers emerged.

The American Press Institute's Jane Elizabeth found that accountability journalists, those who engage in investigations, fact checking, or other forms of impactful reporting, share the trait of a "high level of curiosity" that "propels them to adapt to new platforms, audiences, technology, and content with unusual willingness and a sense of necessity and practicality."[21] As a result, these journalists are on the forefront of impactful journalism that is meaningful for their audiences.

Of course, you do not have to adopt new technologies. Not everything will work for your journalism practice. But it is important to be curious about emerging tools and opportunities and to explore how they might benefit your work.

The moral of this story is to face new ideas, technology, and circumstances with curiosity. This can allow you to see possibility, promise, and benefits, rather than closing yourself off and missing out.

WHERE can we practice curiosity & WHERE can our curiosity take us?

You can practice curiosity anywhere and everywhere, and you never know where your curiosity may take you. A 2013 article from the National Center for Business Journalism called curiosity "our killer app."[22] Curiosity is something we always have control over, even in the face of resource cuts, challenging sources, and faltering technology. We drive the journalistic process – newsgathering, story generation, source interviews, story crafting, and public engagement – and curiosity drives us.

An example of just where curiosity can take you comes from Patrick Lee Plaisance, a former journalist turned ethics professor at Penn State University. In a *Psychology Today* article, he shared how as a young journalist, he followed his curiosity, asked questions, and discovered a major local news story he was not even pursuing.

> I was talking to the finance director for a municipality in central New Jersey (about tax rates), and when he candidly said he didn't know the answers to my questions, I suggested I should go chat with the tax collector. My suggestion was met with a smirk. "You can try," the finance director said. I tried. And tried. I failed to ever meet the tax collector. It turned out that he hadn't been in the office in years. He had helped rewrite the local statutes long before, to turn his job into a sinecure that never actually required him to work or show up.[23]

Plaisance discovered that even the tax collector's own employees never saw him, and they had nicknamed him "The Phantom." Needless to say, publication of this story led the public to express outrage and call for changes, which led the city to let the tax collector go.

Curiosity earned the *Miami Herald* a Pulitzer Prize in 1993.[24] In the wake of Hurricane Andrew in 1992, an editor at the *Herald* did a flyover and saw the devastation below. An incurious journalist might take note, move on, and write the requisite story about how bad this hurricane was and how many people were affected. But curiosity led this editor to *wonder*, did all of those houses lose their roofs because of the severity of the hurricane? Or were all of those houses built with shoddy roofs? Curiosity led to exploration and investigation, which led to uncovering permitting practices that allowed sub-standard construction of countless roofs. Publication of this story led to changes in the permitting process, sparing future residents from hurricane damage that could be prevented (Figure 2.1).

I've discussed how a loss of curiosity can be detrimental to journalism. But curiosity inside us can also wane, and it is important to be aware of that and counter it when possible. For some journalists, especially veterans who have suffered the slings and arrows of holding power to account, or endured cutbacks and downsizing, curiosity may suffer as they burn out, have difficulty finding time to be curious, or get tired of covering the same thing and seeing little to no result.

Figure 2.1 "Apartment Complex Destroyed by Hurricane Andrew, Cutler Ridge" by StevenM_61 is licensed under CC BY-NC-ND 2.0.

For a journalist just starting out, frustration may mount as they face roadblocks to getting a story covered, including sources who may not respond, a lack of resources or support from their newsroom, or an editor who seems to regularly turn their story ideas down. This can be disheartening and discouraging, leading some to wonder why they bother. In this frame of mind, curiosity can wane.

When faced with roadblocks, I encourage you to get even more curious. Get curious about how you can pitch the story differently, how you can articulate an angle that is fresh and of interest to listeners, how you can overcome objections over legal concerns, how you can get your editor to a yes. Let your curiosity lead you to defend your ideas, evolve your presentation of those ideas, and fight for their contribution to informing your audience. You may not win the argument, but you will hone your skills and continue to learn about your audience.

Ideas for cultivating curiosity:

- Get out of the newsroom
- Go somewhere new – at least once a week
- Talk to someone different from you – at least once a week
    - This could lead to the cultivation of a new source or simply a greater understanding of others
- Get out of your car or off your transit system at a stop you don't usually take
- Regularly ask people on social media what they would like to see covered
- Keep a journal of ideas and half-thoughts as they come to you
- Follow up on old ideas
- Read, watch, and listen to other reputable news outlets, including those you might not generally include in your news consumption routine
- Break your routine[21]

If you are reading this book, then you are likely a journalism student and have been asked to find a story for your class or the student newspaper or website. Now that you're near the end of this chapter, where do you begin on your own newsgathering quest?

Begin by getting curious! How do you get curious? Well, start exploring …

What events are coming up on campus? In the nearby community? You can find event calendars by searching online and exploring city, school, and organization websites. Sign up for newsletters of organizations or entities you think might offer newsworthy content. These newsletters will send event info and other potentially newsworthy content right to your inbox.

Also, change your routine. Take yourself to places you've never been. Talk to people who are different from you. When you're on public transit, talk to the person standing next to you. When you're studying at the library or café, look up and notice what's going on around you.

The point is to get curious, and as you continue to give curiosity a try, you will get better. You will hone this skill, and your journalism can only benefit.

Key takeaways

- Curiosity is necessary for strong journalism, and without it, we run the risk of failing to create impactful, informative journalism.
- Curiosity influences every aspect of journalism, including story generation, research, and interviewing.
- New technology, social media, anxiety, and fear can negatively impact curiosity.
- Cultivate curiosity by looking up from social media or that video game, being still, and paying attention to the world around you.

Discussion questions

1. What could you do to break up your daily routine? Where might you go in your local vicinity that you have never been to before? Explain why you chose this place. Whom might you talk with that is different from you? Explain why you chose this person.
2. Find a news article that interests you and was published in the past two weeks. Discuss how curiosity may have informed the story, the sources chosen, the newsgathering process, and any other aspects of the article. Where in the story was curiosity lacking? How would applying curiosity have helped with that aspect of the story? Do you think lack of time or resources played a role? Why or why not?
3. How does curiosity inform your daily life? Give a specific example of when you were curious and what came of it. What did you do to satisfy your curiosity? If you did nothing, why?
4. Have you ever decided NOT to ask a question or speak up about something? If so, what stopped you? How did you feel about the fact that you did not ask? How did you find the information you were curious about? If you had the opportunity again, would you ask/speak up? Why or why not?

Exercises

1. Slow down, set down your phone, get up, and look around.
    Take a look around your current environment or out the nearest window. If that does not pique your curiosity, then step outside. Take a walk. Observe the world around you. What do you see, hear, smell?
    a. Write down your observations.
        i. Preferably on pen and paper – leave the phone at home!
    b. List the questions you have about those observations.

    c. For each observation, come up with at least one story idea you could pursue.
    d. BONUS: List the sources you may use to develop the story.
2. Practice asking WHY.
    a. Choose a substantive news article from the past two weeks (i.e. at least 1,000 words or at least 03:00 – can be longer!).
    b. Grab a pen and paper, or open a Word doc, Google doc, etc. on your laptop or mobile phone.
    c. As you read, watch, or listen to your chosen story, take every opportunity to ask WHY and HOW (as well as WHO, WHAT, WHERE, and WHEN). Jot down on your paper or digital document the specific questions that come up for you.
        NOTE: Challenge yourself to come up with at least five questions. For a real challenge, go for ten+!
        i. Ex: Questions about the coverage:
           1. Why did the reporter talk with that source?
           2. How did the source discover the information?
           3. Who else could add an important perspective to this story?
        ii. Ex: Questions about the story itself:
           1. Why have people not spoken up until now?
           2. Why did the city budget its funds in this particular way?
           3. How did this organization secure an expensive office space?
    d. Once you've listened to/watched/read your chosen story and completed asking questions, take a look at what you've written. Use those questions to develop one-to-three story ideas you could pursue.
3. Take exercise #2 and apply it to your daily life. Throughout the day, practice observing your environment, focusing on something, and asking WHY, HOW, and other curiosity-provoking questions.
    a. At the end of your first week of practicing asking WHY, list the items that prompted you to ask WHY (at least three to five – the more, the better).
    b. Explain why those items piqued your interest or curiosity.
    c. Do some research and endeavor to answer your questions. At the very least, write down which sources may help answer the questions you had.
4. BONUS:[25]
    a. Hang out with a child under eight years of age. Young children are naturally curious, often asking WHY something is the way it is or HOW it works. (NOTE: Even if you are unable to hang out with a child, you can still complete the below exercise.)
        Take note of what children in your life are curious about and use that to drive your own thought process.
    b. Whether or not you are able to spend time with a child, consider anew things you may have always taken for granted (see partial list

below). There are plenty of processes, structures, and systems that we take for granted.

Once you've chosen something (or many things), explore how those processes, structures, or systems are set up in other communities, other cities and towns, other states, and even other countries. Chances are, you'll discover so many other ways of doing things, and this will likely lead to one or more story ideas.

Options for city processes include, but are not limited to:
i. Street maintenance
ii. Neighborhood makeup
iii. Incarceration in relation to community demographics
iv. Animal welfare
v. Schooling (including school demographics, district boundaries, education choices, funding and budget decisions, etc.)
vi. Utilities (power, water, and gas) and access
vii. Fire and police services and community communication
viii. Libraries (including services, availability, funding, etc.)
ix. Zoning for houses and commercial use
x. Garbage services

Options for schools include, but are not limited to:
i. How student fees are spent
ii. Parking services
iii. Housing for students
iv. Food service
v. Classroom and lab allocations
vi. Community engagement with surrounding neighborhoods
vii. Book sales

The list goes on – explore what interests you ... get curious!

5. Journalism Scavenger Hunt.
   Get into groups of three-to-five people with your fellow journalism students and see if you can beat the other groups on this journalistic scavenger hunt.
   Your professor may customize this list to better match your campus, but here are some scavenger hunt items to collect:
   a. Go to your theatre, dance, or other performing arts center or department and collect one or more flyers for upcoming shows. Find a staffer, professor, or student and interview them about a performance. Ask three-to-five questions.
      If no performance is coming up, interview someone about what the department offers.
   b. Visit a science or engineering department and interview someone about something that the department offers.
      i. BONUS: Research the department online first. Be sure to ask specific questions.

42 *Cultivating curiosity*

   c. Interview three-to-five students whom you do *not* already know about why they decided to come to this campus, what they like about campus, and what they'd like to see improved.
   d. Choose a student club and reach out to the student leaders and/or faculty advisor via email, social media, and/or phone – or in person, if you can find them. Interview them about what the club offers and why it exists on campus.
   e. Go to the counseling or writing center on campus and collect information about what the center has to offer. Write two-to-three tweets and/or Instagram posts about what you learned that you think would be helpful for other students. Be sure to take photos and include them.
   f. Visit the website of your campus president or provost. Choose one item from that site and explain it in your own words via a short audio podcast.
   g. Visit the website for your academic senate. Find out what was discussed at the previous meeting. Choose one item and write a tweet about it. Then, find out when the next meeting is scheduled and write a tweet about that. BONUS: If there's already an agenda for the next meeting, include an item that may be of interest to fellow students.
   h. Visit the athletic center and get information about an upcoming sporting event. Snap some photos, seek an interview, and write a 200–400-word news story about the game and players.
   i. Player's choice: Choose one other department, office, or agency and learn something about it that you could report on. Collect any relevant flyers or other info and grab some photos for social media.
   j. Surprise your professor! During your outing about campus, jot down notes about something that you did not already know or that you think might be worth exploring and researching as a potential story. Pitch it to your professor.

(*The Journalistic Scavenger Hunt exercise appears courtesy of Anne Belden.*)

6. Get curious about a classmate.
   Many of you have likely done the ice breaker where you're asked to interview a classmate. Let's give it a journalistic curiosity twist.
   a. Have everyone in class write down:
      i. Three things about themselves, two things that are true and one a lie
      ii. What they wish they could have done on their most recent vacation
      iii. Something they are proud of
      iv. A goal they have in life
   b. Get into groups of two and begin discussing your answers. For each answer, get curious and ask at least two follow-up questions to discover more about each answer.

c. Then, write a 200–400-word inverted pyramid story (or a 60-second audio story).
  d. BONUS: Write a tweet or Instagram post.
7. Watch or listen to an interview or press conference conducted by a journalist at a local daily news outlet.
  a. As you listen, jot down the question you would ask next, as well as any follow-up questions that come to you based on interviewee responses.
  b. Note which questions the interviewer did ask.
  c. Which questions would you ask that the interviewer missed?

Notes

1 Gallop-Goodman, Gerda. Diane Sawyer. p. 95: Turtleback, 2001.
2 Vanessa Nevarez (news assignment editor at KGTV), in conversation with Gina Baleria, February 2020.
3 Janice Wright (Anchor & Reporter at WCBS), in conversation with Gina Baleria, February 2020.
4 Schulz, Kathryn. "On Being Wrong." *TED*. TED Conferences, LLC, March 2011. https://www.ted.com/talks/kathryn_schulz_on_being_wrong.
5 Anne Belden (Journalism Instructor at Santa Rosa Junior College), in conversation with Gina Baleria, February 2020.
6 Rick Brunson (AssociateInstructor at the University of Central Florida), in conversation with Gina Baleria, February 2020.
7 Julian Rodriguez (Lecturer at University of Texas at Arlington), in conversation with Gina Baleria, February 2020.
8 Laura Smith (Lecturer at the University of South Carolina), in conversation with Gina Baleria, February 2020.
9 Dodge, D., D. Donato, N. Kelly, A. La Greca, J. Morganstein, J. Reser, J. Ruzek, S. Schweitzer, M. M. Shimamoto, K. Thigpen Tart, and R. Ursano. "Ch. 8: Mental Health and Well-Being. The Impacts of Climate Change on Human Health in the United States: A Scientific Assessment." U.S. Global Change Research Program, Washington, DC, 2016, 217–246. doi: 10.7930/J0TX3C9H.
10 "CURIOSITY: Meaning in the Cambridge English Dictionary." Cambridge Dictionary. Accessed March 1, 2020. https://dictionary.cambridge.org/dictionary/english/curiosity.
11 "Curiosity." Merriam-Webster. Accessed March 1, 2020. https://www.merriam-webster.com/dictionary/curiosity.
12 Niles, Robert. "What Is 'Journalism?'" *Robert Niles*, March 2007. Accessed February 11, 2020. https://www.robertniles.com/journalism.
13 Terry Conway (former News Radio editor & writer), in conversation with Gina Baleria, February 2020.
14 Peter Finch (Anchor & Reporter), in conversation with Gina Baleria, February 2020.
15 George Kiriyama (Managing Editor at KTNV), in conversation with Gina Baleria, February 2020.
16 Geraghty, Jim. "The Incurious Reporters." *National Review*, January 6, 2017. https://www.nationalreview.com/2017/01/pickup-trucks-media-reporters-lack-curiosity/.
17 "Most Americans Think Their Local News Media Are Doing Well Financially." Pew Research Center's Journalism Project. Pew Charitable Trusts, March 26, 2019. https://www.journalism.org/2019/03/26/most-americans-think-their-local-news-media-are-doing-well-financially-few-help-to-support-it/.

18 Conner, Robert. "Can Student Journalists Save Struggling Local News?" *News Decoder*, April 10, 2020. Accessed February 11, 2021. https://news-decoder.com/student-journal ists-local-news/.
19 Dory Culver (Retired Managing Editor at KCBS), in conversation with Gina Baleria, February 2020.
20 Sloan, W. David, and Lisa Mullikin Parcell. *American Journalism: History, Principles, Practices*. Jefferson, NC: McFarland & Co., 2002.
21 Elizabeth, Jane. "7 Characteristics of Effective Accountability Journalists." American Press Institute, December 20, 2016. https://www.americanpressinstitute.org/publications/rep orts/white-papers/characteristics-effective-accountability-journalists/.
22 "Essential Tool for Journalists: Curiosity Is Our Killer App." Reynolds Center. Donald W. Reynolds National Center for Business Journalism, June 22, 2015. https://busines sjournalism.org/2013/03/forgotten-essential-tool-for-journalists-curiosity-is-our-kil ler-app/.
23 Plaisance, Patrick L. "Why Is Curiosity Critical in Good Journalism? Just Ask!" *Psychology Today*. Sussex Publishers, December 10, 2014. https://www.psychologytoday.com/us/ blog/virtue-in-the-media-world/201412/why-is-curiosity-critical-in-good-journalism -just-ask.
24 "1993 Pulitzer Prizes: Journalism, The Miami Herald." The Pulitzer Prizes, 2013. https ://www.pulitzer.org/prize-winners-by-year/1993.
25 Ritchie, Josh. "Council Post: Five Ways to Cultivate Curiosity and Tap into Your Creativity." *Forbes*, November 21, 2017. Accessed February 11, 2021. https://www.for bes.com/sites/forbesagencycouncil/2017/11/15/five-ways-to-cultivate-curiosity-and -tap-into-your-creativity/#38ecd8b11fd6.

3 Empathy, solidarity, & compassion
Covering subjects fairly & countering echo chambers

> You never really understand a person until you consider things from his point of view... until you climb inside of his skin and walk around in it.
> – Atticus Finch in *To Kill a Mockingbird* by Harper Lee[1]

As a young news intern in Los Angeles, I was handed a story I dreaded. A family dog had been killed horrifically in the family's backyard. Apparently, someone walking in an alley behind the house had thrown a Molotov cocktail into the yard. I was (and am) a vegetarian who also avoids wearing animal products, and at the time, I was young, naïve, and sheltered. To cover the horrific killing of a pet was going to be difficult for me. My supervisor initially did not want to send me, because I was still just an intern, and she did not want to risk traumatizing me. She looked for someone else to take the story, but I knew everyone else was busy, and so I volunteered to go.

When my **photog** and I arrived on the scene, we were met by a mother and daughter. The neighborhood where it happened was lower on the socio-economic scale, and residents dealt with violence, gang activity, and a lack of attention from city leaders. I had grown up in a middle-class suburb, and my naivete led me to assume their lives were completely different from mine. And, my empathy for the dog was on overdrive, leaving no room for anyone else. I was, in essence, blinded by my all-consuming thoughts of the dog, forgetting that the family I was about to meet was experiencing their own feelings of grief over their dog's violent death.

But, as my interaction with the mother and daughter unfolded, my feelings of empathy evolved and broadened to include them, as well. I saw that they were (rightly) more upset than I, because it was their dog, a member of their family.

As I began to actually focus on the people who should be centered in this story – the mom and daughter – I was able to get outside of my own feelings and listen. The daughter, it turned out, was exactly my age, and we shared a love of animals. I began to feel a bond with her.

As the interview progressed, I saw that this was not just a story about a senseless attack on a defenseless pet. The mom and daughter both said they felt unsafe, because there were no streetlights in the alley behind their house. They were worried about robbery, sexual assault, and other violent crimes that may harm them or their neighbors. The community had repeatedly asked the city to do something about it, had seen no action, and now their pet was dead.

I began my newsgathering with the idea that this was going to be a story about a poor sweet dog and some heartless monster who killed for kicks. But, because I allowed myself to listen and *hear* the family's story, I could see commonality, recognize connection, and share their humanity with viewers. I learned that I could tell this story to help lead to a solution. I could point out that the city could do something to make people in the neighborhood feel more secure, and reach out to city officials to get them on record. While nothing could bring back the dog, perhaps the tragedy could inspire solutions that would benefit not only the mother and daughter, but their entire neighborhood, such as placing streetlights in the alley.

This story I dreaded covering ended up being a formative moment for me in my evolution as a journalist. I learned to listen. I learned to get outside my own feelings, thoughts, and biases – to take myself out of the equation. I learned to practice empathy – not the singular empathy that blinded me to all but one thing (the dog), but all-encompassing empathy that reminds me to challenge my assumptions and see the humanity in everyone involved in a story. This led me to practice better journalism that seeks to inform the public, hold power to account, and identify solutions. It has been nearly 25 years since this moment, and I still think of the daughter often. I still feel connected to her. This experience reminds me every day to seek out, listen to, and illuminate stories and perspectives that may bring context, inform audiences, and improve communities.

WHAT is empathy?

Psychology Today defines empathy as:

> the ability to recognize, understand, and share the thoughts and feelings of another person, animal, or fictional character. Developing empathy is crucial for establishing relationships and behaving compassionately. It involves experiencing another person's point of view, rather than just one's own, and enables prosocial, or helping behaviors that come from within, rather than being forced.[2]

In a 2018 report from the American Press Institute (API) on empathy strategies for newsrooms,[3] author P. Kim Bui wrote, "empathy is an essential skill in accurately portraying any community you cover,"[3] and she identified three types of empathy: cognitive, behavioral, and affective.

Cognitive: The ability to see the world through another person's perspective.

Behavioral: The verbal and nonverbal communication that indicates someone understands another person or their perspective.

Affective: Involves physically and emotionally experiencing another person's emotions.[3]

Cognitive empathy could help us tell the story of a nursing home worker threatened with deportation to Guatemala if she did not work extra hours without pay.[4] Cognitive empathy allows us to see the injustice and understand how the nursing home worker might feel. It allows us to tell her story so our audience can glimpse inside her world. These stories have the potential to affect policy, perhaps leading to worker protections for people like those profiled. To practice cognitive empathy, cultivate your curiosity (see *Chapter 2*) and ask questions. Do your best to avoid making assumptions, and approach the story with wonder and an openness. Instead of thinking you know how a person thinks and feels, ask them. Follow questions where they lead and explore the answers and additional questions that come up as you pursue your story.

David Finkel, national enterprise editor for *The Washington Post*, said empathy goes hand-in-hand with curiosity. Through curiosity, we are driven to understand, and through empathy, open ourselves to learning about, imagining, and vicariously experiencing what we seek to understand. "When you're underway and you're immersing yourself, that's when empathy really starts," Finkel told the API. "I genuinely am interested, I don't have an agenda, I'm curious about something, I want to understand something. That's empathy all the way."[3]

Behavioral empathy allows us to interview the nursing home worker mentioned above with compassion. It allows us to hear and see this human being as she shares her story. For example, note how her facial expressions change as she talks about her realities versus her desires, or how her shoulders tense as she describes her working conditions. Observing and taking in cues beyond just the words spoken, such as from body language and the environment, help us ask questions to illuminate the story for our audience. To practice behavioral empathy, look someone in the eye, physically mirror their posture and body language, pause and just listen without jumping to the next question, and then consider their words before moving on. Instead of having your next question ready, ask the question that comes up as you listen. Pay attention to how you are showing up in the moment and whether your questions are infused with judgment or simply curiosity. Removing judgment and instead genuinely inquiring can help people feel heard and understood and give audiences a deeper understanding.

Affective empathy is where journalists may find challenges. When we physically and emotionally experience another person's emotions, such as the pain, anguish, exhaustion, and fear of the nursing home worker, we run the risk of seeing only that worker's point of view. We run the risk of losing perspective by missing other aspects of the story that also need to be included. We run the risk of letting our empathy turn into tunnel vision, and thus into bias. Affective empathy may blind us to a bigger picture that the audience needs to know. Of course, it is OK to feel strong emotions and perhaps even strong connections during your work. But be aware of whether those feelings are hindering your news coverage, and if so, work to manage them and identify other important aspects of the story.

It is also important to understand the distinction between empathy and sympathy. When we feel sympathy, we are often feeling pity or remorse – how sad we are that a person is going through something and likely thankful that we are not in their shoes. This can lead us to look down on someone or separate ourselves. With empathy, we're seeking understanding and offering recognition, which can help keep you and your subject on equitable ground.

But true empathy can only be achieved with awareness and understanding of a story's broader context. As Kyle Harland wrote for the Center for Journalism Ethics at the University of Wisconsin-Madison:

> A real sense of empathy requires understanding the spectrum of ideas, events, and communities related to a story. Regardless of a reporter's intelligence or skill, if they are thrust into a situation and have had a short time to conduct background research, they cannot be expected to be as empathetic as someone familiar with a particular community or situation.[5]

This is why **beats** can be so effective, because they allow a journalist to get more deeply acquainted with a topic area. Then, by sharing stories, we seek to cultivate empathy in our audience. We see this, for example, in stories of individual athletes during the Olympics. We may not care to watch a sport we know nothing about, but once we get to know the person involved in that sport, we become more familiar, both with the person and the sport, having vicariously experienced the sport from the athlete's perspective. This connection leads us to tune in and follow that story to its conclusion.

To further illustrate, let's explore an example of a systemic failure in journalists' cultivation of empathy.

In 1989, when five young Black and Brown teenagers in New York were charged with raping a jogger in Central Park, news and tabloid coverage framed the story as guilty kids facing justice. Tabloid headlines included: "Wolf Pack's Prey" (*New York Daily News*);[6] and descriptions of the teens included blatantly racist words and phrases such as, "bloodthirsty," "animals," "savages," and "human mutations."[7] The teens were even depicted as a gang, by being dubbed, "The Central Park Five."[6]

The nonprofit journalism school and research organization the Poynter Institute explored how the media misjudged the case and the accused. "The tabloid press, desperate for details in the midst of a breaking story, benefitted from a cozy, trusting relationship with police," wrote NYU professor, former journalist, and author Julia Dahl. "At some level, the press got it wrong in

1989 because police got it wrong."[7] The news media centered the police narrative, even in the face of details that clearly conflicted with the law enforcement account, such as the fact that the victim lost more than 75% of her blood, but the boys had no blood on them.

The boys accused of the crime, instead of being seen as young, scared children who did not get due process, were seen as evil monsters. For police, the media, and the mainstream community, the five boys "quickly became symbols of the criminal menace that white New Yorkers felt had captured their city."[7] The facts – that the boys told conflicting stories, that police had no physical evidence tying any of the boys to the crime, and that one of the boys was not even a suspect, but simply went with his friend to the police station – were not highlighted on front pages or in top news stories, even if some reporters did explore those avenues.

Jim Dwyer, a columnist for Newsday in 1989, told Poynter, "I don't remember there being a lot of reflection about the truth."[7]

Of course, we now know that those five boys did not commit that horrendous crime. Another person confessed to it in 2002, leading to the boys' release from prison, and subsequently a book, a documentary, and later a movie about their experience. This case, and others like it, have led to reflection throughout the industry on the importance of empathy – for the victim, of course, but also for every other person in the story's orbit, including the accused. This can keep us open to all sides and avenues of a story, even when the case appears straightforward, and especially

Anita Varma & solidarity journalism

While good journalism can evoke feelings of empathy, this may not always bring audiences a full picture of a situation, plight, or systemic challenge. Instead, Anita Varma, PhD, assistant director of journalism and media ethics at the Markkula Center for Applied Ethics at Santa Clara University, says journalists should take a solidarity approach.

Solidarity Journalism is "where journalists humanize not by emphasizing similarities and not by emphasizing this model minority discourse, but instead by emphasizing people's perspectives," Varma said.[21]

Varma's research on coverage of the Bay Area homeless population[44,45] revealed that empathetic coverage often frames issues as individual problems, leaving audiences to believe they cannot help. However, solidarity coverage can advance social justice by framing issues in systemic, societal, and policy contexts, thus engendering empowerment.

In much coverage of people outside the mainstream audience, said Varma, "the basic assumption of human dignity is often unfortunately when the cultural context breeds bias, as it did in the racially charged context of New York City in the late 1980s. Failure to do this has led more than once to coverage that misleads and harms, rather than informs and gives context.

Empathy using more of a solidarity approach (see Sidebar) may have led to an investigation of how NYPD conducted the interrogations, including the fact that the boys were held for hours into the early morning without access to their parents or an attorney. It may have led journalists to seek out psychologists to discuss how this interrogation approach often leads to false confessions. It could have led more quickly to the arrest of the actual perpetrator, which would have saved other women from harm. In short, a broad-based empathy could have led journalists to provide important context. It may have even led to the clear picture that these kids were not perpetrators, rather victims caught up in a media and law enforcement frenzy.

Unfortunately, coverage without empathy continues to occur – in police shootings involving people of color, protests and demonstrations, and other stories. For example, in 2012, when teenager Trayvon Martin was killed while walking home in Sanford, FL, the fully grown adult male who killed Martin said he did it in self-defense. Much of the news media placed their empathy with the non-Black participant and went with this narrative. However, a few journalists of color questioned it and through dogged, curious, empathetic reporting were able to reveal a fuller picture of what happened the night Trayvon Martin was killed.[8]

not applied." One potential pitfall of humanizing to evoke empathy is,

aiming to humanize communities that respond to certain stigmas that privileged groups have put on them. That's where we get into model minority stuff. "So, you may think that everyone in this community is lazy and just lives off of public funds. But I'm here to tell you that Suzy Smith is not like that." That can be quite patronizing.[21]

Varma explained that empathy has a place, but journalists need to adjust their approach to help audiences understand systemic and social justice issues. "When we empathize and we see, let's say children suffering, we can feel very much for them. And then after a while, it can be a stark drop-off. And one reason for that is that empathy is fatiguing," said Varma. "So, we try to reconcile it." For example,

the world must be a fair place, and how could this fit into fairness? Well, I'm going to say their parents probably didn't work hard enough, or I'm going to say that they just aren't doing all their schoolwork. And that kind of victim-blaming can also come up as an attempt to reconcile. If you view the world as a fair place or want to view the world as a fair place, then it can be very hard to come to terms with the idea that there's entrenched and institutionalized unfairness all around us.[21]

WHY do journalists need to cultivate empathy?

A quote attributed to former Soviet dictator Joseph Stalin reads, "a single death is a tragedy, a million deaths are a statistic."[9] Stalin is known for leading with terror and brutality. He was responsible for the deaths of an estimated 20 million of his own people.[10] One way he was able to do this was to convince his followers to see those he harmed not with empathy, but as inhumane – *other* – and not worthy of empathy or compassion.

What happened under Stalin is one result of taking a lack of empathy to its logical conclusion, and it illustrates why cultivating and practicing inclusive empathy is so important. I say inclusive empathy because our empathy must extend both to **in-groups** and **out-groups** – people we perceive as like us, as well as people we perceive as part of another group. When we do not feel empathy for a person or group, we are more likely to vilify, marginalize, dehumanize, and *other*,[11,12] which can lead to horrific consequences, such as allowing the mass killings or large-scale imprisonment, mistreatment, or brutalization of groups. We have unfortunately seen such consequences far too many times around the world, including the killings of Stalin's political enemies; the Armenian genocide in the early 20th century; the WWII holocaust targeting Jews, LGBTQ+, academics, and political rivals; the Rwanda genocide in the early 1980s, which led to the massacre of 800,000 Tutsis and some moderate Hutus; US slavery and Jim Crow in the 17th–20th centuries; the genocide of Indigenous people in the US; and abuse of the Rohingya in Myanmar and Uyghurs in China.

Varma recommends avoiding the standard convention of reporting, which can lead to empathy fatigue:

"Here's the exemplar. Here's the best one of the lot. She's so good you wouldn't even know she's from a marginalized community." That's where the reporter's lens is betrayed as trying to assimilate this community into the mainstream. Trying to assimilate them into being more like *us* when *us* is assumed to be the dominant group.[21]

Instead, Varma recommends centering the voice, perspective, and narrative of the subject. "Think about the people at all times," she said.

Who are the people who are not only making the decisions – those might be isolated to a handful of people in government or corporations. But who are the people affected? Who are the people speaking up against how things have been done for the most part in the past, and what are their stories? That's where we start to get a more complete picture of any issue.[21]

To have empathy, we must find familiarity and commonality, and it's difficult to do that with a large, impersonal number, such as one million.[13] Think about the COVID-19 pandemic. What does it mean to say there have been nearly 600,000 deaths in the US and more than three million deaths worldwide as of May 2021? The scale is too large and abstract. But what if I say that someone named Olivia Cortez died – a young woman who worked at a local grocery store and helped patrons find the chocolate chips or mango slices. She always smiled when checking people out and even covered the partial cost of groceries for a woman who had lost her job. Cortez also played soccer for her local high school and volunteered as a children's soccer coach. Whether you shopped at Olivia's store or not, you can relate to a human being who helps people and goes the extra mile when someone is in need. You can picture an Olivia-like person in your own life playing a sport, working with kids, interacting with people at work. That familiarity breeds a connection. That is why one death is a tragedy. It can cultivate empathy in a way that a larger number, a statistic, cannot.

"Empathy is a tool that allows for connection with other human beings," explained Emmy- and Murrow-Award-winning journalist Cristina Mendonsa, host of the podcast *A Fresh Agenda*. "It leads to the type of understanding and soulful storytelling that not only draws viewers in but keeps them there with you, soaking in the information as they invest in the story."[14]

Journalistic empathy seeks not to make excuses for someone, agree with them, or overly identify. It seeks to help the audience understand – for example why someone joined a gang, why someone voted a certain way, or why someone chose to post something hurtful on social media. If consequences are in order, our empathetic reporting is not out to help any subject avoid accountability. Often, empathetic reporting can reveal aspects of a story that are important to know, even if they are not flattering or positive. Again, you're not pursuing an agenda or condoning an activity or action, rather you're shedding light on an issue, situation, or topic.

By understanding why or how someone ended up in a gang, you learn about the challenges they face and the systemic issues at play. Perhaps your coverage motivates community members to address those issues. You are not condoning any problematic or criminal activity the subject may have committed. When we talk with people who vote differently, we learn why, and often we find that they are concerned about the same things – their children's safety, the cost of education, or the inability to pay rent or a mortgage. They just saw a different path to dealing with the issue. Or, their worldview and motivations become clearer, giving audiences critical information to navigating their communities and those with whom they share community spaces.

Studies show that practicing broad-based empathy, solidarity (see Sidebar), or seeing can lead to positive outcomes in journalism and beyond. For example, doctors who were trained to increase the use of empathy in their practice saw better patient outcomes, fewer medical errors, a decrease in malpractice claims, and patients who felt more satisfied and heard.[15] In one study on the benefits of empathy in medical practice, the author wrote, "One legacy of medical education is overvaluing scientific measurement and undervaluing subjective experiences."[16]

This trend can also be seen in journalism, where we often over-value data-driven and official responses and under-value source material that falls outside of these purviews. We saw this phenomenon in the Central Park Five – now Exonerated Five – case discussed above, which privileged the narrative coming from the NYPD. When covering a shooting, fire, or city hall policy, we are likely to draw heavily from official news releases and news conferences. Accounts from the community that may run counter to these sources are scrutinized more heavily and often not given the same weight until they can be verified by an official source. This is not to say that verification is not important – it is critically important. But it behooves us to consider how we might also invest time and effort to verify information coming from unofficial sources that is pertinent to a given story. Research suggests that narrative journalism centering voices of those who are marginalized or *othered* can help create empathy among readers, viewers, or listeners[17] and result in a more balanced story.

WHO deserves the empathy of a journalist?

Everyone who ends up within the orbit of a news story deserves to be treated with empathy. This does not mean you are taking a side or excusing alleged behavior – merely that you are helping audiences understand, providing context, and offering information that can help communities make decisions about how they want to be governed, approach challenges, and deal with issues.

"Empathy compels fair treatment of all sources" because it compels the journalist to "seek to understand the *other*, not produce agreement with the *other*," wrote Janet Blank-Libra for Poynter. It is "the moment within which one connects with the *other* in an effort to see through his or her eyes, to know something through its meaning for that person."[18]

As P. Kim Bui wrote in the API empathy report, empathy can sometimes involve pointing out something "that the subject prefers not to acknowledge"[3] but the journalist can see because of the perspective we have on the story. We can see it because we empathize and seek to understand.

There are, of course, ethical challenges inherent in navigating this issue. For example, by covering a white supremacist[19] are we giving voice to an abhorrent movement?[20] Anita Varma, PhD, assistant director of journalism and media ethics at the Markkula Center for Applied Ethics at Santa Clara University, cautions that any subject can be humanized, but it is important to consider which subjects have historically *not* been given this courtesy and which sources have. One pitfall journalists may fall into is failing to make this distinction.

> One that keeps me up at night was a *New York Times* profile of (Syrian President) Bashar al-Assad. Assad that summer (2015) had been accused of gassing his own people. And the conditions in Syria were becoming worse and worse under his control. *The New York Times* published a beautiful profile of him that emphasized how he thinks about Syria, how charming and approachable and kind he is – It was really a humanizing profile of Assad. But those exact same techniques that can be used to humanize

54 *Empathy, solidarity, & compassion*

people we think of as the *other*, were now being used to humanize someone who mounting evidence had shown that the number of deaths in Syria – his hands are not clean of that.[21]

Varma's example highlights an important point. We need to ask ourselves which voices we are centering and which voices we are ignoring or de-emphasizing. Varma recommends assessing whether or not your subjects have power. "When you're out to humanize the top elected or appointed official – the people who have the most power – that's where things can become problematic (because we) humanize people to make them seem more like us."[21] While it's important to recognize the humanity of those in positions of power, it may require more intentionality to also include voices of those who do not hold power in communities. We need to do the work to ensure that all subjects caught in the matrix of a given news story are empowered to add their voices to the narrative while ensuring that we do not over-value the voices of those who hold power or influence.

It is also worth remembering – just as there are usually multiple facts involved in a given story, there are likely multiple truths, and sometimes all have validity. To illustrate, if someone draws a number on the ground (see Figure 3.1), and one person standing on one side of it says "it's a six (6)" and the person

Figure 3.1 6 or 9? Seeing someone else's perspective. (Designed by: Joyce Cheng.)

standing on the other side says "it's a nine (9)," they have two options. They could argue about it and try (with utter futility) to convince the other person. I mean, they can clearly see the number on the ground. From where they're standing, there's no ambiguity, right? How ridiculous that someone could see it differently. Or, they could stop, take a breath, and listen to the other person's perspective. Perhaps walk in their shoes, which in this case may involve walking from where they're standing to the other side of the number written on the ground and look at what the other person is seeing. By doing this, each person sees the other's perspective. It does not mean they are then somehow wrong. It means that there can be multiple perspectives. Empathy involves representing those perspectives fairly, accurately, and honestly, to ensure that the reader understands this and can draw their own conclusions.

HOW can journalists practice empathy?

As a journalist, you will cover all types of stories, some in contexts familiar to you, and others completely alien. For some stories, you'll understand the motivations, feelings, actions, and behaviors of those involved, and for other stories, you will not. In fact, there may be some people you cover whose motivations, feelings, actions, and behaviors you find abhorrent. How do you apply empathy to all people (and other beings) involved in news stories?

First, a reminder that empathy is not agreement. Just because you feel empathy for someone does not mean you are suddenly on their side. Covering all relevant perspectives and contexts allows your audience to make their own decisions about how they feel, what they might want to do about it, and how they can help or take action.

One way to practice empathy in your news coverage is to listen; not just for the soundbite – listen to *learn*. This type of listening involves hearing, processing, and allowing the information to add to your knowledge, inform your perspective, and take you in new directions.

We saw journalists grapple with empathetic listening during the #BLM protests following the death of George Floyd in May 2020, along with several other Black victims of police violence and racism. The temptation exists to cover these protests in a short-hand fashion – focusing on clashes between protesters and police, looting, and large marches down city streets. Though each of those aspects is important, they do not tell the full story. To start, of the more than 10,600 protests that occurred between May and August 2020 (#BLM, COVID-19, and others), 10,100, or more than 95%, of them were peaceful.[22] And, of the fewer than 5% that involved an act considered violent, those acts included tearing down Confederate statues. "In many cases, violent or destructive demonstrations have specifically targeted statues seen to represent the country's legacy of racist violence, such as monuments celebrating colonial figures, slave owners, and Confederate leaders," read a report from the Armed Conflict Location & Event Data Project (ACLED).[22] The report went on to say:

Despite the media focus on looting and vandalism, however, there is little evidence to suggest that demonstrators have engaged in widespread violence. In some cases where demonstrations did turn violent, there are reports of *agents provocateurs* – or infiltrators – instigating the violence. During a demonstration on 27 May in Minneapolis, for example, a man with an umbrella – dubbed the "umbrella man" by the media and later identified as a member of the Hells Angels linked to the Aryan Cowboys, a white supremacist prison and street gang – was seen smashing store windows.[22]

This is not to say that the violence that did occur is unimportant or should be minimized. People suffered harm, including business owners and residents of the affected neighborhoods. But, while including that angle, we need to also include the rest of the story. Images of violence, broken windows, and confrontations may make for compelling content and represent a valid and important angle, but they do not tell the full story. I posit that approaching this story and those involved with empathy could lead to more contextual reporting, which could perhaps lead to systemic and policy shifts.

Journalists who delved into the story and sought to understand the perspectives of those on the streets learned that, by and large, protesters wanted to give voice to their frustration, anger, sadness, and exhaustion over the state of affairs in the US by exercising their First Amendment rights of freedom of assembly, freedom of speech, and freedom of expression. By contrast, several cases of violence involved people who came from outside an area specifically to steal from businesses, wreak havoc, and take advantage of the situation. Examples include a white teen charged with traveling from Illinois to Kenosha, WI, to shoot and kill two people after the police shooting of Jacob Blake;[23] and a white man (mentioned above), later identified as a Hell's Angel member, filmed breaking windows of a Minneapolis auto parts store[24,25] in the early hours of protests in response to the police killing of George Floyd. And also, some looters were protesters. By covering the story with empathy, showing up, and listening to those involved in the story, many reporters were able to differentiate between protesters seeking justice and bad actors causing harm, and to bring those nuanced narratives to light.

Another way to engage in empathy is to do something as simple as looking someone in the eye (as long as that is culturally appropriate). When we look someone in the eye, it's difficult to see them as anything other than a human being. It can also keep you accountable to doing right by your sources and the communities you cover, even if you are covering a story that may be unflattering to a given community. If looking someone in the eye is not appropriate for your cultural context, then learn the community's cultural norms and practices. Once we see the humanity in someone, it becomes difficult to revert to defining them as a one-dimensional stereotype.[26,27] Looking someone in the eye may also remind you that there are human beings within the story – behind the headline and social media post.

When I was a young assignment editor in Los Angeles, a story broke involving a little girl who'd gone missing. The story captured the attention of Angelinos throughout the region, and every news outlet dedicated significant time and space to the story. A reporter at my station made a deeper connection with the family than other reporters. He led with empathy, and so they came to trust him. This relationship born of empathy led the family to speak to our reporter first, invite him to the house, and continue to let him in after they learned a horrible truth – that the little girl had been killed by a member of their family. The reporter asked the hard questions and covered all the developments. But he also treated the people caught in the story's matrix with humanity. Thus, his coverage helped audiences relate to and empathize with the family.

In the API empathy report, Keith Woods, vice president for newsroom training and diversity at National Public Radio (NPR), described empathy as "understanding the perspectives of the people in that community and letting them tell their own stories."[3] Woods recounted that when he was a young journalist, he found that, even though sports were not his first love, he could effectively cover the sports teams at three nearby historically Black colleges and universities (HBCUs), because he had empathy for the players and fans. He focused on their stories, their reactions, and their narratives, leading to compelling coverage.

One structural way to improve the use of empathy in reporting is to reintroduce beats. Reporters on beats – such as education, city hall, health, business, etc. – will achieve a level of familiarity with the people and issues related to that beat. Familiarity breeds empathy. A pitfall of this is over-empathizing with only one or a handful of perspectives on a given beat. Thus, beat reporters must do the work of engaging both official sources and those affected by or in the orbit of the beat.

Beat reporting can help achieve empathetic coverage, especially when a story is breaking. During a breaking story, beat reporters can lean on their connections, knowledge, and experience to provide context in real time. Beat reporting also prompts journalists to revisit stories, issues, and communities, keeping issues in the public eye and helping present a more well-rounded, nuanced, and contextual perspective to audiences.

You can also use immersive journalism, such as virtual reality (VR), augmented reality (AR), and 360 video, to evoke empathy among your audience.[28,29] Immersive technologies allow audiences to experience alternative perspectives, thus cultivating empathy. For example, journalist and documentarian Nonny de la Peña, who's been called "the Godmother of virtual reality,"[30] uses VR in her work because she wants her audience to be *in* the story, to experience it first-hand.

VR "is such a visceral empathy generator," de la Peña said in an interview with *Engadget*. "It can make people feel in a way that nothing, no other platform I've ever worked in can."[30]

De la Peña's work tends to feature marginalized voices, and she seeks to give the public greater understanding. For example, *Project Syria* drops viewers into Aleppo, Syria, where they experience a rocket blast and a refugee camp. She has also created VR stories centering on the homeless in Los Angeles and immigrants at the US-Mexico border. "VR has a unique power to place viewers on the scene of an event – instead of watching it from outside – and that's a really powerful way to engage them emotionally," De la Peña said. "It's also particularly suited to certain kinds of stories, where one significant event takes place in a defined space."

De la Peña explained the power of immersing yourself in a VR space. "You're faced with people in there – to look in their eyes. The sense of connection to the story was like nothing I'd ever seen."[31]

The danger, of course, is crafting an immersive story that over-emphasizes one perspective, leading the audience to feel affective empathy for only one side. Thus, ethical practices should be developed and adhered to when using immersive technologies, including safeguards against exploiting subjects or audience members, as well as an articulated understanding of the journalistic goals and reasons for covering a story using immersive technology.

EXERCISE BREAK

1. Go to *The New York Times* site profiling people who died from COVID-19 or the main NYT obituary page.
   a. https://www.nytimes.com/section/obituaries
   b. https://www.nytimes.com/interactive/2020/obituaries/people-died-coronavirus-obituaries.html
2. Choose one person and read their story.
3. Write 300–500 words *or* record a 60–90 second audio or video podcast
   a. Discuss your reaction to the story, including what you learned about the individual.
   b. Include your observations about how the NYT obituary writers use empathy to tell these stories.

WHEN do journalists need to engage in empathy?

The simple answer to when journalists need to engage in empathy is all the time. But, specifically, you want to intentionally apply empathy when you feel yourself glossing over a piece of a story, walking in with assumptions about a story, or after you've gotten one angle or side and are pursuing other angles. This is because we often over-identify with the first frame we receive, in a phenomenon called **anchoring bias**[32] or **anchoring effect** (see *Chapter 4*). For example, in the 1996 US Olympic Park bombing in Atlanta, the frame that took hold was of a security guard trying to look like a hero by planting a bomb and then clearing the area to save the day. In fact, security guard Richard Jewell *was* a hero who noticed a suspicious backpack and cleared the area before the bomb detonated, saving countless lives. But the first frame clouded all frames that came after it, and even after Jewell's name was officially cleared, that frame lingered.

We need to counter this phenomenon by intentionally and deliberately learning more about other frames and information while managing our bias toward the initial frame. Had we interviewed someone else first or read or viewed a different piece of content, we may have started with a different baseline bias. Deliberately choosing to be empathetic in your subsequent newsgathering can help allow the story to develop and other relevant views to be fully represented. The alternative is to close yourself off to new information, miss parts of the story, and present incomplete and potentially biased reporting.

Another time to intentionally apply empathy is when you are covering people or situations that may not be part of your everyday world. For example, the protests in the wake of the police killing of George Floyd saw an aggressive police response with police in riot gear confronting unarmed protesters. However, just a couple of weeks prior, people with guns stormed the Michigan statehouse in Lansing. Their protest? They did not want to wear masks to protect themselves from COVID-19, and they were unhappy that businesses were closed. In that situation, there were no police confrontations and no riot gear.

In both cases, a group of people were unhappy with an action taken by a governmental body and used their First Amendment rights to gather and make their feelings known, but both police treatment and news coverage differed. In one case armed protesters were allowed to conduct their activities with little interference, and coverage focused on their grievances. In the other case, protesters were thwarted as they conducted their activities, and coverage shifted quickly from their grievances to how they were protesting. What is the difference in each of these two situations? For one, in the first, most of the protesters were white males. In the second, many of the protesters were either Black or other people of color.

When we explore why coverage differed in these and other examples, we find that US newsrooms are comprised primarily of Caucasian men. A 2018 Pew Research Survey found that newsrooms are actually less diverse than the US population. More than three-quarters (77%) of reporters, editors, photographers, and videographers are non-Hispanic whites, and 61% are men.[33] In comparison, 60.1% of the US population is white and 49.2% male.[34] We tend to understand our own social groups, and so coverage is infused with the white male perspective. If someone is a member of a group with which reporters may not have had a lot of contact or about which they have little understanding, coverage can reflect that.[35,36]

Research finds that strong empathy for our **in-groups** – those like us and with whom we relate – can lead to a lack of empathy for **out-groups** – those we consider not like us or *other*.[37,38] In addition, studies indicate that our empathy can go into hyperdrive,[37,38] leading to over-identification with our in-group or **echo chamber**, and *othering*, villainizing, and scapegoating anyone outside our circle. For example, a study found that high empathy for a specific partisan perspective caused participants to show empathy for those in their in-group who subscribed to the same perspective, but a lack of empathy for people in their out-group who subscribed to a different political perspective.[36] Another study found that fans of a specific soccer team felt more empathy for a fellow fan from the same team who was hurt than for a fan of a rival team.[38] This phenomenon has led to actual harm. In March 2011, San Francisco Giants fan Bryan Stow was beat up after an LA Dodgers versus Giants game, apparently because he was rooting for the opposite team. Stow sustained severe brain injuries, and had to re-learn how to walk and talk.[39] Violence against rival fans has also been seen at soccer matches in Europe,[40] Indonesia,[41] and Argentina.[42]

This presents a challenge that journalists may be uniquely suited to address. On the one hand, empathy can help people feel as if they belong, cultivate trust, and lead to humanization, rather than stereotyping and *othering*.[43] But, on the other hand, a lack of empathy in any form can be damaging to relationships, community connection, and societal function. Couple that with research indicating that empathy is waning among the US population,[44] possibly because we gather less and engage with our digital spaces more, and we find that it may be time to become more conscious and aware of how we employ our empathy.

Journalists may find answers in research indicating that people must be motivated to want to empathize, but will respond to specific interventions.[45] This can include using a solidarity approach to introduce people to empathetic portrayals in news stories that center marginalized and under-served voices and the role of systems.[46,47]

This is not easy work. Deepening silos, echo chambers, and tribal politics in the US and around the world have led to a climate in which facts and truth are challenged and disbelieved. Deliberate efforts among some world leaders and other nefarious players to mislead and stoke distrust have led many to question journalists' motives. In this climate, journalists are vilified, *othered*, harassed, and harmed.

For example, on January 6, 2021, a group of white supremacists and other Trump supporters mobbed the US Capitol building in an insurrection to stop the count of the electoral votes that would name Joe Biden president. Five people died. This over-identifying empathy for Trump and the false narrative of a stolen election led to a complete lack of empathy for Congress, citizens who believed the false narrative of a stolen election, and the injury or death of several Capitol police officers. This phenomenon also occurred in Myanmar in 2014, when rampant disinformation about the Rohingya on social media led to a clash between Buddhists and Rohingya Muslims in Mandalay that turned fatal.

Many journalists have been hesitant to embrace the practice of empathy because they worry it will lead to bias. But a lack of empathy can also lead to bias – usually toward the dominant narrative. In fact, empathy for people we vilify can lead to better understanding and thus long-term solutions. For example, many stories have been written seeking to understand those who turn to white nationalist or conspiratorial thinking. As we saw with the January 6, 2021, US Capitol insurrection, this thinking can be dangerous. In one such story, *The New Yorker*'s Ronan Farrow used empathy to get a source to talk who had played a pivotal role in the US Capitol insurrection.[48] Farrow was neither seeking to get readers to agree with this source's beliefs nor condone her actions. Rather, he hoped to shed light on how seemingly normal people fall into conspiratorial or cult-like thinking, and prompt audiences to contribute toward finding solutions. Here, Farrow combined empathy with clarity of purpose to inform and contextualize.

Thus, not only can empathy be used as a valuable tool to help avoid allowing assumptions and biases to take hold in your reporting, empathy can also be used to bring out honest responses in your sources and encourage the seeking of systemic solutions.

WHERE can empathy go wrong?

Though empathy is an important tool for journalists seeking to fairly and fully cover their communities, there are reasons many journalists are uncomfortable with the idea of embracing empathy as part of their journalistic practice. These concerns include risking humanizing someone who allegedly did something monstrous or horrific, absorbing the horrors of the job and taking them home with you, further marginalizing groups by misrepresenting a group member, and being blinded by feelings and allowing bias to creep in. In addition, affective empathy can lead to **burnout**, which may prompt you to leave the profession.

These concerns are real. Burnout has led many journalists to leave the field and pursue other work.[49,50] And, in the US at least, we hold fast to the (false) ideal of objectivity. Objectivity leaves no room for empathy because, under this construct, empathy could lead to bias. (As we'll read in *Chapter 4*, bias is inherent in all of us; objectivity is not.)

It's time to reframe exactly what empathy means, why it's important to the practice of journalism, and how to practice it without falling victim to its pitfalls.

"Empathy doesn't mean getting sucked in or becoming an activist," said Mendonsa. "It is a portal for experience, not for absorption. It is not helpful to story subjects for the journalist to be overwhelmed by the experience."[14]

Ira Glass, host and producer of *This American Life*, said, "reporters tend to find in others what they are suited to find, so there is a whole school of reporting where they are cynical about the world and everything reinforces that."[51] This comment describes the opposite of empathy. It describes pre-conceived notions; seeing only what we *want* to see or are *primed* to see, rather than what's truly there. This can lead us to potentially miss the story or fail to cover it well. In this case, journalists are not blinded by empathy, but by their inherent biases. Empathy would allow them to counter their biases by letting another perspective in.

"A journalist without empathy is a cold practitioner not unlike a doctor with questionable skill and poor bedside manner. That journalist stands apart from the story subject in a lecturing 'well that sucks for you' stance," said Mendonsa. By the same token,

> a journalist (who) allows empathy to cross into activism or over-identification infects the story until it is no longer journalism. The story becomes commentary .... The skill comes in walking the line between those two extremes, using empathy as a tool to open that conduit of connectedness (to) tell the story as it deserves to be told.[14]

Empathy can also lead to pitfalls in our writing and presentation of stories. Affective empathy can turn a journalistic approach into a manipulative one. Empathy can be used as a weapon to manipulate the emotions of readers, listeners, and viewers. If the audience over-empathizes with one side, they may display a lack of empathy for another. We saw this play out in the Central Park Five – now Exonerated Five – story involving a rape and assault victim and five innocent, falsely convicted boys. Much of that coverage over-empathized with the victim, and instead of leading to justice and the capture of the actual perpetrator, led to a climate in which five more victims were created. I'm not arguing here that we avoid empathizing with the victim. The victim deserves empathy, compassion, and justice. She got two of those. Justice was thwarted because empathy went into hyperdrive, blinding journalists, law enforcement, and community members, and leading to a lack of empathy for other people who also deserved empathy. This is not journalism.

Another pitfall of empathy is that it takes something out of us – sometimes journalists don't have the time or emotional capital to spend. Resource cutting and layoffs have left newsrooms unable to give too much time to any one thing as journalists rush to cover multiple stories a day. In this context, applying empathy can feel like too heavy a lift. Audiences can also experience "**empathy fatigue**,"[52] as they, too, face busy lives and limited attention capacity. If I have to study for multiple tests, write a paper, care for an ailing parent or grandparent, tutor my younger sibling, and/or work a full-time job to pay rent, then deeply engaging with a news story will not be high on my list of priorities. Empathy can also cause us to feel distressed, which we may not want to feel. So, we turn to escapist content and avoid the news.

Consider the 2019 and 2020 protests in Hong Kong as mainland China tightened its efforts to exert control. People around the world watched the protests with distress. But we as individuals could not change the outcome. So, many chose to disengage. To counter empathy fatigue, Varma suggests keeping a solidarity approach in mind (see Sidebar), which can allow audiences to feel empowered, rather than despairing.

Empathy is a key intangible journalistic skill, because it helps us hear, see, understand, and convey the experiences of others. When covering stories in which someone has been through something horrific, when someone is in grief, or to understand people in communities with which we may not have had personal experience, empathy can help us center the perspectives of those affected and thus better convey more nuanced, contextual stories to our audiences. As we cover our communities in an ever more fractured national and global political context, empathy may help us more fully contextualize stories and cultivate understanding, rather than polarization.

Key takeaways

- Empathy is an essential skill for journalists, allowing us to see the world through another person's perspective, and engage in verbal and non-verbal communication that conveys understanding.
- Empathy can help journalists see beyond initial, stereotypical, or oft-used frames to potentially discover other important angles or voices.
- Beats, immersive journalism, and simple eye contact can help cultivate empathy among sources and audiences.
- Empathy should be practiced whenever journalists engage with a source or news gather.
- Pitfalls of empathy include over-emphasizing one perspective, empathy fatigue, or the temptation to soften ethical principles in service of one perspective.

Discussion questions

1. Choose one of the following scenarios. How might you pursue and tell this story using empathy, while avoiding the pitfalls of appearing to agree with or condone the subject's actions, i.e. describe techniques you would use to interview based on the three types of empathy:
   a. A high school senior who hacked her school's grading system to alter grades for herself and her friends.
   b. A young trans woman who finds themselves in jail after being arrested for beating up a man they say had been following them from store to store, while making hate-filled comments.
   c. A Trump supporter who was arrested after the insurrection at the US Capitol on January 6, 2021, for trespassing and says he was swept into the chambers by accident.
   d. A protester seen on video throwing a live tear gas canister back toward police during the January 6, 2021, US Capitol insurrection.
2. Discuss how empathy can enhance journalistic coverage, as well as how it can hinder or harm journalistic coverage. Get specific about the aspects of empathy that lead to strong coverage, as well as problematic coverage.
3. What is your opinion on the role of immersive technologies in journalism? How might you use VR, AR, or 360 video to tell a story? What are the pitfalls or dangers of this approach?
4. Should a journalist share their own perspective or experience as a way to cultivate empathy? Why or why not?

64 *Empathy, solidarity, & compassion*

Exercises

1. Find a hard news or feature story that goes in depth on an issue – such as education; health care; technology; business; climate; transportation; or school, city, or county budgets. Read, watch, or listen, and answer the following questions:
   a. How does empathy play a role in this piece of coverage?
      i. If you do not detect empathy, explain how you do not.
   b. Based on the journalist's descriptions of people, places, and circumstances, what types of empathy might they have employed in the process of reporting and writing this story (i.e. cognitive, behavorial, affective)?
   c. Does the story leave you feeling empowered to help? Or, does it leave you feeling powerless or overwhelmed? Describe your reaction and why you think you're having such a reaction.

2. Choose one of the below stories, and discuss how you might employ an empathetic approach to your coverage. Answer:
   a. Which sources would you choose?
   b. Which angles would you pursue?
   c. How would you challenge your own assumptions and biases?
   d. How would your approach lead to empathetic coverage?
   e. STORY OPTIONS (or your professor may have other options):
      i. COVID-19
         1. Hospitalizations
         2. Death data
         3. Impact on medical professionals
         4. Essential workers
         5. Mask wearing
         6. Vaccines
      ii. Civil protest, unrest, and insurrection
         1. #BLM & #DeFundThePolice
         2. #MeToo
         3. QAnon and white supremacy
         4. Hong Kong protests
         5. Nigeria protests
         6. Anti-Asian Hate and violence
      iii. Societal issues
         1. Homelessness
         2. K–12 public education funding
         3. Drinking water
         4. Housing

3. Choose a news story from the past two weeks that involves someone who took an action or exhibited a behavior that you neither understand nor relate to.
   a. Write down all the reasons you can think of as to why the person may have taken these actions or engaged in this behavior.

i. Include sarcastic reasons, skeptical reasons, but also challenge yourself to include reasons that you would not define as evil or selfish. Truly engage in the mental exercise of allowing this subject to have humanity.
ii. NOTE: You do not have to agree with these reasons – simply acknowledge that they could have been motivating factors for this individual.
   b. From your list, choose one of your reasons, and answer the following questions:
      i. Why did you choose this reason?
      ii. How does this reason reflect on the individual?
      iii. How does this reason reflect upon the societal or systemic context?
      iv. What consequences (if any) should the individual face, given the reason you chose?
      v. How might the audience feel after reading your story (i.e. powerless, empowered, disgusted, motivated, etc.)?

4. Go to a public place and observe the people around you. Choose one person and imagine that you and this person have switched places in life. Imagine what your life is like as this person. Answer the following questions about you as this person, as well as others that occur to you, and write up a one- to two-page summary of who you are and what's important to you.
   a. Why are you in this location?
   b. Why are you wearing the clothes you're wearing?
   c. If you're with anyone, who?
   d. Where did you just come from?
   e. Where are you going after this?
   f. Where do you live? With whom?
   g. What do you do for a living?
   h. Where do you see yourself in five years?
   i. What is your name?
   j. Etc.

5. Humans of your campus or community
   a. Find a student, faculty, or staff member on campus and ask if they are willing to talk to you. Identify yourself as a student journalist and say that you are collecting Humans of Campus stories. Ask if they are willing to participate.
      i. NOTE: you may have to approach ten people to find one or two who are willing. Do not take rejection personally.
   b. Ask questions designed to get at their life story. Here are some examples:
      i. Full name
      ii. Age
      iii. Did you grow up here? If not, where are you from?

iv. When did you start college?
v. What brings you to this campus? What do you hope to achieve?
vi. Do you have any hobbies?
vii. What's the most difficult thing about your life right now (i.e. balancing work and school)? How do you cope?
viii. What's the best thing about your life right now?
ix. What motivates or inspires you every day?
x. What are your life dreams or plans for yourself?
xi. Tell us something about yourself that most people would be surprised to hear.

c. Take a portrait. Try to find interesting angles and poses and take close-range and mid-range shots.
  i. NOTE: Do not take only one photo. Take several so you have a selection to choose from.
d. Write 200–400 words about your subject and include at least one quote from the subject. Your goal is to give us a picture of **who** this person is, **where** they are from, **why** they are here, **when** they started school, **what** they plan or dream for their future, and **how** they are managing to do this.
e. Be prepared to discuss with your class how empathy played a role in your process.

(*The Humans from Campus Exercise appears courtesy of Anne Belden.*)

Notes

1 Lee, Harper. *To Kill a Mockingbird*. Philadelphia and New York: J. B. Lippincott & Co., 1960, 30.
2 "Empathy." *Psychology Today*. Accessed February 11, 2021. https://www.psychologytoday.com/us/basics/empathy.
3 Bui, P. Kim. "The Empathetic Newsroom: How Journalists Can Better Cover Neglected Communities." American Press Institute, June 09, 2020. Accessed February 11, 2021. https://www.americanpressinstitute.org/publications/reports/strategy-studies/empathetic-newsroom/single-page/.
4 Nelson, Rob. "AG: Immigrant Health Aides Who Complained about Pay Threatened with Deportation." *ABC7 New York*, September 13, 2019. Accessed February 11, 2021. https://abc7ny.com/immigrant-aides-who-asked-for-full-pay-threatened-with-deportation/5537517/.
5 Harland, Kyle. "Practicing Compassion in an Unbiased Journalism." Center for Journalism Ethics, June 17, 2008. Accessed February 11, 2021. https://ethics.journalism.wisc.edu/2008/06/16/practicing-compassion-in-an-unbiased-journalism/.
6 Gentle, Don, and Don Singleton. "Wolf Pack's Prey." *Nydailynews.com*, April 09, 2013. Accessed February 11, 2021. https://www.nydailynews.com/services/female-jogger-death-savage-attack-roving-gang-article-1.1304506 .
7 Dahl, Julia. "We Were the Wolf Pack: How New York City Tabloid Media Misjudged the Central Park Jogger Case." *Poynter*, October 10, 2018. Accessed February 11, 2021. https://www.poynter.org/newsletters/2011/we-were-the-wolf-pack-how-new-york-city-tabloid-media-mangled-the-central-park-jogger-case/.

8 Froomkin @froomkin, Dan. "Truth or Consequences: Where Is Watchdog Journalism Today?" *Nieman Reports*, April 17, 2014. Accessed February 11, 2021. https://niemanreports.org/articles/truth-or-consequences-where-is-watchdog-journalism-today/.
9 Tirman, John. *The Deaths of Others: The Fate of Civilians in America's Wars*. New York: Oxford University Press, 2015, 316.
10 "Joseph Stalin." *History.com*. A&E Television Networks, November 12, 2009. https://www.history.com/topics/russia/joseph-stalin.
11 Young, B. "Not There Yet: Women in Educational Administration." In Y. L. Jack Lam (Ed.), *The Canadian Public School System: Issues and Prospects* (pp. 85–102). Calgary: Detselig, 1990.
12 Johnson, J., Bottorff, J., Browne, A., Grewal, S., Hilton, B., and Clarke, H. "'Othering and Being Othered in the Context of Health Care Services." *Health Communication* 16, no. 2 (2004): 255–71. doi: 10.1207/S15327027HC1602_7.
13 Lee, Seyoung, and Thomas Hugh Feeley. "The Identifiable Victim Effect: A Meta-Analytic Review." *Social Influence* 11, no. 3 (July 20, 2016): 199–215. doi: 10.1080/15534510.2016.1216891.
14 Mendonsa, Cristina. "The Importance of Empathy in Journalism." *Mendonsa Media*, November 8, 2017. http://www.cristinamendonsa.com/2017/11/08/importance-empathy-journalism/.
15 Riess, Helen, John M. Kelley, Robert Bailey, Paul M. Konowitz, and Stacey Tutt Gray. "Improving Empathy and Relational Skills in Otolaryngology Residents." *Otolaryngology–Head and Neck Surgery* 144, no. 1 (2011): 120–22. doi: 10.1177/0194599810390897.
16 Riess, Helen. "Empathy in Medicine—A Neurobiological Perspective." *JAMA* 304, no. 14 (October 13, 2010): 1604–5. doi: 10.1001/jama.2010.1455.
17 Oliver, Mary Beth, James Price Dillard, Keunmin Bae, and Daniel J. Tamul. "The Effect of Narrative News Format on Empathy for Stigmatized Groups." *Journalism & Mass Communication Quarterly* 89, no. 2 (March 14, 2012): 205–24. doi: 10.1177/1077699012439020.
18 Blank-Libra, Janet. "Compassion Is not Journalism's Downfall, It's Journalism's Salvation." *Poynter*. The Poynter Institute, November 25, 2014. https://www.poynter.org/reporting-editing/2012/compassion-is-not-journalisms-downfall-its-journalisms-salvation/.
19 McCoy, Terrence. "'I Don't Know How You Got this Way'." *The Washington Post*, February 23, 2018. https://www.washingtonpost.com/news/local/wp/2018/02/23/feature/i-dont-know-how-you-got-this-way-a-young-neo-nazi-reveals-himself-to-his-family/.
20 Lacey, Marc. "Readers Accuse Us of Normalizing a Nazi Sympathizer; We Respond." *The New York Times*, November 26, 2017. https://www.nytimes.com/2017/11/26/reader-center/readers-accuse-us-of-normalizing-a-nazi-sympathizer-we-respond.html.
21 Anita, Varma. "Ethically Navigating Major Ongoing News Stories," interview by Gina Baleria, *News in Context* (podcast), July 2020. https://exchange.prx.org/pieces/329891-dr-anita-varma-on-ethically-navigating-major-ongo and https://exchange.prx.org/pieces/330668-ethically-covering-major-ongoing-stories-w-dr-ani.
22 Kishi, Roudabeh, and Sam Jones. "Demonstrations & Political Violence in America: New Data for Summer 2020." Armed Conflict Location & Event Data Project (ACLED), January 21, 2021. https://acleddata.com/2020/09/03/demonstrations-political-violence-in-america-new-data-for-summer-2020/.
23 Levenson, Eric, and Alisha Ebrahimji. "Illinois Teen Arrested in Fatal Shooting at Kenosha Protest, Police Say." *CNN*, August 26, 2020. https://www.cnn.com/2020/08/26/us/kenosha-wisconsin-wednesday-shooting/index.html.
24 Macfarquhar, Neil. "Minneapolis Police Link 'Umbrella Man' to White Supremacy Group." *The New York Times*, July 28, 2020. https://www.nytimes.com/2020/07/28/us/umbrella-man-identified-minneapolis.html.

25 Pagones, Stephanie. "Minneapolis 'Umbrella Man' Who Sparked AutoZone Fire Is Hells Angels Member: Police." FOX News Network, July 30, 2020. https://www.foxnews.com/us/minneapolis-umbrella-man-autozone-fire-hells-angels-police.
26 Bennett, M. J. "Towards a Developmental Model of Intercultural Sensitivity." In M. Paige (Ed.), *Education for the Intercultural Experience*. Yarmouth, MA: Intercultural Press, 1993.
27 Chavez, A. F., F. Guido-DiBrito, and S. L. Mallory. "Learning to Value the "Other": A Framework of Individual Diversity Development." *Journal of College Student Development* 44, no. 4 (2003): 453–69. doi: 10.1353/csd.2003.0038.
28 Bujić, Mila, Mikko Salminen, Joseph Macey, and Juho Hamari. "'Empathy Machine': How Virtual Reality Affects Human Rights Attitudes." *Internet Research* 30, no. 5 (June 30, 2020): 1407–25. doi: 10.1108/INTR-07-2019-0306.
29 Sánchez Laws, and Ana Luisa. "Can Immersive Journalism Enhance Empathy?" *Digital Journalism* 8, no. 2 (2020): 213–28. doi: 10.1080/21670811.2017.1389286.
30 Volpe, Joseph. "The Godmother of Virtual Reality: Nonny De La Peña." *Engadget*, January 24, 2015. https://www.engadget.com/2015-01-24-the-godmother-of-virtual-reality-nonny-de-la-pena.html.
31 Garling, Caleb. "Virtual Reality, Empathy and the Next Journalism." *Wired*. Conde Nast, November 3, 2015. https://www.wired.com/brandlab/2015/11/nonny-de-la-pena-virtual-reality-empathy-and-the-next-journalism/.
32 "Anchoring Bias - Definition, Overview and Examples." Corporate Finance Institute, April 15, 2019. https://corporatefinanceinstitute.com/resources/knowledge/trading-investing/anchoring-bias/.
33 Grieco, Elizabeth. "Newsroom Employees Are Less Diverse than U.S. Workers Overall." Pew Research Center, May 30, 2020. https://www.pewresearch.org/fact-tank/2018/11/02/newsroom-employees-are-less-diverse-than-u-s-workers-overall/.
34 "U.S. Census Bureau QuickFacts: United States." Census Bureau QuickFacts, 2010. https://www.census.gov/quickfacts/fact/table/US/PST045219.
35 White, Kailey, Forrest Stuart, and Shannon L. Morrissey. "Whose Lives Matter? Race, Space, and the Devaluation of Homicide Victims in Minority Communities." *Sociology of Race and Ethnicity*, September 17, 2020. doi: 10.1177/2332649220948184.
36 Stillman, Sarah. "'The Missing White Girl Syndrome': Disappeared Women and Media Activism." *Gender & Development* 15, no. 3 (November 2007): 491–502. doi: 10.1080/13552070701630665.
37 Simas, Elizabeth N., Scott Clifford, and Justin H. Kirkland. "How Empathic Concern Fuels Political Polarization." *American Political Science Review* 114, no. 1 (October 31, 2019): 258–69. doi: 10.1017/S0003055419000534.
38 Hein, Grit, Giorgia Silani, Kerstin Preuschoff, C. Daniel Batson, and Tania Singer. "Neural Responses to Ingroup and Outgroup Members' Suffering Predict Individual Differences in Costly Helping." *Neuron* 68, no. 1 (October 10, 2010): 149–60. doi: 10.1016/j.neuron.2010.09.003.
39 Baig, Yousef. "'I Want to Stop Bullies from Hurting Anyone Else': Students Hear Powerful Message from Injured Giants Fan." *Santa Rosa Press Democrat*, December 7, 2019. https://www.pressdemocrat.com/article/news/bryan-stow-beaten-8-years-ago-at-dodgers-stadium-delivers-anti-bullying-m/.
40 CNN, By Steve Visser. "Euro 2016: Dozens Injured as Crowds of Rival Fans Brawl." CNN, June 11, 2016. https://www.cnn.com/2016/06/11/world/euro-2016-england-russia-brawl/index.html.
41 NDTV.com. "Indonesian Football Fan Beaten To Death By Rival Supporters, 16 Arrested." Accessed April 10, 2021. https://www.ndtv.com/world-news/football-fan-in-indonesia-beaten-to-death-by-rival-supporters-1921245.
42 NDTV.com. "Indonesian Football Fan Beaten To Death By Rival Supporters, 16 Arrested." Accessed April 10, 2021. https://www.ndtv.com/world-news/football-fan-in-indonesia-beaten-to-death-by-rival-supporters-1921245.

43 Johnson, James D., Nelgy Olivo, Nathan Gibson, William Reed, and Leslie Ashburn-Nardo. "Priming Media Stereotypes Reduces Support for Social Welfare Policies: The Mediating Role of Empathy." *Personality and Social Psychology Bulletin* 35, no. 4 (January 22, 2009): 463–76. doi: 10.1177/0146167208329856.
44 Konrath, Sara H., Edward H. O'Brien, and Courtney Hsing. "Changes in Dispositional Empathy in American College Students Over Time: A Meta-Analysis." *Personality and Social Psychology Review* 15, no. 2 (August 5, 2010): 180–98. doi: 10.1177/1088868310377395.
45 Weisz, Erika, Desmond C. Ong, Ryan W. Carlson, and Jamil Zaki. "Building Empathy through Motivation-Based Interventions." *Emotion*, November 19, 2021. doi: 10.1037/emo0000929.
46 Varma, Anita. "Evoking Empathy or Enacting Solidarity with Marginalized Communities? A Case Study of Journalistic Humanizing Techniques in the San Francisco Homeless Project." *Journalism Studies* 21, no. 12 (July 8, 2020): 1705–23. doi: 10.1080/1461670X.2020.1789495.
47 Varma, Anita. "When Empathy Is not Enough." *Journalism Practice* 13, no. 1 (November 14, 2017): 105–21. doi: 10.1080/17512786.2017.1394210.
48 Farrow, Ronan. "A Pennsylvania Mother's Path to Insurrection." *The New Yorker*, February 2, 2021. https://www.newyorker.com/news/news-desk/a-pennsylvania-mothers-path-to-insurrection-capitol-riot.
49 Reinardy, Scott. "Newspaper Journalism in Crisis: Burnout on the Rise, Eroding Young Journalists' Career Commitment." *Journalism: Theory, Practice & Criticism* 12, no. 1 (January 2011): 33–50. doi: 10.1177/1464884910385188.
50 Liu, Huei-Ling, and Ven-hwei Lo. "An Integrated Model of Workload, Autonomy, Burnout, Job Satisfaction, and Turnover Intention among Taiwanese Reporters." *Asian Journal of Communication* 28, no. 2 (September 27, 2017): 153–69. doi: 10.1080/01292986.2017.1382544.
51 Raushenbush, Rev. Paul Brandeis. "Ira Glass, Religion and the Empathetic Power of Storytelling." *HuffPost*, May 25, 2011. https://www.huffpost.com/entry/ira-glass-and-the-empathe_b_806048.
52 Plaisance, Patrick Lee. "The Dilemma of Empathy and the News." *Psychology Today*. Sussex Publishers, May 9, 2019. https://www.psychologytoday.com/us/blog/virtue-in-the-media-world/201905/the-dilemma-empathy-and-the-news.

4   Good stewards

Facing our implicit & unconscious biases

> Neutral "objective journalism" is constructed atop a pyramid of subjective decision-making: which stories to cover, how intensely to cover those stories, which sources to seek out and include, which pieces of information are highlighted and which are downplayed. No journalistic process is objective. And no individual journalist is objective, because no human being is.
> – Wesley Lowery, correspondent, 60 Minutes/CBS News[1]

As the COVID-19 pandemic intensified in fall 2020, a nurse from South Dakota turned to Twitter on November 14 to share what she described as patients seemingly in denial that they were suffering and dying from COVID-19.

The nurse's thread began:

> I have a night off from the hospital. As I'm on my couch with my dog I can't help but think of the COVID patients the last few days. The ones that stick out are those who still don't believe the virus is real. The ones who scream at you for a magic medicine and that Joe Biden is going to ruin the USA. All while gasping for breath on 100% Vapotherm. They tell you there must be another reason they are sick. They call you names and ask why you have to wear all that "stuff" because they don't have COVID because it's not real. Yes. This really happens.[2]

The thread went viral. In two days, it garnered 200,000 likes, and more than 50,000 people re-tweeted it.[3] Many news outlets jumped on the story and interviewed her, including CNN,[4] *The Washington Post*,[5] *USA Today*,[6] and *Newsweek*.[7]

And, of course, the nurse's words captured attention. They coincided with a significant increase in infection rates, hospitalizations, and deaths. Her words also affirmed a narrative held by many non-conservatives that many people in red states were in denial about the severity of the virus and not taking precautions to protect themselves and those around them.

Let me say, there is no reason to think the nurse was being untruthful. In fact, other nurses in other parts of the country have since come forward to share similar experiences.[8] This is not an accusation of falsity, rather an example of unconscious and **implicit bias** in reporting. It illustrates that many news media outlets covered this story uncritically – without doing their due diligence to independently verify the facts before reporting on them because the nurse's tweet fit a narrative.

CNN and other outlets did include the numbers – data illustrating that South Dakota was among the states particularly hard hit, and survey information confirming that many South Dakotans were skeptical of warnings and resistant to calls for mask wearing and social distancing.

But none called the hospital where this nurse worked, or any other hospital in the state, to see if other nurses were experiencing anything similar with their patients ... except *Wired*.

On November 18, 2020, *Wired* published an article detailing its newsgathering and research and admonishing other news outlets for failing to do their jobs. Before writer David Zweig presented his fact finding, he reminded readers:

> There's no doubt that we owe a deep debt of gratitude to [the nurse] and all the frontline medical personnel dealing with the current surge in COVID cases. The work they do is truly heroic. Still, the manner in which [her] account of her experience has been reported and circulated should give people pause.[9]

Zweig wanted to make clear it was *journalists* he was taking to task – for allowing their biases to lead them to cover the story largely uncritically – not heroic nurses dealing with horrific, intense, and emotionally taxing experiences day in and day out as they worked to care for patients.

Zweig went on to write that he called several hospitals in South Dakota in an effort to independently verify the story and assess how widespread this issue may be.

> An ER nurse told me, "I have not had that experience here." At my request ..., the VP for communications and marketing at Huron Regional Medical Center, one of the four medical facilities where [the nurse] works, spoke with several nurses .... None said they'd interacted with Covid patients who denied having the disease. "Most patients are grateful, and thankful for our help," one told her. "I have not experienced this, nor have I been told of this experience, ever," another said. This in no way means that [the nurse]'s account is untrue. But it provides, at minimum, some important context that was completely absent from the CNN interview and from all the media amplification that followed. Little or no effort was made to assess the *scope* of the problem .... No one bothered to find out.[9]

Subsequent coverage did include nurses from all over the country describing incidents similar to the experience shared on Twitter. But, prior to this independent verification, what we saw was the unconscious, implicit bias of journalists who chose to cover the nurse's tweet uncritically, because it confirmed their assumptions about how people in red states might respond to a COVID-19 diagnosis. The moral of the story here is that journalists always need to do their due diligence, and not succumb to implicit biases, even if they end up being right. That's not journalism. That's just luck.

We all have biases, and we're all susceptible to sharing and repeating information that confirms our biases. Journalists must hold themselves to a higher standard. The nurse's perspective is important, but the scope of the problem is also important. When practicing journalism (and ideally in all aspects of your life), resist the urge to allow information to carry you away, no matter how much it fits with your worldview.

WHAT is bias?

Bias is hardwired into all our brains. **Biases** are basically shortcuts our brains take to simplify and make sense of the world. They are based on our experiences up to that point[10] and are informed by the societal and cultural contexts, power structures, and value systems in which we exist. "None of us can be fully aware of how our beliefs and behaviors are being affected by a lifetime of direct and indirect messages about one another,"[11] said Karen Yin, founder of the Conscious Style Guide.

However, unexamined or implicit biases and the assumptions they bring can sometimes prevent us from seeing things from different points of view. National Public Radio (NPR) Chief Diversity Officer Keith Woods describes this as "the unchallenged, (uncritical) point of view."[12] Unchallenged, biases can lead to unfair, prejudiced, or stereotypical assumptions[13] and discriminatory practices. Our goal as journalists is to make our biases explicit – meaning we are aware of them and work to ensure they are not detrimental to our journalistic work.

People often fail to recognize, acknowledge, and mitigate their biases. Some famous examples include an increase in the number of female musicians chosen for orchestras after major orchestras began conducting blind auditions;[14] and a study showing that when identical resumes are given Black- or white-sounding names, resumes with white-sounding names are more likely to get called for an interview.[15]

In journalism, we see examples of unconscious, implicit bias because journalists and those who run newsrooms are also human beings, and may not have done the work of examining their own biases. Female politicians are often stereotyped or minimized in journalistic coverage.[16] People who are Muslim or have darker skin are generally labeled terrorists more quickly than white perpetrators who commit similar acts.[17,18,19] Examining our biases can minimize their subconscious influence on our reporting.

Consider the *Pittsburgh Post-Gazette*'s decision to remove reporter Alexis Johnson from covering the 2020 Black Lives Matter protests. On May 31,

Johnson, who is Black, tweeted pictures of trash strewn about the pavement, with the caption:

> Horrifying scenes and aftermath from selfish LOOTERS who don't care about this city!!!!! ... oh wait sorry. No, these are pictures from a Kenny Chesney concert tailgate. Whoops.[20]

Johnson said she was told her tweet violated social media policy and that she would be taken off protest coverage. However, a white male colleague who also tweeted something that violated social media policy around the same time was initially only given a warning but allowed to keep reporting on the protests. He was only removed from coverage after the union questioned newspaper management about the discrepancy.[20]

This example illustrates how Johnson's actions were seen as inherent to who she was — biased — while her white male colleague was assumed to be an objective journalist who made a slightly biased misstep — not something inherent to his very being.

"That's the way these things happen, not because the person who makes that assumption is Black, but because the person who makes that assumption is not," said Woods. "Until we are able to see through a clear lens ..., we'll continue to have those sorts of ridiculous things happen in the profession of journalism."[12]

As a first step toward grappling with and managing biases, so we can effectively inform the public, consider how journalists might describe people who took to the streets in mid-2020, in response to the police killing of George Floyd in Minneapolis, MN, and several other Black men and women around the US. What words were used to describe them? Protesters? Demonstrators? Rioters?

What about the activity they engaged in? Unrest? A riot? A demonstration? A protest?

What about the description of the act that led to these actions? The death of a man in police custody? The police killing of a Black man? The murder of George Floyd by a police officer?

Now think about the people who stormed the US Capitol on January 6, 2021. What words would you use to describe them and their actions? Protest? Riot? Insurrection?

Each of the words and phrases mentioned above carries the implicit biases we each hold and carry with us everywhere we go. The words you initially gravitated toward represent your implicit biases at work. Our implicit (and explicit) biases frame and inform our perceptions and interpretations of reality — the actions we witness, read about, listen to, watch, and cover.

In the Movement for Black Lives example, for those who gravitated toward riot, your implicit bias may be that you see these actions as going too far, as possibly unfair to the police officers who you see doing a good job. For those who gravitated toward protest or unrest, your implicit bias may be that you see these actions as justified, maybe even necessary – that those involved in the action of taking to the streets have good reason to do so, and even if there are officers who do a good job, the system in which they work will not allow for fair treatment of those considered outside the mainstream community, or accountability for officers who break the rules and cause harm.

If you used different words for the US Capitol insurrection than you did for the Movement for Black Lives, ask yourself why? Here, I deliberately and intentionally use the word insurrection to describe the actions of the rioters (another deliberately chosen word) on January 6. While my own implicit biases may influence me to gravitate toward one word or another, I attempt to counter that by recognizing and acknowledging my biases, and then doing research on how these actions have been defined in other contexts – such as other nations and other moments in time. I also consider the dictionary definitions of each word and pay attention to experts, noting both their political and ideological leanings, as well as how they are discussing the issue. I weigh their biases and assess how to utilize their perspectives in my coverage. It is this research that helps me choose words that have precise meanings to convey what I mean to convey. I don't leave it up to my knee-jerk reaction.

There are many types of bias that we need to be aware of and counter:[21,22,11]

1. **Affinity bias:** Bias *in favor* of someone. We are drawn to them because they are like us.
2. **Bias of balance:** Presenting "both sides" of an issue to try to show we're being fair. NOTE: Any "side" needs to be assessed for journalistic relevance to a given story.
3. **Confirmation bias:** When we are drawn to information that reinforces or confirms our existing beliefs.
4. **Anchor bias:** When we rely too much on the first piece of information we receive, allowing it to frame how we view any additional information we uncover without question.
5. **Bandwagon bias:** When we embrace information because it is trending or popular, such as doing a story just because every other outlet is doing it, rather than because we think it is newsworthy for our audience.
   "Group think" or "pack journalism" are forms of bandwagon bias. This also applies to stories that are easy or expected,[15] such as the annual holiday toy drive or obligatory "most popular Christmas toy" story.

In addition, there are biases explicitly associated with how journalism and communications content is presented, including a list of media bias types from AllSides, an organization focused on revealing bias in media:[23]

1. **Spin:** The use of vague language and general claims involving vivid adjectives that signal how a reader, listener, or viewer *should* feel, such as "major, serious, or meaningful." Spin might imply or stir emotions, rather than informing and contextualizing.

2. **Unsubstantiated claims:** The statement of something as fact without providing proof or evidence that it is indeed verified.
3. **Statements of opinion presented as fact:** Statements that the writer or speaker believes to be true and presents as true, but that in reality represent a perspective.

    Generally, you want to assess whether or not the statement can be *proven* as true. For example, while you may agree (or disagree) with whether something is good or bad, you would need to provide actual proof of *why* – or else it is opinion.
4. **Sensationalism/Emotionalism:** Presenting information in a tone that foments drama and emotion, such as shock or outrage. An example is the over-use of the term "breaking news" when a story is not really breaking anymore, rather it's developing.
5. **Mudslinging/Ad hominem:** Involves attacking the character or motivations of a person or group, rather than dealing with the issue at hand. This is often seen in talk-show content. For example, calling someone a "snowflake" dismisses a potentially valid argument on an important issue and reduces it to a personal attack.
6. **Mind reading:** Assuming you know what someone else thinks. Please never do this. As a journalist, your job is to ask the questions and find out. DO NOT ASSUME.
7. **Slant:** Telling only one part of a story, cherry-picking only information that supports your narrative, and ignoring other valid perspectives.

    Public relations content may involve slant and cherry-picking. It is your job to uncover and tell the fuller story, and not just repeat what's in a press release or what one source tells you. To avoid slant, put each perspective through a journalistic process involving fact-finding and verification. Be able to defend your work if challenged.
8. **Flawed logic:** Involves jumping to conclusions or making false associations to assert something that's not borne out by fact-checking.
9. **Bias by omission:** Leaving out specific viewpoints or failing to cover stories. For example, covering that student debt increased may be important, but it should include the fact that the government changed how it calculated student debt, which affects the numbers reported but not the amount of actual debt. A story that omits this is misleading.
10. **Omission of source attribution:** Whenever possible, name specific sources to be transparent with your audience. Avoid identifying sources as a monolithic group of people, such as "immigrants" or "police officers" or "students" or "critics."

    Of course, there may be times when you need to keep a source's identification confidential – such as to protect safety or livelihood – but that decision should be made in consultation with your newsroom and explained to your audience.
11. **Placement bias:** Where a story is placed and how much time or space it's given on a website, in a newspaper, or within a broadcast can indicate

bias. A story near the beginning of a broadcast or near the top of a page will get more attention than a story at minute 17 or on a page that takes three clicks to find. Having clear guidelines for how and why stories are placed and ordered can provide a foundation for consistency and mitigating bias.

12. **Market-oriented bias:** When we cover a story just because we think our audience might want it. While it's great to consider your audience, the story must have journalistic purpose.

Our **implicit biases**, how we frame our world, can translate to vastly different perceptions. Unconscious and unexamined biases can lead us to seek out certain viewpoints while minimizing others, often without realizing we're doing so.

Woods said all journalists must recognize and acknowledge their biases, and then go through a journalistic process to counter them.

> Here's a bias of mine. I think the death penalty is wrong – period. In spite of the fact that there are people I would advocate for being put to death, I believe it's wrong and therefore can't in the end support it. That's a bias that comes into play any time I'm about to have a conversation about the subject or about a story about the subject.
>
> So, if I'm reporting against my biases, I am making sure that I am talking to reasonable people who see things differently than I do. Whatever the subject of that story, whether it is an impending case or legislative decision to do away with it or reinstate it, I am talking to people who have the counter point of view.
>
> Where American journalism has been getting it wrong so often is when they simply think that the opposite point of view is all you need. You will remember that I said *thoughtful and reasonable* – that I'm talking to people who have a basis for the point of view they have that extends beyond their opinion …. If in the end my judgment, based on all that I've taken in, points me toward one framing for that story, then I'm confident in my ability to defend the choices I made.[12]

In recognizing his own bias against the death penalty, Woods becomes aware of the choices he might make covering such a story. He makes sure to talk to people with different points of view who "have a basis for the point of view that they have that extends beyond their opinion." He also conducts research that may run counter to his biases and pertains to the story at hand, so he can better understand it. Then, in his reporting, he reports on the story, his sources, and the context. His bias is mitigated.

If Woods – or any of us – fail to acknowledge and examine our biases, then those biases may come out in the stories we cover. For example, if Woods were to cover a story about the death penalty un-critically, he may inadvertently reach out only to sources who agree with his bias against the death penalty, or he may minimize or exclude relevant information from sources who disagree. In his writing, Woods may use words and phrases that convey his bias, rather than provide journalistic context, and he will have failed his audience by failing to fully inform them or help them understand the story. Or, Woods may cover the story once but fail to do any follow-ups, which could result in audiences receiving limited information, rather than full context.

WHO is biased?

Everyone is biased. As mentioned above, it is the natural human condition because we all have our own experiences and backgrounds, which frame how we interact with the world. Our brains evolved this way to help us categorize and make sense of the world. But unexamined biases can lead to harm, and a journalist's responsibility is to minimize harm.

Often, the knee-jerk reaction to being called biased is to quickly and vehemently deny it. Studies show that, while people recognize bias exists out in the world, they often rate themselves as far less biased, or not biased at all.[24,25] But, let's be clear, again, before we move on – we are all biased. It comes with being human. No one is immune. So, our goal is not to rid ourselves of bias, rather to learn what our biases are (to the extent that we can – this is a lifelong journey), make them explicit, and then work to minimize them in our reporting.

To illustrate implicit bias, consider a non-journalistic example involving two co-workers at a firm that revised resumes for clients. Nicole Lee Hallberg and Martin R. Schneider did the same work, but it seemed to take Hallberg longer to get the same amount of work done. Their boss complained to Schneider that Hallberg was not working with clients as quickly as he thought she should.

Before we go on, what is your initial assumption as to why this was? Schneider had more experience? Hallberg was just slow? Women can't keep up? Their boss thought Hallberg's gender played a role.

Ok, keep reading.

One day, Schneider started having trouble with a client who had thus far been no issue at all. He wrote in a Twitter thread in 2017:

> I'm emailing a client back-and-forth about his resume and he is just being IMPOSSIBLE. Rude, dismissive, ignoring my questions.
>
> Telling me his methods were the industry standards (they weren't) and I couldn't understand the terms he used (I could).
>
> Anyway, I was getting sick of his shit when I noticed something. Thanks to our shared inbox, I'd been signing all communications as "Nicole."
>
> It was Nicole he was being rude to, not me. So, out of curiosity, I said "Hey this is Martin, I'm taking over this project for Nicole."

IMMEDIATE IMPROVEMENT. Positive reception, thanking me for suggestions, responds promptly, saying "great questions!" Became a model client.

Note: My technique and advice never changed. The only difference was that I had a man's name now.[26,27]

This gave Hallberg an idea to swap email signatures for a week.

For Hallberg, it was the most productive week she'd had. "I had one of the easiest weeks of my professional life. [Martin] ... didn't."[28]

"Folks. It fucking sucked," Schneider wrote. "I was in hell. Everything I asked or suggested was questioned. Clients I could do in my sleep were condescending. One asked if I was single."[27]

Schneider realized that Hallberg had to spend time he did not convincing clients to respect her advice and approach. "I wasn't any better at the job than she was, I just had this invisible advantage."[27]

But, when they told their boss, he did not believe them. His implicit biases were so ingrained that their explanation simply did not make sense to him. This tracks with the research mentioned above showing that, while we can see and recognize bias out in the world, we tend to think we are not as susceptible to it.[24] In addition, anchoring theory posits that once we are introduced to one frame, it is difficult for us to accept other frames because we are biased toward the first one.[21] This means biases can be hard to overcome, even in the face of clear evidence, which has significant implications for our ability to remain open-minded, trust information, and avoid conflict.

WHERE did the false dichotomy between bias & objectivity come from?

It is impossible to discuss bias, at least in US journalism, without addressing **objectivity**. The idea of journalistic objectivity took hold in the early 20th century, around the same time as the scientific method. Walter Dean wrote for the American Press Institute that it grew

> out of a growing recognition that journalists (as humans) were full of bias, often unconsciously. Objectivity called for journalists to develop a consistent method of testing information – a transparent approach to evidence – precisely so that personal and cultural biases would not undermine the accuracy of their work.[22]

This was also a time when public relations (PR) began to take hold as people began to recognize that truth could be manipulated. An objective method could help journalists critically assess PR claims and assertions. Also, during this period, neurologist and psychoanalyst Sigmund Freud revealed that our unconscious may not be as reliable as we assumed. Thus, an objective process was seen as critical to countering our unreliable mind and to practicing fair, impactful journalism.

But, as time marched forward, the idea of objectivity came to be assigned not to the method but to journalists themselves, who were expected to exhibit personal objectivity. This has actually led to uncritical reporting, such as the well-known and maligned approach of getting "both sides" of a story and falsely claiming balance without critically assessing the claims of each side.

What we call "objectivity" is actually the set of biases of the dominant or mainstream culture, or as Woods called it, "the bias of the majority or the bias of the powerful." This set of biases has been given the status of neutral. However, in reality, it's simply another perspective, and not neutral at all.

> Those are the people and institutions that create a narrative, which is why the idea of objectivity has come under such scrutiny and assault more recently. At some point people realized that in order to have an objective view of something, you have to have a beginning point, a standard. And then you begin asking simple questions like who set the standard, and things start to reveal themselves.[12]

Unexamined biases are likely to exert influence on your newsgathering and story crafting, playing a subconscious role in your choices of which stories to pursue, which sources to interview, phraseology, and other decisions. "Journalists who select sources to express what is really their own point of view, and then use the neutral voice to make it seem objective, are engaged in a form of deception," said Dean. "This damages the credibility of the craft by making it seem unprincipled, dishonest, and biased."[22]

At the newsroom management level, let's examine the story of same-sex weddings in San Francisco. On February 11, 2004, then-Mayor Gavin Newsom held the first same-sex wedding in the US at City Hall. Reporters from all over rushed to San Francisco to cover the story, interview couples being married, and talk with the mayor. However, not every reporter was given an equitable chance to cover the story.

Two *San Francisco Chronicle* journalists, city hall reporter Rachel Gordon and photographer Liz Mangelsdorf, "were forbidden to cover the handing out of marriage licenses at City Hall in San Francisco because they married each other,"[12,29] explained Woods.

> The assumption was that because of their orientation and interest in the subject, they couldn't be fair and unbiased. And it assumes that a straight journalist going to cover the same event has no opinion whatsoever on same-sex marriage, which is ridiculous on its face.[12]

In this example, the assumption is that not applying for a marriage license, or applying for a marriage license as a straight person, meant that you were somehow more objective, more neutral, more journalistic than if you had applied for a marriage license as a gay person. What remains unspoken here is that some people who covered the story may not have supported gay marriage. It would not make them any less able to cover the story, as long as they were working against their biases; it would not make them more qualified, either. But, because their biases matched what was considered the mainstream sentiment at the time, they were positioned as neutral or objective.

In today's digital media environment, biases often remain unexamined, and many newsrooms still name objectivity as a goal without explaining whether they are referring to the method or the journalist. For example, *The New York Times* social media guidelines state: "Our journalists should be especially mindful of appearing to take sides on issues that *The Times* is seeking to cover objectively."[30] This may mean that many journalists and other information providers are proceeding with biases unexamined, leading to a media landscape where non-journalistic voices also with unexamined biases compete for attention and peddle opinion, tabloid sensationalism, misinformation, disinformation, and a lack of diverse voices. This has damaged the credibility of all content, including well-practiced journalism.

This has also damaged journalism's relationships with its audiences and turned the word bias into a weapon. "Bias" is now levied as an accusation and a challenge to credibility – i.e. the news media is biased against X point of view. Generally, people use "bias" in this way when they see information that does not conform to their beliefs or worldview – i.e. does not conform to their own implicit, unconscious, and unexamined biases. In the process, the acknowledgment of bias as a part of humanity is lost.

This interpretation of bias has now permeated national and global discourses, leading to suspicion of journalists, distrust of information, and even violence perpetrated against those working to inform the public. We saw this phenomenon after the 2020 election, when Trump and many other conservative officials repeated false accusations that the election was rigged, leading many of his supporters to not only call the mainstream media biased but to threaten news practitioners and even physically assault journalists at protests and riots.

EXERCISE BREAK

1. Go to the RSF Press Freedom Index (https://rsf.org/en/ranking).
2. Choose one nation below 25 on the list (i.e. 26–180).
3. Research how the news media operates in your chosen nation.
   a. What challenges do they face?
   b. How does the government treat the press?
   c. How do the citizens treat the press?
   d. How do citizens and government support journalists' work?
4. Record 60–90 seconds of video or audio on your smartphone sharing what you found and your reaction (or write 200–400 words).

CBS News and 60 Minutes correspondent Wesley Lowery has suggested that we instead accept that we are all biased and follow the advice of journalist Alex S.

Jones, who said we should avoid "trying to create the illusion of fairness by letting advocates pretend in your journalism that there is a debate about the facts when the weight of truth is clear."[1] Jones also called "he-said/she-said reporting, which just pits one voice against another," as "the discredited face of objectivity."[1]

Lowery recommends being explicit with your audience.

Instead of promising our readers that we will never, on any platform, betray a single personal bias – submitting ourselves to a life sentence of public thoughtlessness – a better pledge would be an assurance that we will devote ourselves to accuracy, that we will diligently seek out the perspectives of those with whom we personally may be inclined to disagree and that we will be just as sure to ask hard questions of those with whom we're inclined to agree.[1]

This approach can help build trust with your audience. It can also provide a guide for how audiences can engage to help improve story coverage by pointing out any biases they see and suggesting additional angles or sources.

WHY does it matter that we recognize & examine our biases?

Unchecked implicit bias can impact how we practice journalism, including what we choose to cover and not to cover, which sources we include

Keith Woods, chief diversity officer at NPR

For Keith Woods, chief diversity officer at National Public Radio (NPR), the purpose of journalism is to support and protect democracy.

"I think journalism today, even in its current tattered state, remains one of the truest supporters of democracy that there is, and I think that's really important," Woods said. "It is also one of the last remaining reliable sources of justice in the country, and that's what keeps me engaged. I am in perpetual pursuit of exploiting journalism's ability to deliver justice for people."[29]

In his role, Woods leads NPR's efforts to increase diversity and inclusion, and supports the work of NPR's 260+ member stations, or as he said when he was promoted to his current role, to bring "more of the public to public radio."[31] One way Woods does this is by helping journalists and newsrooms understand and report against our own individual biases, because biases can lead to harm.

"When we're thinking about issues of bias, we need to step back and think about all the ways that its existence in our work is harming the truth or harming the audience or the public in some kind of way," Woods

82 Facing our biases

and exclude, where we place stories, how much time we give to stories, which visuals we choose, and how we frame our coverage.

Implicit bias can affect the journalism industry by opening the door for:

- Stereotypes
- Assumptions
- Interviewing the same sources over and over again, and failing to include diverse voices
- Overlooking people who should be hired

Unexamined, unconscious, implicit bias can lead to omission and stereotyping, misleading audiences, and at worst real harm. When we stereotype, we fail to see humanity, which can lead us to make assumptions, for example whether someone is guilty or innocent. In *Chapter 3*, we discussed the Central Park Five – now the Exonerated Five. The media embraced and accepted the idea that five kids were guilty of rape before a trial was conducted, based in large part on biases about race and socio-economic status that led to stereotyping of the accused teens and thus failure to see their humanity. Acknowledging, examining, and working to counter our biases can potentially mitigate harm and lead us to tell richer, more nuanced, more truthful stories.

Award-winning journalist and war correspondent Lara Logan said it's important to approach your work with "an open mind, an open heart and a million questions. There is nothing more human than opinions and bias. To say we have none is dishonest. But what we do have as said. "That's where our passion and our greatest focus need to be."[12]

The challenge is that journalism in the US has come to value objectivity, which usually does not mean objectivity at all, rather the acceptance of the biases of the mainstream or dominant group as neutral.

"I think that where we have failed in our conversation, especially when we're talking to students about bias, is beginning with the notion that it is possible to be free of it or to have journalism that's free of it," Woods said. In actuality, "everything is about mitigation and minimizing, because the act of being human guarantees the existence of bias."[12]

One way to mitigate bias is to lead with the facts as we know them and also provide context.

"When we are trying to convey something that is powerful to people, the facts are often more powerful than the adjectives and the verbs." We need to "allow the facts to be the lead in the work," said Woods. But just reporting the facts is not enough. You must also report the context. Failure to do this "is where we have seen some of the biggest misinformation over the last couple of years."[29]

Woods got into journalism in college, but he said he did not *choose* the profession until years later.

I fell into it completely by accident. I was a writer. I joined my college newspaper staff at Dillard University, (and) the only beat available when I joined was sports. So, I became a sportswriter, having never actually attended most of the games that professional journalists is a simple standard to get us past that."[32]

Logan told the *New York Post* that media bias can lead to shoddy reporting and fuel assumptions, pointing out the example of a *Time* reporter erroneously tweeting in January 2017 that a bust of Martin Luther King Jr. had been removed from the Oval Office after Trump began his term. "The news went viral. But the writer did not follow the most basic rule of journalism – pick up the phone and ask the White House if it was really gone,"[32] said Logan. Though the reporter did within an hour of the initial tweet make that call and correct himself – tweeting "The MLK bust is still in the Oval Office. It was obscured by an agent and door,"[33] – the knee-jerk initial tweet revealed a bias. When he did not see the MLK bust right away, he made an assumption based on the belief that the 45th President would remove it as an act of racism.

Biases often manifest when we do not take the time to deal with them. This can happen when we're under pressure to get things done quickly or in a certain way; when we are tired, hungry, or stressed out; or when we find ourselves in an unfamiliar situation or feel threatened or insecure.[21] In these cases, so much energy is given to processing the situation that we fall back on preconceived ideas, judgments, or narratives. This is when we need to stop, take a breath, and intentionally look for bias in our newsgathering and writing.

For a journalist on deadline or expected to communicate regularly on social media, it's easy for biases to

I was about to start reporting on. That led to a weekend stringing job with the local newspaper, *The Times Picayune* reporting on high school athletics, which led to a part-time job, which led to a full-time job. So, I was pulled inexorably into the profession one little job classification after another.[29]

After eight or nine years, "it really did come to a moment when I had to actively choose it, instead of being chosen by it," said Woods. That moment was when he realized there was an opportunity to make changes, to improve the profession, and in turn improve the lives of people. "There's never been a day, from the moment that I made the choice, when it was only about reporting and writing and telling stories. It was always about changing something bigger than journalism."[29]

And Woods said he's still energized by the work.

This is hard work for anybody who has a stake in it, and there are emotional costs to staying this close to the fire. But I also have a particular joy that comes from some of this work. So, it isn't all energy going out. There's energy coming in, as well.[29]

In addition to his work in public media, Woods gives workshops on handling diversity matters to journalism schools and news outlets.

Woods also co-edited the book, *The Authentic Voice: The Best Reporting on Race and Ethnicity*.

creep in. While we want to cover a story well, we're also looking for shortcuts to help us meet that deadline and feed the social media churn. The temptation exists to fall back on our limited understanding of a situation, person, community, or event – on our stereotypes and prejudices, the foundations of our implicit, unconscious biases.

Though we all make mistakes, when we find ourselves rushing to judgment instead of fact checking and verifying, we need to take a moment to examine our process and change course before barreling forward and having to correct ourselves later.

Bias can be such a driver of misinformation and harm because it is so inherent to our being. When someone looks, acts, or thinks differently, especially in our current socio-political climate, we may see them as *other*, and vilify them. "Biases are often based on stereotypes, rather than actual knowledge of an individual or circumstance. Whether positive or negative, such cognitive shortcuts can result in prejudgments that lead to rash decisions or discriminatory practices."[13] Bias and stereotyping often affect historically marginalized or underserved groups, based on race, ethnicity, gender, sexuality, socio-economic status, or ability. "This type of bias can have harmful real-world outcomes."[13]

A non-journalistic example of implicit bias is when Amy Cooper, a white woman walking her dog in New York's Central Park in May 2020, responded to the reasonable request of a Black man bird-watching in the park to leash her dog by threatening to call the police – leveraging her gender and his race. In smartphone video taken by birdwatcher Chris Cooper, she said, "I'm going to tell them there's an African American man threatening my life."[34] Amy Cooper has been described as a progressive who voted for President Obama. In her response apologizing for her actions, she insisted that she was not racist, but her declaration does not match her actions in the park. So, what's going on here? One answer is that Amy Cooper has internalized the systemic ways Americans define each other, and her knee-jerk response was to act on these constructs when someone asked her to do something she felt she should not have to do.

In another example of implicit bias leading to stereotyping, in June 2020, a white couple approached a Filipino man who was stenciling "Black Lives Matter" in chalk on a retaining wall in a posh San Francisco neighborhood. The couple, Lisa Alexander and Robert Larkin, were white. They assumed James Juanillo did not live at the house where he was stenciling and accused him of committing a crime. Juanillo recorded the entire exchange, which quickly went viral. On video, he asked whether he would be committing a crime if he lived at the residence. The couple conceded that no he would not, but Alexander insisted that she knew the homeowner and therefore knew that Juanillo did not live there. It turns out that Juanillo did live there. The couple called the police, and when the police arrived, they recognized Juanillo, exchanged a few words, and left.

"What she did was everyday. It's polite racism. It's respectable racism," Juanillo told KGO-TV. "Respectfully, sir, I don't think you belong here at all."[35]

Alexander's and Larkin's implicit biases were so strong that they falsely assumed someone who looked differently than they did was not a resident or neighbor – must be an outsider. Alexander went so far as to falsely assert that she knew the owner, because she assumed she must be right that this Filipino man did not belong in her community.

As Juanillo told KQED, "They're wrong. And they rode that racial bias all the way off a cliff."[36]

Though these examples may seem particularly egregious, it is important to recognize that we are all capable of allowing our implicit biases to lead the way. As these examples illustrate, the results can be ugly, harmful, and potentially deadly.

Alexander "decided to call men with guns because of my chalk art," Juanillo told KPIX.[37] If the officers had not recognized him, then the situation could have ended differently, as it has in so many other instances, including Philando Castile, 12-year-old Tamir Rice, 13-year-old Andy Lopez, and many others.

News outlets across the country are doing more to recognize, acknowledge, and grapple with their biases. For example, in recent years, many local news outlets have abandoned the practice of publishing mugshot galleries.[38] Even if outlets still use mugshots in stories, many have developed guidelines to avoid perpetuating and fueling stereotypes. For example, WCPO in Cincinnati only uses mugshots in stories where a suspect is still at large, not to identify a victim of a crime.

"We've come to realize that without context, the galleries have little journalistic value and may have reinforced negative stereotypes,"[38] wrote Tribune Publishing to readers.

St. Louis Post-Dispatch editor, Gilbert Bailon told Poynter, "This is a first step in reimagining our coverage of crime and justice (and making) our crime and justice coverage more meaningful for our digital readers."[38]

The Boston Globe and other papers have addressed this issue by allowing people to request that past crime coverage online be removed or anonymized. "Our sense, given the criminal justice system, is that this has had a disproportionate impact on people of color," said *Boston Globe* editor Brian McGrory. "The idea behind the program is to start addressing it."[39]

The Kansas City Star took the extraordinary step of acknowledging its historical biases in December 2020, when it apologized for how it historically covered – or failed to cover – its large Black community. In the published apology, *Star* President Mike Fannin detailed how biased coverage since the paper's founding in 1880 perpetuated divisions in the region.

"For much of its early history – through sins of both commission and omission – it disenfranchised, ignored and scorned generations of Black Kansas Citians. It reinforced Jim Crow laws and redlining," Fannin wrote. "Decade after early decade it robbed an entire community of opportunity, dignity, justice and recognition."[40]

Fannin went on to detail how a team of *Star* reporters investigated the *Star*'s own coverage, including talking with community members and comparing what they found with coverage from Black local papers.

Reporters were frequently sickened by what they found – decades of coverage that depicted Black Kansas Citians as criminals living in a crime-laden world. They felt shame at what was missing: the achievements, aspirations and milestones of an entire population routinely overlooked, as if Black people were invisible. Reporters felt regret that the paper's historic coverage not only did a disservice to Black Kansas Citians, but also to white readers deprived of the opportunity to understand the true richness Black citizens brought to Kansas City.[40]

By uncovering, facing, and grappling with historic biases, the *Star* recognized that biases persist unless and until they are named and challenged, and that biases can cause real harm to entire communities.

HOW can we minimize bias in our newsgathering & reporting?

We minimize implicit, unconscious bias through awareness, intentionality, listening, seeking out alternative viewpoints, and making explicit, deliberate changes to our journalistic practice.

Awareness encompasses how we present stories. "Your tone and your biases are carried in a lot of ways into the content," said Woods.

> If you're in broadcast, everything from an inflection to an expression can carry some of it. And in the written word, the adjectives and the verbs, it's a piece of everything that you do. It isn't a single utterance that will reveal a bias.[12]

One of the best ways to minimize bias is to get acquainted with your biases. This can involve engaging the empathy strategies you learned in *Chapter 3*, as well as having people with different perspectives and backgrounds read, watch, or listen to your work with the goal of rooting out any biases they encounter. You should also read news and information from outlets with various perspectives. It's easy to do this when we're talking about political bias – i.e. Fox News and MSNBC or *The Telegraph* and *The Independent*. But when seeking to uncover different perspectives or other biases, consider looking at multiple publications focused on your beat; explore other local news outlets in your market, as well as news outlets in different communities, regions, states, and nations, and reputable digital sources with differing perspectives.

For example, early in my journalism career, I worked at a TV station in Palm Springs, CA. The region had several tribal casinos, and coverage of the casino industry was largely positive. But when I moved to a TV station in

Sacramento, the approach to covering tribal casinos was quite different. It was more critical, more in depth, and included voices from the wider community more often. I realized that I had settled into a bias in Palm Springs without even realizing it. Had I explored how tribal casinos were being covered in other regions, I may have been able to go more in depth on the stories we covered in Palm Springs, thus providing a greater benefit to the community by offering additional context, perspective, and information.

In addition to exploring other news outlets, examine your go-to sources and be sure they don't all come from official entities such as local government, the school district, or the sheriff's department. Find voices among community organizations, student and parent groups, and others to help round out your coverage. Also, have conversations with colleagues who have different perspectives than you, and listen to audience feedback on possible blind spots and stereotyping. (We'll discuss more in *Chapter 6*.)

You can also expand your own network. Assess your current network of friends, sources, and professional connections and note whether they have similar belief systems to yours. Do they look like you? Think like you? Have similar philosophies to you? Did they grow up with a similar socio-economic or religious or spiritual context? In high school and college, did they partake in similar types of activities? Conduct this assessment every once in a while, and if you see too much similarity, then do the work of expanding your network to bring other perspectives and experiences into your reporting.

Note which sources you gravitate toward. Ask yourself why? Are they all men or all women? Are they predominantly white? Do they all come from official agencies or organizations? Do they all ascribe to a similar perspective? For example, if you are a business or finance reporter, you may find that many of your sources share the perspective that online advertising revenue should be protected, and any efforts to limit it should be questioned. Whether or not you share this point of view, if most of your sources ascribe to it, then you may lose sight of the fact that other perspectives exist. If your sources were primarily students or young professionals, these sources might ascribe to the perspective that online ads are too pervasive and need to be regulated. You need to incorporate a spectrum of valid perspectives when working to understand an issue, as well as avoid framing something as a zero-sum scenario. In the online advertising example. Business professionals may assume that consumers critical of ads want to do away with ads entirely. While many may desire this, there is an understanding that ads pay the bills. So, what online ad critics may actually seek is moderation. Coverage that includes all relevant perspectives may contribute to consensus among disparate parties who come to understand each other better through your coverage. Given that official sources are more accessible, you may need to make an effort to include sources affected by the decisions of businesses, governments, and other institutions, in addition to sources from businesses and beneficiaries.

If you are an education reporter, you could explore organizations that focus on an audience of teachers versus administrators versus students. If you are a

88 Facing our biases

crime reporter, you could expand your circle from police and prosecutorial sources to organizations working to reduce crime or police violence through community engagement.

Expanding our universe of sources may require us to make changes to how we practice journalism. Perhaps it means making deeper connections with segments of the community that we had not yet gotten to know. Perhaps it means reaching out to organizations we had not yet spoken with. Perhaps it means reading new books. Often, it means getting out of our comfort zones and making ourselves uncomfortable. Whatever expanding your universe means for you, take the time and make the effort to do it.

It is important to acknowledge that external pressures can contribute to this issue, such as the demands of your news director or managing editor.

"News organizations, specifically managers, are often responsible for promoting unconscious bias, because they often want a specific angle to a story and can be unrelenting in not accepting anything that falls short of their demands," said former KCBS reporter Dave Padilla. "I've had numerous encounters with this issue. I've gone to stories where what I saw didn't fit" with the assignment. "Yet I was pressured to find the 'desired' angle promoted by news managers and anchors on the air who were following the news manager's dictates."[41]

In this case, it may be difficult for you to counter the biases of your supervisor. Though there is no easy solution, finding allies in the newsroom with whom you can discuss issues and hopefully a boss whom you can speak frankly with are some ways to try to address these newsroom pressures. Joining communities of care on social media or via organizations may also help (more in *Chapter 9*).

Using your imagination is another way to counter bias. For example, when covering a story or subject, put yourself in the shoes of the people impacted by the story to see their perspective.[42,43] Imagine living their life. Visualize their day from waking up through going to bed. What is the first thing they do? Who is the first person they talk with? How does the issue at hand influence their moment-to-moment life? What are their hopes and dreams? If you have any trouble visualizing any aspect of a subject's experience, then go and ask questions, so you can learn and fill the gaps.

You can also imagine that the person you are covering is the opposite of a stereotype you may hold. They may indeed *be* the opposite of the stereotype you hold – but you may not be able to see that until you use your imagination. If you are a man, imagine that a woman affected by job loss is a man affected by job loss during COVID-19.[44] If you are white, imagine that the Latino boy shot by police while playing with his toy gun was a white boy shot by police while playing with his toy gun – or a white girl.[45] Doing this may help change the way you think about a story – i.e. reveal and allow you to counter your biases.

We also need to identify and recognize when we might be most susceptible to implicit, unconscious bias. Is it a particular type of story? A specific type of situation? A particular state of mind? Perhaps we're under time pressure and unable to stop and think critically about our choices or assess the full breadth of the story at hand. In these situations, it could be helpful to develop and practice mindfulness. One way to do this is to take long, slow, deep breaths. This can help reduce your heart rate, mitigate stress levels, and reduce the chance that you'll make a quick decision. You can also keep a decision journal to help you reflect on the choices you made when covering a story and improve your process next time. The more aware we are of both our biases and our points of susceptibility, the greater our success will be in minimizing bias and more fairly, fully, and equitably covering the stories of our communities.

WHEN might bias be appropriate?

Is there ever a time when a journalist might *want* bias to seep into a story or into their newsgathering process?

Our biases can inform our values and may lead us to story ideas that we think are important and are not getting coverage. This is how many investigative, explanatory, and feature pieces begin – with a journalist tapping into their biases for or against a certain issue or person or phenomenon and then looking into it.

The same bias that may cause one journalist to dismiss a source who calls or emails a newsroom in a frenetic or pushy tone may cause another journalist – with a different set of biases – to instead hear urgency and pain. That journalist might take that call or respond to that email, which in turn could lead the journalist to look into the seemingly far-fetched claims made by the caller and uncover a big story that bias may have caused another journalist to overlook.

For example, in 2009, two reporters at the *Cleveland Plain Dealer*, Rachel Dissell and Leila Atassi, were covering a story in which the bodies of 11 women had been found around the home of the person who would become known as the Cleveland Strangler. This was a major story, and many news outlets covered it. They covered the find, who the Cleveland Strangler was, who the women were, and what happened during the trial. But most reporters did not cover the deeper story of how serial killers – or serial criminals in general – operate, or how law enforcement tracks and investigates crimes against women.

Dissell and Atassi *did* wonder about the larger context of serial criminals and police approaches to crimes against women, and so they asked Cleveland police officials how they handled sexual assault cases.[46]

Why did Dissell and Atassi ask this question, when no one else did? Is it because they are that much better at their jobs than other reporters covering the story? They are indeed strong reporters, but so were many other people covering this story. So, why then? One possible explanation is that they leaned into their biases. They are women, and most, if not all, women have thought about how to protect themselves when walking or jogging alone. Most, if not all, women have faced the possibility of having to deal with a sexual assault and have taken steps to minimize that possibility. This is something men generally do not have to think about as they move through the world. Therefore, one's life experiences as female will inform how they (we)

90 *Facing our biases*

view information, events, and people. Most men are biased in the opposite direction. Their life experiences as male lead to different biases in how they might view information, events, and people. The same goes for transgender individuals – their life experiences lead them to have biases that may help them see important news stories that people without those life experiences and perspectives will not see.

In this case, Dissell and Atassi discovered that the Cleveland Police Department had a backlog of 4,000 rape kits, and the state of Ohio nearly 14,000 – yes, 14-*thousand*.[47]

Dissell and Atassi's reporting led Ohio Governor Mike DeWine to demand that untested rape kits be sent to state labs for processing. Many were nearly 20 years old, the statute of limitations for sexual assault cases, which meant law enforcement investigators were now scrambling to track down victims and witnesses in an effort to prosecute these cases. Law enforcement discovered that 1/3 were committed by serial offenders, which meant that acting on the rape kits sooner would have led to earlier arrests and thus fewer women harmed.

"I've been in this business for 43 years and I thought I knew something about it," said Cuyahoga County prosecutor Timothy McGinty, who created and oversees the rape kit task force, to the *Columbia Journalism Review*, acknowledging his own bias. "I was astonished."[48]

Dissell and Atassi stayed on the story, reporting on the process, the people involved, and the outcomes of the effort. Had they not leaned into their perspectives and experiences as women, these cases would have gone unprosecuted, the women harmed would have not had an opportunity to receive justice, and potential serial rapists may have continued to go undiscovered, leading to the harm of even more women in the community.

Keep in mind, it was bias that led to this situation in the first place. The bias of predominantly male law enforcement officials to characterize sexual assaults as less serious crimes led to a deprioritizing of rape kit testing. The traumas of 4,000 women were put on a shelf. A consequence of this inaction was that serial rapists went undetected and harmed more women.

So, in this case, bias helped uncover a major story. This was not the type of bias that can lead to exclusion or dismissal of another person's point of view or perspective. Rather, this type of bias can push back on mainstream biases that may have claimed a place of neutrality.

Key takeaways

- Bias is part of the human psyche. We all have unconscious and implicit biases. The goal for journalists is to learn their biases and then balance them in their reporting.
- Objectivity applies to the process of newsgathering, NOT to journalists themselves.
- Unexamined bias can lead to stereotyping, *othering*, marginalizing, and harm.

- Mitigate your biases by seeking different perspectives, examining your source list and seeking out perspectives you are missing, consuming content from outlets in other communities, and recognizing when you are most susceptible to implicit bias.

Discussion questions

1. Think of the five people you trust the most. Discuss how they are similar to you. How are they different from you? How do they help you challenge your biases, if at all?
2. Take the Implicit Association Test (https://implicit.harvard.edu/implicit/iatdetails.html). Discuss your results. What surprised you? What was expected? What will you take from the experience to help address your own implicit biases?
3. In your view, how should journalists approach dealing with bias? How do you think biases influence coverage at your student newspaper? A local news outlet? A national news outlet? How do they influence and inform your own coverage? (The answer is NOT that they do not influence you.)

Exercises

1. Building your rolodex:
   a. Choose a beat.
   b. Then, create a list of at least ten sources related to that beat in your local community, using the following steps:
      i. Brainstorm and write down any names or titles you think should be on your list.
      ii. Do some research to identify sources whose names or titles you may not have known as you brainstormed.
      iii. Assess your initial list through the context of bias.
         1. Are your listed sources all from official outlets?
         2. Which perspectives/voices are missing?
         3. What about race, ethnicity, gender, ability, socio-economic status? Are these perspectives represented?
      iv. Address the gaps you identified in your list by researching and adding additional sources who can provide differing perspectives.
2. Find a widely covered news story from a reputable news outlet over the past two weeks.
   a. Answer the following questions:
      i. How does the lead frame the story?
         1. What do you expect to read, see, or hear next?
         2. Upon finishing the story, were your expectations met? Or did the story go in a different direction?
      ii. What biases can you identify that are at play in the article?

iii. How does the journalist address these biases?
iv. How does the journalist *not* address these biases?
b. Using the AdFontes Media Bias Chart (https://www.adfontesmedia.com/), find a news outlet whose bias is in a different quadrant from the one you chose. Then, seek out the same story, and answer the above questions for this article, video, or podcast.
c. How were the two stories different? Were they both factual? What was the framing of each story? Was either problematic? How?

3. As you embark on newsgathering for a story you are covering, do the following:
   a. Before you begin newsgathering;
      i. Write the lead you assume will work for the story.
      ii. Write what biases you expect your sources to have.
      iii. Identify and record your own blind spots (write at least one).
      iv. Write what you expect to learn.
   b. After you write your first draft:
      i. Revisit your initial responses. Answer the following questions:
         1. How did the lead change?
            a. NOTE: If it did not change much, why?
         2. Did the source biases you identified manifest?
         3. How did you overcome your blind spot(s)?
         4. What did you learn?

4. Visit AllSidesConnect (https://www.allsidesconnect.com/), a site that facilitates conversations with people across socially salient differences, such as political leaning or disparate viewpoints on major issues (will need instructor coordination).
   a. Choose a conversation guide.
   b. Set up conversations through the platform (could be with students at your own school or at a school in another part of the country or world).
   c. Before the conversation, write down:
      i. How you expect the conversation to go.
      ii. How you're feeling about having the conversation.
      iii. What your assumptions are about the person you are paired to speak with.
   d. After the conversation:
      i. Discuss how the conversation went for you.
      ii. How did the conversation compare with your expectations?
      iii. How did your paired partner compare with your assumptions?
      iv. What did you learn about your biases?
      v. How do you feel after having the conversation?
      vi. Has your thinking about the bias you discussed changed after the conversation? How?

5. Keep a decision journal (https://www.americanpressinstitute.org/need-to-know/try-this-at-home/using-decision-journal-can-help-make-better-decisions-reduce-odds-hindsight-bias/).

a. For one story you are pursuing for class, keep a decision journal throughout the process. (If you are not currently pursuing a story – choose one to pursue for the purposes of this exercise.)
b. For each step you take in the newsgathering process, record the following:
   i. What you decided.
   ii. Why did you decide as you did?
   iii. What do you expect to happen?
   iv. How do you feel mentally and physically after making the decision?
c. Revisit the decision journal once your story is complete, and again at the outset of covering your next story. Repeat as desired (or as your professor instructs).

Notes

1 Lowery, Wesley. "A Reckoning Over Objectivity, Led by Black Journalists." *The New York Times*, June 23, 2020. https://www.nytimes.com/2020/06/23/opinion/objectivity-black-journalists-coronavirus.html.
2 Orth, Jodi. "I Have a Night off from the Hospital - Thread." Twitter, November 14, 2020. https://twitter.com/JodiOrth/status/1327771329555292162.
3 Jones, Tom. "A South Dakota ER Nurse Shared the Sobering Reality of the Coronavirus in a CNN Interview." *Poynter*, November 17, 2020. https://www.poynter.org/newsletters/2020/a-south-dakota-er-nurse-shared-the-sobering-reality-of-the-coronavirus-in-a-cnn-interview/.
4 Camerota, Alisyn. "Nurse: Some Patients Who Test Positive Refuse to Believe They Have Covid-19 - CNN Video." *CNN*, November 16, 2020. https://www.cnn.com/videos/us/2020/11/16/south-dakota-nurse-intv-newday-vpx.cnn.
5 Villegas, Paulina. "South Dakota Nurse Says Many Patients Deny the Coronavirus Exists - Right up Until Death." *The Washington Post*, November 16, 2020. https://www.washingtonpost.com/health/2020/11/16/south-dakota-nurse-coronavirus-deniers/.
6 Shannon, Joel. "'It's Not Real': In South Dakota, Which Has Shunned Masks and Other COVID Rules, Some People Die in Denial, Nurse Says." *USA Today*. Gannett Satellite Information Network, November 17, 2020. https://www.usatoday.com/story/news/health/2020/11/17/south-dakota-nurse-jodi-doering-covid-19-patients-denial/6330791002/.
7 Watts, Marina. "South Dakota Nurse's Tweets about COVID Positive Patients Who Don't Believe in the Virus Goes Viral." *Newsweek*, November 16, 2020. https://www.newsweek.com/south-dakota-nurses-tweets-about-covid-positive-patients-who-dont-believe-virus-go-viral-1547727.
8 Chapin, Angelina. "Their Patients Have COVID-19 and Still Think It's a Hoax." *The Cut*, November 25, 2020. https://www.thecut.com/2020/11/nurses-are-dealing-with-patients-who-think-covid-is-a-hoax.html.
9 Zweig, David. "Are Covid Patients Gasping 'It Isn't Real' As They Die?" *Wired*. Conde Nast, November 19, 2020. https://www.wired.com/story/are-covid-patients-gasping-it-isnt-real-as-they-die/.
10 Kahneman, Daniel. "Essay." In *Thinking, Fast and Slow*, 8. New York: Farrar, Straus & Giroux Inc., 2013.
11 Yin, Karen. "Beyond Terminology: Zooming Out to Focus on Bias." *Conscious Style Guide*, September 19, 2017. https://consciousstyleguide.com/beyond-terminology-zooming-focus-bias/.

12 Keith Woods, "Addressing Unconscious Bias in News" interview by Gina Baleria, *News in Context* (podcast), January 11, 2021. https://exchange.prx.org/pieces/353968-npr-chief-diversity-officer-keith-woods-on-address.
13 "Bias." *Psychology Today*. Sussex Publishers. Accessed February 15, 2021. https://www.psychologytoday.com/us/basics/bias.
14 Goldin, Claudia, and Cecilia Rouse. "Orchestrating Impartiality: The Impact of 'Blind' Auditions on Female Musicians." *The American Economic Review* 90, no. 4 (September 2000): 715–41. Doi: 10.3386/w5903.
15 Bertrand, Marianne, and Sendhil Mullainathan. "Are Emily and Greg More Employable than Lakisha and Jamal? A Field Experiment on Labor Market Discrimination." *The American Economic Review* 94, no. 4 (September 2004): 991–1013. doi: 10.3386/w9873.
16 Van der Pas, Daphne Joanna, and Loes Aaldering. "Gender Differences in Political Media Coverage: A Meta-Analysis." *Journal of Communication* 70, no. 1 (February 27, 2020): 114–43. doi: 10.1093/joc/jqz046.
17 Betus, Allison E., Erin M. Kearns, and Anthony F. Lemieux. "How Perpetrator Identity (Sometimes) Influences Media Framing Attacks as 'Terrorism' or 'Mental Illness.'" *Communication Research*, November 30, 2020, 1–44. doi: 10.1177/0093650220971142.
18 Morin, Aysel. "Framing Terror." *Journalism & Mass Communication Quarterly* 93, no. 4 (July 29, 2016): 986–1005. doi: 10.1177/1077699016660720.
19 Elmasry, Mohamad Hamas, and Mohammed el-Nawawy. "Can a Non-Muslim Mass Shooter Be a 'Terrorist'?: A Comparative Content Analysis of the Las Vegas and Orlando Shootings." *Journalism Practice* 14, no. 7 (July 23, 2019): 863–79. doi: 10.1080/17512786.2019.1643766.
20 Romine, Taylor. "Pittsburgh Newspaper Accused of Removing Black Journalist from Protest Coverage after She Posted a Tweet about Looting." *CNN*, June 7, 2020. https://www.cnn.com/2020/06/07/us/pittsburgh-newspaper-black-journalist-looting-tweet/index.html.
21 Goldsmith, Naomi. "Unconscious Bias and Its Impact on Journalism." Media Helping Media, August 22, 2019. https://mediahelpingmedia.org/2019/08/22/unconscious-bias-and-its-impact-on-journalism/.
22 Dean, Walter. "Understanding Bias." American Press Institute, July 18, 2017. https://www.americanpressinstitute.org/journalism-essentials/bias-objectivity/understanding-bias/.
23 Mastrine, Julie. "How to Spot 11 Types of Media Bias." Edited by Jeff Nilsson, Sara Alhariri, and Kristine Sowers. *AllSides*, September 13, 2019. https://www.allsides.com/media-bias/how-to-spot-types-of-media-bias.
24 Banaji, Mahzarin R., and Anthony G. Greenwald. *Blindspot: Hidden Biases of Good People*. New York: Bantam Books, 2016.
25 Ditto, Peter H., Brittany S. Liu, Cory J. Clark, Sean P. Wojcik, Eric E. Chen, Rebecca H. Grady, Jared B. Celniker, and Joanne F. Zinger. "At Least Bias Is Bipartisan: A Meta-Analytic Comparison of Partisan Bias in Liberals and Conservatives." *Perspectives on Psychological Science* 14, no. 2 (May 31, 2018): 273–91. doi: 10.1177/1745691617746796.
26 Schneider, Martin, and Nicole Hallberg. "Sexism in the Workplace Is Real: A Story from Two Perspectives." *Vox*, March 17, 2017. https://www.vox.com/first-person/2017/3/17/14950296/sexism-name-switch-tweets.
27 Schneider, Martin R. "Working as a Woman Can #Suck." Twitter, March 9, 2017. https://twitter.com/i/events/839950218099576832.
28 Hallberg, Nicole. "Working While Female." *Medium*, March 9, 2017. https://nickyknacks.medium.com/working-while-female-59a5de3ad266#.ayf8j5vk7.
29 Dignan, Joe. "Should Two Gay Journalists Who Marry Be Allowed to Cover the Same-Sex Marriage Story?" Grade the News, March 31, 2004. http://www.gradethenews.org/feat/makethecall/gaymarriage.htm.
30 The New York Times. "Social Media Guidelines for the Newsroom." *The New York Times*, October 13, 2017. https://www.nytimes.com/editorial-standards/social-media-guidelines.html.

31 Fishel, Ben. "Keith Woods Named NPR's Chief Diversity Officer." *NPR*, January 23, 2020. https://www.npr.org/about-npr/798902420/keith-woods-named-npr-s-chief-diversity-officer.
32 Logan, Lara. "Political Bias Is Destroying People's Faith in Journalism." *New York Post*, February 26, 2019. https://nypost.com/2019/02/26/political-bias-is-destroying-peoples-faith-in-journalism/.
33 Miller, Zeke. "Correction." Twitter, January 20, 2017. https://twitter.com/ZekeJMiller/status/822613421288026112.
34 Aguilera, Jasmine. "Amy Cooper Apologizes for Calling Police on Christian Cooper." *Time*, May 26, 2020. https://time.com/5842442/amy-cooper-dog-central-park/.
35 Alexander, Lisa. "Couple Calls Cops on Man Stenciling Black Lives Matter Message on His Own Property." *ABC News*, June 13, 2020. https://abcnews.go.com/US/video/couple-calls-police-man-chalking-black-lives-matter-71247211.
36 Rodriguez, Joe Fitzgerald. "She 'Rode that Bias Off a Cliff': Man Who Filmed SF Viral Video on Handling 'Karens'." *KQED*, June 15, 2020. https://www.kqed.org/news/11824410/she-rode-that-bias-off-a-cliff-man-who-filmed-sf-viral-video-on-handling-karens.
37 Choi, Kenny. "Black Lives Matter: Pacific Height Man Talks about Viral Video of San Francisco Skin Care CEO Confronting Him over BLM Sign." *CBS San Francisco*, May 26, 2020. https://sanfrancisco.cbslocal.com/video/4589546-black-lives-matter-pacific-height-man-talks-about-viral-video-of-san-francisco-skin-care-ceo-confronting-him-over-blm-sign/.
38 Hare, Kristen. "Update: Even More Newspapers Are Cutting Mugshots Galleries." *Poynter*, June 23, 2020. https://www.poynter.org/reporting-editing/2020/more-newspapers-are-cutting-mugshots-galleries/.
39 Greenberg, Zoe. "Boston Globe Launches 'Fresh Start' Initiative: People Can Apply to Have Past Coverage about Them Reviewed - The Boston Globe." *The Boston Globe*, January 22, 2021. https://www.bostonglobe.com/2021/01/22/metro/boston-globe-launches-fresh-start-initiative-people-can-apply-update-or-anonymize-coverage-them-thats-online/.
40 Fannin, Mike. "The Truth in Black and White: An Apology from the Kansas City Star." *The Kansas City Star*, December 20, 2020. https://www.kansascity.com/news/local/article247928045.html.
41 Dave Padilla (Retired Reporter & Anchor at KCBS), in conversation with Gina Baleria, February 2021.
42 Batson, C. Daniel, Shannon Early, and Giovanni Salvarani. "Perspective Taking: Imagining How Another Feels Versus Imaging How You Would Feel." *Personality and Social Psychology Bulletin* 23, no. 7 (July 1, 1997): 751–58. doi: 10.1177/0146167297237008.
43 Underwood, Bill, and Bert Moore. "Perspective-Taking and Altruism." *Psychological Bulletin* 91, no. 1 (1982): 143–73. doi: 10.1037/0033-2909.91.1.143.
44 Tappe, Anneken, Clare Duffy, and Tal Yellin. "These 5 Charts Show the Pandemic's Devastating Effect on Working Women." *CNN*, December 17, 2020. https://www.cnn.com/2020/12/17/economy/job-losses-women-pandemic/index.html.
45 Alexander, Kurtis. "Inside the Final Minutes before Andy Lopez's Toy-Gun Death." *SFGATE. San Francisco Chronicle*, July 8, 2014. https://www.sfgate.com/crime/article/Inside-the-final-minutes-before-Andy-Lopez-s-5607654.php.
46 Atassi, Leila, and Rachel Dissell. "A Guide to Reinvestigating Rape: Old Evidence, New Answers." *Cleveland Plain Dealer*, August 10, 2013. https://www.cleveland.com/rape-kits/2013/08/reinvestigating_rape_old_evide.html.
47 Dissell, Rachel, and Leila Atassi. "Cleveland, It's Time to Talk about Rape ... Old Evidence Brings New Answers." YouTube. *Cleveland.com*, February 8, 2017. https://www.youtube.com/watch?v=_UFGUWy8ZYo.
48 *Columbia Journalism Review*. "How an Ohio Reporter Helped Convict More than 100 Rapists." Accessed April 13, 2021. https://www.cjr.org/local_news/rape_kit_reporting.php.

5 The intrepid journalist
Tapping into tenacity, doggedness, & resourcefulness

I can tell you this, we are putting out a damn paper tomorrow.
— *Capital Gazette* reporter Chase Cook in a tweet the day a man shot and killed five staffers in the newsroom in Annapolis, MD[1]

WHY tenacity?

When we look back on the stories that stand out — the journalistic endeavors that define the profession — they are often moments of **tenacity**. Edward R. Murrow taking on Senator Joseph McCarthy. Ronan Farrow, Megan Twohey, and Jodi Kantor bringing to light the sex crimes committed by movie mogul Harvey Weinstein. Maria Ressa standing up to authoritarian Philippines President Rodrigo Duterte. Anthony Shadid telling the stories of Iraqi citizens whose lives were thrown into chaos and turmoil by the 2002 Iraq War. Barbara Walters securing a joint interview with feuding Egyptian and Israeli leaders Anwar Sadat and Menachem Begin. Lara Logan persisting in her coverage of the Arab Spring protests and discussing her own sexual assault during protest coverage in Egypt.

When we lose a journalist, either in the line of work or at the natural end of life, the most admired are remembered as "tenacious."[2,3,4] Journalism awards extol the virtues of tenacity and perseverance in their recipients.[5,6] Journalism programs list tenacity as one of the markers of the type of journalist they hope to teach and cultivate.[6,7] In short, tenacity is universally admired in a journalist, because it translates into the fact that these journalists persisted to ensure that their audiences were informed, power was held to account, and stories were pursued to their fullest extent in service of uncovering the truth.

"Most good journalism comes in the digging," said former TV news Executive Producer Danielle Deavours, who now teaches journalism at the University of Montevallo. "It comes from continuing to ask for answers and being curious enough not to quit until the subject is exhausted (which is usually never). Tenacity is critical to getting to the heart of the story and finding what really matters."[8]

KING-5 Seattle reporter Brit Moorer agreed.

Tenacity is critical in this business. I landed my first TV job only after unwavering persistence. That persistence hasn't died. You need tenacity to break into and survive the journalism business. You have to be critical, curious, and have the innate yearning for wanting to learn more.[9]

"When we shine light in the darkest corners is when we present stories that are of most importance and interest to our viewers/communities," said Dana Rosengard, managing editor of NBC NEWS CENTER Maine. "You (reporters, producers, managers) have to be diligent to find those spots and then chase the people who can add authority, credibility, impact, and dimension to what we have found."[10]

It takes a lot of energy, force of will, and perseverance to pursue a story that needs to be told. There may be powerful people who have spent a lot of time, money, and resources to ensure that a given story *won't* be told. There may be records and other information that have been lost to history, destroyed, or tucked away and are difficult to access. There may be sources afraid to speak out or who don't want to relive their experience, and without them the story cannot be told.

Let's take a look at Ronan Farrow, who as a freelance reporter for NBC began to learn of possible sexual misconduct committed by high-level Hollywood producer, Harvey Weinstein. Farrow, of course, began to pursue the story, along with NBC Producer Rich McHugh. While NBC executives were initially supportive – in fact, one had even provided the initial tip – they soon, according to Farrow and McHugh, began to impede newsgathering efforts, culminating in a refusal to air the story.[11] If this were the only thing getting in the way of publication, tenacity would absolutely still apply. Indeed, once Farrow realized that this important story would not see the light of day at NBC, he took it to *The New Yorker*, where it was published and earned Farrow a Pulitzer Prize – shared with *New York Times* reporters Jodi Kantor and Megan Twohey.[12]

But a nervous news outlet was not the only roadblock in the journey to publishing this story. Farrow detailed in his book *Catch and Kill* and in many interviews how Weinstein leveraged his power and influence to threaten, intimidate, discredit, and silence witnesses and reporters.[13] Farrow reports how he was followed by former Mossad agents who were part of an organization called Black Cube; how a woman posed as a sexual assault victim in an effort to get information; and how when Farrow began to fear for his life, he placed copies of all of the information, documents, and recordings he'd gathered into a safe deposit box inside a bank vault with instructions on whom to contact "should anything happen to me," and the entreaty: "Please make sure this information is released."[13]

McHugh corroborated Farrow's experience, detailing in a *Vanity Fair* article how his own phone started acting strangely. When he took it to a security expert, he was told the phone was likely bugged. So, he and Farrow began using burner phones. McHugh also learned that someone had broken into his home and tampered with the landline.[11]

Facing intimidation from Weinstein and his network, as well as a lack of support and what McHugh described as gaslighting from within at NBC, the two journalists had to decide how to proceed. McHugh pushed from the inside, while Farrow took the story to *The New Yorker*, where it did see the light of day, and along with Kantor and Twohey's *New York Times* reporting, led at last to charges against Weinstein and ultimately a conviction.

"We were actually relying on the classic standards of investigative journalism, tools our colleagues across the newsroom use every day," Kantor said. "Careful interviewing, persistent digging, searches for documents, corroboration."[15]

There were many instances when these journalists could have stopped, given up, thrown in the towel. The pressure they faced from within and without felt threatening and insurmountable. They were worried about their families, their livelihoods, their health, and their safety and that of their sources. So, what kept them going? What helped them persist in the face of all this?

Tenacity.

The Guardian called Farrow's work "a breathtakingly dogged piece of reporting, in the face of extraordinary opposition."[13]

Breathtakingly dogged.

Extraordinary opposition.

These words capture this deeply important tenet of strong journalism – tenacity.

At their core, these journalists knew that this story was important, that it would help enlighten readers to a dark underbelly of what men in power can do to women. This story might help prevent future abuses and encourage women who have been harmed to speak up and find a safe, supportive space to do so, rather than what had been the norm: disbelief, suspicion, accusations of wanting attention or money, and ultimately dismissal. Indeed, the publication of sexual assault accusations against Harvey Weinstein helped catapult the #MeToo movement further into the public consciousness. It also contributed to a culture shift in how sexual assault allegations are dealt with. It's not perfect, but we're farther down the road than we would be thanks to this reporting.

These journalists tapped into their tenacity to help them persist. Tenacity also helped them get every fact right, verify every piece of information, and seek additional witnesses and documentation. The instinct toward tenacity prompted these journalists to make the story so airtight that it could not be questioned, could not be doubted, could not be dismissed.

WHAT is tenacity?

Tenacity "is what separates the great journalists from the so-so journalists," said Faith Sidlow, award-winning broadcast journalist and associate professor at Fresno State. "Those who wait for a story to fall in their laps get the leftovers – not the scoops."[14]

"The best reporters are the ones who stay on a story despite efforts to discourage them," said Jeffrey Schiffman, radio anchor and program director turned professor and WVYC-FM Radio station manager at York College of Pennsylvania.[15]

Tenacity is what led newsroom staffers at the *Capital Gazette* in Annapolis, MD, to publish a paper the day after five of their colleagues were killed when a gunman opened fire on their newsroom, as promised in the tweet that heads this chapter. The staffers who survived the attack left the opinion page empty, except for the line: "Today, we are speechless," and the names of their five fallen colleagues, including the opinion editor.[16] Also on the largely blank page was a promise that the page would the following day "return to its steady purpose of offering our readers informed opinion about the world around them, that they might be better citizens."[16]

This is tenacity.

The Free Dictionary defines tenacious as "extremely persistent in adhering to or doing something … relentless."[17] In journalism, it's a willingness to keep pursuing a story, no matter the obstacles, setbacks, or words and actions of people or entities seeking to deter.

It is rare when journalists must draw upon the reserves of tenacity and doggedness that Farrow, McHugh, Kantor, and Twohey did to ensure that the Weinstein sexual assault story saw the light of day. But tenacity plays a significant role in everyday journalism, as well.

Tenacity could be continuing to pursue a story – no matter how big or small – even after it seems all avenues are exhausted. For example, when I was an intern at a TV news station in Los Angeles, I was asked to find a union rep to comment on a particular story. It was the end of the day – just after 5pm – and this was before cell phones and Google searches. I dove into our newsroom rolodex and called all the usual suspects. Most people did not answer, and those who did declined to be interviewed, because the story was seen as somewhat controversial. I then tried some alternative routes. I called people who might know someone in union leadership. I struck out again. I began sending emails that I assumed would not be read until the next day. I then looked again at my contacts to see if there was anyone who could provide a pathway – whether first degree, second degree, or third degree – to a source for this story. It was now just after 6pm.

Meanwhile, the reporter who had been counting on me to come up with an interview for him had gone to the executive producer's (EPs) office to say he would not be able to make the story happen for the 11pm newscast. At that moment, I received a callback. A second-degree contact had come through, and I had secured an interview.

I quickly scribbled down the contact info and ran from the assignment desk across the newsroom to the EP's office. The EP and the reporter looked at me – likely wondering why an out-of-breath intern was interrupting them. "I got an interview for you," I said. The reporter's face went from bothered to lit up. "You did?" he asked and smiled. I handed him the paper with the contact info, and he strode out of the office to make the call. "Good work," the EP said.

I have drawn upon this everyday tenacity daily in my journalism career, refusing to give up on securing an interview or tracking down a piece of information that could help illuminate a story and allow us to tell it fully and faithfully to our audiences.

Lydia Timmins worked in TV news as a producer, writer, and assignment editor before moving into her position as associate professor of journalism at the University of Delaware. She recalled using tenacity every day in the newsroom, whether it was working her way up in the ranks or covering a story, such as road safety, where tenacity and persistence led directly to securing the data she needed to move forward.

> I was working on a story about dangerous intersections in our viewing area. The state Department of Transportation had all the data about number of accidents and causes and everything I would need to do the story – but they didn't want to give it up. They first claimed they didn't have the info, then they said they couldn't give it to me, then it was too hard to pull the data together. (This was 1998, much was on paper.) *Every day* I called the department spokesman and asked for the data. I was polite and professional. After six weeks, they finally agreed (we) could come to the office for an interview. After two hours, they gave us all the information we requested. I was sorely tempted to give up, but I felt the story was important enough to keep at it until I wore them down – and the spokesman admitted he gave in because I wouldn't stop calling![18]

Timmins' persistence to call every day – polite but firm – to pursue the information needed to bring the story to her viewers is a clear example of the everyday tenacity that can mean the difference between getting the story or letting the story get away. It's common, as Timmins noted, to feel like giving up and moving on, but if it's worth it to the story, then draw upon your tenacity and persist.

Investigative editor Ted Bridis, who now teaches at the University of Florida, has been on the forefront of some of the biggest stories in the past 20 years. He was the first journalist to trace Hillary Clinton's private email server to her home; his team was the first to reveal that Paul Manafort and Rick Gates were conducting covert lobbying activities; his investigative team won Pulitzer and Goldsmith Prizes for revealing that the NYPD was spying on Muslim residents; and his analysis in the 2016 presidential election allowed the Associated Press to correctly call the election for Donald Trump. He was also part of the team at *The Wall Street Journal* that received a Pulitzer Prize for coverage of the 9/11 attacks – he witnessed Flight 77 hit the Pentagon and covered the story. Bridis credited his success, in part, to tenacity. For example,

> My investigative team at The Associated Press in Washington ... worked nearly four years to nail down the true story behind the 2007 kidnapping of retired FBI agent Robert Levinson in Iran. We finally were able to

reveal in 2013 that he had been dispatched by rogue CIA analysts on an unauthorized intelligence mission in Iran, and the US government had been openly lying about the situation even as it quietly paid his family more than $2.5 million to keep the story quiet.[19]

Tenacity played a role on many levels here, including having the patience to stick with a story for four years, the resolve to actively track down information veiled behind bureaucracy and cover-up, and the fortitude to weigh the ethics involved. "The story was challenging on a number of fronts, including the ethics of publishing embarrassing information that could result in Levinson's possible death at the hands of his captors," said Bridis.[19]

At its heart, tenacity is the determination and courage to do what is right, rather than what is easy. None of the stories Ted Bridis pursued were easy. Timmins' persistent pursuit of information that would be helpful to her public was not easy. But they drew upon tenacity to persist and bring those important stories to light.

The reporters who broke the Harvey Weinstein story certainly did not have it easy. But they bore the weight of threats, intimidation, gaslighting, and discrediting, because they knew that to give up and walk away would be more harmful. It would mean that a man who harmed multiple women would be allowed to go on harming women. And, it would empower other men to act similarly without fear of being held accountable for their actions. More women and young girls would be put in harm's way. The same is true for the staff of the *Capital Gazette*. Tenacity propelled them to publish a paper in the wake of a horrific act that directly affected them and their colleagues. Given the motive of the shooter to silence the paper, not publishing was not an option. The tenacity each staffer drew upon helped them speak through their publication and counter the horrific act.

In a *New York Times* interview with Kantor and Twohey, Kantor discussed an email she received from their only source who had gone on record at that point in their investigation to say that Weinstein had sexually assaulted her. The source faced a significant medical issue and was thinking of backing out, because that combined with the potential attention, blowback, and trauma from having her name released publicly, as well as having to relive her ordeal, would be too much. But the source told Kantor that she instead sat down with her daughters to share what had happened to her. When she did, her daughters shared their own stories of the sexual misconduct they and their friends had experienced. At that moment, she realized that all women were at risk of being assaulted or harassed – or they had already experienced it – and she had an opportunity to begin to stop the cycle.

So, she wrote to Kantor:

> I feel I am speaking out on behalf of women who can't because their livelihoods or marriages may be affected. I am the mother of 3 daughters and I do not want them to have to accept this kind of bullying behavior in any

setting as "*normal.*" I have been through life changing health issues and know that time is precious and confronting bullies is important. My family are all supportive of my decision.

I am happy to go on record.[20]

This woman was not a journalist, but she drew upon tenacity to persist with her part in the story. Her passion to ensure that this did not happen to anyone else helped her find the determination to speak out and face the public. This is tenacity.

WHEN should you tap into tenacity?

Tenacity should come into play at every step in the journalistic process, starting with breaking into the industry. KING-5's Moorer recalled that she tapped into tenacity from the very beginning.

When I moved from San Francisco to Charlottesville, VA, without a job, I knew I'd have to get creative to break into TV. My previous radio experience helped a lot, but I relied on my tenacity to push me to the next level. I sent emails to at least two news directors on a monthly basis, letting them know that I was moving to their market and I was interested in working at their news stations. I hadn't received one response after emailing them for at least six months. Finally, two months into my move across the country, I received a response from

Nellie Bly: The embodiment of tenacity

Elizabeth Jane Cochran (1864–1922) established herself as one of the top investigative journalists in history under the name Nellie Bly. She was born into privilege, but lost it when her father died suddenly. She and her mom eventually opened a boarding house in Pittsburgh, PA, to pay the bills and take care of Bly's many siblings.

Bly lived at a time when women were seen as lesser than, and this was embodied in societal conventions, laws, and attitudes. Women in the US did not yet have the right to vote (and wouldn't until three years before Bly's death). But to Bly, these attitudes and conventions did not make sense, and when Bly was 18 years old in 1882, she read an article in her local paper, *The Pittsburgh Dispatch*, which intimated that women were good for only domestic duties, and working women were "a monstrosity."[21] Bly wrote a well-articulated and passionate rebuttal, which impressed the paper's managing editor so much, he offered her a job.

But Bly's goals to reveal "the negative consequences of sexist ideologies and the importance of women's a news director who said someone had just walked into his office and given their notice. He remembered all of my emails. Shortly after that, I accepted a producer/reporter job.⁹

Once you've gotten your job, tenacity can help drive your work. At the beginning, when you are formulating your story idea, gathering information, and identifying sources, you need tenacity to keep you on track and help you push through the sometimes tedious process of conducting research and figuring out how to access people and information.

Sidlow recalled her days working her beat at Fresno, CA's NBC affiliate.

> Every day required tenacity. Not giving up when trying to find an interview or a story angle. Waiting outside a building for hours (after my shift was over) to get a soundbite from a politician who didn't want to talk to the media. Never taking no for an answer and always finding a solution to the problem or obstacle.¹⁴

You may also need to tap into tenacity to counter naysayers who may not think the story is worth pursuing. These naysayers may include colleagues, friends, or even your managing editor, news director, or professor. While it's important to listen to any feedback you do receive, because it can help strengthen your approach and reveal any biases you may not have been aware of (see *Chapter 4*), if you believe in your story idea, then continue to pursue it,

rights issues"⁴⁹ were thwarted after a hard-hitting investigative piece in which she posed as a sweatshop worker to expose the horrific working conditions women faced. Though the piece was powerful, when the sweatshop owner threatened to pull its ads from *The Dispatch*, Bly was put on the fashion beat.²² Bly's tenacity would not allow her to settle, so she sought a paper where she could continue her investigative work, and in 1887 she joined *The New York World*.

At *The World*, Bly's tenacious investigative work revealed inequities and abuses, engaged readers, and led to significant policy change. For her most well-known story, she took an incredible personal risk and went undercover in an asylum. She had herself committed to the Women's Lunatic Asylum on Blackwell's Island. To understand just how much risk Bly took, once she entered as a patient, she would not be able to check herself out. She would have to rely on her lawyers from *The New York World*. For ten days, Bly faced the horrors that other women locked up in Blackwell's faced – abuse, assault, degradation, and deteriorating and dirty living conditions. Bly wrote later:

> Take a perfectly sane and healthy woman, shut her up and make her sit from 6am to 8pm on straight-back benches, do not allow her to talk or move during these hours, ... give her bad food and harsh treatment, and see how long it will take to make her insane. Two months would make her a mental and physical wreck.²³

until 1) you can publish, or 2) you realize there's nothing there and it's time to move on.

"Tenacity is valuable when it comes to pursuing a story, but more so when it comes to producing good quality journalism over a prolonged period of time," said Alex Hollings, editor-in-chief of Sandboxx News, described as apolitical news for military veterans, military spouses, and some active-duty members. "Stories on hard days matter just as much as stories on easy ones. Tenacity delivers on both."[24]

"Sometimes it isn't tenacious reporting but tenacious presence, the belief that the work you're doing and the community you're serving is of value, that matters most," said Leslie-Jean Thornton, associate professor of journalism at Arizona State University, who formerly worked as a newspaper editor and reporter.[25]

Overall, said Thornton, "one needs to get contextual and substantive answers, not just answers. That almost always takes time."[22]

Tenacity is also important in the thick of your newsgathering, when you may feel fatigued, you're unsure which direction to explore next, or you've hit a dead end. A key source may refuse to go on the record or share documents, a promising lead may not pan out, or data may not be publicly available. I have faced this in my own career. At one point, a source came forward who desired anonymity but had damning documents about a public official. We were able to verify the source's story through the documentation, but then the source decided to back out and chose not to give us permission to use the documents. We did persist in trying to bring the story to light via other avenues, but we were unfortunately unable to verify it in any other way. I took another job, but those still in that newsroom continued to keep an eye on this story, in the hope of bringing it to light. The point here

What Bly reported was a bombshell. Her reporting led to an investigation by the New York district attorney and significant policy change, including better oversight and regulations to prevent overcrowding and fire hazards.

Bly's tenacity led her to root out poor treatment of prison inmates and factory workers, and corruption in the New York state legislature. But she was not just tenacious about serious, investigative stories. Her tenacity also led her to land interviews with some of the most prominent thinkers of the day, including suffragist Susan B. Anthony. In addition, Bly pursued a massive puff piece, now considered a prominent example of yellow journalism, fighting to be the reporter sent to traverse the world in less than 80 days, in an effort to break the record of a fictional character from the book, *Around the World in 80 Days*. Bly did it in 72 days and wrote her own book about the experience.

Nellie Bly was a pioneer who laid the groundwork for tenacious, transformative journalism. She forged a path for women at a time when few women were given the chance to become journalists, and far fewer allowed outside the fashion or society beats. She is remembered for her tenacity and perseverance, which led to real social change and improvement in the lives of many.

is that we did not give up when our initial source backed out. We persisted. Sometimes this leads to a story and sometimes it doesn't. But, no matter what, a journalist's responsibility is to persist in seeking the truth. Tapping into tenacity may help you push through obstacles and barriers to continue your work.

It's difficult to know when to stop pursuing a story, and perhaps you never really stop – you simply put it on the shelf and continue to pay attention for opportunities to pursue new avenues. As Bridis reminded us, "The best reporting and stories aren't easy to accomplish. If it were easy, somebody else would have reported this already."[19]

The *Times*' Kantor recalled receiving a lesson in tenacity from the paper's Executive Editor Dean Baquet, when she was covering the Obamas. "I wanted to give up," she shared in a *New York Times* profile piece.

> I asked him: "What if I spend all those months reporting and don't learn anything new?" He told me not to make a decision on that basis. At the outset of a reporting project, he said, the only test is whether you're asking good questions – hard ones. Otherwise, the project was not worth doing.[20]

During the writing, editing, and crafting process, you may need to tap into tenacity to persist in telling and sharing your story. Writer's block can derail us, making it easy to step away and leave it for later. But, in those moments, marshal your tenacity to stick with the process, so your story sees the light of day.

Finally, once the story is published, it may take tenacity to respond to audience comments and feedback, pursue follow-ups, and defend your work. Engaging with audiences in social media spaces is critically important. It can indicate to your audience that you stand by your story, can defend it, and care about building relationships with those who read, listen to, or watch your work. But the task can sometimes feel daunting. Tap into tenacity to persist in this process – it should pay off with increased accountability, trust, and communication. Follow-ups are often just as important – if not more – than the initial story. They keep your audience informed about developments and prompt them to turn to you to learn more. For those who are critical of your work, this is your opportunity to show how you gathered story elements. Be transparent about your process and adjust for any criticism that may be valid.

Practicing tenacity may mean that you have to do battle with editors, sources, and even audiences, advertisers, or funders. Edward R. Murrow faced this when he took on US Senator Joseph McCarthy (R-Wisconsin) in 1954. At the time, McCarthy said he was trying to root out Communist subversion, but he often accused people without proof, thus smearing their names. Many were reluctant to take on McCarthy, because they did not want to be falsely accused. But Murrow faced down that fear, tapped into his tenacity and passion for informing the public, and embraced that his duty as a journalist must take precedence. In March 1954, Murrow aired an episode of his show, *See It Now*, in which he was critical of McCarthy. Murrow then invited McCarthy to take the entire 30 minutes of a future episode to respond. When McCarthy took Murrow up on this offer three weeks later, McCarthy did not come off well. Though others had challenged McCarthy leading up to this moment, it was Murrow's direct, unwavering, well-researched, and verified presentation that went down in history as an iconic moment of tenacious journalism.

Murrow's taking on of McCarthy was seen as courageous, and it is characterized as such in writings about Murrow to this day. But, at the time Murrow did it, reaction was mixed. Many lauded Murrow and praised his tenacity and courage. In fact, McCarthy was censured by the Senate soon after, and his reign as the crusader against communism declined. But Murrow's show also took a hit. Advertisers uncomfortable with that level of conflict pulled their ads from *See It Now*, and the show soon went from weekly to every once in a while. Murrow had prioritized informing the public and taking on a powerful and corrupt individual over his show's financial stability. Whether or not you agree with Murrow's decision (and for the record, I do), he made his choice because his journalistic ethical compass would not allow him to do anything else. This is tenacity.

Tenacity is also prominently displayed in the work of Maria Ressa and her online news outlet, Rappler. Ressa and her team have worked tirelessly to hold Philippines President Rodrigo Duterte accountable and bring his atrocities to light. Ressa has been threatened, put in jail, and convicted on what her lawyers call "politically motivated" charges of cyber-libel for a critical piece revealing that a businessman friendly to Duterte had ties to the drug trade. CNN called Ressa's work "unflinching,"[26] and Ressa herself, upon conviction, implored other journalists to keep fighting.

> I appeal to you, the journalists ... to protect your rights. We are meant to be a cautionary tale. We are meant to make you afraid. So, I appeal again, (do) not be afraid. Because if you don't use your rights, you will lose them.[23]

Ressa was named a *Time* Person of the Year in 2019, and she draws upon her tenacity to persist in her work. She told CNN that being a war correspondent on the frontline is easier than fighting for freedom for the press. "At least when you're in a war zone, the gunfire's coming from one side and you know how to protect yourself," she said. "You don't even know where the enemy is here."[23] Ressa taps into her tenacity to keep her audiences in the Philippines and around the world informed and to cling to press freedom in her country.

EXERCISE BREAK

1. Go to the most recent list of Pulitzer Prize winners (https://www.pulitzer.org/prize-winners-by-year).
2. Choose one winner or finalist and write a paragraph or two, or record an audio or video segment, discussing how tenacity played a role in the award-winning coverage.

WHERE might tenacity be a problem?

Sometimes, we get so blinded by our goal that we become myopic, single minded, and blind to important information just outside of our singularly focused view. This is when tenacity veers into stubbornness and when biases may creep in, such as **confirmation bias** – when we process only the information that conforms to our worldview or perspective. The farther down the road we get on a story, the more we begin to construct an idea of what's important, where the story is going, and what the lead might be. If we obtain counter-information later in our process, we run the risk of minimizing its importance.

Thus, an important feature of a tenacious journalist is the ability to continue to be flexible about information coming in. Just as we need to be flexible enough to change directions when a lead does not pan out or when we hit an obstacle, we need to be flexible enough to listen when information comes to light that counters what we have or what we think.

Avoid allowing tenacity to turn into stubbornness. Tenacity and stubbornness are two different things. Stubbornness is clinging to something and refusing to give up an idea, thought, perspective, or approach. Tenacity is actually the exact opposite – steadily, doggedly, patiently moving forward; persisting in the face of obstacles; clinging not to one precious thing but reaching forward to cling briefly to the next peg before stabilizing yourself and reaching out to grab the peg after that. You may cling to your focus but remain open to new information.[27]

We, unfortunately, see examples of stubbornness crop up in journalism. For example, when someone is misidentified as the perpetrator of a crime, such as in the aftermath of the 1996 Atlanta Olympic Park bombing, the 2013 Boston Marathon bombing, and the 2012 Sandy Hook Elementary School mass shooting. In each of these cases, the tenacity to jump in, cover the story, and secure information turned into stubborn over-zealousness and a rush to share information that ended up being incorrect. Journalists in these cases were misinforming. In some instances, the misreporting continued, even as cracks began to appear in the narrative. Stubbornness, hand-in-hand with **anchoring bias**, makes it difficult for us to let go of what we thought was the story – but you have to be willing to let go and change directions when your newsgathering indicates.

Another important tool for a tenacious journalist is the ability to come up for air. It's important to stop, take a breath, assess what you've got, figure out what might be missing, and then bring in an outside pair of eyes – preferably one or more people who have different perspectives from you. Often, when we get too deep into a story, we can lose sight of the big picture, especially in the current digital landscape, in which quick sharing of information is commonplace. Some newsrooms have a process for internally checking stories before they are aired to ensure that all bases have been covered, all sources verified, all perspectives accounted for.

As mentioned above, it is important to know when to quit. Perhaps the story is not what you thought it was going to be. Perhaps the newsgathering yielded innocuous reasons for conditions that at first seemed suspect. Whatever the reason, not every story idea results in a story. The goal here is to give up for the right reasons. If the story is not worthy of being told, then you will need to face that, let it go, and move on. But be sure you understand your reasons for letting go. If you are letting go because the obstacles became too great, then that's when I would encourage you to tap into your tenacity. What might you need to persist in covering a story that needs to be told but where the obstacles have become insurmountable? Support from colleagues? More resources? If so, then find a way to deal with the obstacles, and keep moving forward!

Finally, proceed ethically in your pursuit of news. This includes knowing when to publish information – and when not to not publish information. For example, if you know the name of a sexual assault victim, do you publish it? How does that serve the story? What would the harm be? Most newsrooms do not publish the names of sexual assault or molestation victims, unless the victim wants to identify themselves.

In an international example of whether to publish a name, in 2019, a whistleblower revealed that President Donald Trump had engaged in alleged misconduct in dealings with Ukraine involving holding back aid to that country for a favor. This led to his first impeachment and vigorous discussion and debate in many corners of the nation. In the milieu of this story, some conservative media outlets said they had identified the whistleblower. A name was revealed in far-right media circles and even mentioned by a handful of conservative lawmakers and a contributor on Fox, but the whistleblower's identity was never confirmed. The law provides a whistleblower with certain protections, including anonymity to prevent retaliation. In this context, journalists from mainstream outlets decided not to print the purported identification of the whistleblower. This tenet was taken so seriously, even beyond journalism, that US Supreme Court Chief Justice John Roberts declined to read a question during the Senate impeachment trial because that question contained the purported name.[28]

HOW do you practice tenacity?

In addition to passion, persistence, doggedness, and determination, tenacity also involves taking initiative, having a thick skin, and being able to handle pressure and persist in hostile situations.

Tenacity is the mindset that you will get that story in some way. It is the belief that there is a path forward, that you just have to persevere and continue exploring to find the pathways that lead you to the ability to publish and inform the public.

Journalists who engage in tenacity don't just try one thing and then give up. They call, email, and DM multiple sources; research multiple websites, organizations, and outlets; get out of the newsroom. In short, they seek to complete the maze, and if there's a dead end, find another path until they make their way through it.

Journalists who engage in tenacity are also flexible. They have a plan, but they're not so rigid as to lose all hope when the primary pathway does not work out. This is called **anticipatory coping**[29] – how one finds their way around obstacles in their path.

Thornton said she was "born stubborn. But I also had a marvelous role model in one of my editors who helped me differentiate between being productively tenacious and non-productively stubborn."[22]

Moorer shared that she developed tenacity by identifying what she cares about. "I think tenacity is attached to your passion. If you're passionate about something, you'll do what it takes to reach your goal."[9]

Tenacity is knowing something is hard but persisting anyway. It is feeling discouraged, defeated, or exhausted, and still pushing through. So, grounding your journalism in strategies to complete tasks and get through projects can be helpful.

"Journalists have to *want* to know the full story, all the facts, everything they can," said Timmins.

> And that stuff isn't just sitting there waiting to be discovered. A journalist has to dig. And follow up. And call again. And not take no for an answer. If the story is important and needs to be told – it needs to be pursued with tenacity.[18]

To cultivate and maintain tenacity, including and especially when things aren't going the way we would like, try the following strategies:

- Specifically define what you're trying to do. Some real-life examples include:
    ○ Find out why certain communities are paying more for the same amount of water usage.[30,31]
    ○ Inform audiences about how your city allocates funds for public safety.[32]
    ○ Explore data about COVID-19 infections based on whether schools met in person or remotely.
- Find a way to make the story idea or tip meaningful to you.
    ○ While you may be assigned a story and not have chosen it, find a way to make it meaningful. At the most basic level, you are trying to inform your audience.
- Break your work into smaller, manageable tasks and specify steps in the process.
    ○ This helps you feel as if you're getting somewhere and makes it easier to move to the next step.
- Do something to advance the story every day.
    ○ This builds consistency and routine into your process.

- Celebrate small achievements throughout the process.
    - This helps you feel accomplished.
- Get curious in your newsgathering process.
    - Ex: The protester hair story on social media (I'll explain in a moment).
    - Ex: Jimmy Kimmel and scented candles (see below).
- Remind yourself of the bigger picture.
    - *Why* are you doing what you do?
    - Keeping sight of the value of our work can keep us on track.
- Remain flexible and seriously consider any well-intentioned critique you receive.
    - Often, well-intentioned critique – no matter how hard to hear – can reveal important things. So LISTEN to it.
- Reframe your setbacks – SETBACKS ARE NOT SETBACKS.[33]
    - Ask – what do I need to do differently to move forward?
    - Look at your issue through a different frame.
        - Talk with someone who thinks differently from you. They may see a way forward that you do not.
- Surround yourself with people who can support you.
    - Sometimes, just sharing your frustrations or setbacks can help relieve the burden and re-energize you to persist (see *Chapter 9*).
    - You can also bounce ideas off of your support network or seek advice.

These suggestions for cultivating tenacity[34] focus on the *process* rather than the outcome. It's in the process that we cultivate this critical journalistic skill. Hopefully, your professor, news director, or managing editor will create an environment that allows you to fully explore and embrace your capacity for tenacity, but if not, you will need to develop that environment for yourself. Use the tips above to help do this.

At first, it will likely be far easier to give up, stop pursuing, and move on to something else. But, like a muscle, the more you work tenacity, the more capacity you will have to engage it. Start small – if you fail to secure a source for a story, do some research and find one-to-two other sources. With each success comes a feeling of accomplishment, prompting you to want to feel that positive feeling again, so you will be more inclined to do something tenacious next time.

Think about the last time you got curious – the last time you said, "huh, I wonder…." Did you do anything about it? Did you seek out an answer to your musing? If you did, then that's great! Tenacity has begun to be cultivated in you. If not, that's OK – but the next time you find yourself saying, "I wonder…," take at least one step to start trying to figure it out. That step may lead to another step, another step, and then another step, until you have an answer, and hopefully the satisfaction of discovery.

Let's discuss the protester hair story mentioned above, which shows how tenacity can be sparked by curiosity. A TikToker with the screen name

Rebabeba posted a TikTok video in April 2020 after a protester in Michigan piqued her curiosity. The woman was protesting the stay-at-home order put in place due to the COVID-19 pandemic. "Specifically, this woman caught my eye because of her insane roots," Rebabeba said about the protester whose roots were prominently showing. "That looks like a lot of growth for the duration of the stay at home," Rebabeba mused. However, instead of letting this pass by, she got curious and decided to figure out how long it takes, on average, for roots to get that visible. "I did some research." She discovered that the stay-at-home order was implemented in Michigan on March 24, 2020 – about 28 days before the protest. She then researched how fast hair grows, on average. Then, she estimated how long the woman's roots were by comparing the woman's index finger, which was next to her head, to the average length of an index finger. Then, Rebabeba did some math and discovered, "she started the stay-at-home with 2.7 inches of visible root. AKA, she has not got her hair done since October." Thus, the stay-at-home order was not the reason for her roots.[35]

Another example of employing tenacity to satisfy curiosity involves negative reviews about scented candles on Yankee Candle's Amazon page. In this case, the curious observer did not employ tenacity. Rather, they posted their wonderment by tweeting, "There are angry ladies all over Yankee Candle's site reporting that none of the candles they just got had any smell at all. I wonder if they're feeling a little hot and nothing has much taste for the last couple days too,"[36] in reference to COVID-19 symptoms. Kate Petrova, a research assistant with the Harvard Study of Adult Development at Bryn Mawr College, read this tweet and also got curious. Petrova then employed tenacity to satisfy her curiosity. She scraped 20,000 Amazon reviews for various scented candles and crunched the data, discovering a correlation between the onset of COVID-19 and an increase in negative candle reviews. She tweeted her findings:

> I couldn't just walk past this Tweet, so here is (a) fun #dataviz Scented candles: An unexpected victim of the COVID-19 pandemic.[37]

Tenacity may also be employed in real time, such as during an interview or as news breaks and develops. For example, consider Axios reporter Jonathan Swan's interview with then-President Donald Trump on August 3, 2020. Swan was lauded for holding Trump accountable during the interview, fact checking in real time, and questioning Trump's assertions. Certainly, Swan did the basic preparation required of any journalist – he researched issues and topics that were likely to come up, he asked the five W's and H, and he asked basic follow-up questions to get clarification, challenge, and explore. But, given that it took three years for any journalist to be lauded for a hard-hitting interview with Donald Trump, clearly Swan carried something else into this interview, too – tenacity. He had the perseverance to remain on task as Trump tried to obfuscate, change the subject, or move on after giving only general responses. (We'll talk more about this example in *Chapter 8*.)

Leadership Consultant Dan Rockwell wrote tenacity is driven by terror, hope, and joy,[38] which I find an interesting way to frame tenacity. Terror could include the fear of not breaking the story, the fear of failing to help the community, the fear of being scooped, or the fear of letting down your audience. In this context, we might theorize that Ronan Farrow's fear of failing to get information out to the public or failing to prevent more sexual assaults outweighed his fear for his own personal safety. Then, there is hope – that you might make a difference or meaningfully contribute to the public discourse with your story – that you might make things better for your community. I have found hope to be an intoxicating and significant driver of my own tenacity, and many journalists do, because we are often driven by mission. Then, there is joy. As soon as you publish a story you worked hard on to inform your audience, the joy of that experience will likely drive you to seek it again.

So, when you face the process of newsgathering, investigating, researching, and discovering, ask yourself what you're afraid of, what you hope to achieve, and how you'll feel both if you get the story and if you don't. When you have a setback, ask yourself how it will feel to find a path forward, and how it will feel to drop it and let that setback win. Facing and recognizing how it will feel to give up can drive you forward.

Fear does not mean worry. Worry is more an internal factor of our worth and everything bad that might happen to us. It can consume us and cause us to lose a lot of time. Fear should tap into our desires but should be defined in terms of achieving and failing to achieve, publishing and failing to publish, informing the community and failing to inform the community.

WHO may challenge your tenacity?

Challenging or hostile situations may happen during the newsgathering process or once the story is published. Reporters who hold power to account may face harassment and threats via social media and in real life. Harassment is often about preserving or asserting power.

For example, when a group of journalists at *The Boston Globe* began looking into allegations of priests sexually abusing minors, they came up against a powerful Catholic Church that had sought to keep accusations of abuse secret by convincing the courts to seal documents, and shuffling accused priests to other dioceses. *Globe* reporter Walter Robinson explained on *Fresh Air*, a radio talk show:

> There was always a pressure in Boston on the *Globe,* and every other institution, by the church. The church was the most important and politically powerful institution in Boston .... The church had such power that if legislation it didn't like was before the Massachusetts Legislature, they could get it killed. And so there was always that sense that when you approach the church, you had to be very, very careful because of its power, and in this case it meant for us getting documents.[39]

The team of reporters tenaciously persevered for months, seeking to unseal documents and interview victims and priests. Their persistence and commitment to getting the full story paid off, bringing an important story to light and earning the journalists a Pulitzer Prize.

"All over the country there were instances [of abuse]," said *Spotlight* movie director Tom McCarthy on *Fresh Air*, "but this story, this reporting, it connected the dots, and that is what sort of blew the roof off of this crisis."[37]

Tenacity was also at play when journalists Ajai Shukla and Sushant Singh brought to light the incursion of Chinese troops into the disputed Ladakh region, claimed not only by China but also by India and Pakistan. Until they published, media outlets were not covering the story, because of pressure in India to pass on critical reporting. Former *Financial Times* Hong Kong Bureau Chief Rahul Jacob wrote in *Business Standard* that Shukla "covered the Chinese incursions with … tenacity."[40]

Efforts to silence, intimidate, and harass journalists have become more prevalent in the age of digital media, especially female journalists and journalists of color. Social media allows for easy access via public posts and DMs, and systemic misogyny and racism play out on these platforms. In addition, trolls and bots exploit our social constructs and send automatic messages filled with hate, vitriol, and even threats. This can lead journalists to self-censor, and could lead to physical or mental harm.

Washington Post media columnist Margaret Sullivan wrote in March 2021 that harassment against female journalists is "increasingly hard to endure," because it is relentless, menacing, and can also target your family members. "Digital harassment is pervasive, and it is destructive to the lives and careers of female journalists," Sullivan said. "It's simply an unhinged rage that women dare to have a voice."[41]

In an interview with *The Hill*, CBS White House correspondent Weijia Jiang said harassment and threats target the person, rather than the coverage. Indeed, many female reporters have reported facing intense harassment and threats, even when they share a byline with male colleagues, who do not receive such messages. Jiang said:

> When I share some of the notes that I get in my DMs and inboxes with my male colleagues, they are stunned because they cannot imagine somebody going there, somebody attacking you for the way you look or for the vile thoughts they might have about you or for your roles as a wife and as a mother.[42]

A troll may be an individual with mental health issues or low self-esteem. In this case, they are mostly men, and their targets are mostly women. These trolls "show high rates of psychopathic, sadistic and narcissistic behavior."[43] They are motivated by boredom, revenge, attention seeking, and a political agenda, and they derive pleasure from seeking pain.[44]

But trolls may also be part of organized groups known as troll armies created to divide and sew discord. Troll armies in the Philippines have harassed and threatened journalists who are critical of President Duterte, such as Rappler's Ressa.[45] Russian troll armies have employed similar tactics to silence journalists and critics, including Finnish broadcaster Jessikka Aro.[46] Or, they may not be human at all. A 2020 Carnegie Mellon study found that nearly 50% of all accounts tweeting about "reopening America" during the COVID-19 pandemic were likely bots.[47]

Trolls generally want to disrupt conversations, sow discord, be provocative to get under your skin, be relevant, and/or advance an agenda. In short, they want attention in some way, and they may go to great lengths to get it. To do this, trolls will often deliberately misread or misinterpret posts, take things out of context, ignore rational argument or evidence, and use anything someone says against them.[48] Their tone will often be abusive, threatening, racist, misogynist, and/or partisan. This issue has gotten so bad that Reporters Without Borders (RSF) Secretary-General Christophe Deloire issued a statement on online harassment:

> Online harassment is a phenomenon that is spreading throughout the world and now constitutes one of the gravest threats to press freedom .... We have discovered that information wars are not just waged between countries at the international level. Journalism's predators also deploy troll armies to hunt down and harass all those who investigate and report the facts honestly. These despots let their mercenaries train their guns on journalists on the virtual terrain as others do in actual war zones.[49]

Indian journalist Rana Ayyub has faced concerted harassment because of her critical reporting of Indian Prime Minister Narendra Modi. "I've been called Jihadi Jane, Islamo fascist [and] ISIS sex slave," Ayyub said. "My face has been superimposed on a naked body, and my mother's photograph has been taken from my Instagram account and photoshopped in the most objectionable manner possible."[45]

Australian journalist Ginger Gorman published an investigative piece and wrote a book about online predator trolling, which led to threats against her own family. She found that common myths about trolls did not hold up. They are not "uneducated losers," rather they are often well educated. In addition, they are not generally alone in their mom's basement. Trolls often work together in coordinated groups and specifically target potential victims. In addition, Gorman found that trolls do not always stay in the digital space. They do harm in real life, such as psychological harm, threatening family and friends, publishing home addresses, showing up where their target is, and inspiring others to pile on.[50]

If you face a troll or troll army, you may need to marshal as much tenacity as you can. Be aware of the three stages of trolling, as outlined by RSF: disinformation, amplification, and intimidation. With disinformation, trolls flood social media feeds with fake news. Then, these posts are artificially amplified through paid accounts or bots. Finally, intimidation, when trolls target and seek to intimidate journalists in an effort to discredit and silence them. Trolls tend to learn all they can about you, so their communications have an effect.

When a troll – a solo actor – attacked writer, comedian, and activist Lindy West, he learned everything he could about her, so he could exploit her at her most vulnerable. He posted about her weight, but even more nefarious, he created an online persona of her deceased father and began targeting her as this persona. For West, this hit home. She did something I do not recommend, but in this one case, it paid off. She responded to him, as she discussed in an episode of *This American Life*. It led to him apologizing and having a conversation with her about why he did it – in essence because he was at a low point in his life and did not like her confidence and seeming fearlessness. For West, this brought her some solace, but also the realization that a troll could be anyone.

> It's frightening to discover that he's so normal. He has female co-workers who enjoy his company. He has a real live girlfriend who loves him. They have no idea that he used to go online and traumatize women for fun. Trolls live among us. I've gotten anonymous comments from people saying they met me at a movie theater and I was a bitch or they served me at a restaurant and my boobs aren't as big as they look in pictures. People say it doesn't matter what happens on the internet – that it's not real life. But, thanks to internet trolls, I'm perpetually reminded that the boundary between the civilized world and our worst selves is just an illusion.[51]

The reason West's troll gave is a common reason for trolling – to silence women's voices.[52] West's case is a rare outcome. The prevailing wisdom is that you do not want to feed the trolls, often because they are engaged in targeted, coordinated attacks, rather than lone wolf, low-self-esteem musings.

Though trolls are part of the digital landscape, there are things you can do to minimize their reach and effect. First, disable comments sections where people can post anonymously, such as on YouTube. If you allow comments, be sure users identify themselves. Also, develop and post policies on what is acceptable and what isn't. This makes it easier to moderate and hold commenters accountable.

If trolls do breach your digital space, you can ignore them, block the accounts, or respond directly using the troll's real name (one journalist even alerts trolls' moms).[53] This last tactic may or may not work, depending on the troll's motives. They may be shamed, but they may like the attention or be a bot. Finally, and most importantly, report trolling to the platform, your outlet, *and* the police if trolls post anything threatening. You must also capture screenshots to document offending posts and save all communications. Though, if you're dealing with a troll army, this may take a lot of time and become impossible.

116 *Tapping into tenacity*

Why does this matter? Because trolls can break down our tenacity. Harassment and threats can lead us to pass on or stop pursuing a story. We also may decide to stay away from spaces where our audiences are commenting, thus losing that connection and engagement with actual audience members. Trolls can have a **chilling effect** on journalistic endeavors and thus public discourse.[54] Given that one of the tenets of journalism is to hold power accountable and inform the public, silencing journalists can threaten the health of societies.

Do take care to differentiate between harassment and criticism. Harassment is attacking *you* or your family. Criticism involves ideas and content. We welcome criticism, because it encourages discussions about ideas and may reveal new story angles, ideas, and sources.

In addition, take care of yourself. Even – perhaps especially – the most tenacious journalists take breaks to recharge (see *Chapter 9*). If you're dealing with a troll or troll army, get out of the spaces where trolls are communicating. Spend time with loved ones, talk to a psychologist, meditate, and exercise. We will discuss self-care more in *Chapter 9*, but these are all ways to keep your state of mind healthy and replenish your reserves of tenacity.

Key takeaways

- Tenacity is a foundational aspect of impactful journalism.
- Tenacity can help drive you forward in the face of setbacks, resistance, or other challenges.
- To build tenacity, reframe discouraging setbacks as opportunities, find what you are passionate about in the story you're covering, and explicitly identify why this story could matter to your audience.
- Journalists must be careful to ensure that tenacity does not turn into stubbornness. This can cause us to make missteps, because we cling to our ideas, rather than approaching the story with an open mind.

Discussion questions

1. What is something you have done or created that you are most proud of?
    a. Why are you proud of this accomplishment?
    b. What were the challenges involved?
    c. How did you overcome them?
    d. Why do you think you pushed through the challenges?
    e. Discuss how you might find more opportunities to achieve this feeling again.
2. Recall a moment in your life when you faced an obstacle. How did tenacity play (or not play) a role? What was the outcome?
3. Describe why you want to be a journalist and what kinds of stories make you feel passionate or inspire you to pursue this career.

Exercises

1. Using pen and paper, your mobile phone, tablet, or computer, answer the following:
   a. What do you care about?
   b. Why do you care about this?
   c. How can you take action to demonstrate you care?
   d. What do you want?
   e. Why do you want it?
   f. How can you begin down your path to attaining what you want?
      i. Include three to five specific steps.

   Your answers to these questions can serve as a foundation for your desired beat. You can also revisit when you lose sight of what you defined and expressed.

2. With a small group of fellow students, brainstorm challenges, problems, or issues you can identify at your school or in the local community. Answer the following
   a. What is the problem, issue, or challenge?
   b. Why is it a problem?
   c. When did it become a problem?
      i. You may not know this. If that is the case, then answer when it became a problem in your eyes?
   d. For whom is it a problem?
   e. For whom is it NOT a problem? Which groups are either unaware of this issue, uninterested in solving it, or benefit from it?
   f. From your perspective, how might you approach solving the problem?
   g. Whom could you talk with to learn more about the problem?
   h. Where could you go to learn more about the problem?
   i. What about this issue are you passionate about?
   j. Why would you spend time pursuing this story?

   Once you've completed this exercise, discuss with your professor whether you can make this into a story pitch for a long-term (i.e. semester-long or year-long) story.

   Then, develop a timeline with roles, responsibilities, and small, actionable steps to begin down the path. Note places where you will reward yourself or where the professor will reward you with points.

3. Think about something that you have been curious about, and discuss.
   a. What was it?
   b. What did you do to satisfy your curiosity?
      i. If nothing, why?
   c. What challenges did you face?
      i. i.e. slow internet, confusing search results, etc.
   d. What did you do when faced with the challenges?
      i. If you discontinued your exploration, why? How did it feel?
   e. If you reached the point of satisfying your curiosity, how did it feel?

Notes

1 Cook, Chase. Twitter Post, June 28, 2018, 3:38 PM. https://twitter.com/chaseacook/status/1012465236195061766.
2 Hilsum, Lindsey. "On the Tenacity and Bravery of a Great Journalist." *Literary Hub*, November 12, 2018. https://lithub.com/on-the-tenacity-and-bravery-of-a-great-journalist/.
3 Davenport, Anne Azzi, and Jeffrey Brown. "Remembering Jim Lehrer." *PBS*, January 23, 2020. https://www.pbs.org/newshour/nation/remembering-jim-lehrer.
4 Editorial, Chicago Tribune. "Time Cover Spotlights Journalists' Tenacity." *Denton Record-Chronicle*. Chicago Tribune, December 17, 2018. https://dentonrc.com/opinion/editorials/time-cover-spotlights-journalists-tenacity/article_b7ddbd86-0491-53ad-a2d0-6cac67827045.html.
5 "'Courage, Tenacity and Integrity'." Nevada Press Association, December 21, 2017. https://nevadapress.com/wabuskamangler/courage-tenacity-integrity/.
6 "Journalism Scholarships." Central Michigan University Wordmark, 2020. https://www.cmich.edu/colleges/cam/JRN/ForStudents/Scholarship/Pages/default.aspx.
7 "Programs." UC Berkeley Graduate School of Journalism. Accessed February 14, 2021. https://journalism.berkeley.edu/programs/.
8 Danielle Deavours (Mass Communication Instructor at University of Montevallo), in conversation with Gina Baleria, January 2021.
9 Brit Moorer (Reporter at KING-5 Seattle), in conversation with Gina Baleria, January 2021.
10 Dana Rosengard (Managing Editor of NBC NEWS CENTER Maine), in conversation with Gina Baleria, July 2020.
11 McHugh, Rich. "'Stand Down': Ronan Farrow's Producer on How NBC Killed Its Weinstein Story." *Vanity Fair*, October 1, 2019. https://www.vanityfair.com/news/2019/10/how-nbc-killed-its-weinstein-story.
12 Farrow, Ronan. "From Aggressive Overtures to Sexual Assault: Harvey Weinstein's Accusers Tell Their Stories." *The New Yorker*, October 23, 2017. https://www.newyorker.com/news/news-desk/from-aggressive-overtures-to-sexual-assault-harvey-weinsteins-accusers-tell-their-stories.
13 Brockes, Emma. "Ronan Farrow on Investigating Harvey Weinstein: 'When Family Issues Are Thrown at Me, It's a Dirty Move'." *The Guardian*, October 12, 2019. https://www.theguardian.com/media/2019/oct/12/ronan-farrow-on-investigating-harvey-weinstein-family-issues-thrown-at-me-is-a-dirty-move.
14 Faith Sidlow (Associate Professor at Fresno State), in conversation with Gina Baleria, January 2021.
15 Jeffrey Schiffman (Lecturer & WVYC Radio Station Manager at York College of Pennsylvania), in conversation with Gina Baleria, July 2020.
16 "Today, We Are Speechless." *Capital Gazette*, June 29, 2018. https://twitter.com/capgaznews/status/1012625503986044928/photo/.
17 "Tenacity." The Free Dictionary. Farlex. Accessed February 14, 2021. https://www.thefreedictionary.com/tenacity.
18 Lydia Timmins (Associate Professor of Journalism at the University of Delaware), in conversation with Gina Baleria, January 2021.
19 Ted Bridis (Lecturer at the University of Florida), in conversation with Gina Baleria, January 2021.
20 Clarke, Rebecca. "The Reporters Who Exposed Harvey Weinstein." *The New York Times*, September 13, 2019. https://www.nytimes.com/2019/09/13/us/the-reporters-who-exposed-harvey-weinstein.html.
21 Editors, Biography.com. "Nellie Bly." *Biography.com*. A&E Networks Television, November 12, 2020. https://www.biography.com/activist/nellie-bly.

22 Spooner, Alicia, ed. Nellie Bly. Accessed February 14, 2021. https://www.u-s-history.com/pages/h3938.html.
23 Bernard, Diane. "She Went Undercover to Expose an Insane Asylum's Horrors. Now Nellie Bly is Getting Her Due." *The Washington Post*, July 28, 2019. https://www.washingtonpost.com/history/2019/07/28/she-went-undercover-expose-an-insane-asylums-horrors-now-nellie-bly-is-getting-her-due/.
24 Alex Hollings (editor-in-chief of Sandboxx News), in conversation with Gina Baleria, January 2021.
25 Leslie-Jean Thornton (Associate Professor at Arizona State University), in conversation with Gina Baleria, July 2020.
26 Griffiths, James. "Philippines Journalist Maria Ressa Found Guilty of 'Cyber Libel' in Latest Blow to Free Press." *CNN*, June 15, 2020. https://www.cnn.com/2020/06/14/asia/maria-ressa-philippines-cyber-libel-intl-hnk/index.html.
27 Haaff, Brian de. "The One Important Career Skill You Are Likely Overlooking." *Inc.*, December 21, 2018. https://www.inc.com/brian-de-haaff/the-one-important-career-skill-you-are-likely-overlooking.html.
28 Mattingly, Phil, Manu Raju, Paul LeBlanc, and Chandelis Duster. "John Roberts Publicly Rejects Rand Paul's Whistleblower Question in Senate Impeachment Trial." *CNN*, January 31, 2020. Accessed February 11, 2021. https://www.cnn.com/2020/01/29/politics/rand-paul-whistleblower-senate-impeachment-trial/index.html.
29 Pam, N. "What Is ANTICIPATORY COPING? Definition of ANTICIPATORY COPING (Psychology Dictionary)." *Psychology Dictionary*, June 25, 2015. https://psychologydictionary.org/anticipatory-coping/.
30 Gregory, Ted, Cecilia Reyes, Patrick M. O'Connell, and Angela Caputo. "Why Our Water Rates Are Surging – And Why Black and Poor Suburbs Pay More." *The Water Drain*. *Chicago Tribune*, October 25, 2017. http://graphics.chicagotribune.com/news/lake-michigan-drinking-water-rates/index.html.
31 Zamudio, Maria, and Will Craft. "In Cities on the Great Lakes, Water Pipes Are Crumbling and Poor People Are Paying the Price." So Close, Yet So Costly. *APM Reports*, June 19, 2020. https://www.apmreports.org/story/2019/02/07/great-lakes-water-shutoffs.
32 Koeze, Ella, and Denise Lu. "The N.Y.P.D. Spends $6 Billion a Year. Proposals to Defund It Want to Cut $1 Billion." *The New York Times*, June 20, 2020. https://www.nytimes.com/interactive/2020/06/20/nyregion/defund-police-nypd-budget.html.
33 Steger, Michael F., Bryan J. Dik, and Ryan D. Duffy. "Measuring Meaningful Work." *Journal of Career Assessment* 20, no. 3 (February 19, 2012): 322–37. doi:10.1177/1069072711436160.
34 Cineas, Judi. "Five (5) Tips for Building Tenacity (Develop Follow Through)." March 8, 2017. https://www.youtube.com/watch?v=9FPW9OYg5Aw.
35 "Rebabeba", Rebecca. "My Math Could Be off Because I Actually Used the Average Bass Player's Pointer Finger #covid19 #Quarantine #Michigan #Coronavirus #Stayhome." TikTok, April 20, 2020. https://www.tiktok.com/@rebabeba/video/6817992292691971333?is_copy_url=1&is_from_webapp=v2#/@rebabeba/video/6817992292691971333.
36 Ingraham, Christopher. "Analysis | What Negative Candle Reviews Might Say about the Coronavirus." *The Washington Post*, December 1, 2020. https://www.washingtonpost.com/business/2020/12/01/covid-scented-candle-reviews/.
37 Petrova, Kate. "I Couldn't Just Walk Past this Tweet, so Here Is Some Fun #DatavizScented Candles: An Unexpected Victim of the COVID-19 Pandemic 1/n Https://T.co/xEmCTQn9sA Pic.twitter.com/tVecEiX5Jc." Twitter, November 27, 2020. https://twitter.com/kate_ptrv/status/1332398737604431874.
38 Rockwell, Dan. "How to Develop Unstoppable Tenacity." *Leadership Freak*, July 22, 2013. https://leadershipfreak.blog/2013/07/21/how-to-develop-unstoppable-tenacity/.

39 Gross, Terry. "Film Shines A 'Spotlight' On Boston's Clergy Sex Abuse Scandal." *Fresh Air*. NPR, October 29, 2015. https://www.npr.org/2015/10/29/452805058/film-shines-a-spotlight-on-bostons-clergy-sex-abuse-scandal.
40 Pubby, Manu. "The Two Veterans Who Unmasked the Chinese Incursions 'with the Tenacity of the NYT Reporters Who Broke the Pentagon Papers.'" *IJR. Indian Journalism Review*, June 20, 2020. https://indianjournalismreview.com/2020/06/20/the-two-veterans-who-unmasked-the-chinese-incursions-with-the-tenacity-of-the-nyt-reporters-who-broke-the-pentagon-papers/.
41 Sullivan, Margaret. "Perspective | Online Harassment of Female Journalists Is Real, and It's Increasingly Hard to Endure." *Washington Post*. Accessed April 11, 2021. https://www.washingtonpost.com/lifestyle/media/online-harassment-female-journalists/2021/03/13/ed24b0aa-82aa-11eb-ac37-4383f7709abe_story.html.
42 Petre, Linda. "Online Harassment Is Ugly and Routine for Women in Journalism." Text. TheHill, March 24, 2021. https://thehill.com/homenews/media/544628-online-harassment-is-ugly-and-routine-for-women-in-journalism.
43 Buckels, E. E., P. D. Trapnell, and D. L. Paulhus. "Trolls Just Want to Have Fun." *PsycEXTRA Dataset* 67 (September 2014): 97–102. doi: 10.1016/j.paid.2014.01.016.
44 Pierre, Joseph M. "No Comment: 3 Rules for Dealing with Internet Trolls." *Psychology Today*. Sussex Publishers, September 1, 2016. https://www.psychologytoday.com/us/blog/psych-unseen/201609/no-comment-3-rules-dealing-internet-trolls.
45 Story, Coda, and Lynzy Billing. "Duterte's Troll Armies Drown out COVID-19 Dissent in the Philippines." Rappler, July 22, 2020. https://www.rappler.com/technology/features/philippine-troll-armies-coda-story.
46 Higgins, Andrew. "Effort to Expose Russia's 'Troll Army' Draws Vicious Retaliation." *The New York Times*, May 30, 2016. https://www.nytimes.com/2016/05/31/world/europe/russia-finland-nato-trolls.html.
47 Young, Virginia Alvino. "Nearly Half of the Twitter Accounts Discussing 'Reopening America' May Be Bots." Carnegie Mellon School of Computer Science, June 24, 2020. https://www.cs.cmu.edu/news/nearly-half-twitter-accounts-discussing-reopening-america-may-be-bots.
48 Chatfield, Tom. "How to Deal with Trump, Trolls and Aggressively Emotive Untruths Online." *The Guardian*, August 2, 2016. https://www.theguardian.com/culture/2016/aug/02/how-to-deal-with-trump-trolls-online.
49 "Online Harassment of Journalists: Attack of the Trolls." Reporters Without Borders (RSF), July 25, 2018. https://rsf.org/sites/default/files/rsf_report_on_online_harassment.pdf.
50 Valentish, Jenny. "'It Was Like Being Skinned Alive': Ginger Gorman Goes Hunting for Trolls." *The Guardian*, January 27, 2019. https://www.theguardian.com/books/2019/jan/28/it-was-like-being-skinned-alive-ginger-gorman-goes-hunting-for-trolls.
51 West, Lindy. "Ask not for Whom the Bell Trolls; It Trolls for Thee." *This American Life*, January 23, 2015. https://www.thisamericanlife.org/545/if-you-dont-have-anything-nice-to-say-say-it-in-all-caps/act-one.
52 Ferrier, Michelle, and Nisha Garud-Patkar. "TrollBusters: Fighting Online Harassment of Women Journalists." In *Mediating Misogyny: Gender, Technology, and Harassment*, 1st ed., 311–32. Palgrave Macmillan, 2019.
53 True, Everett. "The Gaming Journalist Who Tells on Her Internet Trolls – To Their Mothers." *The Guardian*, November 28, 2014. https://www.theguardian.com/culture/australia-culture-blog/2014/nov/28/alanah-pearce-tells-on-her-internet-trolls-to-their-mothers.
54 Ferrier, Michelle, and Nisha Garud-Patkar. "TrollBusters: Fighting Online Harassment of Women Journalists." *Mediating Misogyny*, February 14, 2018, 311–32. doi: 10.1007/978-3-319-72917-6_16.

Part 2
Looking outward

6 Community engagement

Identify, connect, & engage
(but don't pander!)

> I'm just advocating ... the Mexican American community ..., which, by the way, the general community has totally ignored. And so, someone must advocate that.
> – Rubén Salazar (1928–1970), Chicano journalist, *LA Times* and KMEX[1]

It's one o'clock in the morning in Tiburon, CA. A husband and wife are at their store with a friend to do inventory. The lights are on. An officer checking on businesses along the street notices the lights and approaches the store. The husband comes to the door and unlocks and opens it. The officer says, "Hey guys. I've never seen you open this late. You just restocking?" Yema Khalif, who is Black, responds, "No, we're just doing our thing." When the officer asks, "What's your thing? I've never seen anyone in the store this late," Khalif responds, "Is there a problem?"

Body cam footage of the ten-minute interaction goes on to show Officer Isaac Madfes trying to elicit proof from Khalif that it is indeed his store and information about what exactly the three of them are doing there. But when he asks, "Is it your store?" Khalif responds that he is not required to prove he belongs there.

When two other officers arrive, one insists that Khalif place his key into the lock to prove it's his store. Only when a neighbor, who is white, yells, "That's his store!" do officers immediately say, "Thank you very much. That's all I needed to know." One officer does continue to demand that Khalif put his key in the lock, but Khalif continues to refuse.[2]

Though this is a story about policing and not journalism, it is instructive for us because of the narratives generated from such a story that we must parse, fact check, and portray in our coverage. The narrative that has historically taken precedence is that of the good cop protecting the community. And, one officer draws on this narrative, saying, "You should be grateful that we're being as diligent as we are to look out for the street. That's all we do."[2]

Though this is an important and fair narrative to consider and include, it is not the whole story. Notice that this narrative breaks down when another person, who is not Black, simply called out, "That's his store," to prompt officers to back down. They do not then approach this other person to ask what *he* is doing up at this hour and whether *he* belongs in his building. They take his word, accept his right to be in the neighborhood, and allow him to validate the Black store owner.

"It took a white man across the street — who did not come down to show his identification and prove who he was — to de-escalate the situation and make it go away," Khalif told KPIX. "That tells you something."[3]

As journalists, we need to ask ourselves and our sources why officers chose to detain one person and not the other. We also need to ask how situations like this are handled with other store owners on the street, who are largely white, in a community that is predominantly white. When other store owners are unloading inventory in the early morning hours, are there records of police officers arriving to confirm that they belong in their stores? Is there body-cam footage, so we can compare the interactions? If so – or if not – then we have important context.

Another narrative that often takes hold is that the officers were polite, and indeed they were. This is not an example of police brutality or physical mistreatment. Thus, a question we as journalists should ask is – does the fact that officers were polite mitigate the fact that they singled out one person for questioning and not the other? The officers in this story made a determination that one person may not belong and another person did. We must be deliberate and intentional to be sure we do not do the same thing. We must be sure that we cover all members of our coverage area as part of the community, and ensure we work to give all community groups a voice and perspective in stories that reflect, affect, or matter to them.

Another question is, what other behaviors were the officers exhibiting in the video that might undermine politeness? Khalif's business partner and wife Hawi Awash told KPIX, "One of the police officers had his hand on his gun, which was the most terrifying part for me."[3] While it is prudent for an officer to keep a hand on or near their gun or taser in a developing situation, what does that physical action do to belie the politeness the officers exhibited. To an average citizen going about their business, it can be intimidating and frightening.

Khalif told KPIX that his experiences as a Black man in a predominantly white community influenced his reaction, "but that's what happens when trust is lost and the actions of everyone — citizens and police officers alike — are seen as being 'suspicious.'"[3] As journalists, we can break this pattern of suspicion and seek instead to include all salient and relevant perspectives, including those involved in the incident, as well as uninvolved third parties, such as a sociologist doing research in this area. This can provide a broader picture of societal context and valuable information for the audience. In addition, we can work to avoid contributing to the extreme perspectives that often come with such a story by reporting on the nuances and context.

WHAT is community engagement?

Community engagement involves identifying, recognizing, and truly seeing the people in your coverage area throughout the newsgathering process. This becomes even more important when covering people or community groups that may generally be marginalized, under-served, less understood by the mainstream or dominant members of said community, or otherwise different from you.

Community engagement also involves engaging with all communities we cover, building relationships with people, organizations, and representatives; learning about issues important to your audience; understanding the history of community relations, including systemic and structural decisions that may play a role; and getting to know people in communities. This includes official sources, such as city council members and public safety officials, as well as groups or people attempting to challenge the status quo. They generally attend city council and other governance meetings to give public comment, organize demonstrations, and otherwise challenge systems that may not be working for them or their community. Critical to this process is doing this work *before* news breaks; *before* a story needs to be covered; *before* the community comes under a journalistic spotlight.

To illustrate this approach, let's explore how WPLN reporter Meribah Knight authentically and effectively covered stories out of Cayce Homes, Nashville's largest public housing project.

Knight's approach was featured on an episode of the *HowSound* podcast, entitled "Journalism of Empathy."[4] Host Rob Rosenthal explored two different approaches to covering the economically disadvantaged neighborhood in Nashville – the first approach repeated the missteps mainstream newsrooms have made again and again in their failure to fully cover a community, and the second involved authentic community engagement to mitigate bias and increase empathy. In the first example, Rosenthal discussed the *Tennessean* newspaper's series on the Cayce Homes. Two reporters went undercover, posing as an unemployed factory worker and aspiring manicurist. The goal of using the undercover tactic was to blend in so residents would speak freely. The reporters and the outlet believed that if they revealed themselves as reporters, then no one would talk authentically with them.

Before we go on, consider when the undercover tactic is generally used in journalism. Given the responsibility of the news media to be transparent and minimize harm, going undercover is rare. It is generally used to catch someone in the act and lull them into a false sense of security so they reveal something potentially damning or incriminating. Given its somewhat gotcha nature, going undercover can increase mistrust of journalists. With this in mind, ask yourself whether you would make the same decision to go undercover when pursuing a story about a housing project. I suppose it depends on your goals. Are you trying to investigate a series of crimes? Are you trying to reveal something about that community? Are you trying to humanize community members or use them as fodder for the mainstream, dominant audience (i.e. look how different *they* are from *us*)? Ask yourself, do you consider this community part of *your* community? Or, are they *other*?

EXERCISE BREAK

1. When would you go undercover as a journalist?
2. List the reasons you might use the undercover strategy in news.
   a. What are its benefits?
   b. What are its pitfalls?
3. List the types of stories where you think going undercover is never appropriate.
4. Discuss why it would not be appropriate.

I encourage you to ask yourself these or similar questions any time you cover a story involving a community with which you are not familiar. Otherwise, instead of actually *seeing* and engaging with the human beings in front of you, you run the risk of allowing your biases to frame your story, as the *Tennessean* reporters did.

The first story in the *Tennessean* series was headlined, "Little Love, Less Hope, Lost Lives," painting a bleak picture of the community. Residents of Cayce responded with anger about how their community was portrayed. They did not feel heard or listened to, rather they felt exploited and duped. In this case, reporters went in with preconceived ideas – or biases – about what life must be like, without taking the time to really get to know the community and its humanity. Even the characters that the reporters assumed revealed their biases.

WPLN's Knight, who covered the story very differently several years later, told Rosenthal that the *Tennessean* articles reflected that the rest of the city saw Cayce "as this foreign place, as this place that was completely isolated, that you had to put on an armor or another identity to 'go in' … it was so dangerous or so different."[4]

Knight's coverage of the same community for her podcast, *The Promise*, took a different approach. First, Knight, who is white, went into this largely Black community as herself and spent time getting to know people. Often, she did no reporting. She did not record anything or take photos or videos. She simply showed up, was present, and participated. To counter any biases she carried into the space, Knight asked people to describe their experiences for themselves. She also deliberately sought and found commonality by recognizing common experiences or responses, such as how a parent must feel when their child faces danger or scary information.

The result was a more nuanced and richer portrait of the community – a more human presentation. For example, Knight talked about one woman who was accepted to move into a brand-new condo complex. Knight went with the woman as she visited the new home and got excited about its amenities. Knight also sat with the woman on the porch at her current home as she chatted with passersby, waved at kids walking to and from school, and enjoyed the community ambience. Because Knight authentically, respectfully, and honestly documented this woman's life, listeners developed a connection. Thus, when the woman decided to remain in her current home rather than move into a brand-new condo, instead of the audience being shocked at why anyone in their right mind wouldn't get out of a bad situation into a better one, listeners from outside Cayce Homes could understand *why* the woman made the choice she did. They could relate to the idea of not wanting to move away from neighbors they were fond of and relationships they had built. In short, all listeners could connect.

Knight could have walked into the community with her assumptions and preconceived notions, and when faced with information that ran counter to her biases reject it. Why not? We all do it to some extent. But, thankfully, she did not. She listened. She heard. She saw. When she did not understand, she asked. When she was confused, she clarified. The result was a gift for listeners, both those who were not yet acquainted with the people who lived in Cayce Homes, as well as those from the community or a similar community, who felt heard, listened to, understood, *seen*.

Research shows that when we foster connection and build relationships with people who are different from us, it becomes difficult to continue to see them as a one-dimensional or stereotypical *other*.[5,6] We start to see them as fully formed humans, worthy of respect and consideration. Part of this process involves finding and recognizing commonality – common experiences, common backgrounds, or even a resonant lesson learned via stories that appear different at first. As the developers of the Framework for Individual Diversity Development wrote, "consciously searching for at least one commonality may be the first bridge toward valuing and validating others …. Once individuals accept the possibility of relativism, it is difficult – if not impossible – to retreat to dualism."[5] That is not to say that this process is easy. It can be fraught with challenges, "including fear of letting go of a previous mindset, guilt over betraying people who taught previous beliefs and practices, and uncertainty about how to engage with people who are different."[7] But it is a process journalists must undertake to ensure they are seeing, validating, and adequately covering communities outside the mainstream. This should take place when cultivating sources, newsgathering, hiring fellow newsroom staffers, and considering story pitches.

"If you want coverage that represents a wide array of perspectives, your newsroom must mirror the community," wrote P. Kim Bui in a report on empathy for the American Press Institute (API). "An inclusive, diverse newsroom is actually a means to an end. The true goal of diversity is to understand different kinds of communities and portray them more richly and accurately."[8]

Retired KCBS reporter Dave Padilla said this ideal has often been difficult to achieve, given the fact that newsrooms are generally made up of predominantly white males.[9,10]

> Still in this day and age, communities of color are often subjected to assumptions and falsehoods from those who are not part of those communities.

128 *Community engagement*

> Having covered stories in East and West Oakland, the Sunnydale and Army Street projects in San Francisco and East Palo Alto, I can say that most of the people I interviewed were working-class people who just wanted what everyone else wants – happiness, peace of mind, and financial stability. And yet, if you have a reporter with a particular bias of Blacks, Latinos, and Asians then that reporter will most likely find something that fits their preconceived notion. People of color are *not* novelties and yet they're still treated as such.[11]

Acknowledging that you are there to learn and to authentically cultivate relationships may open a door to building connections that can lead to stronger, more comprehensive coverage.

WHY is community engagement important?

Engaging and cultivating relationships with people in all communities is critical to the success of a journalist for many reasons.

For one, connecting with your communities will help you cultivate sources, leads, and story ideas, as well as combat any implicit biases you may have as you acquaint yourself with different experiences and perspectives.

In addition, connecting with both in-person and digital community spaces relevant to your audience can help journalists build trust and credibility. This foundation can serve both you and your audience well when news does break and you are able to rely on – and respect – that trust as you share a more nuanced and holistic story and ensure all voices are heard.

But Bui cautioned that newsroom decisions and choices can help or harm this effort.

> A newsroom's relationship with under-served communities can be harmed by all sorts of editorial and business actions: mishandled interactions between reporters and sources, story selection that takes a one-dimensional view of some communities, continual downsizing in the newsroom, diversity in entry-level positions but not on the masthead …. Those problems can persist even with a press for diversity.[8]

These issues have led to severe consequences for marginalized communities, and for the abilities of communities within a society to work and exist together, and see each other as fully formed human beings. Coverage that stereotypes, minimizes, assumes, and applies the mainstream frame – in essence fails to express the full humanity of a given group of people or community – exacerbates these issues.

Some coverage of violence against Asian Americans in spring 2021 worked to counter this. For one, many news stories included voices from Asian communities who could discuss the issue from their perspective and experience. Stories also offered more information about the victims of these crimes and the community members working to protect each other, which helped humanize them.

In addition, when a gunman shot and killed eight people at several Atlanta, GA-area spas in March 2021, six of whom were Asian women, police said at a news conference that the supect told them it was about sex addiction, and not about race. However, instead of taking this official quote at face value, printing it, and moving on, many journalists questioned the narrative and sought nuance to more fully contextualize the murders and framing of them. This included interviewing sources who were experts in sociology, sex addiction, and religion, as well as Asian American community leaders, who could discuss the intersectionality of race and sex, and point out that the race of the women may have played a role in the suspect's sex addiction.

Padilla said news directors and other newsroom leaders contribute to championing or hindering fair and equitable coverage of communities that fall outside the mainstream.

> News organizations should do their level best to cover communities, especially those of color, in ways that speak to the community and its welfare. The problem is that many news organizations still have white news managers who may not understand the significance of things that happen in these communities, and therefore, the communities are left without proper representation. It's often a struggle in news organizations for reporters to convince their white news managers that certain stories need wider or deeper coverage in communities of color. If there's a drive-by or murder in communities of color, there's almost no hesitation in covering that story or at least doing a "reader" on it. But, oftentimes, positive stories in communities of color get short shrift and are minimized.[11]

Journalist Soledad O'Brien concurs that news coverage often privileges the perspective of the dominant mainstream audience.

> Everyone from architecture critics to real estate writers, from entertainment reporters to sports anchors, talk about the world as if the people listening [to] or reading their work are exclusively white. There are simply not enough of us in the newsroom to object effectively – not in TV, print or online, certainly not in management.[12]

In a 2020 op-ed for *The New York Times*, O'Brien detailed how diversity was approached during her time working in daily news, including at CNN:

> People of color were rarely included in reports unless they were about crime or tragedy or poverty. Deeper reporting on our community was often limited to Black and Hispanic history months – a "special report" that often felt more marginalizing than special. When CNN responded to internal pressure for more coverage of people of color and their

communities, it created the series "Uncovering America," as if the network were revealing some secret world.[12]

NPR Chief Diversity Officer Keith Woods said we find ourselves here because mainstream media has historically focused on a white, middle-to-upper-income, middle-aged person, both because those in newsrooms may also come from this perspective and because the same demographic may hold financial resources and is thus also the focus of advertisers.[13]

Thus, current framing tends to **exceptionalize** those covered in news who are part of historically marginalized or under-served communities, said Woods, meaning they are an exception to the stereotype held by the mainstream. In addition, people of color are often used as sources primarily in stories about race, ethnicity, or social unrest. Data show that people of color, women, trans people, the differently abled, and others from traditionally under-served communities appear far less as sources when the story is about something other than the issue they represent – such as coverage of people shopping for Christmas or back-to-school stories – "The ordinary things – the stories about just regular stuff that happens – that only happens to white people" in much of our mainstream news coverage, Woods said. Truly covering a community "means showing the full truth of that community."[13]

This approach, said Woods, has led to a gap in understanding.

> If the scales fell off my eyes at the end of May or in the middle of July (2020), because of the volume of journalism that was being done about the killing of Black men in this country – if that in fact was an epiphany for me – then it is evidence of how badly you've been telling that story all along; how marginalized that story has been all along; how off the front page it was all along. And that's what you're trying to overcome in your coverage of a community.[14]

Failure to cover the ordinary, everyday moments in marginalized communities can be dangerous to those we cover, because we fail to challenge stereotypes and thus allow stereotypes to stand. Woods said this may lead a community to decide it no longer wants to engage with the news media just to be let down, and will instead tell its own story.

> You're not the first-person who had this idea …. Native Americans on reservations across this country have seen this particular movie a thousand times. Black communities have seen this movie a thousand times. The journalist comes in – the new journalist, the motivated journalist – and says, "yeah, I understand that that was some bad stuff, but this is going to be different. I'm me, I'm not them" – and we try to start over again.[14]

Woods said communities have put themselves through this over and over again, with the hope that a journalist may finally get it right, but that willingness to try again may be fading.

In a lot of these communities, their self-interest directs them to try again and try again and try again with journalists. Because if you get it right, finally, things will improve here. If you get it right, finally, you stop misrepresenting us and tell a fuller and more complete story of us. So, I have to give you another shot, because it's in my self-interest to do this, until the day – and maybe we are there today – when I decide it's no longer in my self-interest. You're hopeless.[14]

Woods thinks the 2020 protests over the death of George Floyd and the ongoing killings of Black men and women by police, as well as access to platforms via digital and social media, may indeed be a turning point at which communities become empowered to tell their own stories. But this does not mean journalists should give up. "When we're told to get lost by the police department, we have to go back and keep trying. When we're told to get lost on the reservation, we have to keep going back," Woods said, "because ultimately, we owe it to everybody, including the people who are avoiding us, to tell that story."[14]

To truly address this ongoing and burgeoning challenge, journalists and newsroom leaders need a plan to ensure that their news coverage is inclusive and acknowledges the humanity of those in the news. "Maybe one of the outcomes of the reckoning is that we begin a far more critical look at who's operating in our organizations, and we start demanding more from them,"[13] Woods said. In addition, newsroom leaders should consider keeping people on beats over the long-term, rather than reassigning them, so that relationships that are built and trust that's cultivated can be sustained.

HOW do we engage meaningfully with all communities?

Covering a community does not just mean spending one day engaging, and then writing a story and moving on. Ideally, we take the approach Knight took when she covered Cayce Homes – spend time getting to know people in the community. Though this can be difficult to achieve in an ever-shrinking mainstream news market with decreasing staff and resources, it's worth fighting for.

But covering communities with humanity does not mean you are only telling positive stories. Said Woods:

> It's also recognizing the consequences of the stories you tell and committing yourself to the full truth of the community, which means you're going to tell the critical stories. You're going to tell the stories that air dirty laundry and all of these things that are true about covering any place. But you are also going to stay long enough to see the ordinariness of my community – see where people fall in love, see where people practice, and enjoy art, and go out for walks, and all of the things that we journalistically tend to associate with people who are not people of color, people who are white, people who are middle class, people who are educated.[13]

Fortunately, there are specific steps we can take to ensure we are intentionally considering all communities in our coverage area; developing relationships and connections within these communities; and ensuring that coverage of these communities is fair, equitable, multi-dimensional, and journalistic.

The questions we want to answer are:

- How do we identify all of our communities?
- Who are our communities?
- How do we cultivate relationships with our communities?
- How do we engage with communities?
- How do we build a diverse source bank?
    - This includes diversity of ethnicity, race, gender, ability, socio-economic status, region, religion, and many other parameters.

It may be worthwhile to start by identifying who you think your audiences are – not who you want them to be – but who they are as it currently stands. If you're working for a local news outlet or your school paper, identify which towns, neighborhoods, and communities are in your coverage area. Document the demographic information of your current audience(s) as you understand them. What is the average age range, ethnicity, income level, education level, etc.? Then, document the geographic information. Does your current average audience live in a house? Apartment? Dorm? Do they rent? Own? Are they rural? Suburban? Urban? Finally, imagine your audiences' psychographics. What are their primary values? What do they do in their spare time? Hobbies? Activities?

Once you've identified your audience as you understand them, take a look and notice who's missing. Identify audiences in communities that may be traditionally overlooked or misunderstood. If you have trouble doing this on your own, then solicit the help of other people in the newsroom or your school, and perhaps reach out to community groups or school, city, or county agencies that work with the public. You can also check out the Open Data Portal to learn about the demographics for a given city or region. Then, begin to identify strategies to rectify this issue.

Once you've identified your communities, begin identifying sources from the various corners of your coverage area. The newsroom rolodex and your personal rolodex are a great start – but take every opportunity to expand your contacts to include people and organizations across ethnicity, gender, socio-economic status, ability, and region. Even if you have a diverse spectrum of sources, you can still face issues if you go to the same sources over and over again.

Fight the urge to become reliant on the sources you know will respond. Push beyond your comfort zone to integrate new sources with new and different important perspectives – perhaps one new source for every story you cover. Cultivating new sources should be a lifelong career endeavor.

"When we're talking about sourcing, I'm told all the time, 'Well, what happens is that on deadline we go to the same people we've always gone to' – the usual suspects kind of argument," Woods explained. But, we built the list of the usual suspects on deadline. We didn't just wake up one morning and there was a whole Rolodex full of names available to us. So, we created this problem under the same conditions that we are trying to solve it.[14]

Becoming reliant on the same limited number of sources, as well as official sources, is easy to do. Sometimes you need to start your source search by going through the PR or communications department at an agency, hospital, school, or business. Public information officers (PIOs) at official agencies are often extremely helpful, because they have well-developed mechanisms for responding to the news media and know how to get journalists what they need. If I call a state agency, hospital, police or fire department, or educational institution, I can count on the PIO to listen to my needs and use their knowledge to identify a source that will answer my questions. And this often happens in a timely manner. When we're on deadline, time is of the essence, and one role of media departments is to facilitate requests in ways that are helpful to journalists. This serves journalists but it also serves the agency. It builds goodwill, ensures that the agency's perspectives and point of view are included in the news cycle, and creates a dependence between the agency and the journalist.

To develop new sources, ask your current sources to introduce you to people familiar with the same topic. Find groups or follow hashtags and topics on social media. Engage on .patch and .nextdoor. If you need to go through a PIO or communications department, try looking at the staff list and identifying one or two people who may be right for the story, and then ask for those people by name. You can also try reaching out to them directly.

Keep in mind, our networks tend to include those who agree with us, have similar backgrounds and perspectives, and view the world in similar ways. While personal networks and official sources remain important, and ease of contact is a bonus, we cannot stop there. We must also cultivate sources outside the official machine and our existing networks.

If you do connect with a source who can provide a different perspective, that source may defer to a more experienced colleague. It is perfectly OK for you to push back and say you specifically reached out to them because of the perspective they can provide.

NPR's Woods explained that rectifying this situation involves a simple and ongoing approach – learning. Though the challenges of limited resources and experiences are real, they should not be prohibitive.

"It is everybody's responsibility to continue to learn," Woods said.

> We always begin with the limitations of time or human resource, and both of those will be with us as long as we're around in this business. Nothing stops you from learning more every day and therefore being more equipped in the moment to surmount the limitations of your individual experience and background.[14]

Learning should be ongoing, so that a reporter is not cramming to learn everything when a story breaks or a deadline looms. For example, "if you don't understand why it's such a big issue in America that trans women are targeted or that Black trans women are particularly targeted, the information is out there," Woods said.

> All you need to know to understand it sufficiently to tell good stories you can get with a quick Google search. So, the people who hit the deadline and then say, "oh, I didn't know to reach out to that person or to take that angle" and had done nothing in the hours before to learn something, that's the first failure.[14]

This is not to say that the solution is simple. "It is not easy to overcome all of the ignorance and blinders that have created the situation we have," said Woods. "It's not easy to do that on deadline, but there is more possible with vigilance than we have allowed ourselves."[14]

Another major challenge is breaking through an initial, pre-conceived notion of how a story is expected to unfold. By assuming what a story will be, we may miss the actual story in front of us. Research shows that once an initial frame is established it is difficult to introduce a new frame.[15] We will discuss framing more in *Chapter 7* when we explore language, but it is also relevant to the newsgathering process. Woods acknowledged that aligning with an initial frame is human nature, but we must work against it.

> I'm as likely as anybody to fall into the trap of seeing a story or an event pop up, and then thinking, "well, obviously the story is this," and then beginning the framing right there. Then, all of the decisions you make from that point forward are guided by the original frame. We need to get more into the habit of questioning on the front end; bringing in other voices as early as possible to hear the idea that's animating our activities; and propose alternatives or challenge narratives so that we're not doing the repair work on the other end.[13]

Bringing in other voices, other perspectives, and people with other experiences can help challenge the framing you start with – another reason it is critical to develop a source list, newsroom, and network that represent perspectives outside your own.

Finally, when covering communities that are traditionally under-served, be clear to your source about what they can expect from you, the outlet, and the coverage.[16] Never mislead a source. To cultivate the relationship, follow up and reconnect.

WHO are your audiences?

As discussed above, we may assume our audiences are like us. This can help us tell stories using familiar language and perspectives and give us someone to relate to, but it can also lead to blinders that cause us to make assumptions, leave out important explanations, or frame the story for and explain things to only people who think like us.

Though we will discuss writing more in depth in *Chapter 7*, it is relevant here to think about writing in the context of audience engagement. When I teach journalism, to get my students acclimated to the rhythm and progression of the inverted pyramid story structure, I ask them to imagine that they are talking to their best friend. I have them identify the first thing about the story that they would share. That's their lead. I then have them imagine what their friend might ask. This becomes the next piece of information they write, etc. While this method is effective for helping students understand how to identify the lead and order of importance of information, it is less effective at helping students identify alternative frames, points of view, and angles, because their best friend or the person they imagine likely comes from the same frame of reference as they do. This is also true when gathering video. If I am the one taking video, then it is truly from my perspective. Diversifying visual content is a challenge. To get outside of the frames we know, we need to expand our understanding of who our audiences are and become better acquainted with the perspectives, experiences, and priorities of those audiences.

When reporter Julian Brave NoiseCat described the experiences of Indigenous people in North America in an article for the *Columbia Journalism Review*, he used the term "apocalypse,"[17] which may not be a term that a non-Indigenous journalist would use, but that effectively conveys the Indigenous perspective.

> To be Indigenous to North America is to be part of a postapocalyptic community and experience. Indigenous journalists have always grappled with earth-shattering stories: either as historical background to current events or in the deep despair of the still-unfolding legacy of Indigenous dispossession, displacement, and death that brought nations like the United States and Canada into being.[17]

As someone who is considered white and grew up learning in the US public school system, I was not taught the history of North America's Indigenous experience using the term apocalypse, and therefore my understanding of this part of North America's history started from a different frame. The frame I was taught in school involved manifest destiny, battles, and the birth of nations – the perspective of European settlers – or to reframe the word settler – colonizers, defined as: to resettle, confine, or subjugate a population.[18] But, of course, this would not be the perspective of the millions of Indigenous people killed, slaughtered, enslaved, kidnapped, and forced to submit to the will of Europeans or their descendants. From their perspective, the term apocalypse is indeed appropriate and aptly and accurately describes what happened. This is an excellent example of why it is critical to have diverse voices and experiences working alongside each other in newsrooms.

136 *Community engagement*

Stuff, a journalism outlet in New Zealand, makes an effort to include all communities it covers and reaches by incorporating Indigenous language into its charter. First, it names New Zealand as Aotearoa, as the Indigenous Māori call New Zealand. The charter goes on to make a commitment to redressing the wrongs done to the Māori at the hands of colonizers, and to build relationships across cultures to improve representation. Here is an excerpt from the charter:

Treaty of Waitangi / Tiriti o Waitangi

We commit to embed the Treaty of Waitangi principles of partnership, participation and protection in the ethics and practice of our business.

E titikaha ana mātoukitewhakaūingāmātāpono o teTiriti o Waitangi, arā ko terangapū, temahingatahitanga, me tetiakitangakingā tikanga matatika me temahinga o tōmātoupakihi.

Restoration / Whakahaumanutanga

Under those principles of the Treaty of Waitangi, and a sense of what it means to be New Zealanders, we commit to acknowledging wrongs that have been done to Māori through reporting and business practices since our first newspaper began in 1857. We commit to redressing wrongs and to doing better in the future, in ways that will help foster trust in our work, deeper relationships with Māori and better representation of contemporary Aotearoa.

Me tewhaiwhakaarokiērāmātāpono o teTiriti o Waitangi, me teāhua o ngāpūtake o Ngāi Aotearoa, ko ū mātoukitetūtohuingā hara ko utainaki a Ngāi Māori mātepūrongo, me ngāwhakahaerenga ā-pakihi, maiiteorokohanga o tāmātouniupepaite tau 1857. E ū ana mātou kia whakatikaingā hara, kia pai akete mahi heitewā e hekemai ana, māngāara e poipoi ai itewhakaponoki ā mātou mahi, e hōhonuake ai ngāwhakawhanaungatanga Māori, e pai ake ai hokitewhakakanohitanga o Aotearoa o nāianei.[19]

By explicitly committing to building relationships, redressing wrongs, and seeking to better represent this historically marginalized community, *Stuff* lays the foundation for quality and inclusive journalism, and allows audiences to reference this charter when holding the news outlet accountable and comparing its coverage to its commitment. This approach can help build trust, cultivate relationships, and lead to more complete coverage.

Of course, the danger in writing to specific audiences is that you fall into patterns of trying to give them what they want, pandering and succumbing to clickbait and sensationalism. You must work to avoid this. You do not want to contribute to the perpetuation of filter bubbles and echo chambers. Our goal should be to help break through them by comprehensively informing, contextualizing, and being transparent. Keep in sight your mandate to tell people what they need to know – not just what they want to know. Consider how your work can provide value – not entertainment. You may face criticism from audience members with their own biases who may not appreciate a portrayal, but as long as it's truthful, factual, well sourced, independently verified, and transparent, you should be able to defend your work.

WHEN might an audience connect or disconnect?

There are many reasons an audience might express interest in a story. One reason is proximity. If a story such as a fire, car accident, shooting, or natural disaster happens near us – on our block, in our neighborhood, or near where we work or go to school – we're likely to pay more attention to it than if a similar story happened in another city or state, or across the country. We pay closer attention to the weather, traffic, and air quality of our own region than we do a weather forecast or traffic report in another part of the world.

Another reason for audience interest is familiarity. If we recognize or know the person, place, or thing in a story, then we are more likely to pay attention than if the elements of a story are unfamiliar to us.

But a larger factor in audience interest, engagement, and connection is relevancy. As the API pointed out, we take interest in stories when they seem relevant to our own life experiences, emotional experiences, or personal interests,

> from the emotional shock of losing a job or worrying about a sick child to mundane tasks like the weekly trip to the grocery store or filling the car with gas. Readers also identify with their own special interests, whether a hobby or sport or an important pocketbook issue like taxes, interest rates, school quality, crime and safety, health care, or economic development.[20]

A retired senior citizen who relies on social security is likely going to take an interest in stories about its solvency and related Congressional activities. A college student working two jobs to pay for tuition and housing is likely going to be interested in a story on debt relief for student loans or officials contemplating tuition increases. A new parent will likely take interest in a story involving the recall of a child safety seat. Stories relevant to our life experiences matter more to us, because we find familiarity and connect with the emotional proximity.

However, some members of the audience can feel alienated when news organizations *assume* that their audience will find the story relevant. This can happen, as the API pointed out, when we lump audiences into large impersonal groups, such as taxpayers, students, Democrats, Republicans, parents, consumers, and the like.[20] While we may fall into several of these groups, there may not be enough personal connection to really pique our interest. In addition, these groups are often discussed as monoliths. For example, the label Democrats is taken to mean *all* Democrats, Republicans as *all* Republicans, Latinos as *all* Latinos.[21] Within these large demographics are a multitude of individuals with personal preferences, who may or may not agree with each other, and who may or may not relate to the larger demographic label to varying degrees. For example, a January 2021 NBC News poll found that people in the US seem to fall into roughly four political party camps, rather than two,[22] and a deeper dive would likely show even more nuances. So, lumping 330 million people[23] into two distinct categories makes less and less sense upon closer examination.

The disconnect between news stories and audience interest can happen when journalists have little to no connection to groups within their larger market reach. When we don't take the time to forge those connections, then we are more apt to default to our unconscious biases – to generalize, stereotype, assume, and paint a monolithic picture. For example, when we look at US news coverage of Asian Americans, it often lumps all Asian Americans into one generalized persona, even though Americans of Asian descent trace their heritage to more than 40 different countries and have widely varying lived experiences. A 2015 Pew study found that annual income among those who identified as Asian ranged from $36,000–$100,000[24] – representing a vast array of experiences, stories, and perspectives.

The same is true for the monolithic terms Hispanic, Latino/a, and Latinx. People referenced using these terms come from multiple nations, and differ as much as those of European or Asian or Middle Eastern or African descent do. Journalists who gloss over the individual characteristics and humanity of millions of people contribute to the perpetuation of stereotypes and assumptions. Audiences will appreciate and benefit from specificity and precision.

"Asking people how they prefer to be identified, both by race and by pronoun, should become a habit," said Carolyn Copeland, copy editor and reporter at Prism.

> If you're writing about a politician or someone in the news and you're not sure how they want to be identified, sometimes just doing a Google search or watching YouTube clips can give you an answer. For instance, you may not know how US Senator Alex Padilla likes to be identified, but you may be able to find a video of him being interviewed where he says, "As a Mexican American man, I feel like it's my responsibility to...."[25]

In another example, a 2020 report from the Bill & Melinda Gates Foundation found that women's voices and experiences are persistently under-represented in news coverage. The report, titled *The Missing Perspectives of Women in News*, looked at the representation of women in three areas: newsgathering, news coverage, and newsrooms, and included measures such as news stories leading with women protagonists, women as sources of news expertise, and coverage of gender equity issues. Report author Luba Kassova plainly and starkly presented the findings:

The report finds that women's representation in the news has flatlined – if not reversed – in the 21st century. This alarming marginalization is clear in all areas of the news media: women are under-represented in newsroom leadership, gender equality stories are going untold, and men remain the vast majority of quoted experts and sources.[26]

Kassova went on to say that the problem is so entrenched that many people do not see it as an issue at all. "What makes any future advancement of gender equality in the news particularly difficult is the existence of gender blindness amongst the public in different countries. It is hard to fix something that is not seen as broken."[26]

Lack of representation can lead to coverage disparities. For example, a 2020 study examined news coverage of all murders that took place in Chicago during 2016 and found that those who were killed in predominantly Black neighborhoods received less or sparser coverage than those who were killed in predominantly white neighborhoods.[27] Homicide victims killed in Black neighborhoods were also less likely to be covered as complex individuals, i.e. less likely to have their humanity discussed. "Whereas the loss of White lives is seen as tragic, the loss of Black lives and those of people of color is treated as normal, acceptable, and even inevitable."[27] This same trend is seen in coverage of missing children. In a phenomenon dubbed "missing white girl syndrome,"[28] research finds that white missing children receive more coverage and more humane coverage than Black children and other children of color.[29] A 2015 study found that even though 35% of missing children's cases involved Black children, those cases garnered only 7% of media coverage. In another study with similar findings, the authors wrote, "Such things as newsroom diversity, news operation routines, media ownership, and commercial motives of media contribute to race- and gender-related media bias."[30] I would be remiss if I did not acknowledge that coverage of Black murders at the hands of police has increased greatly in the wake of the 2020 Black Lives Matter demonstrations, and it will be instructive to see how this coverage develops.

In parallel with efforts to make newsrooms more representative of their publics, those who currently work in newsrooms, hold leadership positions, or are seeking to enter the field can commit to actively engaging with and getting to know the communities they serve. If you identify as a member of a community that has historically been under-served in news coverage, then use your position to draw diverse sources into the newsroom, pitch story ideas that expand upon the normative approach, and cover everyday stories that come out of under-represented communities. If you are a member of a dominant, mainstream group, amplify the story ideas of your colleagues, diversify your source lists, and seek to challenge your biases. The process may not be smooth, and you may face pushback, but being aware and intentional can take us down the road to more representative, comprehensive, and humane coverage.

WHERE can newsrooms and journalists address this challenge?

When entering a community to cover a story, learn all you can, but don't mistake that for knowing it all. You are not the expert – the community members are the experts. The only way to be an expert in something is to have lived it. Academic experts live their work through study, experimentation, and immersion. Community members live their experiences and realities. You are there to listen, learn, and express their stories. It does not mean you cannot challenge them or their narratives or that you are soft-peddling a story. We challenge experts all the time and should engage our skepticism. But it does mean recognizing humanity.

When approaching news subjects, do as much work as you can – in often admittedly limited time – to learn all you can. Then, acknowledge that you don't know it all. Kat Chow, reporter for NPR's *Code Switch*, told P. Kim Bui as part of the API empathy report, "I do a ton of background reading, (and) I always ask people to tell me what I'm missing."[8]

The simple question – "tell me what I'm missing" – can unlock the door to understanding and context. You might also ask, "Is there anything I have not asked you that you think it's important for people to know?" Some type of question to acknowledge that you do not know it all, that you may not have asked all the important questions – that the interviewee, not the reporter, is the expert here.

Another strategy to help you cultivate more holistic, complex, humane coverage is to get to know the people, organizations, and other entities in a given community *before* any story is being covered there. As discussed above, do some networking, build your rolodex, develop trusted sources and contacts, and cultivate relationships. Connect with people and entities over social media, engage in social media spaces, and respond to those who are also engaging. Be transparent about your role – you are a journalist – and also forthcoming about your desire to listen and learn – and then actually listen and learn.

Engaging the community has other benefits, as well. Research suggests that cultivating digital social interactions may lead to increased readership/viewership.[31,32] In addition, engaging in digital spaces can add to our understanding of what our communities find important.[33] One way to do this is to add links to additional information on the outlet's website, share the links over social media, and ask audiences to contribute any information they have.

Several journalism approaches center intentional and deliberate coverage of angles not generally included in mainstream news coverage, often culminating in a call for change. While this may seem counter-intuitive to journalism's mandate to report without fear or favor, in essence it is adhering to that tenet by reporting on issues without fearing the powers that be or favoring a narrative that minimizes or decenters issues and the audiences affected by them.

Examples of these approaches include:

- **Social justice journalism** involves identifying injustices and exploring how to address issues in coverage. A Poynter Institute analysis of all Pulitzer Prize winners found that more than 100 used a social justice approach.[34]
- **Solutions journalism** focuses on coverage of how people respond to problems, discussing evidence of what's working and where things fall short. The goal is to provide evidence-based information that other communities can use to tackle their own challenges.[35]
- **Movement journalism** was developed in the US South – it is solutions journalism practiced by oppressed and marginalized people, often with an explicit perspective. Movement journalists' expertise lies in knowledge of their communities and the systemic issues they face, as well as the resources and agency communities use to grapple with issues.
- **Solidarity journalism** is "a commitment to social justice that translates into action,"[36] where social justice is "defined as dignity for all (as) a foundational moral principle from which journalis(m)" is practiced.[37]
- **Systems journalism** focuses on how the systems that underpin our societies influence the stories we cover, prompting us to apply different frames to newsgathering and writing.

Ida B. Wells: Prioritizing voices of marginalized communities

For journalist and activist Ida B. Wells (1862–1931), community always came first, and this clarity of purpose led her to dedicate herself to illuminating the stories, issues, and perspectives of Black people in the US, particularly in the South.

Wells, who was born enslaved, is remembered as a journalist, activist, abolitionist, and feminist – an early practitioner of social justice and movement journalism.

Growing up in Mississippi, Wells faced racial prejudice, not just from individuals but from the structures, rules, and practices that framed society. She saw first-hand how Black Americans were treated – not as a detached observer, but as a fellow Black American facing the same discriminatory attitudes and practices.

When she was 16, Wells lost her parents and a sibling to yellow fever. To support her remaining siblings, she convinced the nearby district that she was 18 and landed a teaching job. The family then moved to Tennessee, and she attended Fisk University before settling in Memphis.

Applying systems thinking to your journalistic practice can challenge you to break out of common frames. Systems thinking is thinking consciously and intentionally about how systems affect us, and how the choices we make and actions we take can impact systems — such as social, economic, educational, and others. This approach can provide context and explanation to help audiences understand complex or challenging stories.

Journalism + Design, which developed a systems thinking approach for journalists, explained, "Seeing the world in systems helps us look beyond immediate events and dig deeper into the forces, structures, and values that fuel them."[39]

Creators describe systems thinking by visualizing an iceberg. The tip of the iceberg represents the event being covered — what's happening. This is often where coverage begins and ends. But we know that the bulk of an iceberg sits under water (see Figure 6.1). We could go just underneath the surface to explore trends and patterns that relate to the story, and that is stronger coverage than staying above the surface. But the journalism that truly informs and contextualizes goes even deeper — to the structure of the system — the *how* — the interconnected policies and power dynamics at play that fuel the patterns we see. And, if we go even deeper, we can start to ask *why*. "Why is the system structured this way? What assumptions, beliefs, experiences, and worldviews are driving the system?"[38]

For example, if there are two high schools in a district, and one in an affluent area produces a large

In 1884, Wells experienced a confrontation that would shape the direction of her life. Though she bought a first-class train ticket, as she generally did, this time the train crew ordered her to the car for Black riders. When she refused, they forcibly removed her from the train. Though she won her initial lawsuit against the railroad, the Tennessee Supreme Court overturned it.

Wells had done some writing for local Black papers, but this incident sparked her to turn to journalism full time, so she could give her full attention to addressing political and societal issues. Three years later, when she was 25, Wells became the first female co-owner and editor of a Black newspaper in the US when she purchased stakes in the *Headlight* and the *Memphis Free Speech*.

Another life-altering event happened in 1892, when Wells' friend who owned a grocery store was lynched after a confrontation with white store owners who were unhappy that his store was drawing business away. Wells began focusing her writing on lynching in America, in particular the false accusations perpetrators often made about those they killed, including that the lynching victim had raped a white woman.

An editorial pointing out that white women could find Black men attractive led several white men in Memphis to storm Wells' newspaper offices and destroy the equipment. Wells was in New York at the time and did not return to Memphis.

She continued to write about socio-political issues affecting Black Americans, documenting 728 lynching percentage of graduates who go onto college, while the other high school in a less affluent area has only a small percentage of students go onto college, the tip of the iceberg story is to report the fact that this is happening. Going a bit deeper, just under the water line, we may look at trends over time. Has it always been this way? Have outcomes changed over time? But to truly inform your audience, go even deeper and ask *how* this discrepancy came to be, and *why* students at each school are performing so differently? This systems-based approach will yield new angles and provide important context. Perhaps you discover that the buildings and facilities at the second high school are subpar and need repair. Perhaps this leads you to discover that there is lead in the paint, which affects student learning. Perhaps you also discover that the first school has up-to-date textbooks and a new technology center, and that the second school uses textbooks from 20 years ago and does not have much

cases between 1884–1892, which she wrote about in a series called *Southern Horrors*. This work led to a posthumous Pulitzer Prize in 2020 for her "outstanding and courageous" reporting on lynching.[38]

Wells used the power of writing to take on issues that mattered to her community, and journalistic skill to inform. Today, we call this social justice or movement journalism – illuminating issues, perspectives, and experiences and seeking redress.

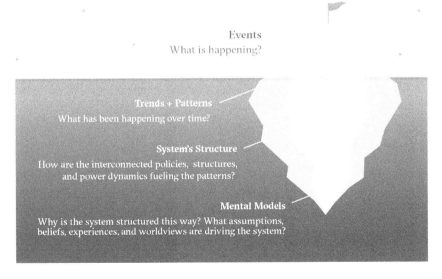

Figure 6.1 Newsgathering down the iceberg. Created by the Journalism + Design at the New School, Bronx, New York, and reprinted with permission.

technology on site. This may lead you to explore how the system contributed to such differing resources being provided to each school. So many story ideas and avenues open up when we get under the surface.

Key takeaways

- It is important for journalists to reach out to and regularly engage with all communities in their coverage area, cultivating contacts, sources, and relationships *before* a story breaks.
- Engaging can help you prevent coverage that stereotypes, minimizes, assumes, or applies the mainstream frame – in essence fails to express the full humanity of a given group of people or community.
- Audience engagement does not mean pandering. Keep your journalistic mandate in mind as you cover communities. Approach the community with the attitude of seeking to learn.

Discussion questions

1. Examine your school news outlet or a community news outlet. Based on the coverage, framing, tone, and language used – who is their primary or target audience? Does that match with the school community or local community? How does it match? How does it not match?
2. Choose one of the journalism approaches mentioned in this chapter: solutions journalism, solidarity journalism, movement journalism, social justice journalism, or systems journalism. How can this kind of journalism be helpful for your community? Are there any ways this kind of journalism could backfire/have a negative effect? Choose a story on your beat and discuss how you would cover it using the approach you chose.
3. How would you balance the need to connect with your audiences against the temptation to pander or sensationalize to get clicks? What could you say to an editor who assigns you a story that seems to be based more on clicks than value to the community?

Exercises

1. Identifying your audience: Select a news organization you would like to work for, or think of your school news outlet. Identify who you think your audiences *are* – not who you want them to be but who they *are* as it currently stands.
   a. Document the demographic information of your current audience(s) as you understand them. NOTE: You can do this for more than one audience group.
      i. Average age range
      ii. Gender

       iii. Ethnicity
       iv. Race
       v. Ability
       vi. Income level/Socio-economic status
       vii. Education level
  b. Document the geographic information.
       i. Does your current average audience live in a house? Apartment?
       ii. Do they rent? Own?
       iii. Are they Rural? Suburban? Urban?
  c. Imagine your audiences' psychographics.
       i. What are their primary values?
       ii. What do they do in their spare time? Hobbies? Activities?
       iii. What is their religion? Do they practice?
  d. Assess your results, and identify where there are gaps – where does your profile not match with the community you serve?
2. Audience engagement strategy: Using the information you compiled in question 1, begin to develop a strategy for engaging audiences that you may not already serve.
  a. Identify which social media platform(s) you will use.
  b. Identify organizations, agencies, and people who are active in the communities.
  c. Discern what may matter to your communities.
       i. Where are there connections and similarities?
       ii. Where are there issues that may matter to one community more than another?
       iii. What is each community's perspective or orientation to the issues you've identified?
3. Systems thinking: Choose an issue on your campus or in your local community, such as homeless encampments, tuition fee increases, poorly performing schools, a high-crime area, flu season, or anything else of interest to you. Apply a systems journalism approach to your research.
  a. Answer:
       i. Basic info
          1. What is the event or incident prompting initial coverage?
          2. Who is being affected by this issue?
          3. Who is involved in creating the issue?
          4. What are the perspectives each side brings? Which are relevant?
       ii. Research
          1. What are the trends over time related to this story?
          2. What has been happening over time? Getting worse? Better?
       iii. Then, answer the following questions:
          1. What has influenced these patterns?
          2. What are the relationships between the elements involved?
          3. How do interconnected policies, structures, and power dynamics fuel or maintain the patterns?

iv. Finally, answer:
   1. Why is the system structured this way?
   2. What assumptions, beliefs, experiences, values, and worldviews do people hold – in the newsroom? In the community? Among those affected?
   3. What beliefs and assumptions have kept the systems in place?
b. The information found at this link can help guide your work: https://www.systems.journalismdesign.com/tools

Notes

1 Navarro, Bob. "Slain Latino Journalist Rubén Salazar, Killed 40 Years Ago in Police Attack, Remembered as Champion of CHICANO RIGHTS." *Democracy Now*, August 31, 2010. https://www.democracynow.org/2010/8/31/slain_latino_journalist_ruben_s alazar_killed.
2 Weikel, Hannah. "Store Owners: Late-Night Encounter with Tiburon Cops Was Racially Motivated." *The Ark*, August 24, 2020. https://www.thearknewspaper.com/single-post /2020/08/24/Store-owners-Late-night-encounter-with-Tiburon-cops-was-racially-motivated.
3 Ramos, John. "Video: Tiburon Police Officers Confront, Question Black Business Owner in His Own Store." *CBS San Francisco*, August 25, 2020. https://sanfrancisco.cbsl ocal.com/2020/08/25/video-tiburon-police-officers-confront-question-black-busine ss-owner-in-his-own-store/.
4 Rosenthal, Rob. "Journalism of Empathy." *HowSound*. Transom, February 6, 2018. https://transom.org/2018/journalism-of-empathy/.
5 Chavez, Alicia Fedelina, Florence Guido-DiBrito, and Sherry L Mallory. "Learning to Value the 'Other': A Framework of Individual Diversity Development." *Journal of College Student Development* 44, no. 4 (2003): 453–69. doi: 10.1353/csd.2003.0038.
6 Bennett, J. M. "Toward Ethnorelativism: A Developmental Model of Intercultural Sensitivity." In R. M. Paige (Ed.), *Education for the Intercultural Experience* (pp. 21–71). Yarmouth, ME: Intercultural Press, 1993.
7 Baleria, Gina. "Story Sharing in a Digital Space to Counter Othering and Foster Belonging and Curiosity among College Students." *Journal of Media Literacy Education* 11, no. 2 (September 1, 2019): 56–78. doi: 10.23860/JMLE-2019-11-2-4.
8 Bui, P. Kim. "The Empathetic Newsroom: How Journalists Can Better Cover Neglected Communities." American Press Institute, June 9, 2020. https://www.ame ricanpressinstitute.org/publications/reports/strategy-studies/empathetic-newsroom/ single-page/.
9 Grieco, Elizabeth. "Newsroom Employees Are Less Diverse than U.S. Workers Overall." Pew Research Center, May 30, 2020. https://www.pewresearch.org/fact-tank/2018/11 /02/newsroom-employees-are-less-diverse-than-u-s-workers-overall/.
10 Thurman, Neil, Alessio Cornia, and Jessica Kunert. Rep. *Journalists in the UK*, 4. Oxford, UK: Reuters Institute for the Study of Journalism, 2016.
11 Dave Padilla (Retired Radio Reporter & Anchor), in conversation with Gina Baleria, February 2021.
12 O'brien, Soledad. "Soledad O'Brien: A MeToo Moment for Journalists of Color." *The New York Times*, July 4, 2020. https://www.nytimes.com/2020/07/04/opinion/soledad -obrien-racism-journalism.html.
13 Keith Woods (Chief Diversity Officer at NPR), in conversation with Gina Baleria, December 2020.

14 Keith Woods, "Addressing Unconscious Bias in News" interview by Gina Baleria, *News in Context* (podcast), January 11, 2021. https://exchange.prx.org/pieces/353968-npr-chief-diversity-officer-keith-woods-on-address.
15 "Anchoring Bias - Definition, Overview and Examples." Corporate Finance Institute, April 15, 2019. https://corporatefinanceinstitute.com/resources/knowledge/trading-investing/anchoring-bias/.
16 Yahr, Natalie. "Why Should I Tell You?: A Guide to Less-Extractive Reporting." Center for Journalism Ethics, 2018. https://ethics.journalism.wisc.edu/why-should-i-tell-you-a-guide-to-less-extractive-reporting/#1553012465523-c22f78df-5121.
17 NoiseCat, Julian Brave. "Apocalypse Then and Now." *Columbia Journalism Review*, 2020. https://www.cjr.org/special_report/apocalypse-then-and-now.php.
18 "Colonizer." The Free Dictionary. Farlex. Accessed February 15, 2021. https://www.thefreedictionary.com/colonizer.
19 Stevens, Mark. "Stuff's Charter; a Brave New Era for NZ's Largest Media Company." *Stuff*, November 30, 2020. https://www.stuff.co.nz/pou-tiaki/our-truth/300168692/stuffs-charter-a-brave-new-era-for-nzs-largest-media-company.
20 Dean, Walter. "Good Stories Prove Their Relevance to the Audience." American Press Institute. Accessed February 15, 2021. https://www.americanpressinstitute.org/journalism-essentials/makes-good-story/good-stories-prove-relevance-audience/.
21 Garza, Mariel. "Opinion: There Is no 'Latino Voting Bloc' Get Used to It." *Los Angeles Times*, November 6, 2020. https://www.latimes.com/opinion/story/2020-11-06/opinion-latinos-arent-homogenous-voting-bloc.
22 Chinni, Dante. "How Many Political Parties in the U.S.? Numbers Suggest Four, Not Two." *NBCNews.com*. NBCUniversal News Group, January 24, 2021. https://www.nbcnews.com/politics/meet-the-press/what-if-america-s-four-political-parties-n1255450.
23 "U.S. and World Population Clock." Population Clock. 2021. U.S. Census Bureau. Accessed February 15, 2021. https://www.census.gov/popclock/.
24 Budiman, Abby, Anthony Cilluffo, and Neil G. Ruiz. "Key Facts about Asian Origin Groups in the U.S." Pew Research Center, May 22, 2019. https://www.pewresearch.org/fact-tank/2019/05/22/key-facts-about-asian-origin-groups-in-the-u-s/.
25 Carolyn Copeland (Copy Editor & Reporter at Prism), in conversation with Gina Baleria, February 2021.
26 Kassova, Luba. Rep. *The Missing Perspectives of Women in News*. Washington, DC: International Women's Media Foundation, 2020.
27 White, Kailey, Forrest Stuart, and Shannon L. Morrissey. "Whose Lives Matter? Race, Space, and the Devaluation of Homicide Victims in Minority Communities." *Sociology of Race and Ethnicity*, September 17, 2020. doi: 10.1177/2332649220948184.
28 Stillman, Sarah. "'The Missing White Girl Syndrome': Disappeared Women and Media Activism." *Gender & Development* 15, no. 3 (November 2007): 491–502. doi: 10.1080/13552070701630665.
29 Kaur, Harmeet. "Black Kids Go Missing at a Higher Rate than White Kids. Here's Why We Don't Hear about Them." *CNN*, November 3, 2019. https://www.cnn.com/2019/11/03/us/missing-children-of-color-trnd/index.html.
30 Min, Seong-Jae, and John C. Feaster. "Missing Children in National News Coverage: Racial and Gender Representations of Missing Children Cases." *Communication Research Reports* 27, no. 3 (2010): 207–16. doi: 10.1080/08824091003776289.
31 Guzmán, Mónica. "How to Build Audiences by Engaging Your Community." American Press Institute, May 2, 2016. https://www.americanpressinstitute.org/publications/reports/strategy-studies/listening-engaging-community/.
32 Mersey, Rachel Davis, Edward C. Malthouse, and Bobby J. Calder. "Focusing on the Reader: Engagement Trumps Satisfaction." *Journalism & Mass Communication Quarterly* 89, no. 4 (September 5, 2012): 695–709. doi: 10.1177/1077699012455391.

148 Community engagement

33 Blanchett, Nicole. "Participative Gatekeeping: The Intersection of News, Audience Data, Newsworkers, and Economics." *Digital Journalism*, January 25, 2021, 1–19. doi: 10.1080/21670811.2020.1869053.
34 Clark, Roy Peter. "Hate and Racism in the South Gave Rise to 'Social Justice Journalism'." *Poynter*, March 23, 2016. https://www.poynter.org/newsletters/2016/hate-and-racism-in-the-south-gave-rise-to-social-justice-journalism/.
35 Solutions Journalism Network. Accessed February 15, 2021. https://www.solutionsjournalism.org/.
36 Varma, Anita. "Evoking Empathy or Enacting Solidarity with Marginalized Communities? A Case Study of Journalistic Humanizing Techniques in the San Francisco Homeless Project." *Journalism Studies* 21, no. 12 (July 8, 2020): 1705–23. doi: 10.1080/1461670X.2020.1789495.
37 Varma, Anita. "Solidarity Journalism." Markkula Center for Applied Ethics. Santa Clara University. Accessed February 15, 2021. https://www.scu.edu/ethics/focus-areas/journalism-and-media-ethics/resources/solidarity-journalism/.
38 "Life Story: Ida B. Wells." New York Historical Society, 2021. https://wams.nyhistory.org/modernizing-america/fighting-for-social-reform/ida-b-wells/.
39 "An Intro to Systems Thinking for Journalists." Systems Thinking for Journalists. Journalism Design. Accessed February 14, 2021. https://www.systems.journalismdesign.com/a-basic-introduction.

7 Inclusive writing & storytelling
Speaking the language of your communities

I became a journalist to come as close as possible to the heart of the world.
— Henry Luce, *Time Magazine* founder[1]

In early 2020, people all over the world began to confront the COVID-19 pandemic, and leaders began to respond to (or downplay) the virus. If you lived in the US, the EU, Nigeria, Malawi, Japan, China, and many other nations, you began to hear and see the steady drumbeat to wear a mask, socially distance, and stay home.

People also began to speculate — about which parts of the world would be most impacted by COVID-19. Industrialized nations assumed that poorer areas of the world would be hardest hit. For example, in Western news coverage from April to December 2020, a colonial bias permeated stories about the continent of Africa, with many viewing the entire continent through a lens of needing patronage and assistance, based on its position outside the sphere of Western society.

On April 6, 2020, the World Economic Forum published an article with the headline: "Africa has a COVID-19 time bomb to defuse."[2] In the article, the writer asserted that "Africa's healthcare systems will be overwhelmed when coronavirus cases escalate," and "There isn't much in Africa standing in the way of COVID-19."[2] In another nod toward colonialism, the writer lumped the entire continent together, rather than discussing the different approaches and circumstances of individual nations. The writer speculated that "Africa, with its long-underfunded healthcare systems, is a time bomb just waiting to explode, (and) deaths from COVID-19 might far exceed what the world is witnessing right now unless major steps are taken,"[2] presumably by those from "benevolent" Western nations.

In most of Africa throughout 2020, this prediction did not occur. By 2021, when a new and more contagious strain mutated, illness and death numbers did rise across many African countries — though as of April 2021, those numbers were still well below many Western nations (115,000 deaths across the entire continent of Africa with 1.3 billion people versus 576,000 deaths in the US with 330 million people; with only two African nations at greater than 10,000 deaths – Egypt at 12,500 and South Africa at 53,000, attributed to a mutated COVID-19 strain) (see Figures 7.1 and 7.2).[3,4]

While a large percentage of people across Africa are young, and there are lower rates of lifestyle diseases, such as obesity and hypertension, leadership also played a significant role in the success of many African nations in limiting and managing the spread of COVID-19. They took the virus seriously from the beginning, re-implementing systems already in place to deal with previous deadly viruses, such as Ebola, and calling for national mask mandates, lockdowns, and other measures to prevent virus spread. Citizens heeded those calls and did what they could to keep each other safe and healthy. For example, public health officials in South Africa went door-to-door to test for the virus, and in Liberia, residents set up their own community checkpoints to take the temperatures of neighbors. Ghana and other nations implemented strict lockdowns very early, and many nations required masks. As a result, infection and death rates were far lower in many parts of Africa than in many other parts of the world.

However, even as news organizations and experts acknowledged that most African nations were faring better than expected, colonial and racist tropes continued to permeate coverage. The BBC reported that "the relatively low numbers in Africa" compared to the rest of the world "have baffled experts."[5]

Washington Post Global Opinions Editor Karen Attiah wrote on September 22, 2020, that there was some cognitive dissonance between what Western officials and media outlets expected and what actually occurred.

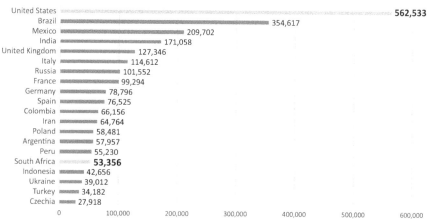

Figure 7.1 COVID-19 deaths by country. Source: Johns Hopkins University Coronavirus Resource Center (https://coronavirus.jhu.edu/data/mortality).

Inclusive writing & storytelling 151

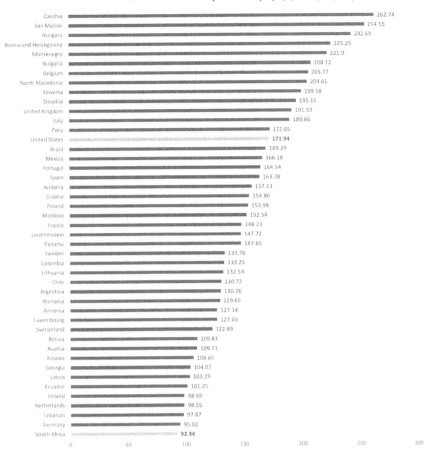

Figure 7.2 COVID-19 deaths by population. Source: Johns Hopkins University Coronavirus Resource Center (https://coronavirus.jhu.edu/data/mortality).

Headline writers seem to be doing their hardest to try to reconcile Western stereotypes about Africa with the reality of the low death rates on the continent. The BBC came under fire for a since-changed headline and a tweet that read "Coronavirus in Africa: Could poverty explain mystery of low death rate?" The New York Post published an article with the headline, "Scientists can't explain puzzling lack of coronavirus outbreaks in Africa." It's almost as if they are disappointed that Africans aren't dying en masse and countries are not collapsing.[6]

In a Deutsche Welle (DW) news report, scientists speculated that parasitic worms could be protecting some Africans,[7] prompting *The Daily Show*'s Trevor Noah, who is from South Africa, to question, "like, all Africans?" and then look down at his stomach and say to an imaginary worm, "I guess I should thank you, Mr. Wriggles."[8]

Instead of covering the fact that many African nations have kept infection and death rates low thanks to strong leadership and informed public health decisions, and then looking to the leaders of those nations for guidance – Western scientists and commentators fell back on colonial and racist framing.

This same racist framing can be seen in coverage of African American populations in the US during the 1918 flu pandemic, as pointed out by Nancy Bristow, professor of history at the University of Puget Sound and author of *American Pandemic: The Lost Worlds of the 1918 Influenza Pandemic*. In an interview on the podcast, *News in Context*, Bristow said,

> In communities where it was reported that African-Americans were dying in higher numbers, white newspaper reporters would (say), "that shows they are inferior." And when they would die in lower numbers, white newspapers would report that "it's because they're not like us." So, they were damned if they did and damned if they didn't.[9]

Biased writing can also be seen in divergent coverage of the two women who married Princess Diana's sons in England. Duchess Kate, who is white and married to Prince William, has been treated well in the news and tabloid media, while Duchess Meghan, who is mixed-race and married to Prince Harry, has been covered negatively for identical behavior. For example, images of both women cradling their baby bumps garnered far different ink. A photo of Princess Kate cradling her baby bump was paired with the headline, "Not long to go! Pregnant Kate tenderly cradles her baby bump while wrapping up her royal duties."[10] However, a photo of Meghan doing the exact same thing came with a far different, more negative headline: "Why can't Meghan keep her hands off her bump? …. Is it pride, vanity, acting, or a new age bonding technique?"[10] In another headline, even though both Kate and Meghan used the same flower – lily of the valley – in their wedding bouquets, that garnered far different coverage, too. The headline for Kate's bouquet read, "Kate Middleton's homegrown bouquet of lily of the valley follows royal code."[10] While the headline for Meghan's bouquet read, "Royal wedding: How Meghan Markle's flowers may have put Princess Charlotte's life at risk."[10]

Both the pandemic and British royal examples illustrate that our societal and cultural biases play a clear and prominent role in our writing, leading those who covered these stories to use framing that reinforced structural racism. In *Chapter 6*, we focused on covering and engaging with communities. In this chapter, we will discuss the power of words, and how journalists can improve their approach to writing so it's more precise and inclusive.

WHAT does speaking the language of the community mean?

Whenever we write, speak, or otherwise communicate, we tailor our communication to fit the audience. It is likely that you speak to your mom or dad differently than you speak to your best friend. You may speak to your significant other differently than you speak to your professor. You use different words and symbols, engage in different body language, and perhaps even use different content delivery platforms. For example, you might send the same message via text to your parents and via Snapchat to your friends. Communication is constructed differently on each platform, thus affecting how you can send the message. When you communicate via text, you're primarily using letters and words – though you may add an emoji or two (or six) or a photo, GIF, or short video. When you use Snapchat, you've got primarily video and graphic options, with text serving as enhancement.

Speaking the language of a given community means you must understand its nuances, which hopefully means you are doing the work necessary to understand community members (see *Chapter 6*). In journalism, the language we use can reveal our biases and include or exclude audience groups. Thus, it is important to be as precise as possible, and aware of how your audience defines and interprets the words and phrases you use.

"It's unavoidable that language carries meaning and carries meaning beyond the literal denotation," said Anita Varma, PhD, assistant director of journalism and media ethics at the Markkula Center for Applied Ethics at Santa Clara University. "Sometimes my students will send me a dictionary definition, and they'll say, 'well, this is what I meant.' And I'll say 'that's great, but that's not all that it means in this context.' Even if the dictionary is on your side, we have all these other levers and discourses going on."[11]

For example, let's explore the words "riot" and "massacre." Writers have often used the word "riot" when describing the incident in 1921 in which white residents of Tulsa went into a Black community dubbed "Black Wall Street" and proceeded to burn buildings, kill Black residents, and bomb businesses. What does the word "riot" connote? Merriam Webster defines it as "public violence, tumult, or disorder."[12] Cambridge defines it as "an occasion when a large number of people behave in a noisy, violent, and uncontrolled way in public, often as a protest."[13] The focus here is on people causing a disturbance, and not on a group of people harming another group of people. Responsibility or blame is distributed among all parties present that day, rather than the group who came into the neighborhood and attacked.

By contrast, the word "massacre" – the way many now refer to the 1921 incident in Tulsa – frames the story differently. Merriam Webster defines massacre as "the act or an instance of killing a number of usually helpless or unresisting human beings under circumstances of atrocity or cruelty."[14] The use of this word to describe what happened in Tulsa in 1921 paints a very different, and more accurate, picture – of a group of people who came into a neighborhood and brutally attacked another group of people who were defenseless to stop it.

When writing, your decision on whether to use the word "riot" or "massacre," "demonstration" or "protest," "non-consensual sex" or "rape," "under-aged woman" or "teen" or "child" or "girl," or some other word or phrase will signal to your audience more than just the word itself. With that word or phrase comes all the history, assumptions, framing, and understanding that have developed around that word or phrase prior to your use of it. Thus, it is important to know your audience's orientation to specific words or phrases, so you don't inadvertently imply, offend, exclude, or mis-report. It is also important for you to pay attention to your word usage, so you can be as precise as possible and convey what you mean to convey.

Varma said the first step is "recognizing that there's a decision you have to make. Trying to not make a decision ends up being a decision in itself."[11] Generally, not making a decision means that your unconscious biases will inform your choice of words and phrases, rather than your conscious, deliberate, and intentional journalistic approach.

For example, in coverage about rape, sexual assault, or molestation, we may use words that soften the horrific actions we are describing, often without realizing it. Though this may be to avoid upsetting the audience (or even ourselves), it actually minimizes the gravity and seriousness of the acts. In an article for The Poynter Institute about how to cover child abuse, Sarah Welliver, former journalist, now public information officer for Utah's Division of Child and Family Services, wrote, "When providing descriptions of any abuse, avoid euphemisms and instead use medical or legal terms."[15] As I noted in the above examples, when you use "non-consensual sex," a euphemism, you are actually describing "rape," an official term, and an act of violence, rather than sex. When you say "under-aged woman" – something that does not exist – you are actually describing a "child," a "girl," or a "teen." The term "under-aged woman" primes us to think of a woman – an adult. "Child," "girl," "boy," and "teen" are more accurate words to use when the victim is under-aged. Welliver also reminded us, if the victim is under the age of consent (which varies depending on the state or country), then the terms "relationship" or "affair" make no sense. The correct terms would instead include, "abuse," "molestation," or "trafficking." "Would the headline 'Man arrested for sexual relationship with 13-year-old boy' be accurate? What about 'Teacher accused of having affair with teen he met online?'" Welliver asked. "Sexual abuse is not a relationship, and repeated sexual abuse is not an affair."[15] To reframe your writing, center the people affected. For example, *The Guardian* produced a film depicting the experience of a rape victim in Australia who was unable to publicly share her own voice because of legal regulations. The film depicts both the crime committed and the subsequent legal battle, centering the victim's experience and voice to help the audience gain a deeper understanding of this perspective.[16]

"The best approach that I've seen some of the most celebrated journalists do is to emphasize the account of the people who are living the experience that you're trying to represent," Varma said. For example, in #MeToo coverage, "do we say that it was the victim (or) survivor *claiming* that there was an unwanted advance? Or do we say that this *person said* they were sexually harassed in the workplace? And the answer has to be the latter." When weighing whether to assert that someone "claimed" or "said," you are privileging one version of events over another.

> If it's someone from the mayor's office (who) told me what happened, that gets taken as fact; and someone who experienced the policy of the mayor's office, for example, are they making claims? There's a disparity there in terms of who's getting privileged and who's not.[11]

Varma went on to explain that an inclusive approach centers the person telling the story. "Say whose story is being told here," she said. "It's also perfectly possible at different points in a story (or in coverage over time) to tell different aspects of the story."[11]

For example, an initial story might be to center the person who said they were sexually harassed. Then, a follow-up story might center the response from communities impacted, including sexual violence prevention groups. A third story might focus on the official investigation. In each story, a different perspective is centered. Of course, critical analysis must be included, but ongoing stories often include multiple relevant voices and multiple relevant perspectives.

The two main questions Varma wants all journalists to ask when they write or produce stories are:

1. "How can we make journalism more inclusive? That can often start with using the language from the people you're talking to and the people who lived it."
2. "Who gets to be a truth teller and who's relegated to making claims?"[11]

Answering these questions can help guide your journalism to a more nuanced, contextual, and informative space.

WHY is it important to speak the language of the community?

It is important to speak the language of the communities you cover, because failure to do so can lead to overlooking and missing important stories, ignoring or misconstruing segments of your audience, and contributing to reinforcing and even amplifying negative stereotypes. This can lead to harm, including further marginalization, exclusion, and even violence.

Varma recommends that when pursuing a story, ask yourself why your public needs to know about this story. "What would serve the public interest right now? And that's not to be confused with what the public finds interesting."[11] A criticism of journalism in recent years is that the focus has been on catering to audience wants and desires, rather than audience needs.[17] This has led to the temptation to use clickbait headlines and prioritize pop culture or frivolous stories over stories that impact audiences. This devalues the journalism that helps communities understand what's happening and make decisions about how to address it.

We see this in headlines used to entice audiences to click. For example, a June 2, 2020, headline reading "Buildings Matter, Too"[18] prompted 44 journalists of color at *The Philadelphia Inquirer* to walk out. They wrote an open letter criticizing the paper for co-opting the phrase "Black Lives Matter" to compare damage to buildings in the unrest following George Floyd's death to the loss of actual human lives. The employees' actions prompted the paper to issue an apology.

A headline changes the *way* people read an article and the *way* they remember it.[20] "The headline frames the rest of the experience," wrote *New Yorker* contributor Maria Konnikova. "A headline can tell you what kind of article you're about to read (and) sets the tone for what follows."[19] Konnikova continued:

> Just as people can manage the impression that they make through their choice of attire, so too, can the crafting of the headline subtly shift the perception of the text that follows. By drawing attention to certain details or facts, a headline can affect what existing knowledge is activated in your head. By its choice of phrasing, a headline can influence your mindset as you read so that you later recall details that coincide with what you were expecting.[19]

For example, a study found that a misleading headline in a fact-based article compromised the reader's ability to recall details from the article, and a misleading headline in an opinion piece affected the reader's ability to reason and infer the larger context.[20] Also keep in mind that many people never get past the headline when scrolling through posts on social media. This drives home the importance of ensuring that your headlines are written with precise language that accurately represents your story.

"Think about the public interest, but (don't) get preoccupied or veer too far in the direction of trying to cater to audience interests, in part because audiences are often interested in what they know they're interested in,"[11] said Varma. Instead, help audiences see what is interesting, relevant, and important.

"Represent what are people going through and what are the gaps," Varma said. "Coronavirus is a great example where we are all living a very interrelated fate." Journalists can help audiences understand why the story is relevant to them and how it affects them. This may start with,

> here's where we are with cases right now, and if what we need is everybody to mask up in order to be able to get back to life as we knew it, then

what are the stories we need? Maybe there's a story about how masks help. Maybe there's a story about what impact they may have and why you would be wearing one. How to get masks. All of those questions are different than getting in the muck of, are masks infringing on my freedom.[11]

If journalists do not do this work of identifying what's in the public interest via investigation and consultation with relevant experts, and then helping contextualize and build understanding among their publics, then people will fail to see the value in journalism. Varma sees this as journalists giving away their position of helping the public ascertain what is newsworthy.

If you're just covering trending topics on Twitter, then why do I need a journalist? I can just see the trending topics on Twitter. So, I think the unique opportunity journalists have is to think about the public interest.[11]

Varma offered one more example of how your writing can affect people – gun violence in Chicago. In *Chapter 6*, we noted a study that found homicide victims in predominantly white neighborhoods received more coverage and more humane coverage than homicide victims in Black neighborhoods.[21] Varma spent time reading about the shootings, the history of gun violence in the area, and how children have been affected. She said she felt both devastated by the situation and concerned about the coverage.

What I didn't have by the end of spending quite a lot of time with that coverage was an understanding of why this violence is happening and who is responsible. And, of course, Chicago is not the only city affected by severe gun violence. Detroit, New Orleans, St. Louis, Pittsburgh, Pennsylvania, where I'm from. So, it's clearly not an isolated issue. And yet, after a solid 90 minutes of trying to find an explanation in news outlets, I really couldn't …. It seems quite shocking to me that there'd be this much coverage and not an answer to that "why" question, which I think often gets lost. And that's where journalists can really serve a need that is not necessarily filled right now.[11]

Karen Yin, founder of the Conscious Style Guide, said providing context is extremely important. Otherwise, people will fill in the blanks using their implicit and explicit biases. "Citing incarceration statistics to demonstrate racial inequality can, instead, reinforce racist beliefs when presuppositions aren't aligned," said Yin. "It's important to practice zooming out from your close perspective to consider the impact or takeaway for readers with different worldviews."[22]

HOW do we speak the language of the communities we cover?

There are many things we can do to bring context and equity to the writing, editing, and producing process, including avoiding use of the passive voice, being specific and precise, and interrogating our use of demographic identifiers when describing story subjects, including suspects and victims. If you are using race or ethnicity to identify one person involved in the story, then why are you not including the race or ethnicity of everyone involved in the story?

One basic thing you can do is be intentional about when you do and do not use racial, ethnic, and gender identifiers. For example, many news outlets no longer use race as the only identifier of a suspect.

"Simply identifying a person as Black is not actually providing any identifying information about them, if you're trying to find them," said NPR's Chief Diversity Officer Keith Woods.

> Why are we still today having to convince journalists, young and experienced, that saying somebody is Hispanic does not physically describe them? But, every day, some police reporter somewhere is going to report that police are looking for a Hispanic male, 5'9", 175 pounds, as though that conjures up an actual image in someone's mind.[23]

New York Times National Editor Marc Lacey wrote for Nieman Reports that "white is the norm"[24] in the US, and thus tends to not be explicitly mentioned in coverage.

> The writer helpfully lets us know when someone or something strays from that norm. The writer points out that the mayor is Black. But the city councilman's race is left unstated two paragraphs later. A neighborhood is described as predominantly Hispanic but another area has no racial identifier at all.[23]

Lacey described this as a blind spot given the fact that the majority of reporters, writers, editors, and other newsroom staff have historically been white.[25] But he acknowledged that things are starting to shift.

> As I read an article in The New York Times the other day about the many potential candidates that Governor Gavin Newsom might choose to replace Kamala Harris as a senator in California …, I knew race was legitimately going to be a factor, and I braced for something to strike me as off. But I couldn't find anything. One reason was because Mr. Newsom's race was acknowledged as a factor: "In fact, political strategists say, the choice will be tricky for Mr. Newsom, a white man who would be replacing a female senator who is Black and of Indian and Jamaican descent in a heavily Democratic state with no ethnic majority and innumerable factions."[26]

Another way to improve inclusion in your writing is to avoid passive voice. As a reminder, passive voice is when we lead with the object of a sentence, rather than the subject.

ACTIVE VOICE: "The police officer tackled the woman."
        S   V   O

PASSIVE VOICE: "The woman was tackled by the police officer."
         O   V   S
– OR –   "The woman was tackled." (by whom?)
         O   V   (no S?)

We want to avoid passive voice in writing anyway because it can weaken a sentence, make sentences more difficult to read, and stymie energy. But it can also obscure, hide, and remove responsibility. Notice in the above example that the second passive sentence does not mention the subject – the actor – at all. Failing to name an actor can lead us to minimize or obscure responsibility.

The reason it is important to avoid passive voice when possible is that readers tend to place emphasis on and assign importance to the beginning of a sentence. If the subject or actor is placed at the beginning using the active construction, then the audience will assign importance to the actor. However, if the sentence begins with the object – the person who received or is affected by the action – then the audience will assign importance to and place emphasis on the object.

Take this example from *The New York Times* on June 20, 2020:

"Just before the city's 7pm curfew went into effect, (protesters) were hit with flash-bang explosions and doused with tear gas."[27]

The question is, by who? Who hit protesters with flash-bang explosions and doused them with tear gas? Though the sentence before mentions that "police officers and National Guard units flooded Lafayette Square,"[26] the passive construction of this sentence obscures their role in and responsibility for the flash-bang explosions and tear gas.

One source of passive voice is news releases, which are often repurposed for use in news. Any news release source will want to place themselves in the best possible light, whether it's a company, nonprofit, or government agency. It is up to the journalist to look at the entire picture. For example, if the news release comes from a law enforcement agency, then that agency, like any organization, will write the news release to both inform *and* present the agency in a positive light. If there is a police shooting, a news release may say:

"A man was injured in an officer-involved shooting as he fled from police."

We must ask ourselves, what exactly is an "officer-involved shooting." It is presumably a shooting that somehow involved an officer. Well, how exactly was the officer involved? The news release should explicitly state that. If it does

160 Inclusive writing & storytelling

not, then it is up to the journalist to ask the question and write the information more precisely and clearly. Another question this sentence brings up is: How did the man and the officers come to interact? What exactly was the man suspected of, if anything? Those are other questions that need answers, so you can tell a more precise and complete story.

An active-voice construction may be written: "An officer shot a man suspected of breaking into multiple vehicles Tuesday night." This construction identifies the subject and places the subject at the beginning of the sentence, identifying more explicitly all parties involved and offering specific information.

As Dana Sitar wrote in an article for Poynter, passive voice can downplay police aggression.[28] Consider this tweet posted by *The New York Times* during the #BLM protests in summer 2020.

Minneapolis: "A photographer was shot in the eye."

Washington, DC: "Protesters struck a journalist with his own microphone."

Louisville: "A reporter was hit by a pepper ball on live television by an officer who appeared to be aiming at her."[29]

This tweet illustrates the minimizing of responsibility when the actor is law enforcement, but highlighting responsibility when the actor is a protester. The Washington, DC, sentence correctly places the protester – the subject/actor – at the beginning of the sentence. It was the protester who struck the journalist with his own mic. However, in the other two sentences – out of Minneapolis and Louisville – it is not immediately clear who the subjects/actors are. We eventually learn in the Louisville sentence that law enforcement is the subject, but the responsible actor is completely missing from the Minneapolis sentence. In both cases, the sentences are written using passive-voice construction, thus minimizing the role of the subject. Active voice would offer a stronger sentence and tell a clearer story. If information is not known, then the reporter needs to explicitly state that.

Now that I've gone over the pitfalls of passive voice, I will acknowledge that it can be used effectively, if you use it deliberately and intentionally toward the goal of providing context. As I say to my students, learn the rules so you know how to break them. For example, in a *Washington Post* article about the January 6, 2021, US Capitol insurrection[30] analyzed by Poynter's Roy Peter Clark, passive voice was effectively balanced with active voice to skillfully call attention to various elements. This can be seen in an opening paragraph:

With poles bearing blue Trump flags, the mob bashed through Capitol doors and windows, forcing their way past police officers unprepared for the onslaught. Lawmakers were evacuated shortly before an armed standoff at the House doors. The woman who was shot by a police officer was rushed to an ambulance, police said, and later died. Canisters of tear gas were fired across the rotunda's white marble floor, and on the steps outside the building, rioters flew Confederate flags.[31]

The active-voice sentences rightly focus attention on "the mob" and "rioters." The passive voice calls attention to other important aspects of this story, including "lawmakers" who "were evacuated," "the woman" who "was shot," and "canisters of tear gas" that "were fired across the rotunda's white marble floor." Each passive sentence was crafted intentionally to draw attention to the first element in the sentence, and the combination of active and passive sentences gives the reader a more nuanced and contextual picture of the event.

To WHOM are we talking?

A good place to start is to ask yourself: Am I writing *about* a given community, or *for* the community? When we write *about*, we run the risk of distancing ourselves and then patronizing, belittling, or marginalizing. When we write *for*, we may be more inclined to write toward understanding, providing context, and seeking to inform.

For example, in 2020, in an effort to ensure that people with intellectual and developmental disabilities were included in communities able to consume news coverage, ProPublica had several of its stories translated into plain language. **Plain language** is "a type of text that uses common words, short sentences, and clear structure to make information more accessible to those with intellectual and developmental disabilities."[32] Of course, writing in this way is also helpful to every reader.

Please read the example in Table 7.1 of ProPublica's original editor's note describing the initiative, which includes both the original explanation and the plain-language version.[31]

Notice that, while the original version is clearly written, the plain language version is more conversational, straightforward, and simple. Each version gets the same information across – nothing is lost in translation.

Becca Monteleone, professor of disability studies at the University of Toledo, did the professional plain-language translations for ProPublica. She told NiemanLab that these translations can give agency to people with disabilities. Without them,

> you can then tell a person with an intellectual disability, "Oh, you don't understand, so I'll make decisions on your behalf." I think that's a really dangerous paradigm to set up. When you write things down in plain language, more people have access to the same information.[31]

These plain-language translations are listed alongside other translations offered on the site, including Spanish and audio.

162 *Inclusive writing & storytelling*

Table 7.1 Plain-language translation of ProPublica editor's note[31]

Original editor's note:	Plain language editor's note:
There's a lot of talk in journalism today about bias, with the assumption being that reporters who believe something can't write about it fairly. Of course, there is some truth to that idea – we would not let our education reporter advocate for school choice, for example. But it's not realistic to believe that journalists are robots without opinions. We have lives and experiences that make our reporting richer, provided we remain vigilant about keeping our opinions out of the stories we publish. The project happened because of Amy's quest to provide a bigger and broader life for her daughter than society told her was possible. Did she come to this project with preconceived notions? Probably, just like the ones we all hold. Did it damage the integrity of her reporting? Just the opposite.	Some people worry that reporters have bias. They think reporters shouldn't write about things they care about. They worry the reporters won't be fair. We think writing fairly is important. But reporters are people. We all have things we care about. We think knowing a lot about the things we care about makes our writing better. We make sure not to write our opinions though. We started writing this story because Amy cares about it. She cares because it affects her family. We don't think caring makes the story less fair. We think caring makes it better.

Though it is recommended that plain-language translations be done by professionals, such as Monteleone, to ensure that they don't come off as patronizing or "infantilizing," the strategies she uses can be employed to help make your writing more accessible in any context.

1. Simplify sentences:
   a. Write using the structure: subject | verb | object
   b. Ex: "The firefighter saved the dog."
           S   V   O
2. Write in the active voice:
   a. YES: Police arrested the shoplifting suspect.
   b. NO: The shoplifting suspect was arrested by police.
3. When writing lists, use bullet points or numbers.
   a. Avoid writing out a list in paragraph form.
4. When new people or elements are introduced in a story, clearly explain who or what they are and what their role is.
5. Avoid unfamiliar words and instead use more commonly known words.
6. Avoid jargon, clichés, or idioms.
   a. If you cannot remove them because they appear in a quote, then clearly explain them.[31]

Sometimes, communities who don't feel heard or addressed in mainstream news coverage will create spaces to share their own content to add to the conversation. For example, the Prison Journalism Project focuses on helping incarcerated people cover news from the perspectives of the incarcerated. The 19th covers stories from the perspectives of women. And Prism covers stories from the perspectives of women of color.

WHEN do we need to be aware of our writing?

While we should always be aware of the phrases and words we use in our writing, the sources from whom and from which we pull quotes and information, and the framing we employ, we must also take stock of our own implicit biases to ensure that we address and counter them (see *Chapter 4*). In addition, we need to critically assess all sources, including official news releases that come into newsrooms from law enforcement, fire, public agencies, PR firms, and other entities.

In the wake of the unrest and protests following the police killing of George Floyd in May 2020, NPR Public Editor Kelly McBride, also senior vice president and chair of the Craig Newmark Center for Ethics and Leadership at Poynter, published an opinion piece that prompted us to take a closer look at a phrase that regularly appears in police news releases and subsequently in news stories – "'unarmed Black man.' In that phrase is the assumption that we have to qualify when a Black man is unarmed and therefore not a threat, as if the natural state of Black men is to be armed and threatening."

"Rooted deep in the collective American psyche is more than armed or unarmed: It's about a false assumption that Black people are more likely to be criminals," McBride wrote. "When a journalist writes or utters the phrase 'unarmed Black man,' she is often honestly trying to quickly convey the key question the audience has: What was the circumstance of the confrontation?"[33]

But McBride breaks down how that logic plays out.

1. Journalist: A white man shot a Black man.
2. Dubious audience member who might dismiss the story: What was the Black man doing that caused the white man to shoot him?
3. Journalist: Well, the Black man didn't have a gun, he posed no deadly threat.
4. Audience: That's important for us to know (because we, (as a white audience) have these hidden biases).
5. Journalist: Right, a white man shot an unarmed Black man.[32]

The assumed audience here is, by default, white. This is the audience who may want reassurance that the Black person in the story was not armed. Audiences of color do not need the same assurance. So, by default, a story written using the phrase "unarmed Black man" is inherently written for a white audience.

What are some other phrases that could be used instead? Innocent? No qualifier at all? Perhaps discuss the specifics of the story? For example, when writing about the 2020 killing of Ahmaud Arbery in Georgia – a Black man who was jogging when three white men began pursuing him, and then one shot and killed him – you might write:

"A man was jogging, and police say three other men began following him in two trucks. The men in the trucks were white and the jogger was Black. Officials believe race played a role in the murder."

Police and community interactions that marginalize or *other* legitimate members of our communities because of how they look, sound, or act can seep into journalism for many reasons, including our own implicit and unconscious biases, lack of time leading to a reliance on standard dominant narratives, and the fact that often the only source we receive is the police news release. Given that any news release is going to represent the perspective of the organization that released it, a news release from a police department is going to use language that sets the department and its officers in the best possible light, while also providing information about a given incident. Some of that language seeps into news writing.

Consider the terms:

"officer-involved shooting"

"unarmed Black man"

"high rate of speed"

Instead of adopting this language, move away from what I call "cop-speak" and rewrite in language we actually use when discussing such stories.

Instead of: "One man was injured in an officer-involved shooting that occurred as police gave chase. They later determined that he was not armed."

Try: "Police shot and injured a man as he ran away from them. The man did not have a weapon."

Instead of: "The vehicle accelerated toward officers at a high rate of speed, prompting them to discharge their weapons."

Try: "Police opened fire on a pickup truck, because they said the driver was speeding toward them."

It's easy when we have limited time to rely on a news release from an official source. Official sources are often assumed to be trusted sources. And, while I will not argue against trusting official sources, I will say that it is always important to be skeptical, ask questions, seek out multiple sources, and verify, verify, verify.

Also at work in our writing is framing. As we touched on in *Chapter 6*, words, phrases, media, sources, and other elements create a specific frame – a perspective from which a story is told.[34] The words we use when we craft our stories can affect how those stories are received and contribute to how audiences grapple with the issues and topics presented. We see examples of this in news stories and talk-show discussions all the time. For example, near the beginning of the COVID-19 pandemic, those who were given the frame that masks can help save lives and cut down on virus transmission were far more likely to wear masks than those who were given the frame that masks were an infringement on individual rights and freedoms.

A 2011 study found that simply changing the metaphor used to describe a social issue led readers to perceive the issue very differently.[33] In a series of experiments, researchers presented study participants with a story on increasing crime rates in a city, and then asked them what the solution should be. Crime stories often contain metaphors, such as "spree," "epidemic," "wave," or "plague." In one experiment, some readers read a story framing crime as a virus, using words such as "infecting" and "plaguing," while others read a story framing crime as a beast, using words such as "preying" or "lurking." Otherwise, the stories were similar. Study participants who read the first article overwhelmingly advocated for implementing social reforms, including dealing with poverty and improving education. Those who read the second article instead proposed increased enforcement to arrest and imprison perpetrators.

Even more interestingly, when participants were asked why they made their recommendations, none mentioned the metaphor. Instead, they pointed to crime statistics, which were the same in each article. This indicated that participants were not aware of how the metaphor influenced their reasoning.

It is also important to tell a story in context, including historical context. In 2020, as more white people in the US began to support the Black Lives Matter movement, coverage focused on white people waking up. Prism copy editor and reporter Carolyn Copeland said the language centered white people, rather than the people most affected, the Black community.

> What those articles failed to mention is that people of color have been advocating for these things for years. Those problems were not new, but much of the coverage centered on the changes white people were making and giving them kudos for something that should have been done years ago when people of color were advocating for it.[35]

Images also frame, and they can be such powerful framing devices that the Bush Administration in 2003 sought to prevent the release of images of soldier caskets from the Afghanistan and Iraq wars.[35] It made this decision because similar images are believed to have contributed to a lack of support among many Americans for the Vietnam War. The hope was that by removing these images from the public eye, the Administration could minimize opposition among the public. It took a **Freedom of Information Act (FOIA)** request – which allows journalists and other citizens to access certain federal government information – and years of follow-up to finally get the images released.[36]

166 Inclusive writing & storytelling

More recently, Sarah Elizabeth Lewis, associate professor of History at Harvard University, wrote an op-ed for *The New York Times* positing that because we don't see many images of people affected by COVID-19, it's harder for us to comprehend the gravity of the situation. "In times of crisis, stark images of sacrifice or consequence have often moved masses to act," Lewis wrote. "It is much harder to picture tragedy of the kind we are now witnessing than it is to visualize one person in pain, or an image that connects with a familiar aspect of the human condition."[37]

As a counter to this, it is important to be aware that the news media is more likely to show upsetting images involving people of color or immigrants than white people or people of the mainstream societal group. For example, the image of a father and daughter who drowned along the US-Mexico border; the image of George Floyd losing his life while pinned under an officer's knee; and the image of the Kurdish Syrian child who drowned while trying to cross with his family from Turkey to Greece in a small boat. Sometimes, these images are shown over and over again without any content warnings. This can lead to racial trauma among people of color as they are re-traumatized over and over again by the images depicted in news coverage.[38] **Racial trauma** is "similar to post-traumatic stress disorder" but "involves ongoing individual and collective injuries due to exposure and re-exposure to race-based stress."[39]

While I do support the goal of publishing images that are newsworthy and may also be upsetting to help those who are unaware face the reality of a situation, it may lead to trauma and harm for those who are not only already aware of a situation but are harmed by it. We can take steps to alleviate harm by adding content advisories, placing upsetting visuals a click or two from the main story, avoiding use of these images as the social media visual or thumbnail, ensuring we are choosing visuals for their newsworthiness and contribution to telling the story, and treating visuals depicting those from the in-group in the same way we treat visuals depicting people from out-groups.

EXERCISE BREAK

1. Search for images and graphics of the COVID-19 pandemic that are used in news coverage.
    a. (NOTE: If this exercise will be triggering for you, ask your professor for an alternate topic, either current or historical.)
2. Answer the following questions:
    a. What images were the most common?
    b. What narratives do you glean from just the images you found?
    c. What images and visuals are missing from the story that would add context?
    d. Why do you think these images should be part of the coverage?
    e. When someone looks back 100 or 500 years from now, what will they assume about this moment in time just by seeing the photos used in news coverage?

We can also address issues of inclusion and community in our corrections. To be clear, you will likely need to make a correction (or two or ten) in your career. Of course, you will do your journalistic due diligence, but we are human and mistakes happen. One marker of a quality journalistic outlet is that it owns and corrects its mistakes in a public way.

Many corrections posted by news outlets include corrections to minor errors of fact, such as a misspelling, incorrect date, and the like. It is important to correct the record on these facts, to ensure accuracy, precision, and clarity. But there are larger errors that may be more difficult to address. Nevertheless, these errors must also be dealt with in a public way.

Take for example *The New York Times Caliphate* podcast, a Pulitzer Prize finalist about an Islamic State (IS) terror group that ended up containing foundational factual errors. In several episodes of the 12-episode series released in 2018, reporter Rukmini Callimachi shared information from a source who said he'd been an IS member and participated in killings in Syria. Soon after the publication of the series, the Canadian Broadcasting Corporation (CBC) interviewed the source, who told the CBC he had lied about taking part in killings. US intelligence officials had also questioned the version of events presented in the podcast. The source was later arrested in Canada on terrorism hoax charges.

Under these circumstances, the responsibility of *The New York Times* is to issue a correction in a very public way, pull the fabricated story, and correct its reporting. But it was not until the *Times* completed its own investigation that it issued a correction as an editor's note,[40] followed a few months later by stories about its investigation and the other external investigations. The magnitude of the correction was the right thing to do. But the *Times* has faced criticism for dragging its feet and not issuing its correction earlier.[41] Indeed, *Caliphate* first began airing in April 2018, and by May of that year the man had admitted to the CBC that he lied, and by September he faced charges. Couple that with the fact that US intelligence officials also expressed concern about the story as reported soon after its release, and one would expect a correction fairly soon. However, the *Times* correction did not come until after the arrest; The editor's note was published on September 20, 2018 – five months after the story aired, and four months after the CBC article.

In January 2021, NBC moved more quickly to make a substantive correction, acknowledging that a story about a Biden appointee making a large donation to a controversial organization "fell short of our reporting standards," because of the lack of on-the-record sources and failure to present other relevant perspectives.[42] Though this type of correction may be embarrassing, publicly correcting mistakes sets reputable news outlets apart from other content providers by offering transparency and accountability to audiences.

WHERE can you turn to improve these skills?

Speaking to all communities means consistently being aware of the language you use; words you choose (and don't choose); tone and inflection; and video, graphics, and images you incorporate into the story. It also means, as discussed in *Chapter 6*, that you need to constantly be learning, seeking out information, and adding to your writing repertoire. In addition, if you make a mistake, own it. Make a correction, apologize, and then do better.

Thankfully, there are many resources available to support you as you seek to become more inclusive in your writing.

For example, in the wake of stories about Anti-Asian violence in the US, the Asian American Journalists Association (AAJA) published several resources to help reporters more inclusively cover these stories, including pronouncers of victims' names, guides for covering Asia and Asian Americans, and a database of Asian experts and journalists to be used as sources. These resources provided a direct and accessible way for all journalists to contextualize their coverage.

Cristi Hegranes, CEO of Global Press and publisher of *Global Press Journal*, wrote that writers too often use vague terms or euphemisms, as we discussed earlier, which gives readers, listeners, and viewers permission to avoid complexity and understanding. We often turn to vagaries when we ourselves are uncomfortable and lack knowledge. Hegranes wrote that this is "a consequence of the lack of diversity in newsrooms," and many journalists have "a genuine unfamiliarity and therefore discomfort with word choice related to race and diverse identities." Vague terms allow us to "write around touchy subjects. We avoid precision and eschew context. But imprecise words send a message to audiences that they don't need to understand the nuances of complicated issues."[43]

One example she uses in her Poynter article is the word "ethnic."

> "Ethnic tensions flared in Minneapolis again today," is a real sentence published by a major news outlet in the United States recently. "Ethnic tensions are common in the border regions of Democratic Republic of Congo," is too.
>
> In the first case, you may be more familiar with the context in which the phrase is used. In the second, you likely are not. In both cases, the subtext of the sentence is clear – this story is about race. It's complicated. But the details aren't important for you to understand.[42]

Instead of using words such as ethnic, which can be too general for many contexts, use specific language. How might you rewrite the sentence: "ethnic tensions flared in Minneapolis again today" – presumably about protests in the wake of the police killing of George Floyd? A more specific sentence might be:

> "Demonstrators filled the streets of downtown Minneapolis again today, as Black community members demanded that the officer who killed George

Floyd on camera be brought to justice and that the city take concrete steps to address what demonstrators say is longstanding mistreatment of Black Minneapolis residents at the hands of law enforcement."

This sentence gives specific information about *who* the protesters are and *why* they are protesting. It also centers them and acknowledges their humanity and inclusion in the community.

What about the sentence: "Ethnic tensions are common in the border regions of Democratic Republic of Congo?" In this case, the word "ethnic" vaguely describes an entirely different group of people in an entirely different region of the world. But a reader, listener, or viewer would come away with no understanding of the specific situation being referenced. This does a disservice to our audiences, the subjects we are covering, and the situation unfolding in the Democratic Republic of Congo. Instead, consider this more specific sentence:

> "16 people have been killed in a militia raid on a village in Northeastern Democratic Republic of Congo, and the United Nations says this and other killings may be crimes against humanity."

This sentence leads with specific information; the people affected are centered; and groups are named, rather than called a general term, like "ethnic."

Conscious style guide

The word choice and language we use to describe and explain carry with them our biases and the frames we bring to a story. As a journalist, it's important to be aware of the power and framing of the words, phrases, and visuals you use – whether they inform, explain, and contextualize or whether they mislead, marginalize, *other*, and exclude.

Karen Yin thinks deeply about the power of language to set the tone and direction of our thinking, and how content and context are intertwined. She created the Conscious Style Guide to help educate writers and raise awareness.

"Conscious language refers to language rooted in critical thinking and compassion, used skillfully in a specific context," Yin said.

Many people confuse conscious language with politically correct language. The approaches and values are entirely different: Whereas PC language is based on fear and adherence to an ill-defined set of rules, conscious language seeks to liberate and illuminate through mindful framing, representation, and terminology.[21]

Yin works to help people understand the nuances inherent in

This is not to say that "ethnic" has no place. Ethnicity plays a role in the tensions and violence in both cases. You do not have to avoid the word "ethnic" – but you do need to get specific, so that you help your audience learn, understand, and grapple with the news and information you are providing. If you find yourself uncomfortable doing this, then explore why and address your discomfort (see *Chapter 4*), so you can better cover the communities and stories on your beat.

Global Press offers a three-point style guide to help journalists move from vague generalizations to precise descriptions.

1. Avoid words that lead readers to make assumptions.
   a. Ex: "Developing Nation" has become shorthand for a place where people of color live in poverty. But the myriad of nations described this way are very different from each other, and the basic short-hand assumption readers make does not come close to telling the full story.
   b. Instead, specifically describe the aspects of the story. Whether it's about vaccine distribution, crop yields, weather, or some other topic, start there. As Hegranes wrote, "Avoid the temptation to dump the majority of the world's population into one giant bucket."[42]
2. Precise, accurate descriptions offer dignity.
   a. Again, set aside vague terms such as "terrorist"

language and the differences between PC language and inclusive language.

Sometimes inclusive language is conscious language, but conscious language and inclusive language are not the same. When all-inclusive language is your goal or default despite ever-changing contexts, it can and will erase the most marginalized. That's why sometimes *exclusive* language is conscious language. For example, saying "Black lives matter" centers Black communities and their experiences, whereas the all-inclusive "all lives matter" oppresses those subsumed by the so-called dominant culture.[21]

The Conscious Style Guide website provides articles and links to resources that can help us be more aware – or conscious – of the influence of the words, phrases, and descriptors we use in our writing. Resources include links to all types of topic-specific style and reporting guides, organized by ethnicity, race, ability and plain language, age, appearance, empowerment, gender and sexuality, health, socioeconomic status, and religion and spirituality.

For example, you can find links to style and reporting guides created by the Native American Journalists Association (NAJA), GLAAD, the Trans Journalists Association, the Center for Disability Rights; the National Association of Black Journalists (NABJ), the Refugee Reporting Guide, and many others.

or "rebel", which prompt audiences to make assumptions, and instead offer precise and accurate descriptions in your coverage. Better yet, go to the source, and let the people centered in the story describe and explain. You do not have to lose control of the narrative. But, by including all voices, you are providing context, not endorsing.

3. Discuss people as people, not labels.
    a. Often, journalists opt for short-hand words, but these words often come with assumptions or generalizations that obscure important context that the public may need to be aware of. Examples include: voters, immigrants, people of color, etc. As discussed in *Chapter 6*, this can reduce people to one specific thing, which means audiences may not recognize or acknowledge the entire humanity of the subject. It is up to us to make sure we acknowledge the humanity of our subjects and sources, if we want our audiences to do so.
    b. To address this, describe the action, the moment, or specific incident, rather than assigning it to the person. Instead of writing, "she is a cancer survivor," write, "she went through six months of chemo and two surgeries, after being diagnosed with breast cancer two years ago." This shift allows us to identify

"Conscious Style Guide's resources tend to be guidelines created by groups serving marginalized communities, including journalists' organizations," said Yin. "The articles tend to be more current, presenting salient points of view that help writers and editors make their own style decisions."[21]

The website (consciousstyleguide.com) even offers a section on making conscious choices when it comes to design and imagery.

A monthly newsletter provides a roundup of debates and developments in the conscious language space.

Other resources to help guide your writing include:

- **Resolve Philly's Reframe Guide** (https://reframe.resolvephilly.org/covid-19/framing/): Helps journalists better understand the news habits of audiences with the goal of reframing COVID-19 stories.
- **Writing with Color** (https://writingwithcolor.tumblr.com/): Provides resources focused on racial, ethnic, and religious diversity.
- **Diversity Style Guide** (https://www.diversitystyleguide.com/about/): Provides precise definitions of various terms to help journalists sensitively cover multi-cultural topics that they may not be familiar with or have experience with.
- **Red/Blue Dictionary** (https://redbluedictionary.org/): Provides multiple definitions for various terms based on political leaning.

the subject as a human who happened to have dealt with cancer, rather than as a label – cancer survivor. (If the subject wants to be called a cancer survivor, let them identify themselves that way.)

- **Citizen's Agenda** (https://www.thecitizensagenda.org/): Helps journalists cover elections, campaigns, and political issues in a way that is more helpful for voters.

Above all, be intentional about the words and visuals you use to communicate. Jay Rosen, professor of journalism at New York University and editor of PressThink, wrote during the Trump Administration, "you cannot keep from getting swept up in Trump's agenda without a firm grasp on your own."[44] His point remains

Resources such as these can help journalists covering political stories decipher what a given source may mean, understand how various audiences may understand the same terms and phrases differently, and recognize when terminology may cause undue harm.

relevant – whatever you are covering, you must understand why you're covering it and what your journalistic goals are. What do you hope to convey? How do you want your audience to respond? In the case of covering politics, social issues, and other major stories, many mainstream news outlets have fallen into a pattern of presenting "both sides," no matter how legitimate or illegitimate a given side may be. In addition, not every story has two sides. Some – most – have many sides and perspectives. Where do you, the journalist, fall in all of this? I argue that you are there to inform, and this means providing context about the various sides and perspectives – not just parroting the responses of those who have an opinion. Jay Rosen, PressThink, and Hearken call this a **citizen's agenda** – centering the citizen who needs to be informed to make decisions about the health of their community and society.[45]

Rosen gives the example of CNN's Jake Tapper, who in 2016 responded to an accusation Donald Trump made that Ted Cruz's father was involved in the John F. Kennedy assassination.

> There is no corroborated evidence that Ted Cruz's father ever met Lee Harvey Oswald, or, for that matter, any other presidential assassin. We in the media don't talk about it because there's no evidence of it. In fact, there is contrary evidence. Well before the picture was taken, Rafael Cruz's sister was brutally beaten by Castro forces and Rafael Cruz had denounced the regime. So, any suggestion that Cruz's father played a role in the Kennedy assassination is ridiculous and, frankly, shameful. Now, that's not an anti-Trump position or a pro-Cruz position. It's a pro-truth position.[46]

How do you interpret Tapper's words? While some said Tapper was being pro-Cruz and anti-Trump, in reality, Tapper was being pro-truth.[31] He was fact checking a statement made by a presidential candidate. The fact that the fact check involved another presidential candidate does not make Tapper pro- or anti- any candidate. It simply means that he was doing his journalistic due diligence in ensuring his viewers knew the facts related to an issue being talked about in the media.

Key takeaways

- Writing for the community involves centering the subjects of your stories, to ensure that you are covering them accurately and fairly.
- Centering the community does not mean pandering. Be sure you are providing journalistic value by informing and contextualizing, so that audiences can better understand issues and events and take part in addressing challenges.
- Consider whether you are speaking *about* or *to* the subjects in your story. And, imagine to whom you are speaking, so you can intentionally make adjustments, if need be.
- When we fail to speak the language of the communities we cover, we run the risk of contributing to their lack of voice and agency, and to perpetuating stereotypes that can lead to marginalization, disenfranchisement, *othering*, and harm.

Discussion questions

1. Choose a news article from the past two weeks. Read and identify words and phrases that convey a specific frame – whether or not it is a frame you agree with. What are the implications of using these frames in this particular story?
2. Read the original and plain language versions of the content on page 162. Discuss how the plain language text differs from the original text, as well as whether or not you believe it conveys the same information. Which is easier to consume? Why?
3. What assumptions do you make when you hear the phrase "developing nation," as mentioned in the chapter? What about the phrase "racial tensions" or "ethnic tensions?" Or perhaps you notice a phrase used in news that you think allows for imprecise and vague coverage that lacks context or precision. Discuss how phrases can lead to assumptions and stereotypes, as well as strategies you can use to avoid this in your own writing.

Exercises

1. Each of the following sentences contains one or more issues covered in this chapter. Rewrite the following leads so that they are precise, and so that generalizations are dealt with:
   a. "A 12-year-old has accused a beloved track coach of sexual misconduct after authorities say he engaged in a non-consensual relationship with the underaged-woman."

b. "Ethnic tensions flared up along the India-Pakistan border over the weekend, leading to skirmishes along the disputed stretch of land."
c. "An unarmed Black man was injured in an officer-involved shooting on Wednesday night, when police say he failed to stop when they tried to detain him."
d. "The victim claimed that a city council member stole their earnings from a fundraiser, but the city councilman said he was never anywhere near the money."
e. "Police describe the suspect as a Hispanic Male in his 20s or 30s."
f. "Taxpayers are frustrated with a new process for filing taxes each year, which requires anyone filing a tax return to do so electronically."

2. Explore a resource or article on the Conscious Style Guide website, and answer the following questions:
   a. Which resource or article did you choose?
   b. What were three primary takeaways from the resource?
   c. How can you apply this resource to your journalistic writing?

3. Using Anita Varma's example of shootings in Chicago on page 157 as your guide, choose a topic or issue that you care about and that is covered in the news. Research at least five stories written about this topic or issue. Answer:
   a. What did you learn from the stories about the context or history underpinning this story?
   b. What was missing?
   c. What do you understand better?
   d. What do you still not understand?
   e. Were any vague or imprecise terms used? If so, what were they? How would you make the content more precise?
   f. Given your experience, what story would you write or produce? From what perspective would you approach this story? Whose voice(s) would you include? Why? What voices might you exclude? Why?

4. You have been assigned to cover a story in which two children (aged 8 and 11) and the family dog were killed when the children's father crashed their car into a guard rail on the freeway. A third child (aged 5) and the father were injured. The mom was not in the vehicle at the time of the crash. The father failed a drunk driving test, and toxicology reports came back over the legal limit.

The mom's statement to police included:
"He just lost his own mother to COVID-19, and they were very close."

"I don't even know how to process what's happened. I feel like my life is over, but my baby still needs me."

The news release from the local police department also stated: "The vehicle was going at a high rate of speed, when it came in contact with the right-hand guard rail."

"No other vehicles were involved in the solo collision."

"Officers responded to find two people deceased. Two others were transported to the hospital, where they are in serious condition."

"The suspect has been charged with two counts of vehicular manslaughter, one count each of endangerment, destruction of property, and DUI. He will be taken into custody once he is released from the hospital."

Write an inverted pyramid story that incorporates lessons learned in this chapter to acknowledge the humanity of everyone caught up in this story while also incorporating the imperative to hold someone accountable for wrongdoing. Avoid cop-speak! Feel free to come up with your own names for the people involved in the story.

Notes

1. "About Time - Time Magazine." Accessed February 25, 2021. https://subs.time.com/about-time.
2. Nyenswah, Tolbert. "Africa Has a COVID-19 Time Bomb to Defuse." *World Economic Forum*, April 6, 2020. https://www.weforum.org/agenda/2020/04/africa-covid-19-time-bomb-defuse/.
3. "COVID-19 Map." Johns Hopkins Coronavirus Resource Center, February 26, 2021. https://coronavirus.jhu.edu/map.html.
4. "Coronavirus -- Home." allAfrica.com, February 26, 2021. https://allafrica.com/coronavirus/#covid19-map.
5. Soy, Anne. "Africa v Coronavirus: A Challenge for the Continent." *BBC*, March 14, 2020. https://www.bbc.com/news/world-africa-51873514.
6. Attiah, Karen. "Opinion | Africa Has Defied the Covid-19 Nightmare Scenarios. We Shouldn't Be Surprised." *The Washington Post*, September 22, 2020. https://www.washingtonpost.com/opinions/2020/09/22/africa-has-defied-covid-19-nightmare-scenarios-we-shouldnt-be-surprised/.
7. Dillon, Connor, Sam Baker, and Gabriel Borrud. "You May Have a Better Chance of Surviving Covid-19 If You Have Parasitic Worms." *Deutsche Welle*, March 9, 2020. https://www.dw.com/en/you-may-have-a-better-chance-of-surviving-covid-19-if-you-have-parasitic-worms/av-54804907.
8. Noah, Trevor. "How Africa Is Leading the World in Corona Response." *The Daily Social Distancing Show*, November 13, 2021. https://www.youtube.com/watch?v=rq29fhtwfC0.
9. Baleria, Gina. "The Tales of Two Pandemics: with Dr. Nancy Bristow." *PRX*, May 15, 2020. https://beta.prx.org/stories/321092.
10. North, Lili, and Mindaugas Balčiauskas. "15 Headlines Show How Differently the British Press Treat Meghan MARKLE Vs Kate Middleton," Bored Panda, 2020. https://www.boredpanda.com/uk-media-double-standarts-royal-meghan-markle-kate-middleton/.
11. Anita, Varma, "Ethically Navigating Major Ongoing News Stories," interview by Gina Baleria, *News in Context* (podcast), July 2020. https://exchange.prx.org/pieces/329891

-dr-anita-varma-on-ethically-navigating-major-ongo and https://exchange.prx.org/pieces/330668-ethically-covering-major-ongoing-stories-w-dr-ani.

12 "Riot." Merriam-Webster. Accessed February 15, 2021. https://www.merriam-webster.com/dictionary/riot.

13 "Riot." Cambridge Dictionary. Accessed February 23, 2021. https://dictionary.cambridge.org/dictionary/english/riot.

14 "Massacre." Merriam-Webster. Accessed February 15, 2021. https://www.merriam-webster.com/dictionary/massacre.

15 Welliver, Sarah. "A Journalist's Guide on What to Write - and What Not to - When Covering Child Abuse." *Poynter*, February 4, 2020. https://www.poynter.org/ethics-trust/2020/a-journalists-guide-on-what-to-write-and-what-not-to-when-covering-child-abuse/.

16 Lucine, Blue. "'Asking for It': Survivor Recounts the Day She Was Raped and Her Fight for Justice – Video." *The Guardian*. Guardian News and Media, January 30, 2021. https://www.theguardian.com/society/video/2021/jan/31/asking-for-it-survivor-recounts-the-day-she-was-raped-and-her-fight-for-justice-video.

17 Kennedy, Dan. "How the Media Blew the 2016 Campaign." *U.S. News & World Report*, November 6, 2016. https://www.usnews.com/news/politics/articles/2016-11-06/how-the-media-blew-the-2016-campaign.

18 Brown, Lee. "Philadelphia Inquirer Journalists Walk out over 'Buildings Matter, Too' Headline." *New York Post*, June 4, 2020. https://nypost.com/2020/06/04/philadelphia-inquirer-journalists-walk-out-over-deeply-offensive-headline/.

19 Konnikova, Maria. "How Headlines Change the Way We Think." *The New Yorker*, December 17, 2014. https://www.newyorker.com/science/maria-konnikova/headlines-change-way-think.

20 Ecker, Ullrich K., Stephan Lewandowsky, Ee Pin Chang, and Rekha Pillai. "The Effects of Subtle Misinformation in News Headlines." *Journal of Experimental Psychology: Applied* 20, no. 4 (2014): 323–35. doi: 10.1037/xap0000028.

21 White, Kailey, Forrest Stuart, and Shannon L. Morrissey. "Whose Lives Matter? Race, Space, and the Devaluation of Homicide Victims in Minority Communities." *Sociology of Race and Ethnicity*, September 17, 2020. https://doi.org/10.1177/2332649220948184

22 Karen Yin (founder of the *Conscious Style Guide*), in conversation with Gina Baleria, January 2020.

23 Keith Woods (Chief Diversity Officer at NPR), in conversation with Gina Baleria, December 2020.

24 Lacey @marclacey, Marc. "Journalists Need to Remember that not All News Readers Are White." *Nieman Reports*, November 2, 2020. https://niemanreports.org/articles/journalists-need-to-remember-that-not-all-readers-are-white/.

25 Thurman, Neil, Alessio Cornia, and Jessica Kunert. Rep. *Journalists in the UK*, 4. Oxford, UK: Reuters Institute for the Study of Journalism, 2016.

26 Hubler, Shawn. "Who Would Replace Kamala Harris in the Senate for California? Let the Jockeying Begin." *The New York Times*, August 13, 2020. https://www.nytimes.com/2020/08/13/us/california-senate-kamala-harris.html.

27 Rogers, Katie. "Protesters Dispersed with Tear Gas so Trump Could Pose at Church." *The New York Times*, June 2, 2020. https://www.nytimes.com/2020/06/01/us/politics/trump-st-johns-church-bible.html?action=click&module=Well&pgtype=Homepage§ion=Politics.

28 Sitar, Dana. "The New York Times Was Accused of Siding with Police Because of Ill-Placed Passive Voice." *Poynter*, June 2, 2020. https://www.poynter.org/ethics-trust/2020/new-york-times-tweet-passive-voice/.

29 "A Reporter's Cry on Live TV: 'I'm Getting Shot! I'm Getting Shot!'" Twitter. *The New York Times*, May 30, 2020. https://twitter.com/nytimes/status/1266935666274906113.

Inclusive writing & storytelling 177

30 Tan, Rebecca, Peter Jamison, John Woodrow Cox, Meagan Flynn, and Carol D. Leonnig. "Trump Supporters Storm U.S. Capitol, with One Woman Killed and Tear Gas Fired." *The Washington Post*, January 6, 2021. https://www.washingtonpost.com/local/trump-su pporters-storm-capitol-dc/2021/01/06/58afc0b8-504b-11eb-83e3-322644d82356_s tory.html.
31 Clark, Roy Peter. "Telling It like It Is: When Writing News Requires a Distance from Neutrality." *Poynter*, January 13, 2021. https://www.poynter.org/reporting-editing/2021 /telling-it-like-it-is-when-writing-news-requires-distance-from-neutrality/.
32 Scire, Sarah. "ProPublica Experiments with Ultra-Accessible Plain Language in Stories about People with Disabilities." NiemanLab, November 10, 2010. https://www.nie manlab.org/2020/11/propublica-experiments-with-ultra-accessible-plain-language-in -stories-about-disabilities/.
33 McBride, Kelly. "'Unarmed Black Man' Doesn't Mean What You Think It Means." *NPR*, May 21, 2020. https://www.npr.org/sections/publiceditor/2020/05/21/859498255/ unarmed-black-man-doesnt-mean-what-you-think-it-means.
34 Thibodeau, Paul H., and Lera Boroditsky. "Metaphors We Think With: The Role of Metaphor in Reasoning." *PLoS ONE* 6, no. 2 (February 23, 2011). doi: 10.1371/journal .pone.0016782.
35 Carolyn Copeland (Copy Editor & Reporter at Prism), in conversation with Gina Baleria, February 2021.
36 Harden, Blaine, and Dana Milbank. "Photos of Soldiers' Coffins Revive Controversy." *The Washington Post*. WP Company, April 23, 2004. https://www.washingtonpost.com /archive/politics/2004/04/23/photos-of-soldiers-coffins-revive-controversy/70cee7b7 -84b0-4663-84ce-c6afce291073/.
37 Lewis, Sarah Elizabeth. "Where Are the Photos of People Dying of Covid?" *The New York Times*, May 1, 2020. https://www.nytimes.com/2020/05/01/opinion/coronavirus- photography.html.
38 Nasir, Noreen. "Images of Brutality against Black People Spur Racial Trauma." *Associated Press News*, June 29, 2020. https://apnews.com/article/e0f960ecf3b1059a8daa50309be8 d6f1.
39 Comas-Díaz, Lillian, Gordon Nagayama Hall, and Helen A. Neville. "Racial Trauma: Theory, Research, and Healing: Introduction to the Special Issue." *American Psychologist* 74, no. 1 (2019): 1–5. doi: 10.1037/amp0000442.
40 Callimachi, Rukmini. "Prologue: The Mission." *The New York Times*, September 20, 2018. https://www.nytimes.com/2018/09/20/podcasts/caliphate-transcript-prologue-the- mission.html.
41 Snyder, Gabriel. "New York Times Public Editor: Callimachi Is not Jayson Blair, but Questions Remain." *Columbia Journalism Review*, December 18, 2020. https://www.cjr. org/public_editor/new-york-times-public-editor-callimachi-is-not-jayson-blair-but- questions-remain.php.
42 "Foundation Linked to Biden Pick for Cybersecurity Gave $500,000 to Pro-Israel Lobby AIPAC." *NBCNews.com*. NBCUniversal News Group, January 27, 2021. https ://www.nbcnews.com/politics/national-security/foundation-linked-biden-pick-cyber -security-gave-500-000-pro-n1255848.
43 Hegranes, Cristi. "Newsrooms Updates to Style Guide Entries Related to Race Are Heartening, but Far from Comprehensive." *Poynter*, July 2, 2020. https://www.poynter. org/ethics-trust/2020/newsrooms-updates-to-style-guide-entries-related-to-race-are -heartening-but-far-from-comprehensive/.
44 Rosen, Jay. "You Cannot Keep from Getting Swept up in Trump's Agenda without a Firm Grasp on Your Own." *PressThink*, May 27, 2020. https://pressthink.org/2020/05/ you-cannot-keep-from-getting-swept-up-in-trumps-agenda-without-a-firm-grasp-on- your-own/.

45 Rosen, Jay. "Key Steps in the Citizens Agenda Style of Campaign Coverage." *PressThink*, June 12, 2019. https://pressthink.org/2019/06/key-steps-in-the-citizens-agenda-style-of-campaign-coverage/.
46 Tapper, Jake. "Trump Pushes Tabloid Nonsense about Cruz's Father and JFK Assassination." *CNN*. Cable News Network, May 3, 2016. https://www.cnn.com/videos/tv/2016/05/03/trump-falsely-connects-cruzs-father-with-jfk-assasination-lead-tapper-live.cnn.

8 Speaking truth to power
Embracing the journalist's accountability role

> Freedom of information is the freedom that allows you to verify the existence of all the other freedoms.
> – Win Tin, Burmese journalist[1]

On June 2, 2016, then-Republican presidential nominee Donald Trump was giving yet another speech peppered with misstatements and factual inaccuracies. Thus far, the news media had been covering these events with a soft touch – in part because many in the US still had not taken his candidacy seriously, and in part because the speeches were so outlandish that his untruths seemed apparent.[23] However, on June 2, 2016, something changed.

On that date, CNN's *At This Hour* played a clip of Trump denying that he had said Japan should obtain nuclear weapons – a statement anyone could counter by simply searching the internet and finding the video of Trump earlier in 2016 actually saying he thought Japan should get nuclear weapons. It was such an obvious lie on Trump's part that outlets had to this point just let them pass by. But not on June 2. On that date, CNN ran a lower-third or chyron (graphic on the lower third of the screen) that read:

"**Trump:** I never said Japan should have nukes (he did)."[3]

This simple act of adding a fact check – "(he did)"[3] – to the lower-third to contextualize the story and call out a falsehood got a lot of attention, in part because until that point lower-thirds had not been used that way. They had simply provided identifying information of the person, event, or issue. Also, up to that point, cable news channels had often run speeches and soundbites as they were with the lower-third simply providing information about the video on the screen, such as someone's name, title, and summary of what they were discussing. But it became clear that lower-thirds could be used in other ways – including to provide an accountability function for events happening on screen.

Why did CNN decide on that date to approach its use of lower-thirds in a different way? *Washington Post* media reporter Paul Farhi explained that cable news anchors and reporters had been unwilling to talk over Trump (or any candidate) during campaign rallies in 2016. In addition, news anchors had not been in the habit of calling out falsehoods in real time. Thus, the lower-third became the only way to convey real-time information. "The chryon became a real-time vehicle for challenging Trump, a candidate and president who is often untethered to the facts," Farhi wrote. "The chyrons do the heavy work of squaring the record while simultaneously adding some winks and eye rolls in the parentheses."[4] They have become a valuable tool in a political reporting strategy that more regularly includes real-time fact checks.

Other lower-thirds that ran on CNN and other outlets after June 2, 2016 include:

"Trump: 'Voters don't care about seeing tax returns.' Poll: 78% say Donald Trump should release his tax returns." (CNN, September 2016)[3]

"Trump: 'I don't support WikiLeaks' (He loved it in 2016)." (CNN, April 2017)[3]

"Trump: 'For the last 17 years Obamacare has wreaked havoc' (Law signed in 2010)." (MSNBC, July 2017)[3]

"Trump: 'We've done a great job in Puerto Rico' (Most of island still without power)." (MSNBC, October 2017)[3]

Many media analysts pointed to the fact that cable news networks had, to that point, allowed Donald Trump free, uncritical coverage – something that no other candidate, Republican or Democrat, had received. Because his rallies were colorful and entertaining – meaning great for ratings and increased ad revenue – cable news networks often carried them. This was not the case when it came to rallies or campaign events of other candidates. Thus Trump, in essence, received a large amount of free, uncritical publicity. The fact that his rallies were treated as entertaining or at the very least unserious, meant that little fact checking was taking place. In the process, a candidate was becoming more popular with voters who saw that candidate over and over again on cable news without much counter-information.[2] To counter that effect, CNN and then MSNBC tried to reclaim their accountability role. Lower-thirds became an effective way to do that.

Critics, including John Amato, co-founder of Crooks and Liars, wondered why CNN was receiving praise for something it should have been doing all along.[5] Others, such as the *Columbia Journalism Review*'s public editor for CNN, Emily Tamkin, criticized CNN for covering some of the stories and giving them airtime and attention in the first place.[6] These are important perspectives, and we must consider them as we forge a path forward for journalism. But, at the very least, fact checks began happening.

What this story can illuminate for us is just how important it is for the **watchdog** role of journalism – or **accountability journalism** – to remain ever present, and for journalists to engage in accountability journalism whenever possible to hold power accountable and inform the public about any misdeeds they need to be aware of to make informed decisions and solve community problems.

WHAT is watchdog or accountability journalism?

The fact checking seen in the lower-thirds discussed above is one element of accountability journalism, as are investigative reporting and explanatory journalism.

Fact-check journalism involves confirming, often in real time or within a day or so, whether what someone says or writes is factual, misleading, or false. It happens on a granular level – i.e. checking specific facts as they are said or written.
Investigative journalism involves deeply investigating a single topic, issue, or aspect of a topic or issue. Investigative stories may take days, weeks, months, or even years to cover and publish.
Explanatory journalism goes in depth on a topic, issue, aspect of a topic or issue, or ongoing story to provide context and make the information more accessible to the audience.

Accountability journalism is, in essence, holding power to account, shining light on deception and misinformation, and representing the voice of the people. It is marshalling all of your tenacity, curiosity, and empathy skills, and your community engagement sensibilities to dig into stories that serve and inform your audience. In the US, journalism is often called "The Fourth Estate," an unofficial nod to journalism's integral watchdog role in the effective functioning of a democratic government. The three official branches of US government are judicial, legislative, and executive. The goal of watchdog journalism is to prevent or halt abuse of power and "warn citizens about those that are doing them harm."[7]

The public agrees that an accountability role in journalism is important. In a February 2020 Pew Research Center survey, 73% of Americans responded that it is important for journalists to serve as watchdogs.[8]

Another example of watchdog journalism is what Dan Froomkin, accountability writer at *Nieman Reports*, called reporting what's in plain sight, "contrasting that with what officials in government and other positions of power say, rebuffing and rebutting misinformation, and sometimes even taking a position on what the facts suggest is the right solution."[9] For example, reporters held the Biden White House to account in February 2021, after it initially suspended then-White House Deputy Press Secretary TJ Ducklo for one week after he verbally threatened a reporter. This suspension contrasted with Biden's assertion that he would fire staffers "on the spot" for "treat(ing) another colleague with disrespect."[10] Coverage of this incident led within days to Ducklo's resignation.

If a public official tells you something, but you have credible information that contradicts or disproves what's being said, then you report that. This is different than "he said/she said" reporting. Finding a talking head to represent a binary two sides to every issue is not journalism. If your goal as a watchdog is to inform and enlighten your audience, then you must give context and do the work of determining whether what a source says is true. If it's not true, then report that. And, of course, be sure to show your work.

Glenn Kessler, editor and chief writer of the Fact Checker at *The Washington Post*, called this "an entry-level way to do basic accountability journalism."[11]

"The big thing is at the end you make a judgment," Kessler said. "With fact checking, at the end you say, 'alright, we've looked at the facts and here's what the truth is.' You want to make sure you have all the information you need in order to make that judgment."[11]

Though every news story involves some level of fact checking and verification, fact checking as a specific type of journalism has gotten more popular in the past two decades as a complement to the traditional story, and Kessler sees its influence throughout the industry.

"I think that fact checking has actually influenced traditional reporting, particularly in the age of Trump, where people feel much more willing to say, 'actually what the President just said was false,' which is not what you saw before," he said. Traditionally,

> there's the news conference and there's a straight report of what was said at the news conference. And then we would take something that the president said and explain why that was exaggerated or not correct. It was a separate thing. But, increasingly in the age of Trump, in the course of reporting the news conference, they will say, "well this is wrong or that's wrong and this is why."[11]

While Kessler calls fact checking an entry-level way in to accountability journalism, a more advanced form of accountability journalism is investigative reporting.

David E. Kaplan, executive director of the Global Investigative Journalism Network (GIJN), said investigative journalism is "about the accountability of power." He compared it to the role of an accountant. "We're the ones trying to balance the books of power in society. If there's too much red, someone needs to blow the whistle, so people can look at that,"[13] Kaplan explained. "When you have people who have power in a given society, whether it's through political or corporate or social means, are they using that power in a way that is accountable to the public?"[12]

Kaplan said investigative journalism is important at all levels of society and across societies.

> You need a public watchdog, because public officials don't always tell the truth, particularly in societies that don't have guard rails for accountability. This becomes even more important, where government lying becomes a

way of life. I think we (in the US) got a glimpse of what that's like during the Trump administration where public utterances bore no resemblance to reality. Our colleagues in places like Eastern Europe and China looked at this and said, "Welcome to the club. We've lived like this for decades now."[13]

Investigative reporting has come to be associated with crime, corruption, and international intrigue. But Kaplan said it can be useful in many contexts, and that even those in power generally understand its important role.

There's a realization among most officials with a public spirit that you need to have an independent source of information. You need an outside watchdog to check whether your stock market is rigged, and whether your businesses can play on an even playing field. Systematic, in-depth reporting could be on any topic: Is the food you eat in the morning healthy? Are the toys your kids play with safe? Is the medicine you take at night counterfeit? It could be about schools and children and how women are treated in a society, the persecution of minorities and dissidents.[13]

One challenge with practicing accountability journalism is that many journalists may not be assigned to a specific beat. Thus, when they are given a story to cover, they must learn all they can in a short amount of time, find people to interview, and

Fact checking: "The only dumb question is a question not asked"

Glenn Kessler has been incorporating what we now think of as fact checking into reporting long before he became *The Washington Post* fact checker.

In 1996, when he was chief political correspondent at *Newsday*,

> I was very frustrated by the fact that I would write these stories on the campaign trail about what Bill Clinton said or Bob Dole said. I'd quote them and then say, "actually this is not right because XYZ," and that would often get cut for space.[11]

Though checking and verifying facts has always been a part of journalism, Kessler's approach differed in that the fact check was the main point of the story. During the Clinton versus Dole presidential campaign in 1996, Kessler wrote what is widely considered to be the first fact check of this type.

I went to the editors and said,

> "before the first debate, why don't I take all those bits and pieces here, all these things they say on the road – because people are going to hear these lines in the debate – and I will

do their best to pull all the information together into a coherent story. In this context, if they are interviewing a source who is uncooperative or makes false claims, that journalist may not be adequately equipped to challenge such information in real time. By contrast, a journalist who works on a specific beat or at an outlet that focuses on a specific beat or topic area is likely to be well informed about the stories, challenges, issues, and topics related to that beat or topic area. That journalist will be able to respond in real time to misstatements, falsehoods, and misdirection, and thus better able to inform the public.

In addition, newsrooms have been shrinking over the past 20 years, and ever fewer and less experienced journalists are trying to cover and hold accountable entities with more and more resources to deliver their messages directly to audiences. On top of that, veteran journalists have either been pushed out or have left journalism, taking their institutional knowledge with them, and often leaving newer journalists to reinvent the wheel. "Journalists face the prospect of being spun or misled or manipulated almost every day by sources," said Tom Rosenstiel, executive director of the American Press Institute (API) in a *Nieman Reports* article. "We see ... more **clerkism**,"[9] the uncritical acceptance of the official version of events.

The rise of PR-based outlets fronting as local news contributes to the problem of misinformation, disinformation, and information overload, threatening to flood out the voices of those doing accountability journalism.

say whether or not what they're saying is correct."

It was a huge hit. Readers really appreciated it. So then when I joined *The Washington Post* and it was the 2000 campaign, "I said, why don't I do something similar," and I did fact checks during and after each debate. I did that in the 2004 and 2008 campaigns, as well.[11]

Trump's tenure in the White House, which involved tens of thousands of lies and misstatements, led to an explosion in the practice of fact checking. There are now more than 400 fact checking organizations all over the world, including India, Turkey, and all across Africa, Europe, and South America.

The first *Washington Post* Fact Checker was Michael Dobbs,

who returned to freelance between books. Editors noticed that there was still tremendous interest on the web in Michael's old fact checks, because people were googling for information. So, (in 2011) the editors came to me and said, "how about if you revive the fact checker." And they made it a regular feature that covered all politicians.[11]

The foundational purpose of the Fact Checker is to provide context for complex policy discussions.

"The fact checker has always been very much a policy-oriented feature. We use a quote as a jumping off point to explain the intricacies of complex

Another aspect of accountability journalism is the explainer. Explanatory journalism deals with both serious and light-hearted subjects, but at the heart of explanatory stories is a focus on helping the audience understand *why* or *how* something happened, a situation is the way it is, or a decision was made.

While investigative journalism involves revealing information to the public, and fact checking focuses on contextualizing and verifying information as it is said or shared, **explainers** take a longer, more in-depth route to help people make sense of the information that comes at them every day, the stories that fill their feeds, and the issues being debated.

"Explainer journalism specializes in the *why* and *how*, so that the *who*, *what*, *when*, *where* make more sense," wrote Qifan Zhang, staff writer for the NYU News Literacy 2016 Project. "The aim is not just to deliver the latest news but to increase the number of people who understand the story well enough to follow future developments in it."[14]

Whatever you wish to illuminate, the goal is to hold power accountable by providing your audience with the information they need to make choices about their community and society.

WHERE is accountability journalism most valuable?

While accountability journalism is indispensable at all levels – local, regional, state, national, and international – and in all arenas – business and finance, politics and government, civic affairs, education, transportation, health care, etc. – it often plays an outsized role at the local level. Often, it is local investigative stories that get attention

government policy," Kessler said. "You delve deeply into (issues), because politicians speak in shorthand, and what we try to do is demystify what they're talking about and explain it."[11]

But under Trump, Kessler said that changed.

"In the Trump era, it (got) a little unmoored from that, because Trump has never been serious about any kind of policies," said Kessler. "One of the reasons why we started the database, which [consumed] our lives, of every factual misstatement he [made] was so we wouldn't get distracted from the core function of writing policy."[11]

That database of Trump's lies led to a book, *Donald Trump and His Assault on Truth*.

When it comes to advice for young journalists, Kessler said the most important things are asking questions and checking facts. "The people I've hired to work with me – generally, I look for people who have a background in covering state or local government and have gotten used to probing and asking questions of politicians," he said. "Particularly for young journalists, you just can't trust it. You have to double check it yourself."[11]

Kessler encourages all aspiring journalists to jump in and do the work.

"You learn by doing, and you just have to keep digging," he said. "The basic rule of journalism: The only dumb question is the question not asked."[11]

at the national and international level, where they are amplified and further investigated.

For example, the Flint Water Crisis story came to light because of strong local investigative work by Curt Guyette of the ACLU[15] and his source, local pediatrician Dr. Mona Hanna-Attisha.[16,17] After hearing from a water expert friend that water from the Flint River was not being properly treated, Dr. Hanna-Attisha became concerned that it could lead to lead poisoning among the children of Flint. Lead poisoning can lead to long-term cognitive impairments and behavioral issues. She told NPR that she decided to review her patients' medical records and discovered that lead levels in her patients increased after the city switched Flint's water source to the Flint River from the Great Lakes, where the rest of the community was receiving its water. In addition to lead poisoning, bacteria in the water were hurting people's eyes, causing skin rashes, and affecting hair. But, when Dr. Hanna-Attisha tried to bring this issue to light, hospital and government officials sought to discredit her and her data. When Guyette began reporting on the data, his stories caught on nationally, leading to investigations and eventually criminal charges against several public officials.[18] This work spurred other local news outlets and public health officials to examine their own water supplies, leading to related stories about water issues in other parts of the country.

Another example of a local investigative story with national implications is a story about a significant backlog of untested rape kits in Cleveland, which saw the light of day, thanks to tenacious watchdog reporting by *Cleveland Plain Dealer* reporters Rachel Dissell and Leila Atassi. Dissell and Atassi began investigating this story in 2009, in the wake of the capture of a serial rapist and the discovery of several bodies buried in his yard. After hearing from a resident that the investigation of her rape case had stalled again, and it had been three years since the incident had happened, Dissell and Atassi wondered why this delay was occurring and why no one had yet been charged. As journalists on the sexual crimes beat, they were also hearing a familiar story about another woman not being taken seriously or receiving justice – several women shared with Dissell and Atassi that they did not feel investigators were listening to them. The message these women were receiving was that they did not matter. So, Dissell and Atassi went to the Cleveland Police Department and sought access to files pertaining to two rapes. While they were granted access, no one from the department would consent to an interview. Through dogged investigative reporting, the pair discovered that 4,000 rape kits in Cleveland – and 14,000 statewide – had never been tested rape kits that would later reveal serial rapists were on the loose and could have been caught before they assaulted additional victims.[19] This story also reverberated nationally and prompted other communities across the country to demand accountability from their own law enforcement officials.[20,21]

Other local stories that have had national impact include Eric Eyre's piece in the *Charleston Gazette-Mail* uncovering the extent that opioids had flooded his community and nearby counties, leading to a spike in overdose deaths.[22] Eyre, a statehouse reporter, was able to bring this story to light, even though he faced significant opposition from powerful players, including pharmacies and drug distributors who were profiting from over-prescribing, and the West Virginia state attorney general, who reportedly had financial ties to the drug company in question. Eyre's work spurred journalists in other communities to explore the effects of opioid addiction, prompting many communities to begin to reckon with the problem.[23,24]

Each of these stories – and many more – show the power of local investigative journalism, not just in the community in question, but the wider influence these stories can have. Unfortunately, while Guyette still worked for ACLU of Michigan and Atassi worked for Cleveland.com at the time of this writing, the other reporters discussed above no longer work for the paper where they made their mark on their communities through strong investigative journalism.

This is an illustration of the state of local journalism today. Many local news organizations are plagued by financial challenges, exacerbated by decreasing ad revenue and subscription rates as people (and thus advertisers) turn to online content sources; as well as corporate owners siphoning profits to shareholders rather than reinvesting in communities. This has resulted in the loss of talented and experienced journalists at the local level like Eyre and Dissell, but many people, organizations, and outlets are working to find solutions. We'll explore some of these endeavors in *Chapter 10*.

In the meantime, the loss or diminishment of local news outlets means a loss of an important front line in accountability journalism. Studies show that people trust their local news outlets more than they do national news.[25,26] In addition, communities with a strong local news outlet see less corruption among local and regional government officials and business leaders.[27,28] This reinforces the adage that sunlight is the best disinfectant. With independent journalists there to shine a light on the activities of those in power, local publics get informed about activities taking place in their communities and can use their voices to reinforce how they want their tax dollars spent, local officials to behave, and citizen priorities handled.

And, it is not just the loss of local news outlets and their accountability role that is concerning. It is also that these losses provide opportunities for those peddling misinformation and disinformation to fill the void. And indeed, filling the void are syndicated outlets that, instead of focusing on curated, ethical journalism, peddle stories commissioned by PR firms, political operatives, and others with a specific agenda and message. Writing these stories are not local journalists but paid freelance writers from around the country and world who have been given story angles and source lists friendly to one perspective.[29] Thus, instead of receiving journalism, audiences in these areas receive PR content shrouded as news and designed to sway sentiment in a certain direction.

In a *New York Times* article from October 20, 2020, reporters Davey Alba and Jack Nicas detailed the existence of a nationwide operation of 1,300 websites fronting as local news outlets. But these sites are not really covering local news. Sure, there is some coverage of local community happenings, but much of the coverage is geared toward reinforcing the messages of specific clients, who have purchased an article or series of articles and given specific directions on whom should be interviewed and how the article should be focused. The *Times* investigation found that the clients were "conservative think tanks, political operatives, corporate executives, and public-relations professionals ... to promote a Republican candidate or a company, or to smear their rivals."[29]

Though there are other, smaller partisan local sites and networks, the network run by internet entrepreneur Brian Timpone is by far the largest, with more than twice as many outlets as Gannett, the nation's largest newspaper chain.[29] Timpone's operation allows clients and investors to have a say in the content of specific news articles. While other partisan networks are problematic, their investors primarily serve as financiers, not content editors. In addition, the sites under Timpone's umbrella, according to the *Times* investigation, often do not reveal who their funders are or that their content is influenced by funders and clients. Instead, *about* pages usually say their goal is "to provide objective, data-driven information without political bias."[29] However, this is belied by internal emails, such as one from an editor to freelancers in April 2020, in which the editor wrote, "clients want a politically conservative focus on their stories, so avoid writing stories that only focus on a Democrat lawmaker, bill, etc."[29]

This network of partisan and PR-based news outlets purporting to practice journalism is highly problematic. But the fact that we know about it and can try to address it is thanks to strong investigative journalism from *The New York Times*.

WHEN should you engage in accountability journalism?

Accountability journalism – whether fact checking a candidate, investigating an agency, or explaining a budget story – should be infused in your journalistic practice, from idea generation to research to newsgathering to interviewing to writing to communicating with your audience to following up on the story.

Let's start with interviewing. Accountability journalism involves effectively, professionally, and calmly holding people to account during interviews, including politicians who want to answer only with talking points; interviewees who challenge, intimidate, or bluster; and those who turn hostile. This task is made even more challenging by the fact that many public officials, corporate leaders, and others go through media training to learn how to get their message out when talking with the news media, and this training is often led by former journalists. In the process, the effective accountability journalist must seek out and find information that a given source may be unwilling to provide. Axios reporter Jonathan Swan provided an excellent example of accountability journalism in his interview with Donald Trump on August 3, 2020.[30]

Swan's 37-minute sit-down interview with then-President Trump garnered attention and praise because Swan calmly, methodically, and directly held Trump accountable. Swan did this in multiple ways, including asking follow-up, clarifying questions; interjecting to clarify information or correct falsehoods; asserting facts in the face of misleading responses; reframing information away from spin and toward public knowledge and context; and visually responding with facial expressions of skepticism, confusion, and disbelief when Trump's answers warranted such responses.

For example, when Trump claimed that the US was doing better than the world when it came to COVID-19 deaths – which was not true – Swan did not get upset, confrontational, or indignant. Instead, he asked Trump to show him proof. When Trump then began waving papers, Swan reached for and was given one piece of paper with data on it, which he was able to look at and assess.

Trump: (indicating a piece of paper) "Right here, United States is lowest in numerous categories. We're lower than the world."

Swan: "Lower than the world? What does that mean?"

Trump: "We're lower than Europe."

Swan: "In what?"

Trump: (handing Swan a piece of paper) "Take a look."

Swan: "Oh, you're doing death as a proportion of cases. I'm talking about death as a proportion of population. That's where the US is really bad – much worse than South Korea, Germany, etc."[30]

When Trump said, "you can't do that," Swan did not say, "yes, I can." Instead, he responded with a simple follow-up question – "why not?"[30] Trump was unable to adequately explain why he was using death as a proportion of cases, rather than the more widely used and illuminating statistic of death as a percentage of population.

Later, when Trump said, "We have a new phenomenon. It's called mail-in voting," Swan interjected to correct the record, saying, "new? It's been here since the Civil War."[30]

When Trump claimed to have done more for African Americans than any president since Abraham Lincoln, Swan responded with another clarifying question, born from his exhaustive research, this time with a little bit of disbelief. "You really – you believe you did more than Lyndon Johnson, who passed the Civil Rights Act?" When Trump answered, "I think I did, yeah,"[30] Swan again asked a simple follow-up question to ascertain the reasoning behind the untrue assertion.

Also, during the interview, Trump bragged that his crowd in Tulsa was larger than news media reported. Instead of allowing Trump to frame the moment and responding that his crowd figures were incorrect, Swan focused on a frame that had more relevance to the moment – that of a crowd gathering during a deadly pandemic. Swan asked, "Why would you have wanted that? Why would you have wanted a huge crowd?" When Trump went on about crowd size and TV ratings, Swan again reframed away from Trump's spin and toward a frame that was more relevant to the public good, saying, "I think you misunderstand me. I'm not criticizing your ability to draw a crowd ... I'm asking about the public health."[30]

At one point, Trump began talking about COVID-19 testing, and Swan again employed the tenets of accountability journalism, asking simple, clarifying follow-up questions to get to the heart of the information.

Trump: "There are those that say, 'you can test too much.' You do know that."

Swan: "Who says that?"

Trump: "Oh, just read the manuals. Read the books."

Swan: "Manuals? What manuals?"

Trump: "Read the books?"

Swan: "What books?"[30]

Trump does not answer and instead begins talking about testing again. This shows the audience that he does not have specific information about anyone saying "you can test too much." Swan's strong, well-researched, informed accountability journalism approach carried the interview away from tit-for-tat framing and toward the realm of informing the public and holding power to account.

In an interview with MSNBC following his sit-down with Trump, Swan told interviewer Ali Velshi,

> My chief takeaway is that he is not confronting reality when it comes to the virus, and he is reaching for data points that are good for publicity or sound good but are not actually the best metrics for revealing what's going on in this country. I think the big one is testing. He talks about this number – the US has done more tests than anyone in the world. That's true, but it's also not a particularly meaningful thing to say (because US hospitalization rates and deaths were higher than elsewhere in the world). Instead of grappling with that and trying to learn the lessons of what went wrong or acknowledge failure, he is searching for the data points that cast him in the most positive light.[31]

Swan's interview has been held up as a model of strong accountability journalism. He did not allow his interviewee to control the discussion. When his interviewee tried to spin the frame, Swan kept calm but firm as he reframed by asking simple, clarifying follow-up questions.

> **EXERCISE BREAK**
>
> Case study: Watch Jonathan Swan's 37-minute interview with Donald Trump (or a portion of it assigned by your instructor) (https://www.youtube.com/watch?v=zaaTZkqsaxY).
>
> 1. Pause the video and take note of each time Swan holds Trump accountable.
> 2. Describe each exchange and how you see it as holding the interviewee to account.
> 3. Which example do you find most effective? Why?

Another excellent example of accountability journalism is NPR's Mary Louise Kelly in her interview with then-Secretary of State Mike Pompeo. On January 24, 2020, Kelly sat down with Pompeo for an interview on *All Things Considered*, which Pompeo ended early, because when he made assertions that were factually untrue, Kelly fact checked him.[32]

When Kelly asked Pompeo whether he owed an apology to Marie Yovanovitch – whom Trump removed from her post as UN ambassador to Ukraine for being disloyal to him – Pompeo said he had not agreed to discuss this topic. Kelly countered, reminding Pompeo that when she set up the interview, this topic was on the list of questions she planned to ask.

> *Kelly:* "I confirmed with your staff last night that I would talk about Iran and Ukraine."
>
> *Pompeo:* "I just don't have anything else to say about that this morning."
>
> *Kelly:* "I just want to give you another opportunity to answer this, because as you know, people who work for you in your department, people who have resigned from this department under your leadership, saying you should stand up for the diplomats who work here."
>
> *Pompeo:* "I don't know who these unnamed sources are you're referring to. I can tell you this – "
>
> *Kelly:* "These are not unnamed sources. This is your senior advisor Michael McKinley, a career foreign service officer with four decades experience who testified under oath that he resigned, in part, due to the failure of the State Department to offer support to the foreign service employees caught up in the impeachment inquiry on Ukraine."
>
> *Pompeo:* "Yeah, I'm not going to comment on things Mr. McKinley may have said. I'll say only this. I have defended every State Department official. We've built a great team. The team that works here is doing amazing work around the world."

Kelly: "Sir, respectfully, where have you defended Marie Yovanovitch?"

Pompeo: "I've defended every single person on this team. I've done what's right for every single person on this team."

Kelly: "Can you point me toward your remarks where you have defended Marie Yovanovitch?"

Pompeo: "I've said all I'm going to say today. Thank you."[32]

Before Pompeo ended the interview, Kelly also worked to hold him accountable on Iran by asking repeatedly for him to answer how he planned to keep Iran from obtaining nuclear weapons after the US withdrew from the Iran nuclear deal. Each time Pompeo dodged the question, Kelly asked it again, until finally establishing that he was not going to fully answer it.

Kelly's excellent journalistic approach during the interview led to what she described as a heated confrontation off-air soon after the interview concluded. Kelly told NPR's Ari Shapiro:

> He shouted at me for about the same amount of time as the [nine-minute] interview itself had lasted. He was not happy to have been questioned about Ukraine. He asked, "Do you think Americans care about Ukraine?" He used the F-word in that sentence and many others.[32]

Pompeo also asked Kelly – a veteran national security correspondent – whether she could find Ukraine on a map. "I said, yes. He called out for his aides to bring him a map of the world with no writing, no countries marked. I pointed to Ukraine. He put the map away. He said, 'people will hear about this.'"[32]

Kelly also told Shapiro that before Pompeo ended the interview, "he leaned in and glared at me."[32] This is, in essence, a form of intimidation. But Kelly was not intimidated. Instead, she kept her cool and continued to do her job, document the ensuing discussion, and report on it. In this situation, Kelly drew upon the tenets of accountability journalism: keeping calm and firmly asking follow-up questions, as well as coming in prepared with research, names, data, and other information to support her line of questioning and counter any false or misleading information that may be levied by the interviewee.

When it comes to writing, consider which information you are privileging. Are you prioritizing the official point of view, even though it may be factually incorrect? If so, then be sure to include the fact check as high up or as soon in your story as possible, so it can serve as a counter-weight to any official spin and contextualize the information for the public.

To practice accountability journalism, Jennifer Brandel, co-founder and CEO of Hearken, and Jay Rosen from PressThink, wrote, it's important to understand your WHY. Why are you reporting on this story? What do you hope to offer to your audience? What does your audience want and need from your coverage?[33] Defining this can give you clarity and help you frame your coverage in ways that better serve, inform, and enlighten your audiences.

Questions you can ask yourself include:

1. Does your approach to the story fully communicate its context?
2. Does your approach fully communicate the story's urgency?
3. Does your approach fully communicate the story's relevance to the audience?
4. How is your framing *helping* any part of your audience?
5. How is your framing *hurting* any part of your audience?

Overall, you should strive to have an accountability mindset every day. This can help you notice the issues, oddities, situations, and events that may need your attention and prompt you to take a deeper look. As we discussed in *Chapter 2* on curiosity, ask basic questions. Even if you think you're already supposed to know the answer, set your ego aside and ask the questions anyway. That ask may reveal a story that needs investigating – a situation that calls out for accountability.

WHY does accountability journalism matter?

One of the most important roles journalism plays in society is as a watchdog to local, regional, and national governments; corporations and organizations; and other entities that may affect citizens and their communities. For this reason, understanding how to practice accountability journalism is integral to your work.

When I asked GIJN's Kaplan why accountability journalism matters, he was blunt:

> For a society to be just and democratic and to develop for all of its citizens, you've got to have those independent and critical voices asking tough questions about accountability, about whether power in that society is used in an accountable fashion.[12]

We saw in the above examples about the Flint water crisis, the Cleveland rape kits, and the opioid crisis in Charleston that accountability journalism can lead to systemic change and the improvement of lives. Of course, examples exist of when accountability journalism should have been pursued and was not. This failure to dig deeper can lead to significant consequences. For example, in the early 2000s, journalists and news outlets were hesitant to hold the US government accountable for sharing false information about weapons of mass destruction (WMDs) in Iraq. By failing to adequately fact check and report on the falsity of this information, journalists missed a chance to better inform the public and head off a deadly, years-long conflict. The second Iraq War and occupation ended up lasting for eight years and led to the deaths of more than 3,000 US troops, hundreds of coalition force members, and an estimated 650,000 Iraqis.[34]

More recently, a lack of accountability journalism focused on white supremacist and other domestic terror organizations in the US amounted to collectively missing the story or misunderstanding its magnitude. The consequence, in part, was an attack on the US Capitol building on January 6, 2021, that led to the deaths of five people. Though the insurrection was put down, reports released following the attack revealed that if it had been successful, it could have been much worse for those inside the Capitol and for US democracy.

While accountability journalism is always foundational to the healthy functioning of a community and society, in our current global political landscape, it has become ever more important, and also ever more dangerous. Accountability journalists may face negative responses from those in power who don't want their activities brought to light or scrutinized. Negative responses may also come from audience members who have taken a side on a certain issue, or government and business officials who are comfortable in the gray area of ethical behavior. Responses can include caustic opinions, name calling, harassment, threats, intimidation, and even physical harm. For example, Jamal Khashoggi, *Washington Post* columnist, and general manager and editor-in-chief of Al-Arab News Channel, was killed in 2018. A 2021 US Intelligence Report found that his assassination was ordered by Saudi Crown Prince Mohammed bin Salman.[35] The purported reason: bin Salman did not like Khashoggi's critical coverage.

In its annual report on journalists who lost their lives in 2020, Reporters Without Borders (RSF) noted that journalists pursuing investigative, accountability stories – such as local corruption, misuse of public funds, and organized crime – were targeted.[36]

"One of the reasons there are so many attacks on journalists today is that we're asking tougher questions with better tools in more places than ever before," said Kaplan. "Investigative journalists have played a key role in putting the issues of accountability and transparency and abuses of power on the global agenda."[13]

Though the dangers cannot and should not be ignored, there is good that comes from holding power to account through the practice of journalism.

"There is world-class muckraking going on all over the world," said Kaplan.

> In the early days of the COVID-19 pandemic, journalists trying to figure out how many people had actually died were not satisfied with the official numbers they were receiving. In Somalia, they interviewed ambulance drivers, in Nigeria gravediggers, and in China truck drivers (driving trucks) loaded with funeral urns – and they found business was booming.[12]

Journalists also looked at public datasets, including comparing CDC morbidity reports from 2020 to previous years to show that official COVID-19 death counts were not accurate.

HOW do we do accountability journalism well?

As was illustrated in the example above of Mary Louise Kelly's interview with Mike Pompeo, practicing accountability journalism means holding power to account and covering the news without fear or favor, even in the face of intimidation, obfuscation, evasion, and other tactics designed to lead inquirers away from the truth.

To do accountability journalism well, you need to approach your work with a healthy sense of skepticism, an active curiosity, and also a recognition that those you interview are fully formed human beings. I say this because none of us as human beings see ourselves or our actions as inherently evil or bad, and sometimes we are working within systems so entrenched that we often do not realize how they influence our behaviors or actions. For example, policies or economic systems may be rooted in racist approaches that need to be examined and held to account, as well as the people who work uncritically or commit wrongdoing within these systems. But, in the course of your coverage, it's important to remember you are dealing with people who have stories, motivations, and information that need to be understood to help tell your story more fully and completely and perhaps spur systemic change.

Marshall Allen, healthcare reporter for the investigative journalism outlet, ProPublica, wrote in May 2020 about how he approaches stories that may need further investigation or scrutiny, providing a guide of sorts for anyone assessing information. It starts with asking questions generated from critical thinking and media literacy.

Allen's column came in response to the discredited Plandemic video, which included misinformation and conspiracy theories surrounding the COVID-19 pandemic. "What surprised me is how easily 'Plandemic' sank its hooks into some of my friends," Allen said. He was thus inspired to create a checklist to help people better assess information, writing, "My goal is to offer some criteria for sifting through all the content we see every day, so we can tell the difference between fair reporting and something so biased it should not be taken seriously."[37]

Allen recommended assessing information by asking the following questions:

- "Is the presentation one-sided?"[37]
  - If so, then it is likely trying to mislead rather than inform.
  - A strong journalistic piece will take into account opposing points of view, acknowledging their strengths, and pointing out their weaknesses.
- "Is there an independent pursuit of the truth?"[37]
  - Propaganda will often allow flimsy or suspect claims to stand unchallenged. This is the opposite of accountability journalism.
  - In the case of the Plandemic video, the main source asserted that she had never been charged with a crime – a claim easily disproven with a small amount of research. Indeed, she had been charged with serious crimes, but the charges were later dropped. This information gives a fuller picture of the human being involved in the story, rather than allowing a preconceived narrative to dictate the direction, often to the detriment of truth.

- Does the story carefully adhere to the facts or not?[37]
  - Precision matters in journalism. You don't want to get it kind of right. You want to get it right.
  - The main source's characterization that she was never charged with any crimes is false. She may never have been convicted, but precision requires a fact check, and verification is critical. Don't just take what any source says as truth – even if the source seems beyond reproach.
  - Allen reminded us that careful verification "distinguishes the craft of journalism from other forms of information sharing. People often speak imprecisely when they're telling their stories. It's our duty to nail down precisely what they do and do not mean, and verify it independently. If we don't, we risk undermining their credibility and ours."[33]
- "Are those accused allowed to respond?"[37]
  - This is a hallmark of strong watchdog journalism. People who are accused of something may choose not to respond, but they must be given a chance to answer the accusations levied against them.
  - "Every time I write a story that accuses someone of wrong-doing, I call them and urge them to explain the situation from their perspective. This is standard in mainstream journalism," Allen said. "Sometimes I've gone to extreme lengths to get comments from someone who will be portrayed unfavorably in my story – traveling to another state and showing up at their office and their home and leaving a note if they are not there to meet me."[33]
- "Are all sources named and cited?" If not, does the writer explain why?[37]
  - Fully identifying sources allows your audience to independently verify the information, do additional research, and make more informed decisions about the content they are consuming.
  - If a source is presented as anonymous, the explanation as to why will help your audience understand the reasoning and draw their own conclusions as to whether they feel the source should be named or considered credible.
- "Does the (piece) claim some secret or exclusive knowledge?"[37]
  - If so, then be skeptical! Of course, exclusive journalistic pieces come along, but chances are, many journalists are pursuing similar stories, or many journalists will work quickly to verify the exclusive and present their own takes with additional nuanced, verified, and helpful information. Anyone claiming to have a lock on some secret truth should be treated with skepticism until the information is verified.

An important consideration is how you present your story. In particular with accountability journalism, people who support one candidate or another, or one policy or another, may not be open to having their mind changed, even if the new information refutes their version beyond any reasonable doubt.

In a 2017 article for the API, writers Jane Elizabeth, Lori Kelley, and Julie M. Elman wrote that even though there are more and more journalists and news organizations seeking to "scrutinize and hold powerful people and institutions accountable," there has also been an "explosion in the distribution of misinformation, attacks on journalists and a free press, and the rise of **fake news** – material that is intentionally false but designed to mimic journalism."[38]

The authors advocate for changing our approach. Rather than just fact checking and presenting narrative content, the authors recommend more visual content, including timelines, charts, fact boxes, or by-the-numbers graphics. The Poynter Institute's eye-tracking research found that visual and non-narrative approaches helped people connect with information, remember it, and answer questions about it correctly.[39]

For example, in 2015, the *Tampa Bay Times* decided to use Lego pieces to explain how a plan to add toll lanes to a busy bridge fell apart.[40] The visuals of the Lego pieces and people gave clarity and provided a familiar reference point for readers, who likely played with Legos as children or had their own children who did so. The question of which party or politician may have been on which side of the issue was secondary to explaining and ensuring understanding of the issue itself.

Focusing on issues and explanation – rather than who said what and how truthful they were – may help mitigate knee-jerk political reactions and accusations of fake news or bias.

Fake news and disinformation outlets effectively compete for attention by simplifying complex issues and tailoring content for their audience. This makes audiences more receptive to that content. The API authors advocate that reputable news outlets consider ways they can also help audiences connect with and access their content.[41,42]

If you engage in accountability reporting, you need to be prepared for any negative reaction you may get. This can include trolling on social media, harsh words, obfuscation, attempts to discredit you, and possibly even threats to you or those you love. Threatening behavior can be even more intense, targeted, and personal for women, people of color, and those in the LGBTQIA+ community, because the posts may not only express disagreement or outrage, they may also be racist, sexist, homophobic, and/or misogynistic, and may directly threaten violence not only to the journalist but to loved ones, as well.[43,44,45]

WHO is doing accountability journalism?

Though, ideally, accountability journalism would take place in newsrooms everywhere, the fact is that it can be resource-intensive, and many news outlets may not have the ability to dedicate personnel to the coverage of in-depth, ongoing, or complex stories, including original investigative work or fact checks or explainers of stories being covered.

The GIJN is one of many organizations seeking to provide resources and support to those doing investigative journalism, including tip sheets, guides, and videos, and serving as a convener for the world's journalists. Kaplan noted that GIJN's resources are used by a growing number of citizen journalists:

> We created an entire guide for citizen investigators. How do you find out who's polluting in your neighborhood? How do you get an asset disclosure form on a local politician? Who owns the property in your community? People are asking these questions. We call them public interest investigators.[13]

Many other organizations are also seeking to support or conduct accountability journalism, including the International Consortium of Investigative Journalists, Investigative Reporters and Editors, and the Center for Investigative Journalism.

Nonprofit news outlets such as ProPublica and Reveal / The Center for Investigative Reporting are doing in-depth and important investigative stories, including ProPublica's work tracking where the money from federal Paycheck Protection Program (PPP) loans went[46] and telling the stories of people affected by COVID-19, including healthcare workers, new parents, and others.[47,48,49,50] In addition, Reveal reported on data showing that migrant children were held at the Southern US border for longer than was acknowledged[51] and talked with US Census workers to discover concerns about how data are being reported.[52]

Another solution is resource sharing via multi-newsroom collaborations, in which several news outlets

Muckrakers: The first accountability journalists

When people think of the iconic vision of a journalist, we often conjure up someone doing accountability journalism. "It's more than a profession. It's a calling," said David E. Kaplan, executive director of the Global Investigative Journalism Network (GIJN). "The practice has always been rooted in social reform."[13]

Accountability journalism goes back more than 100 years to the muckrakers of the late 19th and early 20th centuries – journalists who used the scientific method and meticulous research and reporting to hold power to account.

Muckraker Ida Tarbell at work.

"It was during the Progressive Era when people like Lincoln Steffens and Ida Tarbell were going after the biggest forces for abuse of power in their day," Kaplan said. Tarbell wrote about Standard Oil's antitrust practices over 19 magazine installments of meticulous, detailed reporting, which would eventually become a two-volume book. "Standard Oil was the Google of her day. Steffens exposed corruption in city government. Nellie and organizations work together to bring an investigative story to fruition. A major example of this is the Pulitzer Prize-winning Panama Papers investigation, in which more than 100 media partners collaborated – combing through two separate leaks totaling 12.7 million files covering more than 40 years – amounting to 26 terabytes of data – to discover and report on the biggest leak of insider information in history. The work of these intrepid journalists exposed "offshore holdings of world political leaders, links to global scandals, and details of the hidden financial dealings of fraudsters, drug traffickers, billionaires, celebrities, sports stars, and more."[53] The collaboration led to a series of stories – and the exposure of 214,000 offshore shell companies – a feat that could not be achieved by one news outlet alone.

Bly checked herself into an insane asylum to reveal abuse and mistreatment of patients."[13]
"There's a brilliant investigative reporter in Ghana who – 130 years later – basically repeated Nellie Bly's investigation, going into his country's worst mental health facility with a button camera and documenting unbelievable conditions," Kaplan said. "The only difference was this guy had a miniature camera, but the methodology really hadn't changed."[13]
The muckrakers understood *why* they were doing the work, and they developed strategies and tactics for *how* to get it done. They paved the way for accountability journalism today.

In local newsrooms, even if there is no budget for investigative journalism, simply working on a beat can lead to leads that prompt the pursuit of investigative and explanatory stories, as well as allow journalists to do more in-depth and contextual reporting. A journalist on a beat will become familiar with the players, issues, and quirks of that beat. This knowledge means a journalist can provide context for stories and explain to audiences what is important, why they should care, and how decisions are made. In addition, a beat reporter who has knowledge of a particular topic area will have enough of an understanding to avoid being taken advantage of. The beat reporter can see through spin, ask the right questions, and hold sources to account.

A pitfall is that beat reporters can become too familiar with their sources, which could lead to soft-balling stories that need hard-hitting journalism. Michael Hudson, investigative editor at the Associated Press, said in an interview with *Nieman Reports* that cultivating mid-level and low-level sources can often pay off, because it gives you a different perspective than you get by talking only to high-level sources.[8] One famous example of when access to high-level sources did not lead to a scoop was Watergate in the early 1970s. It was not a reporter from the Washington Press Corps who broke the Watergate story. Instead, it was two metro reporters who began to pursue the story after covering a court hearing on a break-in at the prestigious Watergate Towers in Washington, DC. Couple that with an anonymous source, and the story was brought to light, leading eventually to the resignation of a president.

Key takeaways

- Accountability or watchdog journalism focuses on holding power to account, and it includes fact checking, explanatory journalism, and investigative journalism.
- Accountability journalists may face pressure, intimidation, or threats from those in power who don't want to be held accountable.
- A free and healthy society goes hand-in-hand with journalism that holds power to account and shines a light on corruption. Without a free press, healthy society may flounder.

Discussion questions

1. What role does fact checking play in the journalistic process? When should fact checking be employed? How could the information be presented to ensure audience engagement and understanding?
2. Identify a story you would like to understand better – preferably a local story to you, but a national or international story will also work. What do you want to understand better? What information is missing from your experience with the story? Try to explain the *why* and *how* of the story based on what you do know. Do some additional research, if necessary.
3. How do you think about investigative journalists? What issues and stories would you like to see investigative journalists cover? How might you pursue those stories?

Exercises

1. Find an accountability journalism article / story from the past two weeks (fact check, explainer, or investigative work). If you're having trouble, you can go to *The Washington Post* Fact Checker, the Global Investigative Journalism Network, ProPublica, Reveal, or other outlets and organizations focused on accountability journalism.
    a. Identify why the journalist(s) covered this story.
    b. Identify the issue the journalist was trying to address.
    c. Identify how the journalist went about presenting the information:
        i. Who / what were the sources?
        ii. How did the journalist open the piece?
        iii. What was the tone of the piece?
    d. Whose side do you think the journalist is on?
        i. NOTE: I don't mean politically here. Is the journalist on the side of just one person or is there a larger reason for doing this story? What is the larger reason?
2. Choose a daily news story from a news outlet that's local to you that was published, posted, or broadcast within the past two weeks, preferably

coverage of a governmental meeting, such as a vote at City Hall or the Board of Supervisors or Board of Education.
   a. Conduct a fact check of the issue, as well as the reasons given by sources for why they support their side.
   b. Write an inverted pyramid story about the fact check (not about the event itself).
3. Choose an issue in your local community – for example, potholes in the street, overgrown grass at a local park, cars driving too fast through a neighborhood, or old technology at a high school.
   a. Research the issue and keep notes.
   b. Then, approach the issue by writing answers to the following prompts:
      i. What caused this issue? How did this issue come to be?
      ii. How does this issue impact the community?
      iii. What might be some solutions to this issue?
      iv. Who and what might be able to enlighten you on the cause, impact, and solution?
         1. Identify both official sources and community and non-official sources.
   c. Check out GIJN's 25 Tips for Everyday Digging (https://gijn.org/2016/05/06/25-tips-for-everyday-digging.).

Notes

1 Tin, Win. "Our Values: Reporters without Borders." *RSF*, September 2012. https://rsf.org/en/our-values.
2 Patterson, Thomas E. Rep. *Pre-Primary News Coverage of the 2016 Presidential Race: Trump's Rise, Sanders' Emergence, Clinton's Struggle*. Harvard, MA: Shorenstein Center on Media, Politics, & Public Policy, 2016.
3 Mantzarlis, Alexios. "Why CNN's Fact-Checking Chyron Is a Big Deal - and Why It Isn't." *Poynter*, June 4, 2016. https://www.poynter.org/fact-checking/2016/why-cnns-fact-checking-chyron-is-a-big-deal-and-why-it-isnt/.
4 Farhi, Paul. "Sassy, Self-Aware, Snarky. In the Trump Era, Cable News Banners Troll in Real Time." *The Washington Post*, July 31, 2018. https://www.washingtonpost.com/graphics/2018/lifestyle/style/how-cable-news-chyrons-have-adapted-to-the-trump-era/.
5 Amato, John. "Why Is CNN Being Praised for Doing Journalism?" *Crooks and Liars*, June 3, 2016. https://crooksandliars.com/2016/06/why-cnn-being-praised-doing-journalism.
6 Tamkin, Emily. "CNN Public Editor: No, It Hasn't." *Columbia Journalism Review*, November 14, 2019. https://www.cjr.org/public_editor/cnn-chyrons-trump.php.
7 Coronel, Sheila S. Rep. *The Media as Watchdog*. Harvard, MA: Harvard-World Bank, 2008.
8 Jurkowitz, Mark, and Amy Mitchell. "Most Say Journalists Should Be Watchdogs, but Views of How Well They Fill this Role Vary by Party, Media Diet." Pew Research Center's Journalism Project, August 18, 2020. https://www.journalism.org/2020/02/26/most-say-journalists-should-be-watchdogs-but-views-of-how-well-they-fill-this-role-vary-by-party-media-diet/.
9 Froomkin @froomkin, Dan. "Truth or Consequences: Where Is Watchdog Journalism Today?" *Nieman Reports*, April 17, 2014. https://niemanreports.org/articles/truth-or-consequences-where-is-watchdog-journalism-today/.

10 Mai, H. J. "White House Press Aide TJ Ducklo Resigns over Threats against Reporter." *NPR*, February 13, 2021. https://www.npr.org/2021/02/13/967745623/white-house-press-aide-tj-ducklo-resigns-over-threats-against-reporter.
11 Glenn Kessler, "Accountability Journalism" interview by Gina Baleria, *News in Context* (podcast), December 17, 2021. https://beta.prx.org/stories/351071.
12 David E. Kaplan (Executive Director of the Global Investigative Journalism Network (GIJN)), in conversation with Gina Baleria, December 2020.
13 David E. Kaplan, "Nonprofit Journalism" interview by Gina Baleria, *News in Context* (podcast), January 22, 2021. https://beta.prx.org/stories/355489.
14 Zhang, Qifan. "Explaining the News Builds Audience for It." *News Literacy*, February 28, 2016. https://nyujournalismprojects.org/newsliteracy2016/topics/explainer-journalism/.
15 NOTE: The ACLU is an advocacy organization doing journalism.
16 Holsopple, Kara. "Meet the Investigative Reporter Who Broke the Flint Lead Story." *The Allegheny Front*, March 21, 2016. https://www.alleghenyfront.org/meet-the-investigative-reporter-who-broke-the-flint-lead-story/.
17 Gross, Terry. "Pediatrician Who Exposed Flint Water Crisis Shares Her 'Story of Resistance'." *Fresh Air*. NPR, June 25, 2018. https://www.npr.org/sections/health-shots/2018/06/25/623126968/pediatrician-who-exposed-flint-water-crisis-shares-her-story-of-resistance.
18 Mclaughlin, Timothy. "Six Michigan Officials Criminally Charged in Flint Water Crisis." *Reuters*. Thomson Reuters, June 14, 2017. https://www.reuters.com/article/us-michigan-water-idUSKBN195234.
19 Atassi, Leila, and Rachel Dissell. "A Guide to Reinvestigating Rape: Old Evidence, New Answers." *Cleveland Plain Dealer*, August 10, 2013. https://www.cleveland.com/rape-kits/2013/08/reinvestigating_rape_old_evide.html.
20 Svokos, Alexandra. "Massive Backlog of Untested Rape Kits Is 'a Public Safety Issue' that May Be Letting Offenders Slip Away, Experts Warn." *ABC News Network*, January 26, 2019. https://abcnews.go.com/US/massive-backlog-untested-rape-kits-public-safety-issue/story?id=60540635.
21 Hopkins, Kyle. "After 3 Years and $1.5 Million Devoted to Testing Rape Kits, Alaska Made One New Arrest." *Anchorage Daily News*, December 30, 2020. https://www.adn.com/alaska-news/lawless/2020/12/30/after-3-years-and-15-million-devoted-to-testing-rape-kits-alaska-made-one-new-arrest/.
22 Eyre, Eric. "Drug Firms Fueled 'Pill Mills' in Rural WV." *Charleston Gazette-Mail*, November 21, 2017. https://www.wvgazettemail.com/news/legal_affairs/drug-firms-fueled-pill-mills-in-rural-wv/article_14c8e1a5-19b1-579d-9ed5-770f09589a22.html.
23 Johnson, Julie. "Rise in Fentanyl Overdose Deaths Gives New Focus to Drug Prosecutions." *Santa Rosa Press Democrat*, February 12, 2021. https://www.pressdemocrat.com/article/news/rise-in-fentanyl-overdose-deaths-giving-new-focus-on-opioid-prosecutions-in/.
24 Cutler, Calvin. "Advocates Push for Bills to Stem Opioid Overdose Crisis." *WCAX*, February 17, 2021. https://www.wcax.com/video/2021/02/17/advocates-push-bills-stem-opioid-overdose-crisis/.
25 Guess, Andrew, Brendan Nyhan, and Jason Reifler. "All Media Trust Is Local?" *2018 Poynter Media Trust Survey*, August 10, 2018.
26 Sands, John. "Local News Is More Trusted than National News – But That Could Change." Knight Foundation, October 29, 2019. https://knightfoundation.org/articles/local-news-is-more-trusted-than-national-news-but-that-could-change/.
27 Camaj, Lindita. "The Media's Role in Fighting Corruption." *The International Journal of Press/Politics* 18, no. 1 (November 2, 2012): 21–42.
28 Lessmann, Christian, and Gunther Markwardt. "One Size Fits All? Decentralization, Corruption, and the Monitoring of Bureaucrats." *World Development* 38, no. 4 (April 2010): 631–46. doi: 10.1016/j.worlddev.2009.11.003.

29 Alba, Davey, and Jack Nicas. "As Local News Dies, a Pay-for-Play Network Rises in Its Place." *The New York Times*, October 18, 2020. https://www.nytimes.com/2020/10/18/technology/timpone-local-news-metric-media.html.
30 Swan, Jonathan. "AXIOS on HBO: President Trump Exclusive Interview (Full Episode) | HBO." *Axios*, August 3, 2020. https://www.youtube.com/watch?reload=9&v=zaaTZ-kqsaxY.
31 Velshi, Ali. "Jonathan Swan: Trump Is not Confronting Reality about Coronavirus." *The Last Word*. MSNBC, August 4, 2020. https://www.youtube.com/watch?v=imAzLGMEucA.
32 Welna, David. "After Contentious Interview, Pompeo Publicly Accuses NPR Journalist of Lying to Him." All Things Considered. *NPR*, January 25, 2020. https://www.npr.org/2020/01/25/799562818/after-contentious-interview-pompeo-publicly-accuses-npr-journalist-of-lying-to-h.
33 Brandel, Jennifer, and Jay Rosen. "A Call for Radically Different Campaign Coverage." *Medium*. We Are Hearken, November 28, 2019. https://medium.com/we-are-hearken/a-call-for-radically-different-campaign-coverage-85e62401d0c6.
34 The Editors of Encyclopaedia Britannica. "Iraq War - Occupation and Continued Warfare." *Encyclopedia Britannica*, 2020. https://www.britannica.com/event/Iraq-War.
35 DeYoung, Karen. "Saudi Crown Prince Approved Operation That Led to Death of Journalist Jamal Khashoggi, U.S. Intelligence Report Concludes." *The Washington Post*, February 26, 2021. https://www.washingtonpost.com/national-security/khashoggi-killing-intelligence-report-release-mbs-saudi-arabia/2021/02/26/df5f6e58-7844-11eb-948d-19472e683521_story.html.
36 "RSF's 2020 Round-Up: 50 Journalists Killed, Two-Thirds in Countries 'at Peace': Reporters without Borders." *Reporters Without Borders (RSF)*, December 29, 2020. https://rsf.org/en/news/rsfs-2020-round-50-journalists-killed-two-thirds-countries-peace.
37 Allen, Marshall. "I'm an Investigative Journalist. These Are the Questions I Asked About the Viral 'Plandemic' Video." *ProPublica*, May 9, 2020. https://www.propublica.org/article/im-an-investigative-journalist-these-are-the-questions-i-asked-about-the-viral-plandemic-video.
38 Elizabeth, Jane, Lori Kelley, and Julie M. Elman. "Improving Accountability Reporting: How to Make the Best of Journalism Better for Audiences." American Press Institute, August 8, 2017. https://www.americanpressinstitute.org/publications/reports/strategy-studies/improving-accountability-reporting/.
39 Quinn, Sara Dickenson. "Alternative Story Forms Are Effective." *Poynter*, November 24, 2014. https://www.poynter.org/reporting-editing/2007/alternative-story-forms-are-effective/.
40 Zhang, Eli, Caitlin Johnston, Anthony Cormier, and Martin Frobisher. "How the Plan to Fix Tampa Bay's Most Important Bridge Fell Apart." *Tampa Bay Times*, December 15, 2016. https://projects.tampabay.com/projects/2016/features/howard-frankland-bridge-plan-legos/.
41 "Paying for News: Why People Subscribe and What It Says about the Future of Journalism." American Press Institute. The Media Insight Project, May 25, 2017. https://www.americanpressinstitute.org/publications/reports/survey-research/paying-for-news/single-page/.
42 "'My' Media versus 'the' Media: Trust in News Depends on Which News Media You Mean." American Press Institute. Media Insight Project, May 31, 2017. https://www.americanpressinstitute.org/publications/reports/survey-research/my-media-vs-the-media/single-page/.
43 "Troll Patrol Findings." *Troll Patrol Report*. Amnesty International, 2018. https://decoders.amnesty.org/projects/troll-patrol/findings.
44 Posetti, Julie, Nermine Aboulez, Kalina Bontcheva, Jackie Harrison, and Silvio Waisbord. Rep. *Online Violence against Women Journalists: A Global Snapshot of Incidence*

and Impacts. Paris: United Nations Educational, Scientific and Cultural Organization (UNESCO), 2020.
45 Barton, Alana, Hannah Storm, and Samantha Brady. Rep. Edited by Elisa Lees Muñoz. *Violence and Harassment against Women in the News Media: A Global Picture*. Washington, DC & London, UK: International Womens Media Foundation & International News Safety Institute, 2014.
46 Syed, Moiz, and Derek Willis. "Coronavirus Bailouts: Search Every Company Approved for Federal Loans Over $150k." *ProPublica*, July 7, 2020. https://projects.propublica.org/coronavirus/bailouts/.
47 Johnson, Akilah, and Talia Buford. "Early Data Shows African Americans Have Contracted and Died of Coronavirus at an Alarming Rate." *ProPublica*, April 3, 2020. https://www.propublica.org/article/early-data-shows-african-americans-have-contracted-and-died-of-coronavirus-at-an-alarming-rate.
48 Gillum, Jack, Lisa Song, and Jeff Kao. "There's Been a Spike in People Dying at Home in Several Cities. That Suggests Coronavirus Deaths Are Higher than Reported." *ProPublica*, April 14, 2020. https://www.propublica.org/article/theres-been-a-spike-in-people-dying-at-home-in-several-cities-that-suggests-coronavirus-deaths-are-higher-than-reported.
49 Martin, Nina. "They Didn't Have Coronavirus Symptoms Until after They Gave Birth. Then They Tested Positive." *ProPublica*, March 27, 2020. https://www.propublica.org/article/they-didnt-have-coronavirus-symptoms-until-after-they-gave-birth-then-they-tested-positive.
50 Presser, Lizzie. "A Medical Worker Describes Terrifying Lung Failure from COVID-19 - Even in His Young Patients." *ProPublica*, March 21, 2020. https://www.propublica.org/article/a-medical-worker-describes--terrifying-lung-failure-from-covid19-even-in-his-young-patients.
51 Bogado, Aura, and Melissa Lewis Reveal from The Center for Investigative Reporting October 30. "US Detained Migrant Children for Far Longer than Previously Known." *Reveal*, October 30, 2020. https://revealnews.org/article/thousands-migrant-children-languished-in-us-detention/.
52 Rodriguez, David, and Byard Duncan Reveal from The Center for Investigative Reporting January 12. "Census Workers Raise Concerns about Data Quality, with Bureau Leaning on Records Rather than In-Person Counts." *Reveal*, January 12, 2021. https://revealnews.org/article/census-workers-raise-concerns-about-data-quality-with-bureau-leaning-on-records-rather-than-in-person-counts/.
53 Diaz-Struck, Emilia, ed. "About the Panama Papers Investigation." *International Consortium of Investigative Journalists (ICIJ)*, January 18, 2019. https://www.icij.org/investigations/panama-papers/pages/panama-papers-about-the-investigation/.

Part 3

Contextualizing your practice

9 The importance of stepping away
Managing safety, trauma, & self-care in journalism

> If we really believe in the importance of our work in journalism and our responsibility to the communities we cover, we need a responsible self-care plan.
> – Bruce Shapiro, executive director of Columbia Journalism School's Dart Center for Journalism and Trauma[1]

On Tuesday, September 11, 2001, I woke up to my alarm, as usual. And, as usual, it was tuned to KCBS Radio in San Francisco, where I worked. I was the website producer and usually rolled out of bed, did a quick update of the top morning stories from home, and then got ready and headed into the newsroom. But I did not hear the usual traffic and weather. I heard that a plane had slammed into a building. I momentarily wondered where in the world this had happened. It took my groggy brain a beat to understand that it was our buildings – the twin towers of the World Trade Center in New York City. Soon after I had woken up, a second plane hit the second tower.

I bolted up, flipped on the TV, and called out to my roommates as I quickly powered up my computer. It was time to get to work.

As I began to take it all in and update the KCBS website, I heard the sounds of thuds coming from the liveshot on TV. Those thuds were human beings – people on the floors above where the planes had hit making the grim decision to jump to their deaths rather than be burned alive. I gasped, and intense emotions of grief and pain welled up inside me. I kept working.

Reports came in that another plane had hit the Pentagon, and later that a fourth had gone down in a Pennsylvania field. As I wondered how many more there might be and where they might strike, I kept working.

Then, I heard a rumble and sounds of shock from the anchors. I turned and watched in horror as one of the towers came down. It took my breath away. I kept working.

The next tower fell. More grief. Tears welled up, and I could no longer keep them down. As I cried, I kept working.

Once I had the breaking news up on the site, I took the briefest of showers and got myself into the newsroom. News was still breaking and developing, and now the human stories were coming in. Stories of loss, grief, searching, and apparent heroes who reportedly foiled the plans of one group of hijackers headed for the White House, forcing the plane to crash in Pennsylvania. All on board lost their lives.

For 16 hours, I and my colleagues worked. We sobbed. We struggled for breath as the news developed. We commiserated. We felt the pain of those affected. We talked with friends and loved ones of the presumed and confirmed dead, and we shared the onslaught of grim information with our audience.

At some point late into the night, I went home to grab a handful of hours of sleep and was back at it early the next morning. I worked 14 hours on September 12 and 12 hours on September 13. Every day filled with grief, pain, pride, human suffering, human heroism, human darkness, and a deep feeling of honor to be in a position to be able to inform people and get this important news out.

By Friday, September 14, I felt like an empty shell and a wasteland. I went back to work, this time for ten hours. Thankfully, one of my best friends, who worked down the street from my newsroom, suggested that instead of going home, I go to the gym. Every cell in me resisted. But I battled through it, dragged myself to the gym, and worked out. I was transformed. I then met my friend for a drink and to share about and process the week. That workout (and that friendship) made all the difference. I felt like a new person. My brain worked again. I was still grieving (along with much of the rest of the nation and world), but I could manage it. The world did not feel so hopeless. I could face it again.

Though September 11 was particularly intense, this scenario in some form has played out multiple times in my journalism career – from Columbine, the deadliest mass shooting at a high school to that point; to Hurricane Katrina; to the Boston Marathon Bombing; kidnappings, shootings, fires, and countless other stories. The job can be intense and demanding. It can also put us face-to-face with the worst of humanity, the most graphic crime or accident scenes, someone on the worst day of their life, and the most painful truths about humanity. Some stories may also trigger our own mental health challenges. Through it all, we must do our jobs. We must inform the public.

Self-care is key to being able to persist in the field of journalism. In the example above, specific self-care activities sustained and replenished me – a support system, a workout, a little bit of alcohol (one drink), and eventually some sleep. The goal of this chapter is to discuss what self-care is, how you can find the best self-care options for you, the importance of moderation, and how to make self-care part of your journalism practice.

WHAT is self-care?

Self-care is basically taking care of yourself – not just once in a while, but as a consistent, everyday practice woven into your daily and weekly routines. Self-care can be something you do for yourself, or it can be reaching out for help.

We can think of self-care in journalism both as an individual practice and as part of a newsroom culture that supports the well-being of its team.

Practicing self-care can help you take a break from the relentless beat that is journalism and replenish the mind and body, as well as heal from and process the traumatic events that occur as part of doing the job. Thus, you can refresh and be ready to do the important work of covering your beat and informing your community.

Self-care involves both individual choices you make to take care of yourself, and strategies to deal with the world and the job as they exist. Ideally, your newsroom is also systemically supporting, providing, and encouraging self-care strategies. Self-care can include any activity that helps you, and so everyone's self-care strategy will look different. But strategies fall into a few general categories:

- Connection
- Exercise and fitness
- Mindfulness
- Therapy
- Coping strategies

Connection strategies include having conversations with friends and loved ones; calling your mom or dad; and doing an activity with someone, such as a hike, sharing a meal, or having a drink or coffee. It also includes hugging your dog (or cat, if they'll allow it), taking your dog for a walk, or spending some time to play. Research indicates that receiving emotional support can help people cope and engage in self-care practices,[2,3] and sharing what we're going through can lead to increased social support.[4]

Conntecting with other people, even for the introverts, is something that needs to be done," said Elana Newman, PhD, McFarlin professor of psychology at the University of Tulsa, and research director for the Dart Center for Journalism and Trauma. Dart advocates for and educates about ethical, thorough, compassionate coverage of trauma stories and those affected. "We know that social support is really important – or giving support. Giving it can be really helpful, as well."[5]

Exercise and fitness include anything that gets your physical body moving, whether it's a five-minute walk, a ten-mile hike, a trip to the gym, or even getting up from your computer for two minutes to stretch. Cleaning also counts! In addition, this category encompasses what you put in your body. Self-care can involve choosing a banana over a cookie, drinking water instead of a second glass of wine, or saying no to newsroom food (usually cookies, brownies, pizza, etc.). It also involves eating regularly – not too little and not to excess. Research is clear that fitness can mitigate the effects of stress,[6] trauma,[7] and burnout.[8]

Mindfulness strategies include meditation, looking up from your computer or smartphone and noticing the world around you, or simply breathing slowly and deeply for 30 seconds before you get out of the car or off the train or bus, or in between emails or calls. Reading, organizing, or learning a new skill may also give your mind a break from the job. Research shows that engaging in mindfulness can reduce stress[9] and help with burnout and trauma.[10]

Another important strategy is engaging in therapy or counseling. The job of journalism can be rewarding, fulfilling, and meaningful, but it can also be traumatic, intense, triggering, and relentless. Regularly seeing a therapist can provide a structured environment for you to work through, manage, and learn to cope with the traumas you experience doing the job, as well as any triggers that may come up for you. Research supports the assertion that therapy can mitigate the effects of stress and post-traumatic stress disorder (PTSD).[11,12]

Self-care may also include taking steps to maximize your safety and well-being while on the job and developing coping strategies to deal with story trauma, newsroom culture, and the built-in demands of the job. This can include getting special training, speaking up about issues, and preparing yourself for whatever may come.

At the most basic level, to reduce stress on the job, broadcast and digital journalists who know they may be sent to cover breaking news should have extra batteries for recording equipment, as well as healthy snacks and water in their bags, in case they get sent to a breaking or developing story. Having a mobile charging unit for your tech devices can help ensure that you don't create stress for yourself by allowing the tools of your trade to die on you in the middle of your newsgathering.

But, in a larger sense, more and more journalism leaders and educators are recognizing the need for training in crisis preparedness, coping skills, and boundary-setting; a clear-eyed examination of toxic newsroom culture; and systemic efforts to ensure that everyone in the newsroom can manage the stress and trauma that come with the job. For example, going through specialized training on how to talk to victims of trauma or how to cope with emotional stories can help build your resiliency and give you tools for managing the trauma or stress you encounter on the job. Newsroom leaders who provide resources for coping with stress, encourage staff to engage in self-care, and actively check in after a traumatic or stressful assignment contribute to newsroom well-being.

EXERCISE BREAK

List two to three things you would do to care for yourself in each category:

- Connection
- Exercise and fitness
- Mindfulness
- Coping strategies

WHAT is trauma?

For the purposes of this book, **trauma** is defined both as an experience that is "psychologically overwhelming,"[13] and the "emotional response to a terrible event like an accident, rape, or natural disaster."[14] That response can come from experiencing the event directly or vicariously or by serving as a **professional witness** to that event, such as a first responder or journalist.

Symptoms of trauma-related distress can be both physical and emotional, and include shock or denial in the short term, while longer-term symptoms include headache, fatigue, nausea, emotional outbursts, flashbacks, and even a breakdown of relationships. A person may feel overwhelmed, numb, guilty, angry, hopeless, anxious, and/or depressed.

"Journalists are **professional witnesses**," said Newman. "You are the eyes and ears of society. You are there to tell us and interpret what's happening in the world." Bearing witness can cause trauma-related distress, and many journalists don't know how to cope. "Journalists are trained to record, but are not trained on the emotional impact of bearing witness."[5]

Studies bear this out, showing that journalists have a higher incidence of PTSD[15,16] and depression[17] than the general population, because the job is inherently stressful, and many of the stories we cover are mentally and emotionally fraught. Stress and trauma are not generated just when covering big stories, such as war or mass shootings, but also stories we cover from day-to-day, including fires, car accidents, shootings, and other tales of human suffering and grief. In addition, it's not just journalists in the field who are affected. Those in the newsroom experience **vicarious trauma** as they newsgather, view disturbing images and video, and conduct interviews from the newsroom or remotely.

Freelance journalist Cristiana Bedei wrote, "Interviewing people about their experiences, viewing horrific images on the computer, or covering stories that hit close to home – both literally and metaphorically – might be enough to wreak emotional havoc."[18]

My own experience covering 9/11, as discussed above, is an example of vicarious trauma. Though our region did have a direct connection, given that some of the people on Flight 93 – the plane that passengers brought down in a Pennsylvania field before it could reach its destination – were from the Bay Area, I was not present on site. But I still experienced effects from the trauma of covering the story that persisted for years.

Misha LeClair, a former TV and digital news producer who now works in tech, discussed her own vicarious trauma when she covered the police killing of Oscar Grant on New Year's Day in 2009, as he was returning from New Year's celebrations on BART – the San Francisco Bay Area's metro rail.

"We were the first crew there, because we had a guy who chased the scanners," LeClair said. "When he got there, BART police were like, 'Oh, not a big deal.' He was like, 'no, this is a big deal. I saw him on the gurney.' And then, he dies."[19]

Soon after the incident, in which BART police officer Johannes Mehserle shot and killed Grant on the platform at Fruitvale Station, cell phone video started coming out from many angles. "But in the (initial) videos, it was really hard to tell" what happened, LeClair said. "It's obviously a chaotic scene, but it's hard to say whose bad behavior in those initial videos. And police are just like, 'they were resisting arrest, and they were fighting on the train,' and these blanket statements."[19]

What happened next drove the story forward. LeClair said a man showed up at the newsroom offering video with a different angle of the shooting. LeClair said the video was stunning and upsetting.

> I remember the first time watching it. There's definitely that moment of like, "oh my god," because it was very clear that he was already pinned on the ground. It was very clear that he was shot in the back. (And) you hear everybody's reaction. There's a full BART train of people reacting.[19]

The consummate news professional, LeClair quickly pivoted to how to get this information to the public.

> Very quickly, your instinctual emotional reaction kind of gets turned down, right? Like you have that, "oh my God, what just happened? Why was he shot?" And then you kind of have to move on. Then, it becomes like, okay, we're backing up the video and we're scrutinizing it more and pausing it. Where are people's hands? And all that stuff.
>
> And then it transitions into the debate about handling it responsibly. What can we show and not show? What do we *say* we saw on the video versus *airing*, and what times of day (do we show it) and with what warnings?[19]

The decision about how to air the video came down to its journalistic contribution. "Ultimately, especially because so commonly the police just say they're resisting arrest, and it's like this blanket whatever, we felt it was really important to show it." LeClair recalled that the decision at the time was to air the video in full once with an explicit warning, and subsequently air video only to the moment before the fatal shot, while continuing to air audio of the full clip, so they weren't repeatedly showing someone getting killed.[19]

LeClair explained that the gravity of the story took precedence over her own mental health.

> There's such a sense of responsibility in those moments that, even though you're watching something pretty horrific happen, you feel a sense of responsibility to tell the whole story. We definitely felt the weight of it. There are so many times where people get shot in a confrontation with police, and we don't really know what happened, and we're not there. This time, you can see what happens. So, we can't just not address this. And then it becomes just very much doing the work.[19]

But just because LeClair didn't have an emotional reaction at the time, did not mean watching that content had no effect. When the movie *Fruitvale Station* came out about the incident, LeClair could at first not bring herself to see it. "I didn't watch it until a couple years ago when I was long out of news. I just wasn't sure that I could – that I would want to see that moment again, even though I knew it was going to be fictional," she said.[19]

The cumulative trauma of working in news, coupled with a lack of support from newsroom managers, prompted LeClair to leave the profession and change careers.

We all bring our own experiences with us wherever we go, and some stories may be triggers that affect our mental health. Other first responders, such as police, firefighters, and EMTs, have implemented strategies to deal with the trauma that can result from doing the job, including counseling, training, and resources. Journalists are also first responders to disasters, tragedies, and other traumatic events, but the journalism industry has historically not addressed trauma or self-care.

"In many ways, journalists are the last first-on-the-scene group to start this conversation .... Journalists were very reticent to talk about these issues," Newman said. But, "empathetically engaging with someone who has experienced violence, particularly when you're not trained to deal with all those emotions, is another form of exposure that can be more difficult to manage without tools and training."[5]

Part of the reason for the reticence is that journalists have internalized the mantra that they are meant to be objective observers, documenting history and informing the public. Of course, given that journalists are also human, it is impossible in practice to remain detached from the emotional aspect of covering difficult stories.

Complicating matters is that many journalists thrive on the pace of breaking news and pursuing the story, and are so mission driven that we often put our self-care needs on the backburner to serve our audience and feed our internal need to get the story, provide information, hold power accountable, and shine a light on complex processes. Thus, whatever may be nagging at us gets pushed down on the priority list in service of the job.

In addition, the job itself can be both a source of stress and a source of satisfaction. Research has found that covering a story well may help mitigate PTSD, depression, and other negative factors.[20] For example, when I covered 9/11 and its aftermath, I took great pride in the fact that I was seeking out, verifying, and sharing information with my audience. I also felt this way during coverage of the Columbine shooting, the Atlanta Olympic Park bombing, the Boston Marathon bombing, and countless other stories over the course of my career. That feeling of being helpful through informing my audience – i.e. doing my job well – made all the difference in how I perceive and remember those experiences, mitigating some residual trauma.

Research has found that this is a common feeling among journalists. For example, a study on Mexican journalists found that those who stopped covering drug cartels because of threats, intimidation, or violence often had a greater incidence of PTSD and/or depression than those who persisted and continued to cover cartels in the face of the same threats, intimidation, and violence.[18]

HOW do journalists generally approach self-care?

Self-care sounds straightforward, but it can be difficult to actually do on a regular and consistent basis, and journalists in particular are quintessentially bad at taking time for themselves or disconnecting from work. But this can lead to negative outcomes.

"You shut it off, but it comes out somewhere. It just comes out in unhealthy ways," LeClair said.

> You see a lot of journalists drinking a lot. You see in the newsroom that we're really rude to each other. We can be very aggressive and mean. We make really irreverent and awful jokes, because it has to come out somewhere. It just does.[19]

The job can be intense, and journalists often cover stories involving death, trauma, violence, people harming other people or animals, people taking advantage of others, and other stories involving human suffering.

"You would be a mess all the time if you felt all the feelings about all the stuff that happens," LeClair said. "I don't think you can necessarily perform the job if you're always feeling all the things. There has to be an outlet, and that's definitely something that I didn't have or realize I needed until later."[19]

In March 2019, *LA Times* Reporter Sonali Kohli shared her own struggles to engage in self-care in a Twitter thread. Thousands of Twitter users – many of them journalists – responded to Kohli's thread with gratitude and with their own stories. She had struck a chord.

Kohli's tweets included her efforts to delay self-care, as many journalists do.

> About a year ago, after covering two mass shootings and deadly fires across California, my therapist told me I had post-traumatic stress symptoms and I should take a month away from work to address them, before they became PTSD. I did not listen. /2

> My logic: I had covered those tragedies from the office. My secondary trauma couldn't be as bad as it was for the journalists in the field, or the people living it. So instead of a break, I took on a new project on the high schools surrounded by the most homicide. /3

> I'd take a break after that published, I said. So I reported on these killings of children, and was working on the stories when another mass shooting

happened last fall. More victims to memorialize. The same week, more deadly fires. More heartbroken families. /4

The insomnia was back, and when I could sleep I had nightmares. Hearing ambulances or seeing police helicopters hovering made my heart race. Candles and bonfires terrified me. Every space I entered, I imagined how it could be the next target of a fire or shooting. /5

Again, my therapist told me to take at least three weeks off. Ever the haggler, I took one, then worked 12–16 hour days for weeks covering the LA teachers strike with my brilliant colleagues. Then I jumped straight back into the project about killings near schools. /6

As soon as those stories published last week, I became more sick than I have gotten in years. It was like my body went on strike, demanding rest. And now I'm finally going to take that extended time off to give my brain some rest, too. /7[21]

Kohli's logic and actions leading up to her body rebelling are the same logic and actions I have taken countless times over the course of my career. They are the same logic and actions practiced by many of my colleagues and fellow journalists. And, they led to many of the same results. I, too, at times experienced difficulty falling asleep, got sick easily, experienced agitation or discomfort in spaces that resembled those I covered, and felt as if my brain was not firing on all cylinders.

Exacerbating this issue is that journalists tend to always be on the job. Even when not at work, we're paying attention to our surroundings, ready to find and pursue a breaking, developing, or promising story idea. We're reading, watching, and listening to the news in case something breaks and we're needed. We've always got our mobile phones close by. This means we're never totally disconnecting or recharging. Over the long term, this can take a toll on our mental and physical well-being.

Journalist Melody Kramer discussed the conflict many journalists feel when they actually do take a vacation. "Cutting myself off cold turkey was revitalizing in a way I hadn't quite expected. But it still felt wrong, in some ways," she wrote in an article for Poynter. "As journalists, we're expected to be 'on' in ways other professions aren't. As a result, I think it's more difficult to break away and easier to feel conflicted about it."[22]

Journalists Kramer spoke with felt similarly and also faced challenges to fully unplugging.

"Checking emails and Slack on vacation is a bit of a necessary evil when you're a journalist. You've just got to set aside time to take care of it," said Gerald Rich, interactive graphics producer at Vocativ.[22]

Sarah Baicker, morning show co-host on the Comcast Sports Network, Philadelphia, told Kramer,

I can't think of a time when I'm entirely disconnected. When I take vacations, generally, I'll check in with my email once a day ... of course, my work email goes right to my phone (which I almost always have on me) so that makes it tricky. Really, what I try to do is, for at least a few hours each day, make sure NOT to have the phone on me.[22]

When an Asiana Airlines plane crashed at San Francisco International Airport on July 6, 2013, I was the assistant news director at a San Francisco radio station. Within moments of the crash, reporters, producers, and writers were calling in to the newsroom to ask whether they were needed and what they could do. Several of my colleagues rushed to the newsroom to handle coverage from there, and several others took it upon themselves to head to the crash site. Our team's coverage that day garnered an APTRA award, an annual award given by the Associated Press. Every single person who responded to the story was ready. Even though most were not scheduled to work that day, even though it was a weekend, and even though many were with family or friends, a part of each of them was tuned to the needs of the newsroom, and when the story broke, they responded without hesitation. They fulfilled the mission they all committed to when they entered the profession – to inform the public. While this contributes to great journalism, it is not conducive to ensuring that journalists take time for self-care, healing, and refreshing.

HOW do trauma and a lack of self-care affect journalists?

The demands of the job can take their toll, and journalists can become cynical and jaded. In addition, news staffers sometimes deal with a toxic or legacy newsroom culture. These challenges have led many younger journalists and journalists of color to leave the profession after just a few years.[23,24]

"Journalists are notorious for not realizing how hard it is until they leave," LeClair said. "When you leave and you take a look back, you're like, holy cow! You just power through so much stuff that a normal person doesn't."[19]

Newman said journalists have been slow to accept that they must manage trauma and stress through self-care, before they burn out.

> They were more than willing to talk about how to interview a survivor sensitively, but when it came to talking about the impact on oneself, people were very hesitant. The issue of talking about how difficult this work can be was much more stigmatized.[5]

Low pay and a lack of resources also play a role in stress and burnout. But a decision to stay or leave the profession can also take an emotional toll,[25] because many journalists see the job as integral to their identity.[25]

"There's a sense of pride when you can hold your own in that toxic work environment," LeClair said. "It's like celebrated. The crazier the situation you've been in and dealt with, the better. I've had people throw things in the control room. I've had people scream in my face, 'fuck you,' and it's all okay." It's all tolerated.[19]

"It's easy to forget that you're not just a journalist. You're also a human being, and perhaps your most important obligation is to yourself," said veteran reporter and journalism educator Elaine Monaghan in a webinar for IJNet. "You can't tell stories or do your job if you're not ok."[26]

Though trauma and stress can manifest in any story, covering the COVID-19 pandemic significantly impacted journalists' mental health. Several studies illuminate the widespread impact on journalists, including an October 2020 survey of 1,400 journalists from The International Center for Journalists (ICFJ) and the Tow Center for Digital Journalism at Columbia University,[27] and a July 2020 study from the Reuters Institute at the University of Oxford,[28] in which researchers interviewed 73 journalists from established newsrooms all over the world. In both studies, 70% of participants responded that covering the pandemic led to psychological or emotional distress, including anxiety, depression, and PTSD.

Said one Reuters study respondent:

> I am more stressed out because I am unable to cover the outbreak in my country as other countries in the west have done. I feel like a hypocrite because I am only allowed to follow what the government tells me to, and I am not able to shed light on how the rest of the country is handling this outbreak.[28]

Inherent in COVID-19 coverage is coverage about socio-economic status, race and ethnicity, age, ability, gender, and socio-political divides – all of our societal fault lines represented in a story that impacted the entire world. At the same time, working to cover the COVID-19 pandemic also likely meant you were working harder to reach sources, uncover information, and inform your audience, while at the same time potentially having more family responsibilities, including managing schooling for your kids or caring for aging parents. In fact, the Reuter's Institute survey found that 60% of respondents said they were working harder in the pandemic, with younger journalists reporting that they were assigned COVID-19 stories at a higher rate than their older colleagues, given the dangers of the pandemic to older people.

Said another Reuters study respondent, "the combination of working from home and home schooling, while trying to run a home, is impossible."[28]

Journalists covering COVID-19 and other major stories were also tasked with trying to cultivate trust among fractured audiences. "Finding things to document that inform the public [is] extremely difficult with mistrust of the media at an all-time high," another Reuters respondent said. "Gatherings can turn hostile on us in an instant, and the idea that the media has any agenda other than simply documenting this time in our collective history is pervasive."[28]

In this context, journalists, as human beings, will feel the effects, making it important to find ways to weave in self-care, even if you can't do it every day. For example, studies show that respondents who received counseling were less distressed than those who did not.[11]

A May 2020 study from the International Federation of Journalists (IFJ) found that female journalists experienced even greater stress and anxiety than their male counterparts in the wake of the pandemic. Respondents included more than 1,300 journalists from 77 countries.[27]

"We are in a situation where gender roles have been exacerbated and women journalists are no exception to that,"[27] said IFJ Gender Council Chair Maria Angeles Samperio in her survey response.

"A lot of female colleagues are complaining about the difficulty to reconcile work and private life," said Sofia Branco, president of the Portuguese Union of Journalists and a member of the IFJ executive board. "I fear that the ongoing impact of COVID will be more severe on women."[27]

In addition, journalists all over the world face discrimination and harassment from leaders, political actors, and fellow citizens of different demographic groups.

"Journalists used to be the people who were protected. If you said you were a journalist, everyone would try to keep you safe," said Newman. "Now, if you say you're a journalist in many contexts, you're attacked."[5]

Newman cautioned journalists to be realistic about self-care and avoid setting up an unrealistic, over-zealous self-care routine. Balancing work, family, self-care, and other responsibilities sometimes means you won't get to everything every day. "Sometimes you have to work on a breaking news story, and you've got to work for 24 hours, but then you can recover," Newman said. "There's evidence to show that recovery is just as important. Taking time off and doing activities away from work is really important for sustaining you in the long run."[5]

Of course, a tendency among journalists is to focus so much on the job – the mission of informing the public and holding power to account – that we put caring for ourselves on the backburner.

"The problem is that people believe that self-care is extra," said Newman. "It's not an extra. In order for somebody to function, you have to be at your optimal capacity. And if you're going to tell difficult stories with people who have been hurt, you need to be at your best."[5]

Given the COVID-19 pandemic, #MeToo, Anti-Asian violence, and the Movement for Black Lives, as well as the shifting attitudes of a younger generation, Newman thinks the stigma against talking about trauma and stress may be fading.

"Younger journalists are more willing to talk about their reactions," Newman said. In addition, this digital age has led to more "first-person journalism, citizen journalism," which can involve people sharing their own experiences as part of a story. Newman also said journalism coverage of stories related to mental health has contributed to the fading stigma and more general acceptance of conversations about these issues.[5]

WHO is affected by trauma in news coverage?

While all journalists can be affected by news stories that involve traumatic events or scenarios, journalists who fall outside the mainstream demographic group may face greater triggers to trauma and stress than their colleagues, because stories may reflect their lived experiences. As we discussed in *Chapter 7*, racial trauma can be ongoing as stories get covered over and over again and new stories break, and it can cause symptoms similar to PTSD.

For example, Black journalists covering the police killings of George Floyd, Breonna Taylor, and others may carry similar experiences from their own lives, and thus they must both cover the story and live it. Latino and Indigenous journalists in the US covering the death toll from the COVID-19 pandemic do so with the awareness that Latino and Indigenous populations were more affected by COVID-19 illness and death than other demographics. Female journalists covering sex trafficking in Mexico do so likely either knowing someone who has been harmed by sexual violence or having been harmed themselves.

Allissa V. Richardson, PhD, assistant professor of journalism and communication at USC, said on the *IJNotes* podcast,

> We feel the weight of this differently, because we are Black journalists, and when we see old images of civil rights movement protests where Black bodies are being tossed in the air with fire hoses, or even current movements where we see people lying on the street because they have been shot or choked to death, we see ourselves in that.

Richardson said this can traumatize Black journalists and other journalists of color, and so can the response of white colleagues, even if that was not the intention. "Many times, people who are not Black who are in the newsroom, they may be sympathetic, but it's not that same weight, because they don't see themselves as the victim. Nor do they see themselves as the aggressor."[29]

Mobile journalists of color are on the forefront of self-care in journalism, creating communities of care to support each other in the work. "One of the things that I've heard them say often is if they didn't have their communities to retreat to, to talk to, they likely would buckle under much of the pressure," said Richardson.[29]

Though journalists of color may provide richer, more nuanced insights on many stories, in particular, if certain angles are not often represented in mainstream coverage, they may experience trauma or be re-traumatized as they work to tell the story.

In an article for *Self*, political and pop culture journalist Jarrett Hill discussed the challenges Black journalists faced in 2020 and 2021, and whenever stories involving violence against Black people arise.

> There's been fatigue resulting in countless naps and late-morning starts. There's been sadness that's seen me cry four times in a day. There's been

frustration with white people asking me questions I didn't feel the energy or interest to answer. There's been an unexpected resolve in me, regarding where I go from here, what I'm just not willing to do anymore. There's been an anger that lately finds me making my way to the stove, firing up my KitchenAid stand mixer, and turning out baked goods for friends, sublimating my rage into cheesecake. Or banana bread. Or cookies.[30]

NBC LX Dallas host Ashley Holt told Hill she feels a responsibility to do more to get the stories and all relevant aspects told. "I have definitely felt a great responsibility to cover everything in a way that would make people who look like me proud, but that takes a lot, so it's been tough."[30]

CBS-2 investigative reporter Dorothy Tucker told Hill:

> It is just nonstop, and as a reporter, there are so many who are reaching out to you now, [such as] your colleagues in the newsroom, who want your opinion on a story. They want your advice; they want your context. They want your perspective journalistically. It's just truly, truly exhausting, but at the same time, you know you have to put up with it because it is an opportunity to educate, especially your colleagues.[30]

Reporters who cover small or distinct communities may also face trauma while covering the COVID-19 pandemic, anti-Asian violence, and other stories because they are more likely to have some connection to the person or people affected.

For example, in "The People's Newspaper," a short documentary about the *Navajo Times* in Window Rock, Arizona, filmmaker Eléonore (Léo) Hamelin interviewed reporter Arlyssa Becenti for *The New Yorker*, who described what it was like to both cover the pandemic death toll and be affected by it.

> I see the numbers every day and I report on it …, knowing those are my relatives. My mom, she knows everybody. She'll say a name and I'm, like, 'Oh, are you kidding me? I know that person. I just saw that person.' And they're just one of those numbers now, the death toll that I'm reporting on.[31]

While it is important to acknowledge trauma and provide support, it is also important to note that diverse voices in the newsroom can help enrich and expand coverage. For example, Newman pointed out that

> information and news coverage about sexual assault has improved over time, because more women are in the newsroom, because more survivors are in the newsroom, whether they're acknowledged or not, and people have started to tell the stories from the perspective of survivors, from perspectives of family members, as opposed to telling it from the police reports or the perpetrator's voice.[5]

In addition to journalists in specific demographic groups, it is important to consider the impacts of trauma and stress on the ever-growing ranks of freelance journalists, who face not only the stress of covering traumatic stories, but also the stress of worrying about how to afford rent, food, and transportation on meager or irregular salaries.

In an article for the *Columbia Journalism Review* (CJR), freelance journalist Meg Dalton said her first journalism gig offered low pay and just a handful of hours, and even when she landed her first full-time journalism job at the *Greenwich Time*, the salary was just $35,000 a year, meaning she had to keep that freelance gig *and* take on graphic design clients to make ends meet. "My health started to deteriorate. I gained 20 pounds in three months. I developed insomnia. I went back on antidepressants. Taking a step forward professionally meant several steps backward in every other part of my life."[32]

It took a panic attack at a music concert for Dalton to make some changes. She applied to graduate school and decided to stay committed to journalism, but she wrote that she keeps that concert ticket in her wallet, so she can check in with herself every so often. She asks, "*Is it worth it?* So far, the answer has been *yes*. But someday that *yes* may look more like a *no*."[32]

In addition to trauma and stress, burnout is also a very real pitfall for journalists who work longer hours with fewer and fewer resources for seemingly lower pay. Journalists also do their work in the current socio-political context while dealing with accusations of fake news, harassment, and threats from online trolls. These trolls can be disaffected individuals, bots, or troll armies marshaled to put pressure on and silence the voices of those who disagree. Because journalists are a primary target of online trolls, online harassment can greatly contribute to stress and burnout, especially for women,[33] causing many journalists to make the difficult choice of stepping away from what many see as a calling, and leaving the profession.[23,24]

WHY are managing trauma and practicing self-care important?

Employing self-care techniques and engaging in self-care practices can help keep our mental, emotional, and even physical health in optimum condition, allowing us to continue the important work of bearing witness.

"If you look out for yourself, you'll be a better watchdog for the folks you cover," said Heath Druzin, Boise State Public Radio's guns & America reporter, who has covered wars in Iraq and Afghanistan.[1]

Even if your beat feels relatively trauma-free, you never know when you will be called to a breaking news story. For example, on 9/11, reporters covering fashion week in Manhattan were quickly reassigned when the planes hit the World Trade Center towers. Reporters on other beats have also mobilized to cover hurricanes, earthquakes, and other major stories. So, no matter what your beat, trauma and self-care training can help prepare you for any scenario.

Journalists must accept that every difficult story they cover takes a toll. Sometimes it's fatigue, sometimes it's PTSD, and sometimes it's a trigger. Whatever the effect, journalists must come to recognize the importance of stepping away to process and deal with the trauma we witness, sometimes on a daily basis. This allows us to recharge to be ready to face the stories we may have to cover and the potential harassment we may face online for doing our jobs.

The need to address stress and trauma through self-care must become a priority for the journalism industry, because, as Newman pointed out, journalists have a critically important role to play in society.

Telling "compassionate important stories about people who have experienced violence and injustice is such an important task, and it's always been the task of journalists," Newman said.

> Journalists have a role in really explaining the experiences of people and helping people make choices. We have to make a lot of choices about laws that involve survivors, that involve mental health. Journalists have such an impact on societal understanding.[5]

In a way, taking care of yourself can be framed as caring for your audience. If you are unable to work at your optimal level, then your ability to inform audiences and hold power to account will also be affected.

Having emotional self-awareness can help you navigate and manage trauma. This includes, "knowing your coping skills, knowing your vulnerabilities," said Newman. "In other fields, we recognize that, for example, if athletes have broken a leg, they're more vulnerable. We teach them how to do their job" adjusting for their injury. It's important to acknowledge "that we all have vulnerabilities, what extra things do we need to do to keep doing the work?"[5]

Research has also shown that training and preparing can give you a perceived sense of control and make you more resilient.[34] "That's why most first responders drill, so when they're in a chaotic moment, they know what to do," Newman said.[5]

In addition, self-care strategies can help us define and be guided by an ethical and moral compass. Research on first responders who have faced significant traumas, such as losing a limb, shows that those who have a moral code or ethical compass have greater resiliency and can handle trauma and stress better.[35]

Journalists who have not taken the time to intentionally and deliberately develop their own ethical compass run the risk of not only struggling to cope with trauma, but also facing regrets for actions taken or not taken in the field.[36] "There can be a spiritual wound that needs to be healed," Newman explained, such as "when you feel guilt about acts of omission or commission, particularly in war zones." An important benefit of preparing for trauma is that you can prepare an ethical code to guide your response.[5]

As mentioned at the beginning of this chapter, if you are in a position to offer support to a colleague or friend, check in to see how they are and encourage them to engage in an act of self-care. Your support can shore up your colleague. As a side benefit, supporting someone else can also be good for your own well-being.[23]

WHEN should journalists seek self-care?

Though much has been made of the myopic journalist who's only out for the story, in truth journalists are often mission-driven and care deeply about the subjects they cover and the stories they are charged to tell.

In an article with Olga Simanovych, Russian language editor for the Global Investigative Journalism Network (GIJN), Cait McMahon, PhD, managing director of Dart Center Asia Pacific, said a journalist can be re-traumatized throughout the reporting process, specifically at three points:

1. As a witness when covering the event
2. While communicating with victims
3. When telling the story, i.e. sharing the experiences of those affected[37]

When we invest our emotions into a given story, it takes a toll on us. Sometimes, it takes such a toll that we disconnect. This is called **compassion fatigue**, defined as "physical and mental exhaustion and emotional withdrawal experienced by those who care for sick or traumatized people over an extended period of time" and "apathy or indifference toward the suffering of others as the result of overexposure to tragic news stories and images and the subsequent appeals for assistance."[38]

Compassion fatigue is something different from burnout. **Burnout** is a result of dealing with ongoing and/or acute stress, while compassion fatigue deals with taking on and carrying emotional burdens, such as those of the people we cover day in and day out.

Journalists working on a 2014 documentary about family caregivers for Capital Public Radio detailed their experiences with compassion fatigue in an article written by retired editor and producer Catherine Stifter.[39]

> Our photographer Andrew Nixon revealed to me that he'd sat in his car and cried after a photo session with a man caring for his wife with dementia. Andrew told me the couple is about the same age as his parents and they live in the neighborhood where he grew up. The idea that this might happen to his family hit him hard.
>
> A few days later, Katie Orr, who was reporting on a couple in their 50s caring for their severely disabled teenage son, mentioned that it was time to schedule the next recording session. She exhaled a very big sigh and admitted she was putting off calling them and didn't know why.[38]

Signs of compassion fatigue include exhaustion, irritability, insomnia, intrusive thoughts, and headaches, as well as procrastination and emotional outbursts.

You may also experience depression, pulling back from loved ones, and stressful dreams.

Self-care can mitigate the effects of compassion fatigue, burnout, and other traumas. When we take the time to rejuvenate, replenish ourselves, and take a moment away from the demanding job that is journalism, then we can be ready to step back into it with a freshness and sharpness that is lost when we simply persist every day without a break. This benefits us and those we cover.

Journalists should also seek remedies if they find themselves unsupported in their newsroom. Unfortunately, the newsroom culture, while close-knit, intense, and mission-driven, can also be a place that devalues self-care and mental health needs.

"A key strategy in this vein is having good boundaries," said LeClair.

> Speaking up when you feel unsafe or knowing when to pull back from a dangerous assignment – but it goes beyond that, too. When to take extra shifts versus rest; making time for lunch; having healthy boundaries with aggressive or problematic coworkers; as well as establishing boundaries around discussing news or educating people on news stories outside of work.[19]

LeClair faced several incidents of unsupportive managers during her time in news, including after she gave birth to her daughter. "When I went back to work, there was little to no culture around nursing," LeClair said. "I rarely pumped and my milk supply suffered as a result."[19]

> That's one of those things where you should absolutely have a clear boundary. There are legal rules around it, but it's impossible to do on that job. I could not get away enough to do it. I would try. I would try. I would try. I just couldn't. When you're gone for any amount of time, like I would go to the bathroom, and I'd come back to my desk and there'd be three people standing there saying, "where were you? I need something from you."[19]

In the wake of the COVID-19 pandemic, more newsrooms may be acknowledging that journalists need mental health support to do their jobs well. A turning point that made the issue explicit was when CNN's Sara Sidner broke down on the air as she covered yet another story about deaths due to COVID-19. Sidner apologized and tried to compose herself as she said, "this is the tenth hospital that I have been in," and seeing families suffer, "it's really hard to take."[40]

New Day anchor Alisyn Camerota reassured Sidner that no apology was necessary.

"It is a collective trauma that all of us are living through," Camerota said. "Sara, we all appreciate the heart that you bring to this every day, as well as your excellent reporting."[39]

Sidner then added, "It's just not OK. It's not OK what we're doing to each other. These families should not be going through this. No family should be going through this." She implored everyone watching to do what they could to protect each other "and keep this from killing your family members, and your neighbors, and your friends, and your teachers, and doctors, and firefighters. All of these people are here to help you, but you have to do your part."[39]

Sidner's reaction is natural, given the ongoing and collective trauma she experienced as she covered COVID-19 deaths, the Movement for Black Lives, and other traumatic stories. Her response prompts us to reexamine how we approach mental health in newsrooms. She also used her experience to distill the message of the COVID-19 story for viewers.

WHERE can self-care go wrong?

Because the job of a journalist can be so stressful, and because many journalists have not developed healthy self-care regimens or coping mechanisms to deal with stress and trauma, many journalists may turn to habits that can numb them but cause more harm in the long run.

Some of us may become workaholics. By continuing to throw ourselves into the work, we have the illusion of moving forward as we avoid stopping to face the traumas we have yet to deal with. Others may escape into video games or social media, which while fine in moderation can quickly turn to addiction if we have trouble stopping or disengaging.

The Dart Center: Helping journalists deal with the trauma we witness

Journalists may experience trauma as they do their jobs, and also interview people who've experienced trauma. While standard journalism training often teaches how to interview a person in an official capacity – government, business, etc. – the Dart Center seeks to increase training in "ethical, compassionate, victim-centered journalism."

Elana Newman, PhD, is McFarlin professor of psychology at the University of Tulsa, and research director for the Dart Center for Journalism and Trauma.

"The Dart Center offers training in how to bear witness, how to interview people who have experienced trauma, how to care for yourself throughout your journalistic practice, how to recognize the signs that you need a break," Newman said. In addition, the Dart Center develops tools and resources journalists can use to guide their work toward compassionate and victim-centered coverage.[41]

"Traditional journalism has always had very effective tools for talking to people who are empowered," Newman said. "Many of the operating

Of course, if you're intentional about your self-care routine and approach your habits with moderation, then it's perfectly healthy. It's when it turns to addiction and overuse that your habits can lead you astray. For example, if I enjoy watching music videos on YouTube, a healthy self-care routine would be to spend a short and specific amount of time – such as 5–30 minutes – doing this. An unhealthy approach would be to allow my viewing to take me down a rabbit hole from which I do not emerge until hours later. This is not self-care – rather it's procrastination, avoidance, escapism.

When the traumas and stressors become too great to bear, some journalists may turn to substance abuse, and this is exacerbated by a historical glorification of drinking in many newsrooms. It's easy to grab a drink (or two or three or four) with colleagues after work, to commiserate about the day's events and bond over the intense experiences we share. While this may appear to be self-care – after all, we're spending time with friends and colleagues, discussing trauma and stress, and spending time away from work –

---

rules make a lot of sense when you're talking to someone who's in government. They don't make the same sense when you're talking to somebody who's been violated and disempowered." Dart trains journalists to consider "what tools do you need to adjust (your approach)? What do you need to do differently?"[41]

Since its founding nearly three decades ago, Dart has transformed how journalists understand and share people's experiences. Without it, Newman said, "we'd have fewer journalists who continue to tell difficult stories about survivors and victims ..., victim-centered, less compassionate journalism, and newsrooms that are not as flexible and don't sustain good reporting."[41] Overall, without Dart, "citizens would suffer because they weren't getting compelling stories told in new ways."

One of Dart's many resources to help journalists is a comprehensive step-by-step guide to prepare journalists to cover a traumatic story in a way that mitigates trauma and its effects.

For more information, go to DartCenter.org.

---

alcohol consumption can turn problematic. Alcohol serves to dull our senses and numb us to the traumas and stressors we carry. Those who rely too much on alcohol to numb their pain slip into alcoholism, which can cause greater problems throughout someone's life. Alcoholism has led people to lose their jobs, families, and livelihoods. Paired with driving, it could lead to harm of others.

"I think it's a matter of looking at whether your use is problematic," Newman said.

I would say the same thing for eating, sex – there are all sorts of things that in doses bring you pleasure. That is perfectly reasonable. But, when it's problematic, one has to look at it, and one needs to seek help if it really is out of control.[5]

In addition to numbing behaviors, there are dangers that go beyond bad habits and addictions. The quest to manage stress and trauma can cause some journalists to separate themselves from the emotions triggered by witnessing traumatic events. This distancing ourselves from painful and negative emotions can spill over into other parts of our lives, causing us to become cold, unempathetic, disconnected from friends and family, and unable to connect with the sources and stories we cover every day.

To avoid these outcomes, we must face and grapple with traumas and stressors and learn coping strategies. Individual self-care and a newsroom culture that supports self-care can help journalists do that.

HOW do we practice self-care?

The first step in practicing self-care and dealing with the trauma we witness is to admit that journalists are also humans who are affected by stress and trauma, just like anyone else. But, historically, this is not how journalists operate.

"Multiple journalists I talked to felt that their own trauma almost didn't seem legitimate compared to what the people in their stories went through," wrote Kari Cobham, senior associate director of journalism fellowships and media at the Carter Center.

> Yes, it's hard to step back and really think about the personal impact a story or consecutive stories may have had. But don't fall into the trap. Your stress levels, your feelings and your trauma are real and they need to be addressed.[1]

At the very least, develop a list of self-care activities that will work for you, and this list will look different for everyone. Everyday self-care activities can be employed for different goals. If you are feeling lonely or isolated:

- Define, build, and cultivate your emotional support network of friends, colleagues, and loved ones. Then, *use it*!
- Reach out to talk with a friend or loved one (in person or virtually).
- Strike up a conversation with a stranger.
- Journal about how you're feeling and explore why.
- Explicitly ask someone for help.

You can also focus on your physical health and the mind–body connection by doing any of the following:

- Slow breathing in and out for a few minutes
- Deep meditation
- Journaling
- Exercise – whether it's a five-mile run or a one-mile walk
- Hiking
- Five minutes of stretching

Or, you could improve your mood by:

- Taking a break
- Grabbing a piece of fruit
- Drinking a large glass of water
- Taking a nap
- Listening to music
- Hanging out with a pet
- Reading
- Doing something you find fun

To take self-care to the next level, learn to practice mindfulness and meditation. Plenty of apps and YouTube videos will walk you through various different meditation techniques, which can help you slow your heart rate, focus on the present moment, and let go of or reframe stressors or traumas in your life. In addition to meditation, you could explore tai chi, yoga, or Pilates.

Journalist and media consultant Hannah Storm wrote that she defines islands to help manage her own self-care. Islands are

> activities I can look forward to that will help keep me positive and feel less overwhelmed. You could think about islands as something you swim toward if you feel as though you are drowning, a place where you can feel the solid ground beneath your feet.[42]

Some of Storm's islands involve exercising and spending time with friends and family.

Also, define and know your personal mission. Why are you doing journalism? Why are you covering this story? What do you hope to bring to your audience? How and whom will this story help?

If you are covering a traumatic story and need coping mechanisms, Cobham recommends in her Poynter article that you ask yourself a series of questions. Then, based on those answers, act accordingly.

- "Are you isolating yourself instead of connecting with friends or family?
- Are you not enjoying the things you usually do?
- Is your rest fitful?
- Do you spontaneously cry?
- Is it hard to concentrate?
- Has your productivity slipped?
- Do you dread going into work?
- Do you feel disillusioned about work?
- What's your body telling you?"[1]

If you find yourself answering yes to one or more of these questions, then it's likely time to sit down with a therapist or counselor who can address mental health. To find someone, connect with the mental health resources center at your school. If you have health insurance, look into mental health care offerings. Also, check out the resources provided at the end of this chapter.

Some things you can do on your own to mitigate trauma responses are:

- Allow the emotional response to happen. Don't invalidate, deny, or minimize your feelings.
- Calm yourself. Slow breathing is the most direct and immediate way to do this, but you can also go for a brisk walk or run, put yourself into a relaxing situation, or call a friend.

Newman stressed that mental health is just as important as physical health, and the two are intertwined. "Nobody ever says that physical health is optional. Like 'oh no, you can't go to the doctor.' We don't use that language for physical health. It's not optional,"[5] and neither is mental health.

If taking care of *yourself* isn't motivation enough for you, then keep in mind that when you take care of yourself, you can then provide support for a friend, colleague, or loved one who needs it. Also, as Druzin told Poynter, "Figuring out how pain and trauma affect you means you'll have that much of a better understanding of how it's affecting the people you cover."[1] In other words, it will help improve your journalism.

LeClair agreed. "You can't build trust with the communities you're trying to serve, and you're not going to be in a position to do a good job with them," if you are not in a good mental health space. It can hinder your relationships with the communities you cover, "making it that much harder to report on them, that much harder to understand what's really going on in those communities."[19]

Finally, have rituals – of celebration, connection with colleagues, and newsgathering. Celebrate when a story is completed, but also when you complete an interview or when you find an angle. Celebrating successes along the way can motivate us to seek the next celebration point and propel us forward. Rituals of connection – such as a Zoom happy hour, coffee shop meetup, or story pitch session every week or once a month – can keep you connected with colleagues.

Key takeaways

- Self-care is the practice of caring for your physical, emotional, and mental well-being.
- Self-care techniques can help mitigate stress and trauma that can come from doing the work of journalism.
- Journalists are considered professional witnesses, and those who witness trauma can experience trauma vicariously.
- Failing to deal with our trauma can lead to compassion fatigue or burnout, prompting many journalists to leave the profession.

- The practice of self-care, including seeing a counselor, deep breathing, talking with a loved one, or working out, can mitigate feelings of compassion fatigue and burnout.

Discussion questions

1. What do you think of when someone says "self-care"?
2. What do you like to do to relax? Why? If you had trouble answering this question, why did you have trouble?
3. In writing or in small groups:
    a. Discuss a situation in which you experienced stress or trauma.
        i. Did you engage in a self-care practice?
            1. If so, describe what you did and how it affected your well-being?
            2. If not, what was the result and how might you have practiced self-care to avoid negative results?
        ii. NOTE: Please share only what you are comfortable with.
    b. Discuss a situation where you supported a friend or family member who was experiencing trauma or stress.
        i. How did it affect you to witness this person's trauma?
            1. If you were able to help, how did that make you feel?
            2. If you were not able to help, how did that make you feel?
        ii. NOTE: Bearing witness is a key aspect of journalism, so prepare yourself by examining your own life experiences.

Exercises

1. When you experience stress in your life, how do you currently cope? Create a virtual collage, vision board, or slide deck using whatever tool is at your disposal (such as Padlet, VoiceThread, FlipBoard, Google JamBoard, Miro, etc.).
    a. Which of your strategies might you define as negative (i.e. detrimental to you)?
    b. Which would you describe as positive (i.e. helpful to you)?
    c. Challenge yourself to choose a helpful coping strategy, rather than a negative coping strategy to mitigate stress and trauma.

2. Engage in before-and-after assessments of your stress levels.
    a. Write 100–300 words or record 30–60 seconds of audio about your current stress level and state of mind.
    b. After you write, engage in two minutes of deep breathing using the following technique:
        i. Breathe in on a four-count (one-thousand-one – one-thousand-two – one-thousand-three – one-thousand-four).
        ii. Hold the breath in for a four-count.
        iii. Breathe out on a six-to-eight count.
        iv. Repeat FIVE times.

c. After you engage in the breathing exercise, write 100–300 words, or record 30-60 seconds of audio about your current stress level and state of mind.
d. Write an additional paragraph describing how your state of mind changed from before or after the breathing (or add to your audio recording). If it did not, then mention that.
3. Develop a self-care plan.
   a. Take the self-care assessment at the following link: http://socialwork.buffalo.edu/resources/self-care-starter-kit/developing-your-self-care-plan.html
   b. Next, fill out the maintenance sheet.
   c. Identify any barriers that you think might get in the way of you engaging in or maintaining a self-care practice.
   d. How might you deal with the barriers?
   e. Optional: Complete the emergency self-care plan.
4. Revisit your response to the *Chapter 1* discussion question in which you described why you want to be a journalist and what impact you hope to make. Respond to the following:
   a. What aspects of pursuing your goals might lead to the need for self-care?
   b. Compile a list of strategies you might use to care for your mental and physical well-being.
   c. Keep the list in an easily accessible location – so you can reference it when necessary.

Resources

https://www.psychologytoday.com/us/therapists
https://www.lenfestinstitute.org/local-journalism/self-care-advice-for-journalists/
https://www.suicidereportingtoolkit.com/
https://docs.google.com/document/u/0/d/1vszi9-0gfJ3J4m5GcXedfByvyMcr0albtfH5o2r7bYE/mobilebasic
https://journalistsresource.org/tip-sheets/journalist_covering_conflict_staying_safe/
http://www.mediacrimevictimguide.com/selfcare.html
https://ijnet.org/en/story/tips-coping-after-reporting-distressing-and-traumatic-stories
https://docs.google.com/document/u/0/d/1vszi9-0gfJ3J4m5GcXedfByvyMcr0albtfH5o2r7bYE/mobilebasic
https://www.rtdna.org/content/newsroom_mental_health_resource_guide

Notes

1 Cobham, Kari. "How Journalists Can Take Care of Themselves While Covering Trauma." *Poynter*, May 31, 2019. https://www.poynter.org/reporting-editing/2019/how-journalists-can-take-care-of-themselves-while-covering-trauma/.
2 Namkoong, Kang, Bryan McLaughlin, Woohyun Yoo, Shawnika J. Hull, Dhavan V. Shah, Sojung C. Kim, Tae Joon Moon, et al. "The Effects of Expression: How Providing Emotional Support Online Improves Cancer Patients' Coping Strategies." *JNCI Monographs* 2013, no. 47 (December 26, 2013): 169–74.

3 Hubbard, Patricia, Ann F. Muhlenkamp, and Nancy Brown. "The Relationship between Social Support and Self-Care Practices." *Nursing Research* 33, no. 5 (1984): 266–70. PMID: 6566128.
4 Zhang, Renwen. "The Stress-Buffering Effect of Self-Disclosure on Facebook: An Examination of Stressful Life Events, Social Support, and Mental Health among College Students." *Computers in Human Behavior* 75 (October 2017): 527–37. doi: 10.1016/j.chb.2017.05.043.
5 Elena Newman. "Self Care & Trauma in Journalism" interview by Gina Baleria, *News in Context* (podcast), December 3, 2021. https://beta.prx.org/stories/349247.
6 Chen, Runsen, Ke Peng, Jianbo Liu, Amanda Wilson, Yuanyuan Wang, Meredith R. Wilkinon, Siying Wen, Xiaolan Cao, and Jianping Lu. "Interpersonal Trauma and Risk of Depression among Adolescents: The Mediating and Moderating Effect of Interpersonal Relationship and Physical Exercise." *Frontiers in Psychiatry* 11, no. 194 (April 15, 2020). doi: 10.3389/fpsyt.2020.00194.
7 Nilsson, Henrik, Fredrik Saboonchi, Catharina Gustavsson, Andreas Malm, and Maria Gottvall. "Trauma-Afflicted Refugees' Experiences of Participating in Physical Activity and Exercise Treatment: A Qualitative Study Based on Focus Group Discussions." *European Journal of Psychotraumatology* 10, no. 1 (December 6, 2019). doi: 10.1080/20008198.2019.1699327.
8 Gerber, Markus, Magnus Lindwall, Agneta Lindegård, Mats Börjesson, and Ingibjörg H. Jonsdottir. "Cardiorespiratory Fitness Protects against Stress-Related Symptoms of Burnout and Depression." *Patient Education and Counseling* 93, no. 1 (October 1, 2013): 146–52. doi: 10.1016/j.pec.2013.03.021.
9 Stanley, Elizabeth A., John M. Schaldach, Anastasia Kiyonaga, and Amishi P. Jha. "Mindfulness-Based Mind Fitness Training: A Case Study of a High-Stress Predeployment Military Cohort." *Cognitive and Behavioral Practice* 18, no. 4 (November 2011): 566–76. doi: 10.1016/j.cbpra.2010.08.002.
10 Khoury, Bassam, Manoj Sharma, Sarah E. Rush, and Claude Fournier. "Mindfulness-Based Stress Reduction for Healthy Individuals: A Meta-Analysis." *Journal of Psychosomatic Research* 78, no. 6 (June 2015): 519–28. doi: 10.1016/j.jpsychores.2015.03.009.
11 Foa, Edna B., Carmen P. McLean, Sandra Capaldi, and David Rosenfield. "Prolonged Exposure vs Supportive Counseling for Sexual Abuse-Related PTSD in Adolescent Girls." *JAMA* 310, no. 24 (December 25, 2013): 2650–57. doi: 10.1001/jama.2013.282829.
12 Nakimuli-Mpungu, Etheldreda, James Okello, Eugene Kinyanda, Stephen Alderman, Juliet Nakku, Jeffrey S. Alderman, Alison Pavia, Alex Adaku, Kathleen Allden, and Seggane Musisi. "The Impact of Group Counseling on Depression, Post-Traumatic Stress and Function Outcomes: A Prospective Comparison Study in the Peter C. Alderman Trauma Clinics in Northern Uganda." *Journal of Affective Disorders* 151, no. 1 (October 2013): 78–84. doi: 10.1016/j.jad.2013.05.055.
13 Briere, John. "What Is Trauma." Essay. In Catherine Scott (Ed.), *Principles of Trauma Therapy: A Guide to Symptoms, Evaluation, and Treatment*, 1st ed., 3. Thousand Oaks, CA: Sage, 2006.
14 "Trauma and Shock." American Psychological Association. Accessed February 14, 2021. https://www.apa.org/topics/trauma.
15 Aoki, Yuta, Estelle Malcolm, Sosei Yamaguchi, Graham Thornicroft, and Claire Henderson. "Mental Illness among Journalists: A Systematic Review." *International Journal of Social Psychiatry* 59, no. 4 (March 8, 2012): 377–90. doi: 10.1177/0020764012437676.
16 Smith, River J., Susan Drevo, and Elana Newman. "Covering Traumatic News Stories: Factors Associated with Post-Traumatic Stress Disorder among Journalists." *Stress and Health* 34, no. 2 (August 22, 2017): 218–26. doi: 10.1002/smi.2775.
17 Browne, Tess, Michael Evangeli, and Neil Greenberg. "Trauma-Related Guilt and Posttraumatic Stress among Journalists." *Journal of Traumatic Stress* 25, no. 2 (April 20, 2012): 207–10. doi: 10.1002/jts.21678.

18 Bedei, Cristiana. "Tips for Coping after Reporting Distressing and Traumatic Stories." International Journalists' Network, November 5, 2020. https://ijnet.org/en/story/tips-coping-after-reporting-distressing-and-traumatic-stories.
19 Misha LeClair (former TV News Producer), in conversation with Gina Baleria, February 2021.
20 Feinstein, Anthony. "Mexican Journalists: An Investigation of Their Emotional Health." *Journal of Traumatic Stress* 25, no. 4 (July 13, 2012): 480–83. doi: 10.1002/jts.21715.
21 Kohli, Sonali. "Hi Hello? ★Taps Mic★This Is a ~Mental Health~ Thread." Twitter, March 7, 2019. https://twitter.com/Sonali_Kohli/status/1103709956522426373.
22 Kramer, Melody. "When Journalists Take a Vacation, Do They Actually Take a Break?" *Poynter*, July 8, 2015. https://www.poynter.org/reporting-editing/2015/when-journalists-take-a-vacation-do-they-actually-take-a-break/.
23 Reinardy, Scott. "Newspaper Journalism in Crisis: Burnout on the Rise, Eroding Young Journalists' Career Commitment." *Journalism: Theory, Practice & Criticism* 12, no. 1 (January 2011): 33–50. doi: 10.1177/1464884910385188.
24 Liu, Huei-Ling, and Ven-hwei Lo. "An Integrated Model of Workload, Autonomy, Burnout, Job Satisfaction, and Turnover Intention among Taiwanese Reporters." *Asian Journal of Communication* 28, no. 2 (September 27, 2017): 153–69. doi: 10.1080/01292986.2017.1382544.
25 Sherwood, Merryn, and Penny O'Donnell. "Once a Journalist, Always a Journalist?" *Journalism Studies* 19, no. 7 (November 11, 2016): 1021–38. doi: 10.1080/1461670X.2016.1249007.
26 Dorroh, Jennifer. "Key Quotes: Self-Care on the Frontline with Elaine Monaghan." International Journalists' Network, April 15, 2020. https://ijnet.org/en/story/key-quotes-self-care-frontline-elaine-monaghan.
27 Posetti, Julie, and Fatima Bahja. "Journalism and the Pandemic Survey." International Center for Journalists, October 13, 2020. https://www.icfj.org/our-work/journalism-and-pandemic-survey.
28 Selva, Meera. "COVID-19 Is Hurting Journalists' Mental Health. News Outlets Should Help Them Now." Reuters Institute for the Study of Journalism, July 17, 2020. https://reutersinstitute.politics.ox.ac.uk/risj-review/covid-19-hurting-journalists-mental-health-news-outlets-should-help-them-now.
29 Cyprien, D. "Mental Health and Journalism, Part 4: A Conversation with Dr. Allissa Richardson." September 10, 2020. Accessed February 24, 2021. https://ijnet.org/en/story/mental-health-and-journalism-part-4-conversation-dr-allissa-richardson.
30 Hill, Jarrett. "9 Black Journalists on What It's Been Like to Cover—And Cope With—The News." *SELF*, July 10, 2020. https://www.self.com/story/black-journalists-coverage-coping.
31 DenHoed, Andrea. "Covering the COVID-19 Crisis in the Navajo Nation." *The New Yorker*, January 14, 2021. https://www.newyorker.com/culture/the-new-yorker-documentary/covering-the-covid-19-crisis-in-the-navajo-nation.
32 Dalton, Meg. "When the Math Doesn't Work." *Columbia Journalism Review*, 2018. https://www.cjr.org/special_report/journalist-side-hustles.php.
33 Ferrier, Michelle, and Nisha Garud-Patkar. "TrollBusters: Fighting Online Harassment of Women Journalists." In *Mediating Misogyny: Gender, Technology, and Harassment*, 1st ed., 311–32. Palgrave Macmillan, 2019.
34 Robertson, Ivan T., Cary L. Cooper, Mustafa Sarkar, and Thomas Curran. "Resilience Training in the Workplace from 2003 to 2014: A Systematic Review." *Journal of Occupational and Organizational Psychology* 88, no. 3 (April 25, 2015): 533–62. doi: 10.1111/joop.12120.
35 Southwick, Steven M., and Dennis Charney. "Moral Compass, Ethics, and Altruism: Doing What Is Right." Essay. In *Resilience: the Science of Mastering Life's Greatest Challenges*, 1st ed. Cambridge: Cambridge University Press, 2018.

36 Frankfurt, S., and P. Frazier. "A Review of Research on Moral Injury in Combat Veterans." *Military Psychology* 28, no. 5 (2017): 318–30. doi: 10.1037/mil0000132.
37 Simanovych, Olga. "How Journalists Can Deal with Trauma While Reporting on COVID-19." Global Investigative Journalism Network, September 7, 2020. https://gijn.org/2020/03/24/how-journalists-can-deal-with-trauma-while-reporting-on-covid-19/.
38 "Compassion Fatigue." Merriam-Webster. Accessed February 14, 2021. https://www.merriam-webster.com/dictionary/compassion%20fatigue.
39 Stifter, Catherine. "For Reporters Covering Stressful Assignments, Self-Care Is Crucial." Center for Health Journalism. Accessed February 14, 2021. https://centerforhealthjournalism.org/resources/lessons/reporters-covering-stressful-assignments-self-care-crucial.
40 Benveniste, Alexis. "CNN's Sara Sidner Cries during Covid-19 Report: 'We Are Literally Killing Each Other'." *CNN*, January 12, 2021. https://www.cnn.com/2021/01/12/media/sara-sidner-cnn-cries-covid/index.html.
41 Elana Newman (Professor of Psychology at the University of Tulsa), in conversation with Gina Baleria, December 2020.
42 Storm, Hannah. "Navigating My #MeToo Story." *Poynter*, June 19, 2019. https://www.poynter.org/business-work/2019/cohort2/.

10 Navigating & understanding the journalism industry & operationalizing your passion

> The urgent and perplexing issues which confront our country, the new dangers which encompass our free society, the new fatefulness attaching to every step in foreign policy and to what the press publishes about it, mean that the preservation of democracy and perhaps of civilization may now depend upon a free and responsible press. Such a press we must have if we would have progress and peace.
> – 1947 Hutchins Commission Report: A Free and Responsible Press[1]

WHERE do things stand for journalism & the news industry?

While journalism remains critically necessary to healthy, well-functioning societies, the news industry faces myriad ongoing challenges, including financial sustainability, burnout, a reckoning over newsroom diversity, government and corporate influence, harassment and threats of violence, and **information disorder**, defined as the ecosystem of information-sharing issues we face, including **misinformation, disinformation**, and **malinformation**. This includes competition from talk shows, tabloids, and purveyors of misinformation and disinformation – leading to increased audience distrust. Newsroom leaders must tackle all these challenges while engaging in a reckoning over how to navigate expectations of objectivity and balance with an ethical imperative to provide context and perspective.

While it is important for those entering the field of journalism to understand both the industry's challenges and the fact that the work can be grueling, the job of doing journalism can also be rewarding, empowering, exciting, fulfilling, ever-changing, and meaningful; and opportunities are developing throughout the industry to do journalism in new and innovative ways. In addition, you could contribute to solving challenges for both the industry and society.

When we survey the journalistic landscape today, we find that those just entering the field must reckon with job cuts, low pay, and often lack of benefits. Starting pay for a full-time journalism job can be as low as the $30,000s.[2] Young journalists may find themselves freelancing, contracting, or working multiple jobs to make ends meet as they seek a foothold in the industry that may be their calling. Others who study journalism may find themselves writing for non-journalistic publications or working in PR or advertising. Still others may string together freelance or contract work in a combination of these fields.

In addition, women and people of color face persistent roadblocks to ensuring their voices are heard in the newsroom, their stories are told, and their work leads to leadership positions. The Women's Media Center report *The Status of Women in US Media 2019* found that women and people of color still lag in both leadership and rank-and-file roles in newsrooms, and that women receive salaries significantly lower than their male colleagues at several prominent news outlets.[3] These findings are mirrored in other studies, including out of Great Britain, where researchers called their findings "familiar and stark" with a "chronic failure to achieve even reasonable levels of ethnic diversity in journalism," and a failure to cultivate and retain female journalists. There is a "very strong flow of women into the profession – they form a majority among young journalists but are still very much a minority in the senior ranks."[4] Women and people of color also face greater and more intense and threatening incidents of online harassment than their white male colleagues.[5,6]

But, as ever, there are also hopeful and positive signs. Large-scale and legacy news organizations continue to gain access to people, places, and events that allow them to cover important stories that hold power to account, contextualize information, and inform the public. Journalism entrepreneurs – launching both nonprofit and for-profit ventures – are reimagining the field to make room for sharing stories from communities that fall outside the mainstream advertising-driven target market that tends to drive legacy news coverage. Given the massive and multi-faceted digital landscape, there are more ways today than ever before for aspiring journalists to connect with the field.

We see this hope echoed in a 2019 op-ed by *USA Today* intern Allison Weis, who wrote that "journalism jobs are vanishing and the industry is changing, but I still want in."[7] Weis wrote that her journalism professor was blunt about the challenges of pursuing a career in journalism, but also about the rewards, including getting to learn something new every day, meeting people with different backgrounds and experiences, and "hav(ing) an opportunity to make meaningful change in a society that desperately, desperately needs it right now."[7]

"I aspire to influence our public dialogue for the better, by talking to people and sharing their stories," Weiss said. "We are willing to put in the work to be a part of protecting not only the future of the journalism industry, but our democracy."[7]

Journalists and those who study and support journalism are taking novel approaches to navigate and solve issues the industry faces. For example, the nonprofit journalism space is expanding. Outlets such as The 19th, MLK50, The Marshall Project, Reveal, Prism, ProPublica, and others focus on audiences, topics, or beats that often don't get enough coverage or context in the mainstream news space to fully inform audiences. This focus on a single beat or coverage area allows these outlets to go more in depth and provide valuable context and explanation that's not always possible in the corporate or legacy news space. This adds to audience understanding.

In addition, journalism organizations are doing more to support, represent, and train those doing journalism all over the world, with the goal of contributing to a healthy journalism ecosystem. Such organizations include the International Center for Journalists (ICFJ), the Global Investigative Journalism Network (GIJN), Investigative Reporters & Editors (IRE), the Society of Professional Journalists (SPJ), the Institute for Nonprofit News (INN), Local Independent Online News (LION) Publishers, the Online News Association (ONA), the National Association of Black Journalists (NABJ), the Asian American Journalists Association (AAJA), the National Association of Hispanic Journalists (NAHJ), the Native American Journalists Association (NAJA), Journalism & Women Symposium (JAWS), and many others.

This chapter seeks to present a clear-eyed look at both where the practice of journalism and the news industry stand and where we can go from here, providing pathways for journalism students to join this dynamic and critically important industry.

WHAT challenges does the news industry face?

The challenges mentioned above are not insignificant. The news industry faces ongoing financial struggles – or sustainability issues – including how to pay for the work of doing journalism, while preserving the barrier between funding and journalistic independence. Though consumers are accustomed to receiving news largely for free via broadcast TV, radio, and now digital platforms, we were once in the habit of paying for a subscription to our local newspaper and/or donating to our local public broadcasting outlet. However, subscriptions and donations generally count for only a fraction of revenue, with the remainder made up by advertising or foundation support in some countries and taxpayer-funded subsidies in others – or perhaps a combination.

A related challenge is competition from other content generating sources, including tabloids, talk shows, pop-culture sites, and purveyors of misinformation and disinformation. This presents a dual challenge, as these entities draw audience eyes and ears away from legitimate sources of news and information, and advertisers follow to outlets and sites where audiences are spending their time. These entities entice audiences with content that may be more sensational, biased, or outright incorrect and misleading in an effort to manipulate emotions, rather than inform. The resulting information disorder can cause confusion among audiences who may not be able to tell what is or isn't fact-based, as well as set audience expectations toward receiving information that conforms with their beliefs, rather than informs them. This has resulted in increased audience distrust.

"You really can't have a discussion like this without addressing the age of misinformation," said David E. Kaplan, executive director of GIJN. "It's become just an onslaught. I think we woke up just a few years ago to find out we were in a war we didn't even know we were fighting, and we've been getting our asses kicked."[8]

Kaplan said US and other Western journalists can learn from colleagues in other parts of the world, such as China and Russia, where "dictators and kleptocrats" have disseminated misinformation and disinformation in "Orwellian attacks on the media and the public .... It's scary how effective this stuff has been, that you can just keep repeating something and people start to accept it as truth."[8]

These trends have been developing for a while. Tectonic financial, content creation, and delivery shifts have led to a continuing decline in newsroom staff and local news outlets over the past 20 years. The coming of digital media in the late 1990s and early 2000s shifted audiences and thus advertising revenue away from so-called traditional or legacy print and broadcast media to digital delivery platforms. Revenue was further impacted by aggregation, as platforms such as Google, Yahoo!, and others presented content from primary news sources to users for free without permission, without paying content creators, and sometimes without crediting the original source.[9,10]

Between 2008 and 2019 (the year *before* the COVID-19 pandemic hit), the number of people working at US newspapers was cut in half.[11] Though losses at newspapers and radio stations were somewhat offset by hiring increases in other areas of news production, including digital outlets, as well as comparatively stable numbers in broadcast and cable TV news, the overall net was a loss in reporters, editors, photographers, and other newsroom staff totaling 23% or 27,000 jobs.[11]

These issues were exacerbated in 2020, when the COVID-19 pandemic prompted an increase in the number of newsrooms struggling financially, with some cutting production, staff, and resources or shuttering entirely.[12] *The New York Times* reported that 37,000 employees in newsrooms across the country were affected in some way by COVID-19, through layoffs, furloughs, or pay cuts.[13] In addition, Poynter editor Kristen Hare, who kept a running database of newsroom contractions, estimated that at least 60 newsrooms shuttered during the same period (Figures 10.1 and 10.2).[12]

Underlying these challenges is the fact that, throughout the first two decades of the 21st century, corporations and hedge funds increased purchases of legacy news outlets – interested primarily in their assets, such as real estate and advertising and subscription revenue – money that is then siphoned from local markets to shareholders. In the article, "The fight for the future of America's local newspapers," *Financial Times* journalists Anna Nicolaou and James Fontanella-Khan detailed how hedge fund ownership has played out.

> Small and midsized regional and local newspapers, once swimming in cash and an essential service to Americans living outside New York or San Francisco, have been converted into distressed assets boomeranged among investors for short-term profits. Previously an industry stewarded by wealthy families, today about half of America's daily newspapers are controlled by private equity, hedge funds and other investment groups.[14]

Navigating the news industry 239

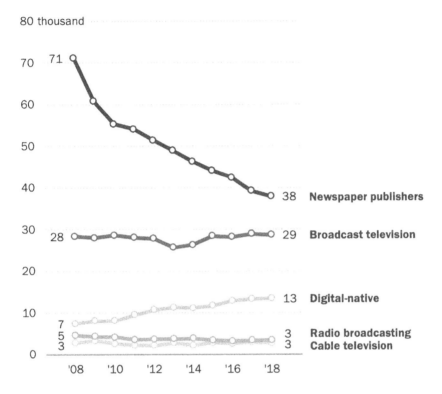

Figure 10.1 Graph of newsroom employment trends (https://www.pewresearch.org/fact
-tank/2020/04/20/u-s-newsroom-employment-has-dropped-by-a-quarter-si
nce-2008/).

Newsroom employees by news industry, 2008 to 2019

Number of U.S. newsroom employees in each news industry

Year	Total	Newspaper publishers	Broadcast television	Digital-native	Radio broadcasting	Cable television
2008	114,260	71,070	28,390	7,400	4,570	2,830
2009	104,490	60,770	28,040	8,090	4,330	3,260
2010	98,680	55,260	28,640	8,090	4,100	2,590
2011	97,350	54,050	28,050	9,520	3,540	2,190
2012	95,770	51,430	27,830	10,750	3,610	2,150
2013	92,240	48,920	25,650	11,250	3,700	2,720
2014	89,820	46,310	26,300	11,180	3,820	2,210
2015	90,400	44,120	28,430	11,710	3,380	2,760
2016	89,220	42,450	28,190	12,830	3,190	2,560
2017	87,630	39,210	28,900	13,260	3,320	2,940
2018	86,100	37,900	28,670	13,470	3,370	2,690
2019	87,510	34,950	30,120	16,090	3,530	2,820

Note: The OES survey is designed to produce estimates by combining data collected over a three-year period. Newsroom employees include news analysts, reporters and journalists; editors; photographers; and television, video and film camera operators and editors. Digital-native sector data is based on "other information services" industry code, whose largest segment is "Internet publishing and broadcasting and web search portals."
Source: Pew Research Center analysis of Bureau of Labor Statistics Occupational Employment Statistics data.

PEW RESEARCH CENTER

Figure 10.2 Chart of newsroom employment trends (https://www.pewresearch.org/fact-tank/2020/04/20/u-s-newsroom-employment-has-dropped-by-a-quarter-since-2008)/).

As an example, Alden Global Capital, the majority owner of Digital First Media (DFM), reported a 17% operating margin and nearly $160 million in profits in 2017.[15] DFM's business model has been to purchase local newspapers or chains and then extract profit for shareholders by cutting staff and selling assets such as legacy newspaper buildings. DFM does not reinvest profits from newspaper sales or ad revenue into the outlets.[15]

In addition to the influence of corporate ownership, we have seen state-sponsored efforts to discredit journalism and encourage violence toward journalists. This has been happening for years in countries such as Mexico, the Philippines, and Russia, and it began escalating in the US in 2015 as Donald Trump entered the 2016 presidential campaign and used verbal attacks on journalists to shore up support among those who felt left behind. Authoritarian-minded leaders stoke negative feelings against journalists in an effort to discredit critical reporting, justify withholding information from news outlets, and wrest narrative control from news.

Journalists all over the globe face increasing threats to their well-being and safety, particularly in nations where press freedom has historically been robust, including the US.[16,17] This trend emboldens those in less democratic nations who feel freer than ever to intimidate and silence journalists working to hold power accountable. In 2020, The US Press Freedom Tracker documented what it called "unprecedented numbers" of assaults on and arrests of journalists, as well as other tactics to impede or prevent journalists from "documenting history," including "Black Lives Matter and anti-police brutality protests." Globally, the situation is also concerning. Reporters Without Borders (RSF), which documents press freedom in 180 countries and territories, wrote upon release of its 2020 World Press Freedom Index that five factors affect press freedom, and they must be addressed in the next decade to maintain a free press.

1. A geopolitical crisis (driven by aggression from authoritarian regimes)
2. A technological crisis (due to a lack of democratic guarantees)
3. A democratic crisis (due to polarization and repression)
4. A trust crisis (suspicion and hatred of the press)
5. An economic crisis (impoverishing quality journalism)

The report noted that these five "areas of crisis" are "compounded by the current global health crisis."[18]

Former journalist Meera Selva, now director of the fellowship program at the University of Oxford's Reuters Institute for the Study of Journalism, said the geopolitical crisis stems from "dictatorial, authoritarian, or populist" leaders "making every effort to suppress information and impose their visions."[19] The COVID-19 pandemic has given these leaders greater cover to restrict the flow of information and take action against journalists whose work may contradict the official line.[19]

The technological crisis stems from the fact that many nations have been reticent to impose "appropriate regulation" on digital platforms, leading to what RSF called "information chaos," where "propaganda, advertising, rumor, and journalism are in direct competition." When people do not understand how to tell the difference between different content types, it contributes to a lack of trust and could lead those in power to pass laws that overreach and restrict journalistic information along with the rest.

In 2020, 17 nations passed laws purportedly restricting online misinformation, some hastily written and vague.[20] While limiting misinformation and disinformation is worthy, having the government in control of determining which information is OK and which is not could lead to dangerous consequences.[20]

> In more autocratic states new laws were written permanently into criminal or civil codes and outlawed all forms of online misinformation, with vaguely defined provisions allowing prosecutors to charge or fine journalists for publishing information deemed untrue or threatening by authorities. Such laws have created new possibilities for authoritarian leaders, and their law enforcement and judicial systems, to place restrictions on speech that may long outlast the pandemic.[20]

Indeed, these laws have allowed dictatorial leaders in countries including Russia, Brazil, Algeria, UAE, Bolivia, and the Philippines, among others, to crack down on legitimate journalists and news outlets.

In addition to passing "Fake News" laws and stoking negative feelings toward journalists, authoritarian regimes have restricted the flow of information during the COVID-19 pandemic by limiting questions at virtual news conferences, suspending requests for information, and cutting internet service.[19] But it is important to remember that, though the challenges are significant, many people are doing impactful and important journalism to counter these efforts.

HOW do these challenges affect the work of doing journalism?

The challenges identified above have impacted the news industry and the practice of doing journalism in many ways. Information disorder has led to misinformed and thus mistrustful citizens, some who gravitated toward conspiracy theories, questioned the advice of scientists and other experts during the pandemic, and embraced content that advocated hate and violence. In the US, this culminated in the January 6, 2021, insurrection attempt at the US Capitol.

With regard to hedge fund ownership, siphoning of profits has left more and more local communities with either emaciated news outlets or no local news outlets at all. Outlets that remain are often unable to adequately cover the news of the area and instead fill pages with syndicated content from other parts of the country that may lack relevance, PR products, or hastily written stories that lack depth given the lack of resources and time. Those unable to withstand the extraction any longer shutter completely.[21] These impacts are detailed in a June 2020 University of North Carolina study on **news deserts**, which measured cuts in staff and losses of outlets.

> In the 15 years leading up to 2020, more than one-fourth of the country's newspapers disappeared, leaving residents in thousands of communities – inner-city neighborhoods, suburban towns and rural villages – living in vast news deserts. Simultaneously, half of all local journalists disappeared, as round after round of layoffs have left many surviving papers – the gutsy dailies and weeklies that had won accolades and Pulitzer Prizes for their reporting – mere "ghosts" or shells of their former selves.[22]

Poynter's Hare, who documented layoffs, furloughs, pay cuts, mergers, and newsroom closures during the COVID-19 pandemic,[9] pointed out that other members of the community were also affected. For example, from March to December 2020, 1,500 people who ran printing presses lost their jobs, as newspapers decreased or ceased print production. "The media isn't just made up of the people who make the news," Hare wrote as she reflected on "what it means – to a town, to an industry and to individual people – when massive shifts like this take place."[23]

In the local news vacuum that's developed, some non-news players have sought to fill the void. Companies with decided points of view, PR-focus, or political bias have developed websites that mimic the look and feel of local news outlets but push a specific agenda, instead. The *Columbia Journalism Review* (CJR) called these "shadowy, politically-backed" information purveyors "pink slime" outlets[24] (in reference to the meat by-product once used by

McDonalds), because they are not covering news; they are pushing partisan talking points and collecting data on those who visit their sites.

The stress of this trend has affected journalists all over the world. In a survey of more than 1,400 English-speaking journalists from 125 countries, the ICFJ and the Tow Center for Journalism at the Columbia Graduate School for Journalism, learned that journalists are struggling with mental health challenges, financial uncertainty, threats of violence, efforts to curtail press freedom, and accusations of peddling misinformation while working to fact-check actual misinformation. Report authors called the results "startling and disturbing."[5] Survey respondents said nearly half (46%) of all misinformation and disinformation came from elected officials, and that their sources have shared that they feared retaliation for speaking to the news media. Respondents also identified Facebook as "the most prolific spreader of misinformation."[5] Nearly 1/3 (30%) told ICFJ that their employer had not provided any personal protective equipment (PPE) to keep them safe during pandemic news coverage, and 70% said mental health was their "most difficult challenge"[5] during the pandemic. The authors went so far as to say that the pandemic, on top of ongoing economic, political, and other challenges, should be seen as a potential "extinction-level event."[5]

If we take this pathway – of siphoning resources from local communities into shareholder pockets, contraction of local newsrooms, and replacement of independent reporting with stories based on partisan talking points – to its most extreme conclusion, then what we face is a deterioration of healthy functioning societies, as well as our ability to make decisions about our health, safety, education, and other issues based on legitimate information. As we discussed in *Chapter 1*, democracies and healthy societies require public participation. With a crippled journalism ecosystem, the public may not be able to follow the activities of elected officials from moment-to-moment, nor may individual members of the public know how or even have time to reach out to public officials, access or decipher government documents, or attend public meetings. Journalists take on these roles and responsibilities and then inform their publics about the activities of elected representatives, appointed officials, and governmental bodies in service to the community.

We already see how lack of information flow affects local and regional ecosystems. Study after study has found that communities that have lost their local paper have seen a decrease in transparency and accountability among governmental and corporate leaders; an increase in corruption; and a deterioration in public knowledge of the activities of city councils, boards of supervisors, school boards, and other governmental bodies. News deserts have also seen a decrease in the number of people running for public office,[25] lower voter turnout,[26] less citizen engagement,[27] increases in partisan polarization,[28] the public becoming less informed,[26] lower quality government,[29] higher municipal borrowing costs,[30] and even increased pollution.[31] Decreased local journalism also leads to a power shift in which elected officials have the advantage, as was revealed in a Pew Research study showing that as local news reporting in Baltimore declined, news outlets produced more uncritical stories based on press releases from elected officials.[32] This means elected officials wield more control over the narrative.

In the wake of layoffs at the venerable *Cleveland Plain Dealer*, former executive Brian Tucker told *Governing*, "No matter what side of the political fence you sit," in the absence of "a decent robust newspaper, politicians are going to do bad things .... Nobody is going to be watching. No one is holding your feet to the fire."[33]

Report for America co-founders Steven Waldman and Charles Sennott, who place and support reporters in local newsrooms, wrote in a 2018 *Washington Post* opinion piece that a lack of local journalism tears at the fabric of a community.

> The reporter shortage means residents don't have the information to make decisions for their families or hold institutions accountable. They don't know if their schools are underperforming or their mayor is corrupt or their courts are fair .... With less local reporting, residents come to understand each other less well. Fellow citizens become caricatures rather than neighbors – and we become more polarized. People rely more on national sources, which tend to be ideologically driven. By contrast, local issues – Why are there so many traffic deaths at Maple and Main? How do our teacher salaries compare with those in the rest of the state? – often cross party boundaries.[34]

Waldman and Sennott said erosion of local journalism in Middle America may be why two major stories went barely noticed until they were entrenched, "the rise of the opioid epidemic in middle America and the political strength of Donald Trump."[34] They also called out cuts in reporting staff as a reason for decreasing trust. "Residents would be less likely to view 'the media' as arrogant, ideologically driven miscreants if they see real reporters at school board meetings until midnight, covering nitty-gritty stories of importance to them."[34]

The issue is so concerning in the US that a *Harvard Business Review* article was headlined: "Journalism's Market Failure Is a Crisis for Democracy." The sub-header drove home the point, saying "Commercial imperatives are at odds with democratic objectives."[35]

As mentioned above, many nations have now passed laws purportedly to control misinformation, laws that may overreach and also affect legitimate accountability journalism. These laws are already having a chilling effect on journalists and sources in many countries, causing some journalists to pass on covering stories or leave the field entirely, and prompting some sources to refuse to speak to journalists for fear of retaliation.[36] A UNESCO report warned, "Heavy-handed responses to disinformation that restrict freedom of expression rights ... could actually hobble the work of journalists and others engaged in vital research, investigation and storytelling about the pandemic, and the disinfodemic that helps fuel it."[5]

The pie chart from the RSF's World Press Freedom Index (Figure 10.3) shows that the situation is deemed "good" in only 8% of nations and territories covered, and satisfactory in just 18%. The remaining 74% are categorized as problematic (35%), difficult (26%), or very serious (13%). The very serious category grew by 2% from 2019 to 2020.[15]

RSF Secretary-General Christophe Deloire said the next decade will be "decisive" for journalism.

The coronavirus pandemic illustrates the negative factors threatening the right to reliable information, and is itself an exacerbating factor .... The public health crisis provides authoritarian governments with an opportunity to implement the notorious "shock doctrine" – to take advantage of the fact that politics are on hold, the public is stunned and protests are out of the question, in order to impose measures that would be impossible in normal times.[15]

Deloire went on to warn:

For this decisive decade to not be a disastrous one, people of goodwill, whoever they are, must campaign for journalists to be able to fulfill their role as society's trusted third parties, which means they must have the capacity to do so.[15]

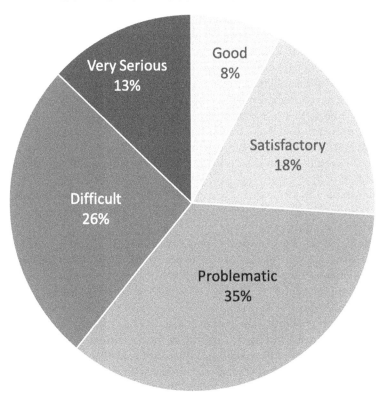

Figure 10.3 RSF 2020 World Press Freedom Index. Source: Reporters Without Borders (RSF) (https://rsf.org/en/ranking).

> **EXERCISE BREAK**
>
> 1. Go to the Newseum's Journalists Memorial Database (https://www.newseum.org/exhibits/online/journalists-memorial/).
> 2. Choose a journalist being honored in the memorial and read their story.
> 3. Create a one-minute video or audio podcast OR write 200–400 words discussing what stood out to you. Include:
>   a. What type of journalism did this person do?
>   b. What country/countries did this person cover?
>   c. How did this person die?
>   d. What was this person's contribution to journalism?
>   e. What else stood out or resonated with you?

WHO is doing journalism that counters and addresses these challenges?

So, that's the bad news ..., but even though challenges abound, the news about the news industry is not all bad. Many "people of goodwill"[15] seek to shore up the industry and ensure that journalists can continue to do the valuable work of informing and thus facilitating free and healthy societies.

As corporate news jobs dwindle, many former journalists from once venerable news outlets have sought out or created new opportunities to inform their publics. Many nonprofit news outlets now fill gaps in mainstream coverage and provide context to overlooked and important stories. For example, Inside Climate News (ICN) was born because major climate stories were either going uncovered or covered at only a cursory level. Founder and publisher David Sassoon wanted to draw attention to stories focused on climate change, energy, and the environment in a way that was accessible to the general public but also valuable and informative for policy makers who have the power to set agendas that can address these issues.

Sassoon told *Nieman Reports* that breaking news is already covered, so ICN focuses on follow-ups and goes more in depth. This explanatory approach garnered the outlet a Pulitzer Prize in 2013. "What seemed to be missing was connecting dots, and context, and also covering news that was sitting there waiting to be reported on."[37] Working on beats or at topic-focused newsrooms can make having an expertise valuable. A reporter with a background studying, working in, or covering a particular issue or industry can draw upon their specialized experience and knowledge to put stories related to that beat into context – to increase public knowledge and understanding.

Former *New York Times* Executive Editor Bill Keller decided to focus on the criminal justice beat and became founding editor-in-chief of The Marshall

Project. The Center for Investigative Reporting has been around since 1977, but the coming of the internet and social media allowed the nonprofit focused on investigative reporting to rebrand as Reveal and increase its reach and methods of conveying information. Reveal's mission statement encapsulates the benefit, promise, and appeal of nonprofit news. It reads,

> We pour the necessary time and resources into unearthing original stories that hold people and institutions accountable for the problems they've caused or benefited from .... As a nonprofit, our bottom line is the public interest. We have the courage, freedom and independence to dedicate our entire newsroom to this work.[38]

In addition to topic-based beats, some news outlets focus on specific perspectives and voices in need of coverage. For example, MLK50 focuses on social justice coverage, specifically naming its goal as seeking to eliminate racial injustice. By defining its audience as those who face injustice, MLK50 seeks to give time and space to stories and perspectives not often covered in mainstream news. In addition, MLK50 explicitly commits to ensuring its staffing, contributors, and "editorial choices and priorities ... reflect the racial and gender diversity of the communities we serve,"[39] signaling to those whose voices have thus far not been centered in most news coverage that their voices may now be more fully included.

Prism, a news site founded in 2018 by women of color, also seeks to center the voices and stories of people of color and women. This focus led Prism reporter Tina Vasquez to break a story involving the forced sterilization of women at a Georgia detention center. Vasquez was able to identify a doctor who was mistreating migrant and rural American women in the region. Notably, Vasquez centered the voices of the affected women, giving them agency to share their stories and reveal systemic injustices and harm. Prism Editor-in-Chief Ashton Lattimore told NiemanLab the outlet's goal is to "shift narratives …. Our approach to culture reporting is, like everything we do, fundamentally rooted in the justice and resiliency of communities of color."[40]

The 19th is another nonprofit news endeavor focusing on women's perspectives. Veteran journalists from *The Washington Post*, ProPublica, and other outlets came together to launch the outlet – named after the 19th Amendment that gave women in the US the right to vote. They hope to provide content that co-founder Emily Ramshaw told Poynter is "by women for women."[41]

In addition, a coalition of journalism organizations released a plan in late 2020 to implement strategies the US government can pursue to shore up and support local news without providing direct funding that many worry could threaten journalistic independence. Recommendations include a $250 refundable tax credit toward local nonprofit news subscriptions. This idea is already in place in France and Canada. Another recommendation in the Local Journalism Sustainability Act would give current owners of local papers a tax credit if they transfer ownership to a nonprofit umbrella. This would be coupled with anti-trust legislation penalizing conglomerate media ownership. In addition, local businesses would get a tax credit for taking out advertising in their local nonprofit news outlet.[42] The hope is that these measures would reinvigorate local journalism without direct government interference. Those in support of the Act hope that Congress will re-introduce it in the current session.

Other exciting initiatives involve funders seeding news outlets in under-served local communities. Canada-based IndieGraf and US-based Tiny News Collective from LION Publishers and News Catalyst give resources and scaffolding to entrepreneurs seeking to launch a local news outlet in a news desert or under-served community. In addition, USC journalism and engineering students teamed up in 2020 to create a data-driven series for 110 different hyper-local newsletters as part of the Crosstown Neighborhood Newsletter Project.[43]

Other ideas to support and shore up local journalism include additional taxpayer funding (with explicit language guaranteeing journalistic independence), which works well in places like England, Canada, Norway, Singapore, and Australia, and to have tech companies fund a portion of local news, given their reliance on content from news outlets (with the same explicit language guaranteeing journalistic independence).[44]

Another trend, according to the International Federation of Journalists (IFJ), is an increase in union activity in countries where journalists have faced sparse protections, such as Kenya, El Salvador, Peru, and Namibia, as well as the Netherlands, UK, US, Australia, and Canada. Unions work to protect journalists, advocate for the designation of journalists as essential workers, and care for those who face financial and mental health issues by providing food and services.[45]

Finally, media development programs funded by UNESCO, USAID, and others provide international aid to support strong local journalism around the world. GIJN's Kaplan likens media development to other foreign assistance, such as for agriculture or industry.

> The World Bank, USAID, the European Union, the United Nations all have recognized that accountability journalism is just as fundamental a building block to a healthy, just, and economically developed society as all these other facets – as having good agriculture and industrial policy and good schools and good cops. You need a watchdog press.

In the midst of all of these endeavors, opportunities abound for young journalists to connect and find support to do journalism that informs, contextualizes, and holds power to account.

WHEN can you launch & build your journalism career?

It is admittedly challenging for budding journalists to make their way in this ever-shifting industry. Entering the field can be scary and exhilarating. But, ideally, it will be rewarding on many levels, including professional fulfillment, financial stability, and longevity.

Journalism's funding model has never really been perfected, and we're living in a moment when this model is in the process of being re-thought again. In the 18th century, journalism was driven primarily by a political patronage model. The 19th century saw the rise of the penny press, which used advertising revenue to reap profits and keep subscription prices low, so the masses could access daily news. In the 20th century, individual and family ownership of news outlets gave way to a corporate model as businesses bought local news outlets and created chains. Now, in the 21st century, we're seeing the downsides of that model and seeking alternatives to sustain a profession that sustains democracy.

Young journalists may choose to seek employment at a mainstream, nonprofit, or public news outlet, or even do contract or freelance work. Finding and securing your dream position may be challenging, but many resources can help, including Poynter's Media Jobs Connection, the Broadcast Education Association's (BEA's) professional job postings, and newsletters that compile full-time and freelance opportunities, such as West Coast Media Jobs, Freelancing with Tim, and Journalism Jobs and a Photo of My Dog. In addition, even though jobs at legacy media outlets may be more difficult to secure, jobs at digital and nonprofit outlets are more plentiful. Also, get creative about finding opportunities to do journalism. Many nonprofits and NGOs that focus on a specific sector are incorporating journalistic practices into their work. For example, Greenpeace and the ACLU are doing investigative journalism.

Newsrooms today consist of all types of positions, including traditional positions, such as reporters, editors, writers, photographers and videographers, producers, news directors, production assistants, and assignment editors; as well as social media managers, graphic designers, social video producers, and audience specialists. This diversity of positions means that whatever your skillset or passion, if you want to pursue journalism, there is a way to do it.

One thing to keep in mind is that larger publications and outlets have historically relied on talent pools coming through the ranks of local journalism, and this increasingly includes student news outlets. Local journalism is still considered the backbone of journalism. It is where stories break that become national. The police killing of George Floyd became a consequential national and international story, but it happened in a local community – Minneapolis. It was local journalists who brought the nuances of the story to life and provided guideposts for national journalists who did not know the community well and did not have a developed network of sources. Every election story or COVID-19 story is part of the national compilation of stories, but they are at their heart local. For example, the story of a nurse who stayed by the bedsides of COVID-19 patients as they took their last breaths, the story of mysterious ballot boxes cropping up in small towns, the story of local community organizers registering people to vote – these are all stories discovered by, broken by, and covered by local journalists. Their resonance gets the attention of national, international, and other local outlets.

As more and more local news outlets are downsized or shuttered, student journalism is filling the void and playing an important role. For example, the California North Bay wildfires were initially covered in large part by students from a local community college.

As Santa Rosa Junior College student Nick Vides, editor-in-chief of the *Oak Leaf* student newspaper, told the *San Francisco Chronicle,* students may not be seasoned journalists, but they make up for it with hometown knowledge. "The advantages are tenfold. You're in my backyard," Vides said. "These major media outlets swarming the area, they don't know the back roads like we do. If I see a roadblock, I know two other roads to safely get to that same place to get our photo and get out."[46] Every year, the *Oak Leaf* garners awards for its coverage, illustrating the value of student journalism to local communities.

Oak Leaf adviser Anne Belden said students also provided a fact-checking service, telling the *San Francisco Chronicle* that "one student saw a need and made his beat dispelling false social media information, reporting with photographic proof that a grocery store rumored to be destroyed was still standing."[46]

Washington Post Fact Checker Glenn Kessler said when he hires, he looks for a local journalism background in someone's resume, particularly experience covering local, regional, or state government, because it means they have experience digging and posing hard questions.

"The guy who's my sidekick now, he previously covered Chris Christie when he was governor of New Jersey, and the woman that had the job before that, she'd previously covered Joe Arpaio in Maricopa County for the *Arizona Republic,*" Kessler said. "They were in the field closely scrutinizing what controversial politicians were doing."[47]

When the *Press Gazette* asked news editors to share what they look for in new hires, most cited tenacity, curiosity, passion, and commitment, in addition to basic skills, such as strong writing and grammar, and knowledge of AP Style. Robin Searle, managing editor at *Travel Weekly*, said she looks for people with solid journalism training and the ability to navigate digital media.

> The majority of our journalists have a background in local, regional or national newspapers – however, the contraction of that particular sector means the pool of available talent coming through the newspaper route is becoming smaller, and respected websites are slowly becoming more reliable sources of quality candidates …. Experience is key, particularly when we are looking for someone who will be capable of immersing themselves in a particular industry and sector and quickly developing a level of expertise to be able to write about and for that market with authority.[48]

Jenny Stevens, commissioning editor on features at *The Guardian*, also held up experience in local news as a plus, as well as persistence and the ability to immerse yourself in your community. "The most important training is going out and finding stories," Stevens said. "Try and get work experience, make contacts with local journalists, seek as much professional advice as you can."[48]

If a local news gig or internship is simply not possible for you, try developing your own stories and pitching them to local, regional, and national news outlets. Though freelance gigs may not always pay well, they do provide exposure and familiarity to those doing the hiring, making it more likely that outlets will give you a shot when an opportunity (or emergency) arises. For example, when journalist and educator Samantha Stanley moved to Longmont, Colorado, she emailed the local paper to ask if they needed any freelance help. "I was assigned a story the same day," she said. She turned the story around for publication three days later. "The next day, they offered me another longer story."[49] If you do decide to pursue freelance or contract work, Stanley recommends getting to know the self-employment laws in your state or country.

Other editors recommend majoring or minoring in a topic that interests you. Developing an expertise can make you a valuable asset in a newsroom and allow you to cover stories on a deeper level. But, as you pursue this other degree, do practice as much journalism as you can on campus and/or in your local community.

If you have trouble landing a position, do journalism anyway. Anyone can set up a website and social media platforms, cover stories, and contribute to the journalistic landscape. Of course, you want to earn a living, and that is the end goal, but putting yourself out there on your own terms can help news organizations see what you can do.

Global Investigative Journalism Network (GIJN): Convening those called to accountability journalism

"The bad guys went international a long time ago," said Global Investigative Journalism Network (GIJN) Executive Director David E. Kaplan. "Globalization had made it easy to move money, people and contraband around the world. The Cold War had taken down borders; cell phones and internet were changing everything. And yet journalism globally had barely changed."[8]

That is why Kaplan has dedicated himself to growing GIJN and supporting investigative and other accountability journalists all over the world.

Before GIJN, investigative journalists largely worked solo or in small teams – essentially without a regional, national, or global network to support the difficult work of holding power to account. Though there were bright spots, it was difficult to compete with a well-networked adversary.

"We have very few troops in the field fighting this war. And then there's so much corruption; so much abuse of power. There's so much

WHY prepare for journalism in the new normal?

As the saying goes, the more things change the more they stay the same. This truism applies to journalism. Change after change, event after event, innovation after innovation have both transformed the practice of doing journalism and highlighted the importance of developing strong foundational skills, such as the ones discussed in this book, as well as skills such as writing, interviewing, and researching. Crises can provide opportunities and reveal solutions, even as they take their toll.

The COVID-19 pandemic prompted an immediate move to remote newsrooms and news coverage. In March 2020, as the pandemic began sweeping across the globe, newsrooms everywhere had to figure out how to keep journalists safe while also effectively covering one of the biggest stories in our lifetime.

Though fully remote news coverage was not expected to last forever, aspects of it were expected to persist. Students entering the field need to be able to do their jobs in this context. It's not the first time a new technology or global scenario prompted shifts in how news was covered. The telegraph in the mid-19th century introduced the tenet of timeliness into our news lexicon. Stories that may have taken days, weeks, or months to reach publishers via foot, horse, train, or ship could be tapped out in seconds or minutes via the telegraph. That new technology led to a shift in the relationship between US Civil War military leaders and journalists, who could now learn about lack of accountability at a time when the press is being hollowed out at an alarming rate," Kaplan said. But, since GIJN's founding in 2003, it has made a difference. "One of the few bright spots has been, we're managing to increase the ranks of people who practice quality investigative journalism. And that's been really exciting."[8]

At the time of this writing, GIJN served and supported member organizations in 80 countries, providing resources, tools, tips, and instructional materials to people doing the journalism of accountability.

It's hard to believe an organization like GIJN – a global hub for the world's investigative journalists – did not exist until the 21st century. Kaplan pointed out that health writers, science writers, and general assignment reporters had established associations early on. But, even though muckraking has been part of journalism since the 19th century, it did not have an established global network. "The journalists who took a lot of the biggest risks, who used the most advanced tools, who went after the toughest stories were kind of loners,"[8] Kaplan said. But, it turns out, they craved connection to others doing similar work.

Kaplan joined a small team led by Brant Houston of Investigative Reporters and Editors (IRE), and Nils Mulvad of the Danish International Center for Analytical Reporting Institute. They decided to hold an investigative journalism conference. "Why don't we invite the world?" Houston suggested. They had no idea if anybody would come. "300 and report on troop movements and strategies within hours, rather than days or weeks. In the late 19th century, as the telephone became ubiquitous, journalists realized that they could call sources (at least those who also had a telephone), rather than trying to track them down in person. Journalists could also stay in the field longer, as long as they could find a phone and call to dictate their story to a copy editor back in the newsroom. The typewriter allowed journalists to type up stories much more quickly. Images allowed journalists to show the public things they could before only imagine. Radio allowed for an even more intimate and immediate news consumption experience. Television brought scenes to life. The internet and social media transformed the relationship between journalists and audiences and added yet another layer of immediacy.

In addition to technologies, global events change how we cover news. Each war, from the Civil War to WWI to WWII to Vietnam and Iraq and all the wars in between, prompted journalists to figure out new ways of seeking out information. The COVID-19 pandemic, too, has left its mark on the profession. Journalists now attend many news conferences via Zoom. This introduces challenges in effectively holding those in power accountable. A local mayor or regional leader can more easily bypass a question or end the news conference when it's held remotely. The journalist cannot yell out that last question, follow the newsmaker to their car, or otherwise seek to hold them accountable the way they were able to do in person. But journalists

journalists from 30 countries came to Copenhagen in what had the feeling of a religious revival. People discovered that they weren't alone; that they had the same problems. They couldn't get access to documents and data, to sources. Officials were stonewalling and corporations were unaccountable."[8]

Kaplan said that first conference electrified the connections among investigative journalists. They "were ready to come together and the thing just took off." In attendee surveys, more than 90% said the organization has helped them build capacity as investigative journalists. "In places like Sri Lanka and Uganda and Peru you can see that these journalists have been empowered; you can see the light bulbs going off over their heads."[50]

But, Kaplan cautions, the situation for journalists remains dire. "We're under assault on multiple levels. Obviously, the financial model has changed. There's a political backlash against not just independent media, but human rights and democracy all over the world. And independent media is one of the first areas these autocrats and oligarchs go after. It's ironic. Just at a time when we're getting more and more people trained, when we're getting them skilled with how to use data and connect with each other across borders, this global backlash hits. So, we've got our backs to the wall, even in places where we thought we were relatively secure, like the United States."[8]

Nevertheless, Kaplan remains hopeful and electrified at the

have been figuring out other ways of doing this, including using Twitter to publicly encourage newsmakers to respond.

Physical distancing and sheltering in place also provided opportunities. Newsmakers who are generally busy in non-pandemic times found themselves sitting at home like everyone else – with more time to grant interviews or make news in some way, such as by raising money for the families of COVID-19 victims, health care workers, or political hopefuls running in local, regional, and national elections.

2020 reminded journalists to be nimble, innovative, and tenacious – that above all else we must seek truth, hold power accountable, and inform our public.

Remote news coverage has also prompted news outlets to reckon with a truth that has plagued the industry for a while. In a piece for NiemanLab, Prism's Lattimore wrote that the pandemic has helped the news industry face that journalists cannot congregate in major cities, such as London, New York, Washington, DC, Paris, Los Angeles, Tokyo, San Francisco, Beijing, or Johannesburg. Journalists should be spread out across regions to ensure adequate coverage beyond these centers of commerce and culture. "Building national news teams with roots in every corner of the country won't just produce better journalism – it'll help diversify and democratize the industry," Lattimore wrote.[51]

Maybe they're working class and can't afford to move to a high-cost-of-living city on an intern's progress that's been made and what's on the horizon. "We're just outgunned," he said. "We're outfinanced, and until recently we've been outmaneuvered. But we're catching up."[51]

"The numbers of hardcore full-time investigative journalists worldwide are only in the thousands. There's not that many of us. But the number of journalists (in general) are in the hundreds of thousands. And they all use investigative skills to some extent. Not only staff reporters and editors, but also book authors, documentary makers, freelancers, and bloggers. The next circle are these citizen journalists and NGOs and good government types. So, there's a formidable army out there ready to use these kinds of skills to go after lack of accountability, lack of transparency, and abuses of power. That's pretty heartening."[8]

But journalists cannot do it alone, said Kaplan. "Obviously you've got to have groups that will take up the call and push for reform, and the political process has to be not completely dysfunctional."[51]

Kaplan's reason for doing the work he does: "Unjust societies fail. If we're going to continue to progress as a species, there have to be people who are exposing the very serious problems that underlie these social maladies. We're not the only solution, but having an inquisitive watchdog media that asks these tough questions is the first step toward solving them."[8]

For more information about the Global Investigative Journalism Network (GIJN), go to GIJN.org.

pittance. Maybe family responsibilities or a partner's job mean they have less geographic mobility, as is true for many women. Or maybe, just *maybe*, they've deliberately set down roots in a part of the country that's not New York City because they love it, or it's where they're from, or they value the local communities of which they're a part.[50]

Lattimore argued that having a dispersed news staff will lead to richer, more nuanced, more diverse coverage and prevent so-called **parachute reporting**, when a journalist from a national outlet flies into a region simply to cover a big story, stays for a few days or a few weeks and then flies back to New York, London, or Washington, DC. Parachute reporting is generally not as rich or nuanced as local reporting. It generally does not capture nor center the voices and humanity of the people from the region. The coverage may be sound, but the nuanced understanding of local issues, concerns, and humanity may be lacking. Local reporters are connected with their communities and sources.

Because the journalism landscape is shifting and evolving, you have the power to influence the direction of the industry and the practice of journalism. There will always be stories to cover – major stories, minor stories, and stories in between. You may report on a hero police dog one day and the next do an exposé on the condition of schools in lower-income neighborhoods. Both stories help inform the public about what is happening and allow them to engage and contribute to the direction they want their community to go.

"Why do we do this? I think it's because we want to leave the world a little better, and that we care about underdogs and people being exploited," said GIJN's Kaplan.

> There need to be people who bear witness to history and document that there is objective truth. And our job is indeed writing a first rough draft of history and making it as accurate and fair and durable as possible. This is what civilization's built on.[8]

Key takeaways

- Journalism faces many challenges, including financial insecurity, lack of resources, harassment and threats against journalists, and misinformation and disinformation campaigns.
- Nonprofit journalism outlets are gaining traction, and many focus on specific beats or perspectives to allow for more in-depth, explanatory coverage.
- There are many ways to do journalism, including working in a legacy print or broadcast newsroom, working for a digital outlet, finding a journalism-oriented position at a nonprofit or NGO, or starting your own journalism endeavor.
- Student journalism can provide a strong foundation for launching your career.

Discussion questions

1. When you envision a career in journalism, what do you envision? How do you expect your career to launch? Where do you see yourself working?
2. If you were to work for a nonprofit journalism outlet or beat-focused nonprofit or NGO, what would your ideal coverage focus be? Why?
3. How do you want to contribute to the journalism (or communications) field? What type of work do you want to do? (The answer is NOT "I don't know." Commit to something – you can always change your mind.)

Exercises

1. Research a nonprofit news outlet or a nonprofit organization or NGO that incorporates journalism into its work. Answer the following questions:
   a. What is the focus area of this outlet?
   b. Why did you choose it?
   c. Research and explain why the founders launched this particular outlet.
   d. Choose one story this outlet covered over the past two months. Answer:
      i. Why did you choose this story?
      ii. How many sources were used in the story?
      iii. What did you learn from the story?
      iv. What do you still want to know?

2. Using the same article from #1 (or a different article from a nonprofit journalism outlet), research and find a story on the same topic covered by a mainstream legacy news outlet, such as *The New York Times*, *The Washington Post*, CNN, ABC, NBC, CBS, BBC, etc. Answer:
   a. How is the coverage similar?
   b. How is it different?
   c. What is the angle for each story?
   d. If they are the same, why do you think that is? If they are different, how are they different, and why do you think they are different?
   e. Which approach held your attention better?
   f. Which article led you to learn more?

3. Go to the site: https://www.usnewsdeserts.com/ to discover whether you live in a news desert.
   a. Find your community on the interactive map (either where you grew up, where you're going to college, etc.).
      i. Answer:
         1. Who owns your community's local newspaper?
         2. Has your community seen outlets disappear in the past 20 years?
         3. Is there a digital presence to fill the void?
            a. If so, is it a news outlet or PR-based outlet?
            b. If you can't tell, do some digging to find out!
         4. Does your community have a public broadcasting outlet?

5. How are marginalized or under-served communities covered in your community?
6. How are racial and ethnic groups covered in your community?
7. What is your reaction to the information you discovered? Are you surprised?

Notes

1 Hutchins, Robert Maynard, Zechariah Chafee, John M. Clark, John Dickinson, William F. Hocking, Harold D. Lasswell, Archibald D. MacLeish, et al. "Essay." The Commission On Freedom Of The Press. In *A Free and Responsible Press*, 1st ed., 105–6. Chicago, IL: University of Chicago Press, 1947.
2 "Average Entry-Level Journalist Salary." PayScale, January 20, 2021. https://www.payscale.com/research/US/Job=Journalist/Salary/e19a87d9/Entry-Level.
3 Chancellor, Cristal Williams, Katti Gray, Diahann Hill, and Maya King. Rep. Edited by Faye Wolfe and Tiffany Nguyen. *The Status of Women in U.S. Media 2019*. New York: Women's Media Center, 2019.
4 Thurman, Neil, Alessio Cornia, and Jessica Kunert. Rep. *Journalists in the UK*, 4. Oxford, UK: Reuters Institute for the Study of Journalism, 2016.
5 Posetti, Julie, Nermine Aboulez, Kalina Bontcheva, Jackie Harrison, and Silvio Waisbord. Rep. *Online Violence against Women Journalists: A Global Snapshot of Incidence and Impacts*. Paris: United Nations Educational, Scientific and Cultural Organization (UNESCO), 2020.
6 "Troll Patrol Findings." *Troll Patrol Report*. Amnesty International, 2018. https://decoders.amnesty.org/projects/troll-patrol/findings.
7 Weis, Allison. "I'm a Journalism Student in an Era of Closing Newsrooms, 'Fake News.' But I Still Want In." *USA Today*. Gannett Satellite Information Network, August 13, 2019. https://www.usatoday.com/story/opinion/voices/2019/08/13/journalism-student-industry-first-amendment-democracy-column/1935675001/.
8 David E. Kaplan, "Nonprofit Journalism" interview by Gina Baleria, *News in Context* (podcast), January 22, 2021, https://beta.prx.org/stories/355489.
9 Isbell, Kimberley. "What's the Law around Aggregating News Online? A Harvard Law Report on the Risks and the Best Practices." NiemanLab, September 8, 2010. https://www.niemanlab.org/2010/09/whats-the-law-around-aggregating-news-online-a-harvard-law-report-on-the-risks-and-the-best-practices/.
10 Wemple, Erik. "Opinion | Google News Failed Us, Says New York Times." *The Washington Post*, June 12, 2019. https://www.washingtonpost.com/opinions/2019/06/12/google-news-failed-us-says-new-york-times/.
11 Grieco, Elizabeth. "U.S. Newspapers Have Shed Half of Their Newsroom Employees since 2008." Pew Research Center, April 20, 2020. https://www.pewresearch.org/fact-tank/2020/04/20/u-s-newsroom-employment-has-dropped-by-a-quarter-since-2008/.
12 Hare, Kristen. "The Coronavirus Has Closed More than 60 Local Newsrooms across America and Counting." *Poynter*, January 6, 2021. https://www.poynter.org/locally/2020/the-coronavirus-has-closed-more-than-25-local-newsrooms-across-america-and-counting/.
13 Tracy, Marc. "News Media Outlets Have Been Ravaged by the Pandemic." *The New York Times*, April 10, 2020. https://www.nytimes.com/2020/04/10/business/media/news-media-coronavirus-jobs.html.
14 Fontanella-Khan, James. "The Fight for the Future of America's Local Newspapers." *Financial Times*, January 21, 2021. https://www.ft.com/content/5c22075c-f1af-431d-bf39-becf9c54758b.

15 Doctor, Ken. "Newsonomics: Alden Global Capital Is Making so Much Money Wrecking Local Journalism It Might not Want to Stop Anytime Soon." NiemanLab, May 1, 2018. https://www.niemanlab.org/2018/05/newsonomics-alden-global-capital-is-making-so-much-money-wrecking-local-journalism-it-might-not-want-to-stop-anytime-soon/.
16 "2020 World Press Freedom Index: Reporters without Borders." *Reporters Without Borders (RSF)*. Accessed February 11, 2021. https://rsf.org/en/ranking.
17 "U.S. Press Freedom Tracker." Quick Facts. Freedom of the Press Foundation, January 6, 2021. https://pressfreedomtracker.us/.
18 "2020 World Press Freedom Index: 'Entering a Decisive Decade for Journalism, Exacerbated by Coronavirus.'" *Reporters Without Borders (RSF)*, April 21, 2020. https://rsf.org/en/2020-world-press-freedom-index-entering-decisive-decade-journalism-exacerbated-coronavirus.
19 Selva, Meera. "How Press Freedom Came under Attack in 2020." *Foreign Policy*, December 30, 2020. https://foreignpolicy.com/2020/12/30/press-media-freedom-2020-journalists-covid-19-pandemic/.
20 Wiseman, Jamie. "Rush to Pass 'Fake News' Laws during Covid-19 Intensifying Global Media Freedom Challenges." International Press Institute, October 22, 2020. https://ipi.media/rush-to-pass-fake-news-laws-during-covid-19-intensifying-global-media-freedom-challenges/.
21 Stites, Tom. "A Quarter of All U.S. Newspapers Have Died in 15 Years, a New UNC News Deserts Study Found." *Poynter*, June 24, 2020. https://www.poynter.org/locally/2020/unc-news-deserts-report-2020/.
22 Abernathy, Penelope Muse. Rep. *News Deserts and Ghost Newspapers: Will Local News Survive?* Chapel Hill, NC: University of North Carolina, 2020.
23 Hare, Kristen. "What I've Learned from Covering a Year of Media Layoffs and Closures." *Poynter*, December 28, 2020. https://www.poynter.org/locally/2020/what-ive-learned-from-covering-a-year-of-media-layoffs-and-closures/.
24 Bengani, Priyanjana. "As Election Looms, a Network of Mysterious 'Pink Slime' Local News Outlets Nearly Triples in Size." *Columbia Journalism Review*, August 4, 2020. https://www.cjr.org/analysis/as-election-looms-a-network-of-mysterious-pink-slime-local-news-outlets-nearly-triples-in-size.php.
25 Rubado, Meghan E., and Jay T. Jennings. "Political Consequences of the Endangered Local Watchdog: Newspaper Decline and Mayoral Elections in the United States." *Urban Affairs Review*, March 2019. doi: 10.1177/1078087419838058.
26 Hayes, Danny, and Jennifer L. Lawless. "As Local News Goes, So Goes Citizen Engagement: Media, Knowledge, and Participation in U.S. House Elections." *SSRN Electronic Journal* 77, no. 2 (2014): 447–62. doi: 10.2139/ssrn.2452076.
27 Shaker, Lee. "Dead Newspapers and Citizens' Civic Engagement." *Political Communication* 31, no. 1 (February 2014): 131–48. doi: 10.1080/10584609.2012.762817.
28 Darr, Joshua P., Matthew P. Hitt, and Johanna L. Dunaway. "Newspaper Closures Polarize Voting Behavior." *Journal of Communication* 68, no. 6 (May 2018): 1007–28. doi: 10.1093/joc/jqy051.
29 Adsera, Alicia, Carles Boix, and Mark Payne. "Are You Being Served?: Political Accountability and Quality of Government." *SSRN Electronic Journal* 19, no. 2 (2000): 445–90. doi: 10.1093/jleo/ewg017.
30 Gao, Pengjie, Chang Lee, and Dermot Murphy. "Financing Dies in Darkness? The Impact of Newspaper Closures on Public Finance." *Journal of Financial Economics* 135, no. 2 (2020): 445–67. doi: 10.1016/j.jfineco.2019.06.003.
31 Campa, Pamela. "Press and Leaks: Do Newspapers Reduce Toxic Emissions?" *Journal of Environmental Economics and Management* 91 (2018): 184–202. doi: 10.1016/j.jeem.2018.07.007.
32 "How News Happens." Pew Research Center's Journalism Project. Pew Charitable Trusts, December 31, 2019. https://www.journalism.org/2010/01/11/how-news-happens/.
33 Greenblatt, Alan. "The Decline of Newspapers Is Bad for Politics, Debt and … Pollution, Studies Show." *Governing*. eRebuplic, April 24, 2019. https://www.governing.com/topics/politics/gov-newspapers-government-studies.html.

34 Waldman, Steven, and Charles Sennott. "Opinion | The Crisis in Local Journalism Has Become a Crisis of Democracy." *The Washington Post*, April 11, 2018. https://www.washingtonpost.com/opinions/the-crisis-in-journalism-has-become-a-crisis-of-democracy/2018/04/11/a908d5fc-2d64-11e8-8688-e053ba58f1e4_story.html.
35 Pickard, Victor. "Journalism's Market Failure Is a Crisis for Democracy." *Harvard Business Review*, March 12, 2020. https://hbr.org/2020/03/journalisms-market-failure-is-a-crisis-for-democracy.
36 Ferrier, Michelle, and Nisha Garud-Patkar. "TrollBusters: Fighting Online Harassment of Women Journalists." *Mediating Misogyny*, February 14, 2018, 311–32. doi: 10.1007/978-3-319-72917-6_16.
37 Froomkin @froomkin, Dan. "Truth or Consequences: Where Is Watchdog Journalism Today?" *Nieman Reports*, April 17, 2014. https://niemanreports.org/articles/truth-or-consequences-where-is-watchdog-journalism-today/.
38 "About Us." Reveal. Accessed February 14, 2021. https://revealnews.org/about-us/.
39 "Editorial Policies." MLK50 - Justice through Journalism, October 6, 2020. https://mlk50.com/editorial-policies/.
40 Tameez, Hanaa.' "Prism, a News Site Led by Women of Color, Centers the Voices of Marginalized People in Its Reporting." NiemanLab, October 20, 2020. https://www.niemanlab.org/2020/10/prism-a-news-site-led-by-women-of-color-centers-the-voices-of-marginalized-people-in-its-reporting/.
41 Jones, Tom. "Meet The 19th*, a New Gender and Politics News Organization by Women and for Women." *Poynter*, August 3, 2020. https://www.poynter.org/business-work/2020/meet-the-19th-a-new-gender-and-politics-news-organization-by-women-and-for-women/.
42 "Rebuilding Local News." *Rebuild Local News*, September 2020. https://www.rebuildlocalnews.org/our-plan.
43 Kahn, Gabriel. "A Newsletter for Every Neighborhood." *Medium*. Crosstown, LA, January 10, 2021. https://medium.com/crosstown-la/a-newsletter-for-every-neighborhood-cc44cd03cb7f.
44 Schiffrin, Anya, Hannah Clifford, Kylie Tumiatti, Allynn McInerney, and Léa Allirajah. "Saving Journalism: A Vision for the Post-Covid World." *Konrad Adenauer Stiftung*, January 11, 2021. https://www.kas.de/en/web/usa/single-title/-/content/saving-journalism.
45 "Fighting Back the Pandemic and Saving Journalism. The Moment Is Now." *International Federation of Journalists*, December 23, 2020. https://www.ifj.org/media-centre/news/detail/category/press-releases/article/fighting-back-the-pandemic-and-saving-journalism-the-moment-is-now.html.
46 Hartlaub, Peter. "'Fire College': As Devastation Revisits Santa Rosa, Student Journalists Find Purpose." *San Francisco Chronicle*, October 3, 2020. https://www.sfchronicle.com/culture/article/Fire-college-As-devastation-revisits-Santa-15614020.php.
47 Glenn Kessler, "Accountability Journalism" interview by Gina Baleria, *News in Context* (podcast), December 17, 2021. https://beta.prx.org/stories/351071.
48 Ponsford, Dominic. "Want to Be a Journalist? Top Editors Share Their Advice: 'Tenacity, Commitment and Passion Are What I Look for'." *Press Gazette*, July 18, 2017. https://www.pressgazette.co.uk/want-to-be-a-journalist-top-editors-share-their-advice-show-you-can-give-100-per-cent-or-it-will-end-in-tears/.
49 Samantha Stanley (freelance journalist & PhD student at the University of Hong Kong), in conversation with Gina Baleria, January 2021.
50 David E. Kaplan (Executive Director of the Global Investigative Journalism Network (GIJN)), in conversation with Gina Baleria, December 2020.
51 Lattimore, Ashton. "Remote Work Helps Level the Playing Field in an Insular Industry." NiemanLab, December 2020. https://www.niemanlab.org/2020/12/remote-work-helps-level-the-playing-field-in-an-insular-industry/.

Glossary

Accountability Journalism: Holding power to account, shining light on deception and misinformation, and representing the voice of the people.
Accountability Journalists: Those who engage in investigations, fact checking, or other forms of impactful reporting.
Affective Empathy: Involves physically and emotionally experiencing another person's emotions.
Anchoring Bias/Anchoring Effect: Relying too much on the initial frame or information you receive, making it difficult to accept new information.
Anticipatory Coping: Preparing strategies for how to handle a stressful event before the event occurs.
Audience: The readers, listeners, and viewers – or potential readers, listeners, and viewers - of the news.
Beat: Journalism focused on a specific topic area, subject area, or perspective.
Behavioral Empathy: The verbal and nonverbal communication that indicates someone understands another person or their perspective.
Bias: Shortcuts our brains take in an effort to simplify and make sense of the world around us based on our experiences up to that point.
Burnout: Emotional, mental, and physical exhaustion stemming from dealing with ongoing and/or acute stress or trauma.
Chilling Effect: The suppression of news or deterring of the work of a journalist based on intimidation, threat, or other discouragement tactics.
Citizen's Agenda: Centering the citizen who needs to be informed to make decisions about the health of their community and society.
Clerkism: Uncritically accepting the official or dominant version without fact-checking or additional newsgathering.
Cognitive Empathy: The ability to see the world through another person's perspective.
Compassion Fatigue: An apathy or indifference toward suffering caused by prolonged exposure to stress or trauma and stemming from mental exhaustion.
Constructed Reality: A perception of the world constructed by the media we consume and the filter bubbles we inhabit.
Curiosity: Wanting to know more about someone or something.

Disinformation: Deliberately disseminating false information to obscure the truth or influence what people think.
Echo Chamber: When a person only encounters information that they agree with or that fits with or reinforces their worldview.
Empathy: Sharing and understanding the thoughts, feelings, and perspectives of another.
Empathy Fatigue: See compassion fatigue.
Exceptionalize: Treating historically marginalized news subjects as the exception to the stereotype held by the mainstream.
Explainer: See explanatory journalism.
Explanatory Journalism: Goes in depth on a topic, issue, aspect of a topic or issue, or ongoing story to provide context and make the information more accessible to the audience.
Explicit Bias: Biases and perspectives you hold of which you are aware and conscious but may be unwilling to address.
Fact Checking: The act of confirming whether or not stated assertions are true.
Fact-Check Journalism: Involves confirming, often in real time or within a day or so, whether what someone says or writes is factual, misleading, or false.
Fake News: False content designed to mimic journalistic content.
Filter Bubble: See Echo Chamber.
Fourth Estate: The unofficial moniker given to the US news media to indicate that they are as important as the official three branches of government, because they represent the people and hold power accountable.
Freedom of Information Act (FOIA) Request: US federal law allowing journalists and other citizens to access certain federal government information.
Implicit Bias: Unconscious or inherent perspectives we hold that we are unaware of but that can influence our decision-making.
In-groups: Those like us and to whom we relate.
Information Disorder: The ecosystem of information-sharing issues we face, including misinformation, disinformation, and malinformation.
Investigative Journalism: Involves deeply investigating a single topic, issue, or aspect of a topic or issue. Investigative stories may take days, weeks, months, or even years to cover and publish.
Malinformation: Intentional and deliberate publication of truthful information that may be private or personal, or the manipulation of factual content to deceive or cause harm.
Misinformation: The spread of false information, but possibly without the intention to mislead.
Movement Journalism: Developed in the US South, journalism practiced by oppressed and marginalized people, often explicitly representing the perspective of these groups.
Native Advertising: Content designed to look like editorial content, but is actually a sponsored ad.

News Desert: A community without a strong local news outlet and therefore no credible source of information or coverage of their community.

Objectivity: The unattainable concept that news will be presented without bias. Objectivity has come to define the human, but it was meant to apply to the process of newsgathering.

Off the Record: Shared in confidence; not to be used for publication.

Out-group: A group with which reporters may not have had a lot of contact or about which they have little understanding. Those we consider not like us or *other*.

Parachute Reporting: When a journalist from a national outlet flies into a region simply to cover a big story that happens to be taking place there, stays for a few days or perhaps a few weeks and then flies home. May not be as rich or nuanced as local reporting.

Photog: a TV news video-journalist.

Plain Language: A translation that makes content more accessible to people with developmental disabilities. Uses short sentences, common words, and a simple structure.

Professional Witness: Someone who works in a profession where they are exposed to traumatic and stressful contexts and are tasked with helping those in distress or reporting on the situation.

Racial Trauma: Similar to "post-traumatic stress disorder" but involves ongoing individual and collective injuries due to exposure and re-exposure to race-based stress.

Self-Care: The act of caring for yourself, including your physical and mental health.

Social Justice Journalism: Involves identifying injustices and exploring how to address issues in coverage.

Solidarity Journalism: Dignity for all as a foundational principle from which journalism is practiced.

Solutions Journalism: Focuses on coverage of how people respond to problems, discussing evidence of what's working and where things fall short, with the goal of tackling challenges.

Systems Journalism: Focuses on how the systems that underpin our societies influence the stories we cover, prompting us to apply different frames to newsgathering and writing.

Tenacity: Persistence, doggedness, a willingness to keep pursuing a story, no matter the obstacles, setbacks, or words and actions of people or entities seeking to deter.

Trauma: Severe mental or emotional distress, caused by an event or ongoing series of events.

Unconscious Bias: See Implicit Bias.

Vicarious Trauma: The negative effects of caring about and for others as we bear witness to traumatic events.

Watchdog: See Accountability Journalism.

Index

Bold denotes tables; *Italics* denotes figures

ABC Australia 3
accountability 11
accountability journalism 179–204; challenges of 183–84; defining 181–85; engaging in 188–93; explainer's role in 185; focus on domestic terrorism 193–94; importance of 182–83, 193–94; locating 185–88; muckrakers 198–99; organizations supporting 198; practicing 192–93; practitioners of 197–200; properly using 194–97
accountability journalists 36, 189, 194, 198, 200, 251
active voice, using 159–61; writing in 162
ad hominem 75
advertising revenue 87, 238, 249
affective empathy 46–47
affinity bias 74
Africa, COVID-19 in 149–150
agents provocateurs 56
air, coming up for 107
Al-Assad, Bashar 53–54
Alba, Davey 188
alcohol 226
Alden Global Capital 5, 240
Alexander, Lisa 84
Algeria, legitimacy in 241
All News 740 35
Allen, Marshall 195
AllSides 74
Amato, John 180
American Pandemic: The Lost Worlds of the 1918 Influenza Pandemic 152
American Press Association (APA) 2
American Press Institute (API) 46, 47, 53, 57, 78, 127, 137, 140, 184, 196–197
amplification, trolling 113–16, 197, 221

anchor bias 74
anchoring bias 58, 107
anchoring effect 58
Andorra, COVID-19 deaths in *151*
anticipatory coping 109
Aotearoa 136–37
"apocalypse," term 135
Arbery, Ahmaud 164
Argentina 60
Argentina, COVID-19 deaths in *150, 151*
Arizona Daily Star 35
Armed Conflict Location & Event Data Project (ACLED) 55
Armenia, COVID-19 deaths in *151*
Armenian genocide 51
Aro, Jessikka 114
Arpaio, Joe 250
artificial intelligence (AI) 35
Asian American Journalists Association (AAJA) 168, 237
Asian Americans, coverage of 34, 128–29, 138, 168
Asiana Airlines Crash 26, 27, 216
assumptions, words leading to 170
At This Hour 179
Atassi, Leila 89–90, 186
Attiah, Karen 150–51
audience: and active voice 159–61; audience interest 137–39; distrust from 235, 237; informing 38, 109, 112, 143, 181, 217; language and 153–55; maintaining trust with 6; psychographics 132
augmented reality (AR) 35, 57
Australia: taxpayer funding in 248; unions in 248
Austria, COVID-19 deaths in *151*

authoritarianism, influence of 96, 240–42, 245
Awash, Hawi 124
Ayyub, Rana 114

Baicker, Sarah 215–16
Baier, Bret 3
Bailon, Gilbert 85
bandwagon bias 74
Baquet, Dean 3, 105
BART 211–12
BBC 3
beat reporting 48, 57, 131, 183–84, 199, 221, 236, 247
Becenti, Arlyssa 220
Bedei, Cristina 211
Begin, Menachem 96
behavioral empathy 46
Belden, Anne 24, 25, 34, 250
Belgium, COVID-19 deaths in 151
Bias 8, 10, 14, 48, 50, 59, 60, 61–62, 126, 128, 152, **162**, 169, 195, 242–43: appropriateness of 89–90; of balance 74; as challenge to credibility 80; defining 72–77; driving misinformation 84; importance of examining 81–86; manifestations of 83; minimizing 86–89; and objectivity 78–81; by omission 75; prevalence of 77–78; types of 74–76; unconscious 138, 154
Biden, Joe 4, 60, 70, 167, 181
Bill & Melinda Gates Foundation 138
Black Cube 97
Black journalists 219
Black Kansas Citians 85
Black Lives Matter 9, 72–73, 84, 139, 156, 165, 170
Black Wall Street 153
Blake, Jacob 56
Blank-Libra, Janet 53
Bly, Nellie 102–4, 199
Bolivia, COVID-19 deaths in 151; legitimacy in 241
Boston Globe 85, 112–13
Branco, Sofia 218
Brandel, Jennifer 192
Brazil, COVID-19 deaths in 150, 151; legitimacy in 241
Bridis, Ted 100, 101, 105
Bristow, Nancy 152
British royalty, coverage of 152
Brunson, Rick 24–25
Bui, K. Kim 46, 53, 127, 140; on community engagement 128

"Buildings Matter, Too" 156
Bulgaria, COVID-19 deaths in 151
burnout 61, 221, 223
Bush Administration 165
BuzzFeed 3

cable news networks 180; employees in 239, 240
Camerota, Alisyn 224
Camus, Albert 1
Canada: taxpayer funding in 248; unions in 248
Canadian Broadcasting Corporation (CBC) 167
Capital Gazette 99, 101
Carnegie Mellon 114
Catch and Kill (Farrow) 8, 97
Cayce Homes 125, 126–127, 131
Center for Investigative Journalism 198
Center for Investigative Reporting see Reveal
Central Park Five see Exonerated Five
charging unit 210
Charleston Gazette-Mail 187
Chicago: murders 139, 157
Chile, COVID-19 deaths in 151
chilling effect 116, 244
China, journalism in 1, 238
Chow, Kit 140
Christie, Chris 250
citizen's agenda 172
Clark, Roy Peter 160–61
clerkism 184
Cleveland, untested rape kits in 89–90, 186
Clinton versus Dole Presidential campaign 183–84
Clinton, Hillary 100
CNN 3, 4, 70, 71, 106, 129, 172, 179–80, 224
Cobham, Kari 227
Cochran, Elizabeth Jane see Nellie Bly
Code Switch 140
cognitive empathy 46
Colombia, COVID-19 deaths in 150, 151
Columbia Journalism Review 90, 135, 180, 221, 242
Committee to Protect Journalists 3
Community engagement 9; audience interest 137–39; defining 124–28; engaging meaningfully 131–34; identifying audience 134–37; importance of 128–31; learning and 133–34; newsrooms approaching 140–44; story assumptions 134

community language: about/for distinction 161–63; awareness of 163–68; blind spots 158; defining 153–55; importance of 155–58; improving on 168–72; points of view 155; questions 156; recognizing diction 153–57; speaking 158–61
compassion fatigue 223–24
confirmation bias 74, 107
connection, desire for 10
connection, self-care 209
conscious language 169–72
Conscious Style Guide 72, 169–72
constructed reality 4
content creators 4–5
Conway, Terry 25–26
Cooper, Amy 84
Cooper, Chris 84
Copeland, Carolyn 138, 166
coping strategies 12, 210, 227
cop-speak 164
corrections, indicating 167–68
Cortez, Olivia 51
coverage, fairness of *see* empathy
COVID-19 1–2, 25, 51, 59, 70, 111, 165, 166, 189, 194, 219–20, 224–25, 241, 252; coverage of 217, 249; deaths caused by 149–51, *150, 151*; losses before 238, 242
crime stories, metaphors in 165
criticism 116
Croatia, COVID-19 deaths in *151*
Cronkite, Walter 1
Cruz, Ted 172–73
Culver, Dory 35
curiosity 7, 47, 110–11; addressing lack of 24–25; becoming curious 29–31; cultivating 27–28, 38–39; defining 25–29; importance of 23–24; influencing journalism 29–31; killers of 28–29; people affected by 32–35; practicing 35–36; wonder in 26–28
Czechia, COVID-19 deaths in *150*

Dahl, Julia 48
Dalton, Meg 221
Dart Center 207, 209, 223, 225–26
Dean, Walter 78
Deavours, Danielle 96
Deloire, Christophe 2, 114, 245
democratic crisis 241
Democratic Republic of Congo 168
depression 211, 213–14, 217, 224
Des Moines Register 3
descriptions, accuracy of 170–71

Deutsche Welle (DW) 152
DeWine, Mike 90
diction, recognizing 153–56
Digital First Media (DFM) 240
digital harassment 113
digital media 238
digital spaces, voices in 5
digital-native, employees in *239, 240*
disinformation 60, 80, 114, 184, 187, 197, 235, 238, 241, 243–44
Dissell, Rachel 89–90, 186–87
Dobbs, Michael 184
domestic terrorism, focus on 193–94
Donald Trump and His Assault on Truth 186
downsizing 6
Druzin, Heath 221
Ducklo, TJ 181
Duterte, Rodrigo 9, 96, 106, 114
Dwyer, Jim 49

echo chambers 4, 7, 60, 136
economic crisis 241
Ecuador, COVID-19 deaths in *151*
education reporter 87–88
Egypt, journalism in 1
El Mundo 2
El Salvador, unions in 248
Elizabeth, Jane 36, 197
Elman, Julie M. 197
emotionalism 75
empathy 7, 125; concerns of 61–63; coverage without 50–51; defining 46–51; importance of 51–53; pitfalls of 62; positive impacts of 52; practicing 55–58; receivers of 53–55; solidarity approach to 49–51; when to engage in 58–61
Engadget 57
England, taxpayer funding in 248
Eritrea, journalism in 1
Europe 60, 183–84, 189
events, newsgathering iceberg *143*
exceptionalizing 130
executive producer (EP) 99
exercise, self-care 209
Exonerated Five 48, 53, 62, 82
explainer 185
explanation, focusing on 197
explanatory journalism 181, 185
eyes, looking someone in 56
Eyre, Eric 187

fact checks 84, 111, 172–73, 179–85, 191, 193, 196, 243, 249
fact-check journalism 181–85

266 Index

fake news 3, 6, 114, 197, 221, 243;
  competition of 197
Fannin, Mike 85
Farhi, Paul 179–80
Farrow, Ronan 8, 60–61, 96–99, 112
filter bubbles 4, 33, 136
Finch, Atticus 45
Finch, Peter 26
Finkel, David 46
First Amendment 56, 59
first responders 211, 213, 222
five Ws 28
flawed logic 75
Flight 77, coverage of 100
Flight 93 211
Flint Water Crisis 186
Floyd, George 55, 56, 59, 156, 166, 168–69, 219, 249; and bias 73, 163; community engagement in response to 130–31
Fonatella-Khan, James 238
Fourth Estate 1, 181
Fox News 3, 4, 108
Framework for Individual Diversity Development 127
France, COVID-19 deaths in 150, 151
Freedman, Wayne 23
Freedom of Information Act (FOIA) 165
freelancing 221, 235–36, 249–51
Freelancing with Tim 249
Fresh Agenda, A 52
Fresh Air (radio) 112–13
Freud, Sigmund 78
Froomkin, Dan 181
Fruitvale Station 212, 213

Gannett–GateHouse (merger) 5
Gates, Rick 100
geopolitical crisis 241
Georgia, COVID-19 deaths in 151
Geraghty, Jim 32–33
Germany, COVID-19 deaths in 150, 151
"getting it right" 25
Glass, Ira 61
global events 253–54
Global Investigative Journalism Network (GIJN) 182, 187–98, 223, 237, 251–54
Global Press Journal 168
Gorman, Ginger 114
Grant, Oscar 211–12
Greenwich Time 221
Guardian, The 3, 98, 154, 250
gun violence, covering 157
Guyette, Curt 186, 187

Hamelin, Eléonore (Léo) 220
Hanna-Attisha, Mona 186
harassment *see* trolling
Hare, Kristen 238, 242
Harland, Kyle 48
Headlight 142
Hearken 172, 192
hedge fund ownership 5, 12, 238–239, 242
Hegranes, Cristi 168, 169
he-said/she-said reporting 81
Hero on the Hudson *see* Sullenberger, Captain Sully
Hill, Jarrett 219–20
historically Black colleges and universities (HBCUs) 57
Hollings, Alex 104
Holt, Ashley 220
Hong Kong, protests in 62
Houston Chronicle 11
HowSound 125
Hudson, Michael 199
Hungary, COVID-19 deaths in 151
Hurricane Andrew, reporting on 7
Hurricane Katrina 208
hyperbole, avoiding 23

iceberg, newsgathering down 142–43; mental models *143*
identifiers, using 158–61
implicit bias 8, 76–77, 157; affecting journalism 82
India, COVID-19 deaths in 150
IndieGraf 248
Indonesia 60; COVID-19 deaths in 150
information: assessing 195–96; chaos 241; disorder 235, 237, 242; laws restricting 241–42; providers 4–5
in-groups 7, 51, 59–60, 166
Inside Climate News (ICN) 246
Institute for Nonprofit News (INN) 237
intangible skills, defining 1–2, 6–13
International Center for Journalists (ICFJ) 217, 237, 243
International Consortium of Investigative Journalists (ICIJ) 2, 198
International Federation of Journalists (IFJ) 218
interviewing 11, 26, 28, 45–46, 70, 82, 111–12, 129, 138, 150, 183–84, 188–93, 211, 225
investigative journalism 98, 100, 102–4, 181, 182–85, 186, 194, 199, 251–54
Investigative Reporters & Editors (IRE) 198, 237

investigative reporting *see* accountability journalism
Iran, COVID-19 deaths in *150*
Iraq War 96
Ireland, COVID-19 deaths in *151*
Islamic State (IS) 167
Italy, COVID-19 deaths in *150, 151*

Jacob, Rahul 113
Japan, journalism in 1
jargon, avoiding 162
Jefferson, Thomas 1
Jewell, Richard 59
Jim Crow laws 51, 85
Johnson, Alexis 72–73
Jones, Alex S. 80–81
Journalism & Women Symposium (JAWS) 237
Journalism + Design 142
Journalism Jobs and a Photo of My Dog 249
"Journalism of Empathy" 125
journalism: accountability 179–204; community engagement 123–49; community language 149–78; constructed realities in 3–4; covering subjects for 45–66; COVID-19 impact on 217; curiosity as influence on 29–31; curiosity in 23–44; developing intangible skills 1–16; employing intangible skills 6; ethical standards of 13–14; focusing too much on job 218; as Fourth Estate 181; funding of 249; lack of empathy in 62; launching career in 249–52; losing journalists 96; mission of 2–3; navigating industry 235–59; navigating information 4–6; necessary evils in 215; preparing for 252–55; self-care 207–234; tenacity in 96–116
"Journalism's Market Failure Is a Crisis for Democracy" 244
Juanillo, James 84–85

Kansas City Star 85–86
Kantor, Jodi 8, 96–99, 101, 105
Kaplan, David E. 182, 183, 193, 194, 198–99, 237–38, 248, 251–55
Kassova, Luba 138
KCBS Radio 25, 35, 88, 127, 207
Keller, Bill 13, 246
Kelley, Lori 197
Kelly, Mary Louise 11, 191–92, 194–95
Kenya, unions in 248
Kessler, Glenn 182–85, 250

KGO-TV 23, 25, 84
Khalif, Yema 123
Khashoggi, Jamal 9, 194
King, Gayle 11
King, Martin Luther, Jr. 83
Kiriyama, George 7, 32–34
Knight, Meribah 125, 131
Kohli, Sonali 214–15
Konnikova, Maria 156–57
Kosovo, COVID-19 deaths in *151*
KPIX 85, 123–24
KQED 85
Kramer, Melody 215

LA Times 3, 123, 214
Lacey, Marc 158
Larkin, Robert 84
Lattimore, Ashton 247, 254–55
Latvia, COVID-19 deaths in *151*
learning 133–34
Lebanon, COVID-19 deaths in *151*
LeClair, Misha 12, 211–16, 224, 229
legacy outlets, purchasing 238
Lewis, Sarah Elizabeth 166
Liechtenstein, COVID-19 deaths in *151*
Lincoln, Abraham 189
lists, writing 162
Lithuania, COVID-19 deaths in *151*
"Little Love, Less Hope, Lost Lives" 126
Local Independent Online News (LION) 237, 248
local journalism: as accountability frontline 187; current state of 187; erosion of 244–45; and spread of misinformation 187–88; supporting 244–49
Local Journalism Sustainability Act 247–48
Logan, Lara 9, 82–83, 96
Lowery, Wesley 70, 80–81
Luce, Henry 149
Luxembourg, COVID-19 deaths in *151*

#MeToo movement 98, 155
Madfes, Isaac 123
Manafort, Paul 100
Mangelsdorf, Liz 79
market-oriented bias 76
Markkula Center for Applied Ethics 49, 53, 153
marriage license, assumptions of 79–80
Marshall Project 11, 13
Martin, Trayvon 50
Massachusetts Institute of Technology (MIT) 5
massacre, word 153–54

McBride, Kelly 163
McCarthy, Joseph 96, 105–6
McCarthy, Tom 113
McClatchy 5
McGinty, Timothy 90
McGrory, Brian 85
McHugh, Rich 97
McMahon, Cait 223
McRaven, William H. 1
media development programs 248
Media Matters 10–11
Mehserle, Johannes 212
Memphis Free Speech 142
Mendonsa, Cristina 52, 61–62
Mental health 113, 208, 212, 213, 217, 218, 222, 224–25, 229, 243, 248
Mexico, COVID-19 deaths in *150, 151*
Miami Herald 7, 37
mind reading 75
misinformation, contributing to 80, 82, 84, 181, 184, 187, 195–97, 235, 237–38, 241, 243
Missing Perspectives of Women in News, The 138
MLK50 247
Modi, Narenda 114
Moldova, COVID-19 deaths in *151*
Monaghan, Elaine
Monteleone, Becca 161
Montenegro, COVID-19 deaths in *151*
Moorer, Brit 97, 102–3, 109
Movement for Black Lives 73–74
movement journalism 141, 143
MSNBC 3, 180, 190
muckrakers 198–99
mudslinging 75
multi-newsroom collaborations 198–99
Murrow, Edward R. 96, 105–6
Myanmar 60

Namibia, unions in 248
National Association of Black Journalists (NABJ) 237
National Association of Hispanic Journalists (NAHJ) 237
National Public Radio (NPR) 11, 57, 72, 81 130, 140, 158, 163, 186, 191–92,
native advertising 6
Native American Journalists Association (NAJA) 237
Netherlands, COVID-19 deaths in *151*; unions in 248
network, expanding 87–88
Nevarez, Vanessa 23

New York Times 3, 8, 13, 53, 80, 97–98, 101, 115, 129–30, 158–60 166; corrections by 167, 188, 238, 246
New Yorker 8, 61, 97–98, 156, 220
New Zealand 136–37
Newman, Elana 209, 211, 213, 216, 218, 220, 222, 225–26, 229
News Catalyst 248
news deserts 242–43, 248
news industry: addressing challenges facing 246–48; challenges facing 237–42; competition in 237, 241; current landscape of 235–37; entrepreneurs of 236; financial issues facing 237; journalists facing challenges to 242–45; nonprofit spaces 236–37; women/people of color entering 236–37; *see also* journalism
Newsday 49, 183
Newsom, Gavin 79, 158
newspaper publishers, employees in *239, 240*
newsroom employees, decline of *239, 240*
newsrooms: approaching community engagement 140–44; layoffs in 62; positions in 249–52; shrinking of 184
.nextdoor 133
NGOs 249, 255
Nicas, Jack 188
Nicolaou, Anna 238
Nieman Reports 158, 181, 184, 199, 246
NiemanLab 161, 247, 254
Nigeria: journalism in 1; silencing journalists in 3
Niles, Robert 25
19th 13, 163, 236, 247
Nixon, Andrew 223
Noah, Trevor 152
NoiseCat, Julian Brave 135
non-conservatives 70
non-news social media 10
nonprofit news outlets 13, 198, 236–37, 246–48
North Macedonia, COVID-19 deaths in *151*
Norway, taxpayer funding in 248
numbing behaviors 226–27
nurse 70–72, 249

O'Brien, Soledad 129–30
Oak Leaf (student newspaper) 250
Objectivity 8, 61, 235: bias and 78–81; defining 79; *see also* empathy

Online News Association (ONA) 237
operationalization 12
Orr, Katie 223
othering 7, 35, 60, 125, 127
out-groups 7, 51, 59, 60, 166
outlets, examining 86–87

Padilla, Alex 138
Padilla, Dave 88, 127–29
Palm Springs, CA 86
Panama, COVID-19 deaths in *151*
Panama Papers, investigation of 199
parachute reporting 255
passive voice, avoiding 159–61
.patch 133
Paycheck Protection Program (PPP) 198
Pelley, Scott 9
Peña, Nonny de la 57–58
penny press 249
people of color 11, 32, 50, 59, 85, 128–9, 130, 131, 139, 166, 170, 197, 236–37, 247
people of goodwill 246
people, discussing 171
people/elements, introducing 162
Perez, Johnny 11
personal mission, defining 228–29
personal protective equipment (PPE) 243
perspectives, seeing multiple 54, 54–55
Peru, COVID-19 deaths in *150, 151*; unions in 248
Petrova, Kate 111
Pew Research Center Survey 59, 181, 243
Philadelphia Inquirer 156
Philippines: journalism in 1; legitimacy in 241; silencing journalists in 3, 9, 96, 106, 114
photog 45
physical distancing, opportunities made by 254
physical health, improving 227–29
"pink slime" outlets 242–43
Pittsburgh Dispatch 102
Pittsburgh Post-Gazette 72–73
placement bias 75–76
plain language 161–63; translations **162**
Plaisance, Patrick Lee 36–37
Plandemic 195
Poland, COVID-19 deaths in *150, 151*
police-community interactions 164–65
Pompeo, Mike 11, 191–92, 194–95
Portugal, COVID-19 deaths in *151*
Poynter Institute 11, 48–49, 53, 85, 141, 154, 160–61, 163, 168, 197, 215, 228–29, 238, 242, 247–49

PR-based outlets 184, 188
press freedom, factors affecting 240–41
Prison Journalism Project 163
professional witness 12, 211
Project Syria 57–58
ProPublica 13, 161–62, 195, 198
Psychology Today 36; defining empathy 46
PTSD 210–11, 213–14, 217, 219, 222
public information officers (PIOs) 133
public interest 157
public relations (PR) 75, 78, 188
Pulitzer Prize 1, 7, 37, 97, 100, 113, 141, 143, 167, 199, 242, 246

quitting 108

R. Kelly 11
racial trauma 166, 219
radio broadcasting, employees in *239, 240*
Rappler 9, 106, 114
Rashtriya Swaroop 2
Rebabeba (screenname) 110–11
remote coverage 254
Reporters Without Borders (RSF) 2–3, 114, 194, 241, 244–45
reporting staff, cuts in 244–45
representation, lack of 139
resourcefulness 8–9
Ressa, Maria 9, 96, 106, 114
reticence 213–14
Reveal 198, 247
Rice, Tamir 85
Richardson, Allissa V. 219
Riot, word 10, 73–74, 153–54
rituals 229
Robinson, Walter 112–13
Rockwell, Dan 112
Rodriguez, Julio Valdivia 2
Rodriquez, Julian 25
Rohingya 60
Romania, COVID-19 deaths in *151*
Rosen, Jay 172, 192
Rosengard, Dana 97
Rosenthal, Rob 125–26
Rosentiel, Tom 184
Russia, COVID-19 deaths in *150*; journalism in 1, 238; legitimacy in 241
Russian Trolls 114
Russian, silencing journalists in 3
Rwanda genocide 51

Sadat, Anwar 96
Salman, Mohammed bin 194
Samperio, Maria Angeles 218

San Francisco Chronicle 79, 250
San Francisco Giants 60
San Marino, COVID-19 deaths in *151*
Sandboxx News 104
Sassoon, David 246
Saudi Arabia, journalism in 1; Saudi Arabia, silencing journalists in 3
Sawyer, Diane 23
Schiffman, Jeffrey 98
Schneider, Martin R. 77–78
Schulz, Kathryn 24
Searle, Robin 251
See It Now 106
self-awareness 222
self-care 12; activities for 227; being realistic about 218; best time to seek 223–25; burnout 221; connection strategies 210; dealing with unsupportiveness 225–27; defining 208–10; effects of lack of 216–218; ethical/moral compass 222; facing regrets 222; importance of managing 221–23; journalists approaching 214–16; mindfulness 209–10; potential harm of 225–27; practicing 208–10, 227–29; reducing PTSD 213–14; reticence 213–14; re-traumatization 223; self-awareness 222; trauma 211–14; vacations 215–16
Selva, Meera 241
Sennott, Charles 244
sensationalism 75, 136
sentences, simplifying 162
September 11, 2001 (9/11) 100, 207–8, 211, 213, 221
sexual assault, word choice when covering 155–56
Shadid, Anthony 96
Shapiro, Ari 192
Shapiro, Bruce 207
shock doctrine 245
Shukla, Ajai 113
Sidlow, Faith 98, 103
Sidner, Sara 224–25
Simanovych, Olga 223
Singapore, taxpayer funding in 248
Singh, Rakesh "Nirbhik" 2
Singh, Sushant 113
Sitar, Dana 160
slant 75
Slovenia, COVID-19 deaths in *151*
Smith, Ben 3
Smith, Laura 25
social justice journalism 141

social media guidelines 80
Society of Professional Journalists (SPJ) 13, 237
Solidarity journalism 49–51, 52, 60, 62, 141
solutions journalism 141
source attribution, omission of 75
sources, expanding on 88
South Africa, COVID-19 deaths in *150, 151*
South Dakota, nurse from 70
Southern Horrors 143
Spain, COVID-19 deaths in *150, 151*
spinning 74
St. Louis Post-Dispatch 35, 85
Stalin, Joseph 51
Stanley, Samantha 251
statements of opinion presented as fact 75
Status of Women in the US Media 2019, The 236
Stevens, Jenny 250
Stifter, Catherine 223
Storm, Hannah 228
Stow, Bryan 60
stress: affected by 219, 221; female journalists and 218; generation of 211, 213; managing 223–26; mitigating 209–10; race-based 166
student news outlets 34, 249
Student Press Law Center 34
Stuff 136–37
subjects/actors 160
subjects, covering 45–66; *see also* empathy
Sullenberger, Captain Sully 26
Sullivan, Margaret 113
Swan, Jonathan 111, 189–90
Sweden, COVID-19 deaths in *151*
Switzerland, COVID-19 deaths in *151*
systems journalism 141–43

tai chi 228
Tamkin, Emily 180
Tampa Bay Times 197
Tapper, Jake 172–73
technological crisis 241
technologies, changes in 252–53
television, employees in *239, 240*
tenacity 8; challenging 112–16; coming up for air 107; concerns of 107–8; cultivating 109–10; defining 98–102; embodiment of 102–4; importance of 96–98; in newsgathering 104–5; practicing 108–12; and quitting 108; and

story publishing 105; stubbornness in 107–8; tapping into 102–6
therapy, self-care 210
This American Life 61, 115
Thornton, Leslie-Jean 104, 109
360 video 35, 57, 63
Timmins, Lydia 100–01, 109
Timpone, Brian 188
Tin News Collection 248
Tin, Win 179
Tow Center for Digital Journalism 217, 243
traditional/legacy media 5, 12, 236–38, 249
trauma 12, 90; racial trauma 166, 219; defining 211–14; effects of lack of 216–18; importance of managing 210, 220, 221–23, 228–29; unhealthy coping 226–27
Treaty of Waitangi 136–37
trends/patterns, newsgathering iceberg *143*
tribal politics 60
Tribune Publishing 5, 85
Troll Armies 114–16
Trolling (harassment) 113–16, 221, 222; intimidation 114; minimizing 115; silencing women's voices 9, 12, 113, 115, 116, 236; stages of 114; power 112, 114, 194
Trump, Donald 3, 4, 33, 83, 100, 108, 111, 172, 240; on COVID-19 deaths/ testing 189–90; July 2, 2016, speech 179–81
trust crisis 241
Tucker, Brian 244
Tucker, Dorothy 220
Turkey, COVID-19 deaths in *150*
24-hour news cycle 3
Twitter 70, 71, 77, 157, 214, 254; lies spreading on 5
Twohey, Megan 8, 96
2012 Sandy Hook Elementary School mass shooting 107
2013 Boston Marathon bombing 107, 208, 213

UAE, legitimacy in 241
Ukraine, COVID-19 deaths in *150*; locating 192; *see also* Kelly, Mary Louise; Pompeo, Mike
umbrella man 56
United Kingdom, COVID-19 deaths in *150*, *151*; unions in 248
United Nations 2

United States, COVID-19 deaths in *150*, *151*; unions in 248; whiteness in 158
Univision 3
unsubstantiated claims 75
upsetting images, showing 166–67
US Capitol, insurrection of 4, 9, 60–61, 73–74, 160, 193–94, 242
US Olympic Park bombing (Atlanta, 1996) 58–59, 107, 213
US Press Freedom Tracker 240–41
USA Today 70, 236

vacations 215–16
vagueness, avoiding 168–73
Varma, Anita 49–51, 53–54, 62, 155–57, 157; and community language 153
Vasquez, Tina 247
Velshi, Ali 190
vicarious trauma 211
Vides, Nick 250
virtual reality (VR) 35, 57–58

Waldman, Steven 244
Wall Street Journal 100
Walters, Barbara 96
Washington Post 3, 9, 16, 47, 70, 113, 150, 160, 179, 182–84, 194, 244, 247, 250; Fact Checker 182
watchdog journalism *see* accountability journalism
Watergate 199
weapons of mass destruction (WMD) 193
Weijia Jiang 113
Weinstein, Harvey 8, 96–99, 101
Weis, Allison 236
Welliver, Sarah 154 Wells, Ida B. 1, 141–43
West Coast Media Jobs 249
West, Lindy 115
White House Correspondents' Association 3
Wired 71
women 8–9, 13, 50, 77, 89–90, 98, 101–04, 113, 115, 218, 220–21, 236–37; Asian Women 129; trans women 134; black trans women 134; women of color 247; missing perspectives 138–39
Women's Media Center 236
Wonder 7, 23, 26, 29, 37, 89, 110–11, 186; jumpstarting 27–28
Woods, Keith 57, 81–83; on bias 72, 73, 76–77, 79, 86; on covering communities 130–34; on identifiers 158; on learning 133–34; on mainstream media focus 130–31
words, conveying meaning of 10

World Economic Forum: on
  COVID-19 149
World Press Freedom Index 3, 241,
  244–45, *245*
Wright, Janice 24, 26–27

Yahoo! 238
Yglesias, Matthew 33

Yin, Karen 72, 157, 169–72
yoga 228
YouTube 115, 138, 226, 228
Yovanovitch, Marie 191–92

Zhang, Qifan 185
Zoom 253
Zweig, David 71